The UNITED NATIONS

In the New Millennium

The UNITED NATIONS

In the New Millennium

RUMKI BASU

STERLING

STERLING PUBLISHERS (P) LTD.
Regd. Office: A1/256, Safdarjung Enclave, New Delhi-110029.
Cin: U22110DL1964PTC211907
Phone: +91 82877 98380/ +91 120-6251823
E-mail: mail@sterlingpublishers.in
www.sterlingpublishers.in

The United Nations: In the New Millennium

ISBN 978 93 93853 17 2

Printed and Published in India

Sterling Publishers Pvt. Ltd.,
Plot No. 13, Ecotech-III, Greater Noida -201306, U.P. India

To
my late friend
Professor Kadloor Savitri,
for all our years together
in the Department of Political Science
Jamia Millia Islamia,
where she taught International Organization,
and it was she who gave me the blueprint
for revisiting my original book
on the seventy-fifth year of the UN.

PREFACE TO THE NEW EDITION

The book attempts to take a fresh look at the United Nations (UN) system and its role in the international arena in the 21st century. The book describes what the UN does and how it operates today, to examine the reforms needed to allow multilateralism to succeed by making the UN a more effective force in contemporary world politics.

Ever since the establishment of the UN, it has attracted as many friends as foes. There have been conflicting opinions about its role in world affairs. Its critics say that the UN has failed to perform its chief responsibility in keeping world peace. It has become little more than an occasional "talking shop" or "a paper factory", where nothing effective ever gets done. Others feel that the UN in its present form is quite irrelevant to more potent factors in world politics—its power diplomacy, regional groupings, international political movements, or even important non-governmental organizations, which are sometimes more effective than the UN.

There is widespread ignorance about what the UN is and what it does in practice. The present book intends to help correct this impression. It aims to provide an up-to-date description of what the UN is, how it works, and how it has evolved over the years—the operational realities it has had to face sometimes while hiding behind an illusory mask of self-proclaimed ideals.

This edition seeks to examine some changes which have greatly affected the working of the UN since the 1990s. These include the advent of new members from the developing world, the impact of changing superpower relations which diminished or enhanced its role from time to time, and the problems of security (interstate and intrastate) as it has played out in the international arena since the early years of the 21st century. Meeting the challenges of balanced growth and human development, is only possible through coordinated and adequately funded national and international efforts. The United Nations family has always led the international community. It is the prime duty of the UN to spearhead the efforts to assist countries in unleashing the positive forces of the global market, attract private capital, accelerate the momentum for Sustainable Development Goal implementation and reduce the risk of increased marginalization and inequality among regions and peoples.

At the global level, the current governance structures, constitute the United Nations agencies, the Bretton Woods Institutions, and the WTO. At present, new players, such as the World Economic Forum, the G-8, the G-20, BRICS, Non-Governmental Organizations (NGOs), and the media, have emerged on the global field. This does not mean that the United Nations and older multilateral institutions have lost their purpose of existence. However, the United Nations needs to revisit and revive some aspects of its mandate, functions, and responsibilities. Firstly, at present, the governance debate is still too narrow, concentrating mainly on concerns regarding economic growth and financial stability. The parity was very unbalanced as the G-8 dominated the discussions till recently. Now the developing world has been included in G-20.

The United Nations has advocated the broadening of equality in terms of issues and contributions. However, to do that, the UN requires the capacity to reclaim its role in development thinking. Simultaneously, when many countries have been undertaking fundamental reforms, the level of development assistance through UN bodies has steadily been lessening. Appropriate and effective aid levels need to be supported to give governments the space they require to put economic reforms on a self-sustaining path. In addition, development assistance needs to be restructured to focus on people-centred, inclusive development. To spell out the Sustainable Development Goals as the Minimum Agenda of Good Governance to be implemented by all signatory states by 2030, the UN has again got into a new kind of development thinking for the 21st century.

It is already clear that governance in the new millennium is unlikely to mean a single framework of international law applied through a unified global authority. More likely, it will be a multi-layered process of interaction between various forms of systems (states, citizens, and markets) and regulation (laws, conventions, and social norms). They will be working together to pursue common goals, resolve disputes and negotiate new trade-offs between conflicting interests.

The UN can help to ensure that the playing field for civic involvement has to encourage the broadest possible range of organizations to participate, especially from the South. Today, actors on the global stage are not only states: the private sector, NGOs, and multilateral agencies increasingly work with governments to find consensual solutions for global problems. With a constrained budget, the United Nations must strive not to usurp the role of these global actors, but to become a more effective catalyst for change and coordination among them, stimulating collective action at the global level. The organization's influence derives not from power but from the values it represents, its role in helping to sustain global norms, its ability to stimulate global concern and action as well as the trust inspired by its practical work to improve people's lives. The United Nations must build on these core strengths and at the same time adopt structural reforms and clearer consensus on priorities among member states. Decisions are needed from the General Assembly, for instance, to include time limits in new mandates and to introduce result-based budgeting. By reforming the Security Council, and expanding the relationship of the UN with civil society organizations and the private sector, the UN can both work effectively and enjoy unquestioned legitimacy. To serve states and people more efficiently, the United Nations must become more representative, more inclusive, and thereby more accessible to the peoples across the globe.

The development choices that we make will mould the 21st century. The successive Human Development Reports of the United Nations Development Programme (UNDP) state that the present era of globalization is characterized by the following distinctive features: (a) shrinking spaces; (b) disappearing borders; (c) growing interstate inequality and inequality within states. The globalization process links people's lives more deeply, more intensely, and more immediately than ever before. It is not only about integrating the economy but also culture, technology, and governance.

Globalization in its current form presents many universal challenges—challenges not only for each country but also for the institutions of global governance. No country or institution can escape from this globalization and its influence. However, in my opinion, the essential question is how to manage the process. Therefore, we need to question different forms of regulation at the national as well as international levels.

Globalization can unleash the positive forces of the global market if effective public action is taken at the national and international levels to develop the institutions and policies that would bring about inclusive growth. In addition, globalization can also facilitate the unleashing of our combined efforts and expertise to reach global solutions to major socio-economic problems. In an interdependent world, the manifestation of extreme poverty and the growing gap between the rich and the poor has decreased the prospects for global integration. The breakdown of peace and security over the years has led to the failure of peacekeeping and the emergence of budgetary crises. The disastrous political conflicts once between the East and the West and now between the North and the South have transformed international relations. The new emerging world order after the disintegration of the Soviet Union and the strategic implications of the demise of the Cold War has led to seminal changes in the power relations in the UN.

In some ways, the UN is coming into its own again. There is increasing recognition of the need for a multilateral approach to world problems—North-South issues, protection of the international environment, and the more immediate threats to peace within and between nations. Demands for UN peacekeeping forces are again widely being made in different conflict areas of the world. There is a new willingness to look to the UN for solutions to the above problems. The people begin to think better of the UN when it succeeds in its efforts. They will have greater hopes of maintenance of peace; the reverse is also true.

The UN has completed seventy-five years. With such a consensus of faith in the UN, the sudden changes in the international climate strengthened it. There is not just a return to the earlier hope that had greeted the birth of the world organization, but a hope tempered by a firmer sense of realities. There seems to be a strong desire to turn over a new leaf, to try innovative approaches to the solution to old problems. There is increasing recognition among the member-states of the UN regarding the futility of war as an instrument of national policy to solve bilateral and other kinds of problems. The East-West ideological debate has now lost its agenda and public appeal. Instead, states must evoke the courage and determination to fight against the causes of conflict, the struggle against economic inequalities, and the causes leading to the degradation of the environment. If anything is clear in the present world situation, it is that wars and preparations for war have dwindling constituencies while peace has a growing one.

In this new climate of optimism, therefore, it becomes almost necessary for us to have a fresh look at the United Nations to see how it can be better adapted to meet the growing demand for world peace that will be imposed on the world organization in future.

Since the 1990s, the member states have drafted new doctrines, such as the Responsibility to Protect, initiated the Sustainable Development Goals, which pursued "holistic" democracy in failing states, addressed issues like terrorism, sectarian violence, climate change, or recently handled a recalcitrant global power like China, while a pandemic-like Covid-19 played havoc with human lives and the world economy!

In the Millennium Summit—the largest-ever gathering of states held at UN Headquarters from 6–8 September 2000, world leaders established clear directions for the organization in the new century. The Millennium Declaration adopted unanimously a series of concrete goals and specific targets for the international community to meet the central challenge of ensuring that globalization becomes a positive force for all in the 21st century.

This revised edition, although delayed, was meant to be published for the seventy-fifth year of the UN. Some additions and deletions are incorporated—this edition will have 5 sections and 22 chapters.

In the end, I would like to thank my students, colleagues, friends, and readers from India and abroad, who have, by their overwhelming response in terms of suggestions, criticism, and overall enthusiasm, kept my energies alive to keep updating and revising the book from time to time. I owe a huge debt of gratitude to Miss Vibhu, Editor, Sterling Publishers for the enormous help and assistance she gave me to improve the quality of this new edition, by way of updating data and editing the last revised draft. Last but not the least, I would like to acknowledge the secretarial help and assistance I got from Rupak Kumar to complete the manuscript in the shortest possible time to meet the publishing deadlines.

Rumki Basu

CONTENTS

Part IV

Part V

INTRODUCTION

Since the 19th century, there was a desire for and a gradual move towards some form of international organization to achieve an objective of world unity. It was a compulsive reality produced by a century of technological change that had tied all the peoples together in an unprecedented intimacy of contact and interdependence. The history of international organization is not a very long one. The growing complexity of international relations has led to the evolution of international organizations. Currently, there are many international organizations – both in the public and private spheres. Although the present international organizations lack much, they are not few either in the public arena or in the private one. These organizations greatly vary in structure, purpose, and areas of operation. They are global and regional, specialized and multipurpose, their concerns ranging from abstract issues of war to concrete measures of peace-building. Others deal with technical measures like health, labour, civil aviation, and problems of refugees, women, and children. Thus, whether or not to organize is no longer a question open to debate; it is an irreversible process.

Before we begin a serious study of the United Nations (UN), it is essential to educate ourselves on how the UN works, what it does, and most importantly, what it could realistically be expected to do. People express disappointment at what the world organization has not been able to achieve. They entertain hopes about what it can be made to perform without any well-founded conception of what capacity the UN might reasonably be expected to have. It is foolish to be hopeful, cynical, or disillusioned, without first exploring the limitations imposed on the organization by the political context within which it operates.

The United Nations is an international agency called into being by states, sustained by states, and directed by states. Therefore, it can hardly be expected to act as an autonomous or independent participant in international affairs, for its very existence is dependent upon the will of states, and its functional capacity is also ultimately subject to their directions.

The progressive development of international organizations represents the additional introduction of features in international relations, which epitomize the characteristics of intra-state rather than traditional inter-state relationships. A popular notion existed for a long time that international organizations can be called successful in the degree to which their tasks increase and their authority strengthened at the expense of the state system which would wither away in proportion to the success of these bodies. However, what is often forgotten is that international agencies represent the efforts of states to further their interests by collaborating in the acceptance of restraint and responsibility and the curtailment of their sovereign power to the extent that would help a multi-state system to survive. Therefore, the agencies of the UN operating within the security sphere are regarded as instruments of assistance rather than as competitors of states. Their success in building a secure world order alone will lead to the protection of the multi-state system.

The history of the evolution of international organizations proves that they were pragmatic devices to achieve specific objectives. An international organization assumes the continuity of the multi-state system and seeks only to provide an effective means for the reconciliation of the conflicts that emerge from it.

The UN is not in any respect a super-state, able to act outside the framework of decisions made by its members. It can serve but is not a substitute for the efforts of its member governments. The United Nations can, therefore, be best defined as a state-serving, state-restraining, and state-protecting organization.

PART I
THE HISTORICAL BACKGROUND

1

THEORETICAL FOUNDATIONS OF INTERNATIONAL ORGANIZATION

Theories of International Relations aim to elucidate and interpret varied aspects of international phenomena and place them within an explanatory framework of models and paradigms. Every theoretical approach is based on a set of core ideas about the nature and roles of the state, and other non-state actors (including individual actors) in interstate interactions and their cumulative impact on global politics.

In international relations theory, one measures and explains the behaviour of states and institutions objectively in the backdrop of real events, through the positivist or rationalist theory, or focuses on the interpretation of the vocabulary and symbols of state interaction through constructivist or non-rationalist theory. The latter approach is especially relevant to global governance today since values, rules, and identities play important roles besides, the earlier traditional factors such as economic and military capabilities and national interest. Each approach and method provides convenient tools to study International Relations, interpret events and explain the objective rationale behind happenings in world politics.

Scholars and critics often think of international relations in binaries, either empirical or normative. In this context, the word "empirical" refers to things as they exist, rather than how they should be. In contrast, "normative" refers to how things ought to be, to standards or preferred norms of state behaviour.

From theory, propositions are hypothesized and tested by observations in the real international political space. For example, normative theory suggests that an international organization needs to grow from a macro technical focus to a broader macro-political vision. These hypotheses are tested against the backdrop of European or Asian regionalism, the history of making UN specialized agencies or tracing of historical and chronological case studies of multistate cooperation through particular institutions. This is the way rationalist theories establish links between independent and dependent variables.

In contrast, constructivism and most critical theories cannot be similarly tested. They can be critiqued regarding whether their assertions are internally logical or help to illustrate the true nature of international institutions. However, many social constructivists argue that for state or non-state actors, identities and interests are the product of debate and interaction, which one could study e.g. the evolution of a normative principle, such as disarmament against the use of force in international relations, explores whether this proposition can be justified or not.

In this chapter, we briefly discuss four major theories – Liberalism, Realism, Social Constructivism, and Critical theories – with particular attention to what each has to say about international cooperation, conflict, and global governance.

Liberalism

Liberalism starts with the core assertion that human nature is good, and therefore, human progress is possible. War and conflict will continue as long as there are corrupt social institutions and unavoidable misunderstandings among the ruling regimes of different states. They can be eliminated through multilateral action and institutional reform. The idea of linear progress and the inevitability of expanding human freedom is a core liberal conviction that liberals believe can be achieved through democracy and market capitalism. Due to their innate faith in human reason and societal progress, liberals have often been termed, Idealists.

The philosophy of US President Woodrow Wilson, (projected best in the "Fourteen Points"), on which the Versailles Treaty (ending World War I) and the Covenant of the League of Nations were established, laid the fundamentals of twentieth-century liberalism. Wilson envisioned the implementation of a system for collective security, promotion of the self-determination of peoples, the delimitation of power politics, and advocacy of international institutions for collective problem-solving to prevent war. The early-twentieth-century liberals were also strong advocates for using international law, arbitration, diplomacy, and mediation to promote world cooperation and peace.

For liberals, individuals are primary actors while states are the most important collective actors. Power relations among domestic and transnational groups and changing international conditions shape national interests and policies. There is no fixed definition of national interest as states' goals vary with their changing perceptions of national interest.

Liberals believe that international cooperation is possible and will grow over time. National power is a reality but should be exercised within a framework of rules, international law, and institutions. Liberals expect an increase in cooperation among states with greater interdependence, knowledge, communication, peace, welfare, justice, and democratization of politics within and between states. To liberals, international organizations are global spaces where states interact and cooperate to solve common problems through rules drafted by consensus. They are the major instruments for framing and maintaining peace and order in world politics.

For liberals, intergovernmental organizations play many crucial roles, including contributing to habits of cooperation and serving as arenas for negotiating and developing coalitions among and between the North and the South. A body of research (devoted to the "democratic peace" thesis) opines that democratization as a process has expanded during the late twentieth century, that democracies normally will not go to war against one another so global regimes of law and cooperation can be developed and then studied as examples of human progress. For liberal idealists, nation-states are only one set of actors in world politics, and they can cooperate through intergovernmental institutions like the United Nations.

Neoliberalism

In the 1970s, liberalism experienced a resurgence following the ascendancy of the realist theory during the Cold War period. An increased international interdependence and an awareness of the vulnerabilities that characterized interdependence were major factors that boosted the revival of liberalism. Robert Keohane and Joseph Nye's book *Power and Interdependence* (1977), which delineated how international institutions constituted a critical response to conditions of complex interdependence, also added an impetus to its resurgence. Neoliberal institutionalists argue that despite serious barriers constraining the willingness of states to cooperate, states can still work together with the support of international institutions. They, therefore, take on a more state-centric and optimistic view of international relations and believe that states are rational actors in a generally anarchic world. States have incentives to cooperate with institutions and liberal states can solve common problems through collective action.

Some initiatives of UN-related institutions, such as the World Bank, the International Monetary Fund, and the World Trade Organization or General Agreement on Tariffs and Trade, brought neoliberalism into sharp focus. The UN affiliates believed that economic integration is a forerunner to political integration, a view espoused by neoliberal theorists as well.

Neoliberalism efforts to integrate the world economy further through regionalism include such initiatives as the North American Free Trade Association (NAFTA), the World Trade Organization (WTO), and proposed free-trade regimes between the Americas (The continents of North America and South America) and the Asia and between the Americas and Europe.

Liberal internationalism emphasizes democracy, equality (of classes, races, ethnicities, religions, and genders), human rights, and dispute resolution via international law and international organizations, such as the United Nations. Liberal internationalism also stresses the benefits of rule-based market capitalism, open-world trade, the cross-border liquidity of finance, and the fluid movement of goods, people, and money internationally as part of globalization.

Keohane's much-read book *After Hegemony* (1984) noted and emphasized the cooperation that states achieved through international institutions and the positive effects of institutions and practices on state behaviour. States benefit because institutions do things for members that cannot be accomplished by unilateral actions of states. Thus, institutions have critical effects on interstate interactions, both by providing information and by framing actions of state cooperation that lead to integration, both economic and political in the long run.

Realism

Within the international system, realists see states as the primary actors, in pursuit of their national interest, to maximize power and security relative to other states. States coexist in an anarchic international system, characterized by the absence of a decisive authoritative single power-wielding agency. As a result, states must rely primarily on themselves to manage their insecurity through the balance of power and deterrence. Each state is concerned with acquiring more power relative to other states. As the competition between states is keen, there is little basis for cooperation.

To most realists, in the absence of an international authority, there are few rules or norms that restrain states, although Hans Morgenthau, generally regarded as 'the Father of Modern Realism,' did include chapters on international morality, law, and government in his path-breaking book *Politics Among Nations*.

For Morgenthau, international organizations are instruments of states to increase or decrease their powers. But they do not affect the basic characteristics of the international system because they reflect the distribution of power among states, they are no more than the sum of their member states. They are susceptible to great-power manipulation. Thus, international organizations have no independent effect on state behaviour or world politics in general, according to the majority of realists. In short, realists argue that "hard" politics is a play for enhanced power acquisition, a competition in which all states indulge and this is the only real constant in world politics, leaving little room for international cooperation.

Neorealism

Among the variants of realism, the most powerful is neorealism, or structural realism, which owes much to Kenneth Waltz's *Theory of International Politics* (1979). The core difference between traditional realists and neorealists lies in the emphasis placed on the structure of the international system for explaining world politics. The system's structure is determined by the ordering principle, namely the absence of overarching authority leading to anarchy, and the distribution of capabilities (power) among states. What matters the most is states' material capabilities, states' identities, and interests which are largely given leverage. Anarchy poses a severe constraint on state behaviour.

The neorealists emphasize relative gains from limited cooperation and those actors with common interests try to maximize their absolute gains. Relative gains may be more important in security matters than in economic issues, making cooperation more difficult to achieve, harder to maintain, and more dependent on states' power since anarchy fuels insecurity. States are wary of becoming too dependent on others. They prefer to exercise greater control and increase their capabilities. Neorealists also believe that international institutions are independent variables in international politics. But the most important point they emphasize is that power politics will never change, prospects for global cooperation and the impact of international institutions will always be limited.

Social Constructivism

Social constructivism has become increasingly an important approach for studying the role of norms and institutions in global governance. All variants of constructivists agree that the behaviour of individuals, states, and other actors is shaped by socially constructed roles and shared beliefs.

At the core of the constructivist approach is a conviction that ideas, values, norms, and shared beliefs matter, how individuals feel about the world shape practices, and that people are capable of transforming the world by changing their mindsets. Realists treat states, interests, and identity as given, whereas constructivists believe they are socially constructed, that is, influenced by culture, norms, and ideas, domestic and international interactions that can and do change. For example, the colonial powers struggled to redefine their identities in the aftermath of decolonization as much as Russia is doing now after the collapse of the Soviet Union. For constructivists, then, states do not have identities or national interests before their interactions with others. As Alexander Wendt explains, theory analyses how processes of interaction produce and reproduce the social structures—cooperative or conflictual—that shape identities and interests of individuals, groups, and states. The constructivist theory emphasizes that norms and culture, which shape a group's identity as a people or nation, play important roles in world affairs. Different cultures, institutions, and norms can affect the way nations interact with each other. In the post-Cold War era, with advancements in global communications, some constructivists believed that the United Nations, supported a multitude of state and non-state actors to push forward the global discourse on issues and norms related to women's empowerment, human rights development, and the issue of North-South divide, among others.

In examining international organizations, constructivists seek to discover the social content of organizations and the dominant norms that govern behaviour and shape interests. They also decipher how these interests, in turn, influence state actors and impact their behavioural patterns.

Thus, to constructivists, international organizations are purposive actors with independent effects on international relations. They have played an eminent role in the process of changing the understandings and behaviour of state actors concerning poverty, humanitarianism, colonialism, slavery, and other problems in human history.

Marxist Theory

Marxism, though largely discredited with the demise of the Soviet Union and the triumph of capitalism, is still a prime approach for describing the class hierarchy in the international system and the role of economic practices in determining that hierarchy. It still influences scholarly thinking in the developing world, whose colonial past and ongoing experience with capitalism are characterized by poverty, inequalities, social divides, and economic marginalization. Marxist and neo-Marxist critical theories contribute important perspectives for understanding international relations and global governance through the frameworks they provide for linking politics, economics, social forces, and structures of world order.

Like Realism and Liberalism, Marxism comprises a set of core ideas that unite its variants. These include a grounding in historical analysis, the primacy of economic forces in explaining political and social phenomena, the particular character of capitalism as a global mode of production, and the important role of social or economic classes in shaping the ideology and societal norms and beliefs.

Marxist opinions about the structure of the global economic system and global governance are rooted in these ideas. Thus, developed countries have expanded economically (and in the bygone era politically, through imperialism), enabling them to sell goods and export surplus wealth that they could not absorb at home. Similarly, developing countries have become increasingly constrained and dependent on the actions of the developed through neo-imperialistic ties in today's post-globalized world.

Marxist theorists propose that the world is hegemonized by a bourgeois class, bent upon maintaining its global monopoly of power through the instrument of the state. The ascendant global elite is not necessarily imperialistic or overtly exercising power. The international bourgeoisie attempts to hegemonize and control through the instruments of foreign trade, aid, investment, and loans besides other instruments.

For Marxists, international organizations like the United Nations can best be studied in a global backdrop wherein an economic struggle takes place between the privileged class and those representing an immediate challenge (such as the Second World of the Soviet region of influence during the Cold War) or those (such as the less fortunate in the developing countries) beneath it. In an era of globalization, the worldwide capitalist class uses international organizations, financial institutions, and competitive markets to maintain its hegemony.

Neo-Marxist Theories

Neo-Marxism emphasizes the varying techniques of domination and suppression that arise from the uneven economic development inherent in the capitalist system Antonio Gramsci (1891-1937), had considerable influence on critical theorists and some neoliberal institutionalists. However, Gramsci's particular interpretation of "hegemony" was understood as a relationship of consent to political and ideological leadership, without implying domination by brute force. Thus, Cox (1992) argued that the foundation of the "hegemonic order" lies in the ideologies of the dominant social strata of the dominant state with the underlying consent of the dominant social strata of other states.

These views have important implications for neo-Marxist theorizing about contemporary global governance. Cox (1986) and Stephen Gill (1994) have emphasized the importance of "globalizing elites" in the restructuring of the global political economy, and hence global governance. These elites are found in the key economic institutions (the IMF, WTO, and World Bank), in finance ministries of G-8 countries, in the headquarters of MNCs, and in private international relations councils (e.g. the Council on Foreign Relations and Trilateral Commission), etc.

Neo-Marxists view international law and organizations as subtle but powerful instruments of dominant states and dominant ideas, in the interests of the capitalist class. Some view them as instruments of capitalist domination imposed on others. According to the Gramscian view, international organizations are a means to get others to consent to domination through shared ideas, which have been instrumental in the development of the modern capitalist state by facilitating industrial change and the development of liberal ideology. Scholars also see them as being concerned with long-term questions of restructuring the global international order and how international organizations can help shape that change in harmony with prevailing majoritarian world views.

Conclusion

In International Relations theory we have come to believe that Realism is about the relentless pursuit of national power and interest by states, that Liberals are votaries of interstate cooperation that Constructivists see norms as critical in explaining state behaviour, and that Marxism is all about the withering away of the state and the forging of proletarian internationalism.

Each of these presuppositions is probably an exaggerated and one-sided oversimplification. All four approaches above are about political power and the realities of national interest – however, one must understand that realism does not monopolize the study of power, just as liberalism should not monopolize the study of national interest. Marxist and Constructivist theories also inhere in power politics and national interests just as much as liberals and realists.

It is also distended to assume that realists are "pessimists" about international cooperation while liberals and/or constructivists are "optimists." These approaches do not unequivocally tell us whether international organizations will enlarge or diminish, will be successful in their outcomes or not. Instead, they can only opine under what circumstances we might expect international organizations to evolve and with what shape. They also outline and interpret with reasons the powers and limits of international organizations.

Finally, it is too simplistic to associate constructivism with international "standard-setting" as distinct from calculations of power and national interest. Constructivists are as concerned with national interest as any other school of theory. What is different about constructivism is its underlying assumption that one should pay attention to how the national actor perceives its self-interest, and how those are shaped by the external environment and by the process of interacting within that milieu or space. All theories deal with common concerns like power, norms, national interest, conflict, and cooperation, but how they use these concerns to interpret state behaviour or interstate action, is what makes each one different from the other.

Cited Works

Baylis, John and Steve Smith, *The Globalization of World Politics: An Introduction to International Relations*, New York: Oxford University Press, 2005.

Burchill, Scott, Linklater, Andrew, Devetak, Richard, Donnelly, Jack, Terry Nardin, Matthew, Paterson, Reus-Smit, Christian, and True, Jacqui, *Theories of International Relations*. New York: Palgrave, 2001.

Cox, Robert., 'Social Forces, States and World Orders: Beyond International Relations Theory,' *Millennium: Journal of International Studies*, 1981.

Cox, Robert W., "Multilateralism and World Order," *Review of International Studies*, vol. 18, no. 2, Cambridge University Press, 1992, pp. 161–80, *http://www.jstor.org/stable/20097291*.

Cox, Robert, 'Gramsci, Hegemony and International Relations: An Essay in Method', *Millennium: Journal of International Studies*, 12 (2): 162-75., 1983

Folker, Jennifer Sterling (ed.), *Making Sense of International Relations Theory*, New Delhi: Viva Books, 2007.

Gill, Stephen. *Gramsci, Historical Materialism and International Relations*, New York: Cambridge University Press, 1994.

Hurd, Ian, *International Organizations: Politics, Law, Practice,* 2nd edition, New York: Cambridge University Press, 2014.

Kadloor, Savitri, "Major Theoretical Approaches to the Development of International Organization, *Jadavpur Journal of International Relations*, Vol.2, 1996, pg. 43-63.

Keohane Robert and Joseph Nye, *Power and interdependence*, Boston, Little, Brown and Company, *1977.*

Keohane Robert, *After Hegemony: Cooperation and Discord in the World Political Economy),* Princeton University Press, 1984.

Moore, John Allphin Jr., and Jerry, Pubantz, *The New United Nations: International Organization in the Twenty-First Century,* 2nd edition, New York & London, Routledge, 2017.

Morgenthau, Hans J., and Kenneth, W. Thompson, *Politics Among Nations: The Struggle for Power and Peace*, 6th edition. New York: Alfred A. Knopf, 1985.

Viotti, Paul R., Mark V., Kauppi, *International Relations Theory: Realism, Pluralism, Globalism*, New York: Macmillan, 1990.

Waltz, Kenneth. *Theory of International Politics. Reading*, MA: Addison Wesley, 1979.

Wendt, Alexander, *Social Theory of International Politics*, Cambridge: Cambridge University Press, 1999.

2

THE EVOLUTION OF INTERNATIONAL ORGANIZATION

There are some universally accepted prerequisites for the development of the international organization. First, the world must divide into independent states; second, they must be aware of the problems arising out of their coexistence; and third, they must approach and recognize the need for the creation of institutional devices to regulate their relations with one another. During the 19th century, these prerequisite findings were for the first time existent in proper order to bring about the birth of a modern international organization.

There are three main categories to classify the direct predecessors of modern international organizations. The first category included international conferences on world politics. There were meetings held at the end of major wars to arrive at settlements for the post-war period or gatherings in peacetime to cope with crises of one sort or another among states. The second category included international conferences organized for the development of international law. The third category included the creation of a chain of functional organizations during the 19th century to deal with technical and administrative matters affecting more than one country. Taken together, these three forms of international cooperation provided an experience that contributed to the growth of two intergovernmental organizations—the League of Nations and the United Nations— established to deal, generally, with political and economic matters affecting all countries in the 20th century.

During the 16th century, the division of Christendom and the subsequent strengthening of national dynasties finally loosened the grip of the declining Roman Empire that gave birth to the modern state system. During the 17th and 18th centuries, the statesmen of different nations negotiated to resolve bilateral and multilateral problems. These conferences paved the way for the growth of an international organization.

The first major European peace conference to restore order after the war took place in 1648; it was the Peace Treaty of Westphalia, which terminated the Thirty Years' War. Almost all of the then-existing nations and states sent their representatives to that conference. These were the states of Europe, the "world" of international politics in the 19th century. Thus, the origin of modern international organizations was founded on European diplomacy, from treaties that led to the emergence of a new *status quo* in Europe. The Treaty of Westphalia set the trend for similar international peace conferences such as the Utrecht Peace Settlement (1713) and the Congress of Vienna (1815), which rebuilt European order after the wars of Louis XIV and Napoleon, respectively. The negotiation of two multilateral treaties which legalized the new order of European international politics was the diplomatic achievement of the Treaty of Westphalia. The Peace of Utrecht shattered imperial aspirations and furthered the creation of several independent sovereignties. Three new dynasties received recognition at the conference: France recognized the Protestant succession to the British throne, Frederick I— the Elector of Brandenburg took the title of King of Prussia, and Victor Amadeus II the internationally sanctioned monarch of Sicily restored Nice.

Some prominent philosophers like Penn, Pierrie, Bentham, and Kant advanced significant proposals and ideas on international organization. These philosophers emphasized peace and equality of people in their works: William Penn in— "An Essay Towards the Present and Future Peace of Europe" (1693), the Abbe de Saint Pierre in his "Project to Bring Perpetual Peace in Europe" (1712), Bentham in his "Principles of International Law" (1843) and Kant in his essay— "Perpetual Peace" (1795).

During the 17th and 18th centuries, some new plans for international organizations surfaced. The Duke of Sully, the Prime Minister of Henry IV of France, in his memoirs proposed a European confederation of fifteen states. William Penn suggested the establishment of a European Diet, Parliament, or Estates in his essay in 1693. Even in the Peace of Utrecht, Abbe de Saint Pierre had called upon the sovereigns to submit their differences to judicial settlement for an everlasting peace among nations. He also proposed that if any recalcitrant state refuses to accept the decision of the court, other states should unite their military forces against it. However, these schemes, containing some significant ideas for the growth of future international organizations found no general acceptance within the 17th and 18th-century state system. The treaties signed at Westphalia and Utrecht temporarily stabilized the western European state system, but two other powers, Russia and Turkey, had been excluded from the treaties. These two powers became parties to a general European Congress only at the Treaties of Carlowitz in 1699.

The Congress of Vienna was the first international conference that played an eminent part in 19th-century European politics.

The system, thus, initiated came to be known as the "Concert of Europe". In comparison with the pre-Napoleonic international conferences, the Congress of Vienna made a remarkable advance towards the international organization in the following ways:

(a) The political settlement reached,

(b) The diversity of the socio-economic- problems treated, and

(c) The adoption of a procedure for Congress itself.

Apart from reinstating the original boundaries of France, the settlement restored territories to those countries that Napoleon had overrun. The Congress of Vienna affirmed the neutrality of Switzerland.

In the socio-economic field, the Congress of Vienna made efforts to abolish slavery. Every international river bounding or traversing upon the signatory states was not only declared open to commerce, but the states also pledged to regulate, by common consent, rules regarding their navigation. An effort was made to protect minorities and human rights and take necessary steps to safeguard the civil status of the Jews in Germany. The Congress gave a threefold classification of diplomatic envoys, the concept of equality thus, formed the basis of negotiations for the European states not only at conferences but also in their day-to-day dealings. The Congress of Vienna also marked a change in the procedure adopted for conducting conference proceedings. The earlier conferences had elected no presiding officers and appointed no committees for their work. That was not the case with the Congress of Vienna, which had Metternich as President and Friedrich Von Gentz as its Secretary-General. All countries, enemies, allies, and even neutrals received invitations. The delegates at Vienna surely laid the foundations of a political and international system that shaped the course of European and, to some extent, world affairs for a century. The "Grand Alliance" of 1815 (Great Britain, Prussia, Austria, Russia, and later, joined by France) to assure that the Vienna accords would be fulfilled, thereby preserving stability in Europe. Between 1818 and 1822, the four meetings held discussions on the problems threatening European peace. The main purpose of the Grand Alliance was to maintain the European *status quo* that had been threatened from time to time by the ambitions of the Great Powers.

The Grand Alliance contributed to the later conceptual development of the international organizations in three significant respects: first, cooperation among states continued after the defeat of the common enemy – France – which joined the Alliance due to her ideology of equality; second, meetings attended by representatives of the Great Powers likely took place from time to time; third, the idea prevailed that peace in Europe, as well as the rest of the world, depended on the reaching of agreements among the major powers. These ideas dominated the Concert of Europe during the 19th century. The major powers – France, Great Britain, Prussia, Austria, and Russia – took decisions, even when the minor powers joined the Grand Alliance (after consultations with them). The issues discussed at the London Conference brought about Greek independence (1829). Belgian independence was the outcome of the London Conference of 1830. The Congress of Paris (1856) was summoned for the Crimean War, due to the territorial expansion of the Ottoman Empire and several issues related to the Russo-Austrian-Turkish conflicts in the Balkans. The last meeting of the Concert of Europe, the London Conference of 1913, also dealt with the Balkans, where the tension among the Austro-Hungarian and Russian empires eventually led to World War I.

The Concert of Europe was an exclusive club of the Great Powers, whose members became the self-appointed guardians of Europe. The purpose of these conferences became more and more varied concerning subjects such as the maintenance of peace, adoption of pacific methods for settlement of disputes, agreements upon ground rules for playing the competitive game of imperialism, and the formulation of general standards for the codification of international law.

The Concert of Europe prevented or limited some potential armed conflicts. Yet it was far from the established international conventions held today in bodies like the United Nations. In the Concert of Europe, there were neither fixed rules and procedures nor periodic meetings. The *ad hoc* nature of these conferences is often complicated and delays international cooperation. The Great Powers sponsor these conferences and send invitations to other states. There was no principle of automatic representation of all states. The consultative system was also rather clumsy in its handling of crises. Besides, the opinions of minor states had no weightage. Yet the Concert of Europe not only laid the principle of collective diplomatic consultation on all major international issues but had also made considerable progress in developing the techniques and psychological prerequisites for successful multilateral negotiations.

The Hague System

During the 19th century, the development of machinery for adjudication of international disputes was a step that led towards an international organization. While diplomats, philosophers, and sovereigns were engaged in thinking of schemes for world peace and the world was alternating between periods of peace and small wars, a significant development took place. The Dutch jurist, Hugo Grotius primarily contributed to the evolution of international law in the 17th-century. Living in a period of war Grotius felt the urgency for peace. In working out a system of international law, he derived his principles based on the Roman ideas of *jus gentium* and *jus naturale*. The synthesis of ideas into a single system of natural law or a body of customs ratified among the states from time to time.

The Hague Peace Conferences were regarded as landmarks in the development of international law and organization. These two conferences of 1899 and 1907 attempted to revise, clarify and codify the whole body of international law affecting the conduct of war, thereby placing international law on a new footing.

In general, the conferences also aimed at improving international relations by such means as disarmament and peaceful settlement of disputes. The Czar Nicholas II of Russia took the initiative to convene these conferences at The Hague. His idea was to hold periodic meetings, establish institutional codes or rules of warfare among nations and use pacific means of settlement. An underlying principle for modern international bodies – universal membership – provided the basis for the conferences. The First Hague Peace Conference in 1899 comprised 26 states, while 43 states took part in the second conference of 1907. The outbreak of World War I prevented further development of the system. The Third Hague Peace Conference, planned for 1915, was cancelled.

Besides introducing the general idea of holding periodic conferences, the Hague meetings also produced some more concrete results. One of them was the establishment of a Permanent Court of International Arbitration. The court consisted of a panel of qualified jurists and mediators who gave binding decisions on international disputes when called upon by governments. A Secretary-General presiding over an international bureau was also a permanent feature of the organization.

The two Hague conferences were assemblies of the major countries of the world held for the sole purpose of developing a body of international law. They provided an elaborate code for land and naval warfare. Without the development of international law, the history of international organizations could not have begun.

Functional Alliance in the 19th Century

The second development of major importance for the later formation of the international organization took place during the latter part of the 19th-century. Therefore, the governments understood that mutual coordination was a necessity for them to carry on various activities— postal and telegraphic services, meteorological condition or data analysis, medical services, and commuting across the globe. Until then, national governments had supported such services. Their programmes, therefore, had, too, a limited range to develop their full potential. The required international coordination demanded institutionalization, rather than occasional *ad hoc* international conferences. In institutions, central bureaus collected information and prepared periodic meetings that took national approaches to resolve common problems. On this basis, governments acted in an organized manner to establish international norms to govern the states.

The creation of international public or administrative unions represented concrete steps towards such permanent institutional arrangements. Between 1865 and 1914, at least 33 of these international unions organized and operated in transport, communication, medicine, and economics. Among the best known are the International Telegraph Bureau (1868), the Universal Postal Union (1874, which still exists), the International Bureau of Weights and Measures (1875), and the International Institute of Agriculture (1889).

The cooperation by private persons through transnational organizations devoted to coordinating activities in many countries also came into being. Examples of this type of activity included the Red Cross movement, founded in 1864 by the Swiss, Henry Dunant; the Inter-parliamentary Union (1888); and the International Olympic Committee (1894. Between 1865 and 1914, a total of 26 law-related organizations were created by non-governmental sponsors. These organizations, of course, often dealt with issues closely related to the work of governmental agencies.

They engaged in a range of activities. They served as clearing houses of information, centres for discussion on common problems, instruments for achieving coordination by agreement of national policies, and agencies for promoting the formulation and acceptance of minimum standards.

These international agencies (governmental and non-governmental) possessed some specific characteristics which may be enumerated as follows:

1. Multilateral treaties created these agencies whose competence was limited to functional areas. These served as a constitution that proclaimed the aims and objectives of the organization. They laid down the institutional structure and defined the rights and duties of the members.
2. They were all voluntary organizations based on the equality of all their member states.
3. The structure of these bodies had a threefold division: a conference of all the members which met at intervals to lay down the basic policy of the organization; a council which was the main executive organ and was limited in membership; and a secretariat which consisted of international civil servants to conduct the routine functions of the organizations.
4. The principle of majoritarianism where all members had equality of voting rights forms the basis of decision-making.
5. Many organizations had a certain legal status that enable them to own property, to sue and be sued, and in some cases enjoy a measure of diplomatic immunity.
6. In budgetary matters, the member states financially supported the organizations. They followed the principle of "ability to pay", "equality" or a formula that was a combination of these principles.
7. Decision-making was carried on in two ways: firstly, by drafting international treaties and secondly, by submitting them to the member states for ratification, or by adopting resolutions and recommending action by member states. Some organizations had administrative and minor policy-making powers.

Thus, we find that the concept of an international organization that evolved during the 19th-century was partly the result of the Concert of Europe which promoted the idea of international consultation. The Hague system provided the rules and regulations for international unions as the symbols of cooperation. Inevitable distinctions that emerged during the 19th century, between political and non-political agencies, between the position of great and small powers, and between regional and geographically undefined organizations—all contributed to the phenomenal outgrowth of international agencies. Therefore, the two factors behind the motivation of international institution-building were:

1. The need to promote coordinated responses by states to the problems of peaceful interaction in an era of growing economic, social and technical interdependence and;
2. The corresponding need for containing and moderating conflict in the political and military spheres also became operative in this period. Without the international consultation and institution-building in the 19th century, the world could never have evolved towards the two major international organizations of the 20th century: the League of Nations and the United Nations.

Cited Works

Claude, Iris L., *Swords into Ploughshares*, New York: Random, 1971.

Goodspeed, S.S., *The Nature and Functions of International Organisation*, New York: OUP, 1967.

Mangone, Gerald J., *A Short History of International Organisation*, New York: McGraw-Hill Book Company, 1954.

Nicholas H., *The United Nations as a Political Institution*, London: OUP, 1975.

Riggs, Robert E. & C. Jack Plano, *The United Nations: International Organisation and World Politics*, Chicago: The Dorsey Press, 1988.

3

THE LEAGUE OF NATIONS

Of all the predecessors of the United Nations, the League of Nations was the most significant one. It contributed innovative ideas, practices, and experiences the United Nations later adopted. The League was the brainchild of President Woodrow Wilson of the United States. In the last of the famous 14 points that set out the war aims of his government, he proposed:

A general association of nations had to form under specific covenants that afford mutual guarantees of political independence and territorial integrity to great and small states alike.

This idea, together with the plans of Great Britain and France, formed the basis of negotiations at the Versailles Peace Conference of 1919. Its outcome was the Covenant of the League of Nations, an integral part of the Versailles Treaty that formally terminated World War I. The principal purpose of the League was to prevent the repetition of such a disaster ever again.

The League of Nations started as a permanent organization and can be understood as the institutional version of the *ad hoc* conferences of the Concert of Europe. Its various organs met periodically at annual meetings. It had a permanent staff headed by a Secretary-General with a permanent headquarters in Geneva. To promote the general purposes of fostering international cooperation and maintenance of peace and security, all members of the League as sovereign states accepted certain obligations. They committed themselves to solve mutual conflicts without going to war. Organs of the League and parties to them dealt with those conflicts put before them. As expected to defer to their decisions, some of which were legally binding. If a state went to war in defiance of the Covenant of the League of Nations, the members could employ diplomatic, financial, and even military sanctions against the offender.

Never before did the establishment of the League had so many meetings at the international level as it did then. It served as an influential unparalleled experiment having both deliberative organs and procedures. Besides its political bodies, the League system included the most ambitious court of law ever established to settle disputes among states and a permanent staff internationally recruited with headquarters in Geneva. A new inroad to simplify the decolonization process was that the League's supervised the Mandatory system. It was one of the most vital functions devised by the League Covenant. The Mandate system was the name given to the method adopted by the League to deal with the colonies taken over from Germany and Turkey after World War I. Under the Mandate system, certain imperialist powers controlled these colonies on behalf of the League. The administrative functions allowed them to protect local interests and rule according to a framework set by the League. The concept of international accountability of colonies was, therefore, introduced by the Mandate system.

The Permanent Court of International Justice, affiliated with the League, had a bench of 15 justices. They enjoyed a stature derived from appointment by the Council and Assembly of the League acting jointly. Many governments referred several landmark cases to the court in which it made significant advisory pronouncements from its chambers at The Hague. Meanwhile, in Geneva, the first Secretary-General of the League, Sir Eric Drummond, put together a skilful permanent staff to build up the first International Secretariat, which laid down the functional principles of what came to be known as the International Civil Service.

The Assembly representing all members concurrently shared the principal responsibility for settling disputes. However, the smaller Councils represented the Great Powers. Both organs had equal authority and could deal with any matter that was either within the jurisdiction of the organization or threatened international peace. Generally, the cases related to the disputes put before the Council at short notice summon. In matters of decision-making, the influence of the old international conference system was felt at work, As the Great Powers could not comply with the mandates of the majority. Consequently, all decisions required unanimity, which in effect meant that every member-state had the right to veto.

Despite this lack of formal authority, the League used elaborated methods to settle disputes and institutionalized diplomatic practices that had frequently served well earlier. Members agreed in principle to subject their cases of disputes to arbitration or to put them before the Permanent Court of International Justice. The cases dealing with disputes submitted to the Council did not require legal treatment by a tribunal. While others for a less specific treatment were submitted to the Assembly.

In handling a dispute, the League Council had to make a serious effort to find a settlement. If it did not succeed in this effort, the Council had to prepare a report on the facts of the dispute and recommended its settlement. Members undertook not to resort to war during a cooling-off period of three months after an arbitral, court decision, or a report by the Council. A resort to war was, thus, considered an attack against all (that was the concept of 'collective security,' a League innovation), invoking automatic sanctions during that period. The Council could organize these actions and go beyond them to supply armed forces to counter the aggressor. The members declared themselves prepared to give each other mutual financial support to take action against the possible aggression. They also enjoyed the privilege to permit the armed forces to act against the violator of the Covenant.

Causes of the Failure of the League

From the very beginning, the League lacked the cooperation of some of the major powers. Since the inception of the League in 1919, an assumption that all states in the world would join it, that is, its membership would be universal proved wrong. President Wilson of the United States, who initiated the institution, had faced utter disappointment. Being influenced by both isolationist and Utopian tendencies, the US Senate refused to approve the Treaty of Versailles. The senators feared that it meant the abandonment of the time-honoured US principle of non-involvement in European affairs. Thus, some major powers never joined the system of collective security.

Without US participation, the predominantly European character of the new organization gained further emphasis. Japan was the only non-European member of any importance. Except for Great Britain and France, which remained members during the entire life of the League, most of the major powers joined it only for brief periods. Germany joined in 1926 but withdrew in 1933 when Japan also left after being condemned for its intervention in Manchuria. The withdrawal of Italy from the League in 1937 after its conquest of Ethiopia. The Soviet Union joined in 1934 but had withdrawn after it attacked Finland in 1939.

The fundamental principles of the League came in conflict with the policy of some states led to the failure to obtain universal membership and the unwillingness to renounce war. Moreover, the members declined to accept the rule. The main idea behind the League's principle of collective security emphasized that an attack on any one of its member-states was considered an attack on all others. The sense of community feeling and confidence needed have achieved positive results in the first decade of the existence of the League. However, singularly lacking a sense of collective security in the 1930s, it failed to repeat its earlier achievement. During the first half of its existence, the League had comparatively more members and fewer disputes. It successfully brought many cases of disputes to an end. These included hostilities between Bulgaria and Greece and disputes between Sweden and Finland over the Aaland Island in 1925.

During the next decade, the League attempted to deal with serious conflicts involving more powerful states, but it did not succeed. Japan gave no heed to demands by the League that it should cease attacking China, and Italian fascist Mussolini directed the conquest of Ethiopia before the sanctions ordered by the League could have any effect.

However, the Abyssinian war was the only time when sanctions were invoked without success. The economic sanctions were imposed against Italy except concerning oil after a great deal of delay. France was almost unwilling to carry out her share of the sanctions due to her eagerness to keep Italy as a potential ally in any future combat with

Germany. Great Britain imposed sanctions half-heartedly and made it clear that it was not prepared to risk any war with Italy. Military sanctions, in any case, were never attempted under the League or the Anglo-French appeasement policy further weakened the League. England and France were so afraid of driving Fascist Italy into the open arms of the Nazis-Germany under Hitler turned a deaf ear to the helpless appeals of Abyssinia. Rearmament of Germany, the Italian invasion of Abyssinia, the Japanese aggression on Manchuria, and the Rome-Berlin-Tokyo Axis, followed by the unprovoked German aggression on Austria, Czechoslovakia, Algeria, and Poland brought about the dissolution of the League.

In fact, after the conquest of Ethiopia and the resignation of Italy, the League had little political significance. The Spanish Civil War never figured on its agenda in a meaningful way, despite the intervention of Italy, Germany, and the Soviet Union. The League at the Munich Conference considered the German demands on Czechoslovakia beyond its power. The expulsion of the Soviet Union for its attack on Finland did little for the embattled Finns. The German attack on Poland in 1939, which was the signal for the beginning of World War II, never came on the agenda of the League.

Many analysts attribute the failure of the League to the unwillingness of the Great Powers (England and France) to use the collective security of the League. The non-universality of membership, itself a crippling blow to collective security, pointed to a broader lack of agreement among the Great Powers than the hesitancies of the British and the French governments. In addition, the unanimity rule of voting in the Council and the Assembly created a structural obstacle to action. Nevertheless, in limited conflicts among small states, the League often found it possible to make a profound impact, even if it could not cope with a deliberate policy of aggression, such as that of Japan, Italy, Germany, and the Soviet Union.

The League could never impose sanctions whenever needed. The major nation-states, who could carry them out, took too much time to decide and withdrew support. There was no way to enforce sanctions as the League did not possess an armed force and, unlike the United Nations, could not play the role of peacekeeping.

The period of the League was one of constant political instability in the international arena, where it was unprepared to deal with such crises. The international system faced one of the worst economic crises. The League performed very few functions in the economic and social spheres. The concept of peace-building was then a relatively neglected area of concern. It attracted interest only after World War II.

The nations believing in old diplomatic practices were suspicious of the new methods of open diplomacy practised by the League. The League Covenant was a part of the Treaty of Versailles and the members, therefore, used the League to fulfil its treaty obligations. Its political fallout is reflected in the working of the League. Any changes in the League Covenant needed unanimity, which was extremely difficult to attain in such a large body as the League.

Moreover, some other potentially burning issues related to the European boundaries and national self-determination had not been settled amicably by the peace treaties, concluded after World War I. The European state system was still in a state of ferment and a general feeling existed that the victorious powers of World War I dominated the League. Unless nation-states enacted a political settlement acceptable to all was made, the League system was bound to face disruptive forces, signalled time and again, by disgruntled elements to whom the Paris Peace Treaties did not appear justified. Coupled with this was the frequent use of the plea for "domestic jurisdiction," by nations, which made it increasingly difficult for the League to interfere in many conflicts. The League's attempts at disarmament (especially in general and comprehensive disarmament) were doomed to failure.

The final analysis stressed that the political environment was not conducive to international peace, while the demands for interdependence were left unrecognized. By far, national interest and state sovereignty were the greatest hindrances to the effective functioning of the League.

Cited Works

Carr, E.H., *The Twenty Years Crisis 1919-1939*, Toronto: Macmillan, 1946.

Rendiner, Elmer, *A Time for Angels: Tragicomic History of the League of Nations*, London: Weidenfield and Nicolson, 1975.

Scott, George, *The Rise and Fall of the League of Nations*, New York: Macmillan 1974.

Webster, C.K. & Herbert Sydney, *The League of Nations in Theory and Practice*, Boston: Houghton, 1933.

Zimmern, Alfred, *The League of Nations and the Rule of Law, 1918-1935*, London: Macmillan, 1936.

4

THE BIRTH OF THE UNITED NATIONS: PURPOSES AND PRINCIPLES

As the League of Nations was a product of World War I, the United Nations was a product of World War II. In the war period, the need for a new major international organization to maintain peace and security in the post-war world era gradually gained popularity among the Allied Powers.

The United Nations' history starts with President Roosevelt's Annual Message to Congress on January 6, 1941, to the Congress of the United States. Four Freedoms delivered in his speech as being of universal importance were:

1. Freedom of speech and expression;
2. Freedom of every person to worship God in his way;
3. Freedom from want; and
4. Freedom from fear.

These ideas formed the basis for the formation of the United Nations. The United States had not initially entered World War II and had no thought of doing so in the immediate future. Despite this, President Roosevelt's interest in the events in Europe gave a boost to the Allied Powers. As a result, six months later, on June 12, 1941, an Inter-Allied Declaration or the Declaration of St. James Palace was signed in London by the representatives of Great Britain, Australia, Canada, New Zealand, and South Africa, with representatives of the exiled governments from Belgium, Czechoslovakia, Greece, Luxembourg, the Netherlands, Norway, Poland, Yugoslavia, and the Free French put their views forward that the only true basis of peace was the willing cooperation among the free nations of the world. To enjoy economic and social security, they would have to be relieved of the menace of aggression if all peace-loving nations of the world worked together, both in times of war and peace.

On August 9, 1941, President Roosevelt and British Prime Minister Winston Churchill met in Newfoundland to draw up a joint declaration to guide their policies.

The outcome was the formation of the Atlantic Charter, mutually signed by the two leaders on August 14, 1941. The basic principles put forward in this were:

First, their countries seek no aggrandizement, territorial or other.

Second, they desire to see no territorial changes that do not accord with the freely expressed wishes of the people concerned.

Third, they respect the right of all peoples to choose the form of government under which they will live; and they wish to see sovereign rights and self-government restored to those who had been forced to deprive of them.

Fourth, they will endeavour, with due respect for their existing obligations, to further the enjoyment by all states, great or small, victor or vanquished, of access, on equal terms, to the trade and raw materials of the world which they needed for their economic prosperity.

Fifth, they desire to foster close collaboration between all nations in the economic field with the object of securing, for all, improved labour standards, economic advancement, and social security.

Sixth, after the final destruction of Nazi tyranny, they hoped to establish peace for all nations, the means of dwelling in safety within their boundaries, which will ensure that all the men in all the lands may live out their lives in freedom from fear and want.

Seventh, such a peace should enable all men to traverse the high seas and oceans without hindrance.

Eighth, they believe that all the nations of the world, for realistic or spiritual reasons must come to the abandonment of the use of force. Since no future peace can be maintained if land, sea, or air armaments continue to be employed by nations that threaten, or may threaten, aggression outside of their frontiers, they believe, pending the establishment of a wider and permanent system of general security, that the disarmament of such nations is essential. They will likewise aid and encourage all other practicable measures which will lighten for peace-loving peoples the crushing burden of armaments.

Four months later, the United States joined the war after Japan attacked Pearl Harbour. The term "United Nations" was coined by President Roosevelt. On January 1, 1942, the Declaration by the United Nations was signed in Washington by the representatives of twenty-six nations.

This "Declaration by the United Nations" stated that the Atlantic Charter would view as a general programme for the Allied States. Its signatories pledged to give each other full support in the war effort and not to conclude a separate peace or armistice with the enemies. Hardly a blueprint, the declaration set out principles (as mentioned in the Eighth point of the Atlantic Charter) for a "wider and more permanent system of general security". Even the use of the term, "United Nations" was considered tentative.

The Casablanca Conference held in January 1943 was another step towards the formation of a new institution. The most remarkable outcome of the Conference was the finalization of Allied strategic plans against the Axis powers in 1943, and the promulgation of the policy of "unconditional surrender." The participants – Churchill and Roosevelt – discussed, among other things, the role their countries would play in the future international system.

The search for a new international institution intensified in 1943. The foreign ministers of the United States, the United Kingdom, and the Soviet Union met in Moscow, where they signed the "Moscow Declaration"; later China also signed it. It explicitly stressed the need to founding, as soon as possible, a general international organization. The organization was to be based on the sovereign equality of all peace-loving states and open to membership by all such states, large and small, for the maintenance of international peace and security. Similar to the declaration made at the Moscow Conference, the declaration at the Quebec Conference of 1943 made a call for "a general international organization, based on the principle of sovereign equality of all nations." Meanwhile, in several capitals, above all in Washington, efforts began, in earnest, to plan a new international organization.

Although the idea of the new international organization got some attention at the Teheran Conference of 1943, which was attended by Churchill, Stalin, and Roosevelt. The most important planning effort took place in Washington from August to September 1944. The Dumbarton Oaks Conference was named after the estate, where the meetings were held. At that conference, the US Department of State made plans that furnished the basis of discussion, the principles of the United Nations, as we know them today, were formulated and approved by China, the United Kingdom, the Soviet Union, and the United States. The conference members at Dumbarton Oaks decided to retain the name "United Nations". It symbolized their intention of maintaining the general purposes of the war and continuing cooperation in peacetime. There was a clear distinction between the powers of the General Assembly, where all members-states represented, and those of the Security Council, whose members originally 11 (5 permanent members and 6 chosen by General Assembly), now 15 (5 permanent members and 10 chosen by General Assembly) specialized duties related to maintaining the peace.

The differences among the conference members persisted at Dumbarton Oaks. The British government opposed any attention paid to its colonial territories, while the United States thought this was a major task for the new organization. The Soviet Union objected to the Anglo-US notion that a party to an international conflict should not vote on such an issue in the Security Council. Britain and the United States argued that this exclusion would help to obtain cooperation from the smaller countries, but the Soviet Union feared it could use it against itself. Its view was clear that the new organization ought to be devoted mainly to defending states, especially the Soviet Union, against outside aggression. To ensure the security of the states, they had to sign an agreement with the major power of the United Nations. The Soviet Union was also unable to get the consent of the conference to its proposal that all 16 component republics of the Soviet Union should be given membership in the new institution on an individual basis. The proposal had responded to Soviet estimates that the United States and the United Kingdom had assured support from Latin American and Dominion governments.

The small state-large state cleavage became visible in the resistance of the former to the unanimity, or veto, rule in the Security Council. But when the major powers made it clear that without this privilege they would not join the international organization at all, the small states accepted the Dumbarton Oaks proposals. In the election of the non-permanent members of the Security Council, the small states accepted the Dumbarton Oaks proposals, which gave them some advantages. Article 23, Repertory, vol. II (1945-54) stated the regard for the contribution of all member states for the maintenance of peace and security and "equitable geographical distribution" in matters of appointment to UN organs.

A complex set of provisions in the Charter put curbs on the exploitation of the colonies by the colonial powers in the post-war world. The division between trust territories and other colonial possessions, implied in the Yalta agreements, became more explicit. On the one hand, the Trusteeship system would apply to only those defined colonies that had been treated as prizes of war or those which entered the system voluntarily. On the other hand, the Trusteeship was applied to those territories as mentioned in the Art. 77 of the Charter.

Furthermore, at the insistence of the US military, a special category of trust territories was created. These supposedly had a strategic value and were to be administered by the Security Council, rather than by the Trusteeship Council. Only the US administered islands detached from Japan were included in this group. For other colonial areas, a declaration on non-self-governing territories was worked out. It placed on the administering states the duty to ensure the political, economic, social, and educational advancement of the non-self-governing peoples.

At the Yalta Conference of February 1945, Churchill, Roosevelt, and Stalin dealt with those issues that remained unresolved at Dumbarton Oaks. As for colonial questions, the Yalta Conference agreed to a system of trusteeship limited to the following three categories:

1. Former mandates of the League of Nations: these were former colonies of Germany and Turkey that had been put under the supervision of the League. Some of them had not yet gained independence.
2. Territories to be taken from Germany and Japan after World War II.
3. Territories that the present colonial powers would voluntarily put under the supervision of the projected United Nations Trusteeship system.

The United Nations reassured the British that it would neither control any part of her empire without the agreement nor would ever disturb her control on her colonies, except as provided for in the Trusteeship system.

Voting and decision-making received much attention at Yalta, where they dealt with the formulae to work out these matters. Each permanent member of the Security Council held the right to a veto, except for issues related to the procedure. In other words, the views of the five Great Powers had to be unanimous for the Council to act. That procedure required a majority of 7 of the 11 members. The Soviet Union agreed that parties to a conflict would have no vote in the Security Council when the issue was a matter of peaceful settlement of a dispute. But when the Security Council considered any enforcement action, the parties to a conflict would have the right to vote.

The United Nations, on membership issues, agreed to admit the Ukrainian SSR and the Byelorussian SSR, in addition to the Soviet Union. France and China would join the United States, the Soviet Union, and Britain as "sponsoring powers" and would get permanent places in the Security Council as Great Powers with a veto. Finally, those nations that had declared war on the Axis powers before March 1, 1945, and had signed the Declaration of the United Nations of January 1, 1942, would be invited to the founding conference of the United Nations.

Potsdam Conference

In the Potsdam Conference of July 1945, the USA, former USSR, Britain, France, and China finally ratified the UN Charter, adopted at the San Francisco Conference. Earlier, in the San Francisco Conference, the UN Charter was formally adopted on June 25, 1945. So, in a sense, the UN came into being from the Potsdam Conference.

The importance of the Potsdam Conference of July 1945 was that the victors of World War II, for the first time, had divided views regarding the economic occupation, and the future structure of Germany. At Potsdam, the Russians, claim for reparations in kind or cash was intense, secured agreement for removals from their zones of occupation to meet Russian and Polish reparation claims, but nothing was settled about the extent of these claims. The conflict was related to disagreements about the political structure of Germany. The hostility between the USSR and the Western allies increase the gap after the Potsdam Conference. Japan refused the surrender terms issued in the Potsdam Declaration of July 26, 1945.

Towards the end of July 1945, Britain, the United States, and the Republic of China at the Potsdam Conference called on Japan to unconditionally surrender. The Japanese response was a decision to press forward resolutely to carry the war to a quick end, yet the Allies decided to use nuclear weapons. On 6 August 1945, the first atom bomb was dropped on Hiroshima and the second atom bomb on 9 August on Nagasaki destroyed both the cities.

An International Military Tribunal for the Far East was set up in Tokyo to carry out the provisions of the Potsdam proclamation that "Stern justice shall be meted out to all war criminals, including those who have visited cruelties upon our prisoners" and those who had formulated aggressive war policies.

President Roosevelt died on April 12, 1945. However, his successor, Harry Truman, declared that the founding conference of the United Nations had to take place as planned. The United Nations Conference on International Organization opened on April 25, 1945, in San Francisco and ended on June 26, 1945, with agreements by fifty nations on the United Nations Charter, the constitutional document of the new international institution, and the Statute of the new International Court of Justice.

The San Francisco Conference

Under the general chairmanship of Edward Stettinius, the US Secretary of State, 850 delegates of 50 states attended the conference assembled at the San Francisco Opera House on April 26, 1945.

In the course of the deliberations at San Francisco, there appeared two important divisions: between large and small states and between colonial and non-colonial powers. Whenever there were signs of disagreements among major powers, the views of small powers gained prominence. Generally, the small states sought to strengthen the powers of the General Assembly, where they would always represent, as against those of the more exclusive members of the Security Council. They also put more emphasis on economic and social cooperation through the United Nations than the Great Powers. As for colonial issues, the non-administering powers generally sought to make the colonial powers more accountable for their administration of colonial territories.

The conference took place from April 25 to June 26, 1945. The process of writing a Charter for the United Nations took two months. Every part of it had to be voted on and accepted by a two-thirds majority. Here is how the San Francisco Conference accomplished its monumental work: using the Dumbarton Oaks proposals and the Yalta agreement as a starting point, the proposed Charter was divided into four sections. The delegates working on each section formed a "Commission." Commission I dealt with the general purposes and principles of the organization, issues relating to membership, the Secretariat, and the subject of amendments to the Charter. Commission II considered the powers and responsibilities of the General Assembly, while Commission III took up the Security Council. Finally, Commission IV worked on a draft for the Statute of the International Court of Justice establishing the judicial organ of the United Nations. This draft had been prepared by a 44-nation Committee of Jurists, which had met in Washington in April 1945.

There was the question, for example, of the status of "regional organizations". Many countries had their arrangements for regional defence and mutual assistance such as the Inter-American System, for example, and the Arab League. How were such arrangements to be related to the new intergovernmental organization? The conference decided to give them a role in bringing about a peaceful settlement provided that the aims and actions of these groups accorded with the aims and purposes of the United Nations.

One issue that provoked long and heated debate was the right of each permanent member of the Security Council (China, the Soviet Union, United States, United Kingdom, and France) to veto any resolution passed by the Security Council. At one point, the conflict of opinion on this question threatened to break up the conference. The smaller powers feared that when one of the "Big Five" menaced the peace, the Security Council would be powerless to act, while in the event of a clash between two powers not permanent members of the Security Council, the "Big Five" could act arbitrarily. They strove, therefore, to have the power of the "veto" reduced. But the great powers unanimously insisted on this provision and emphasized that the main responsibility for maintaining world peace would fall most heavily on them. Eventually, the smaller powers conceded the point in the interest of setting up the world organization. The Charter was formally signed on 26th June 1945 by 51 states. It came into force on October 24, 1945, after the five Great Powers and a majority of the signatory states had ratified it.

The Purposes and Principles

The purposes of the UN are indicated in its Preamble and are laid down in clearer terms in Article 1 of the Charter.

The Preamble (cf. Appendices) shows that the Charter of the UN is born of the experiences of a devastating war and that it holds out hope of lasting peace, based on a recognition of fundamental human rights that have been the casualties of the war, on recognition of sovereign equality of all states, and on better economic and social conditions for the millions who have been victims of oppression and exploitation.

The purposes of the UN, as laid down in Article 1 of the Charter, are:

1. To maintain international peace and security, and to that end: take effective collective measures for the prevention and removal of threats to the peace and the suppression of acts of aggression or other breaches of the peace, and to bring about by peaceful means, and in conformity with the principles of justice and international law, adjustment or settlement of international disputes or situations which might lead to a breach of the peace;
2. To develop friendly relations among nations; based on respect for the principle of equal rights and self-determination of peoples,
3. To achieve international cooperation in solving international problems of an economic, social, cultural, or humanitarian character, and in promoting and encouraging respect for human rights and fundamental freedoms for all without distinction as to race, sex, language, or religion; and

4. To be a centre for harmonizing the actions of nations in the attainment of these common ends.

The maintenance of international peace and security has been quite logically placed at the head of the list of purposes of the UN because in the absence of peace and security none of its other purposes can be realized.

Admittedly, Art. 1.1 (given above) states all negative steps directed towards the maintenance of international peace and security. More positive steps are stated in Art 1.2 (given above). Obviously, in an atmosphere of fear, suspicion, and uncertainty, peace cannot prevail.

Here it must be noted, that reference to "equal rights and self-determination of peoples" does not imply that the UN stands as a guarantor for equality of rights and self-determination for all peoples across the world. The Charter indicates that respect for these ideals should provide the foundation for friendly relations among nations.

The maintenance of international peace and security may describe the political purpose of the UN because of its direct bearing on the struggle for power among nations. Its political purpose remains unfulfilled due to social unrest, economic backwardness, and cultural drawbacks. Therefore, the Charter enjoins that the organization seeks to solve international economic, social, cultural, and humanitarian problems in cooperation among nations to promote and encourage "respect for human rights and fundamental freedoms for all without distinction as to race, sex, language or religion". (Art. 1.3)

The fourth purpose of the UN is to be a centre for helping nations achieve these ends. Though all international activities in the economic, social, and cultural fields cannot pass through the UN; therefore, various other organizations are working in these fields outside the UN. However, the Charter expects that the organization remains at the "centre" of the network for all these activities.

It is a common observation that the authority of the UN is not adequate for the accomplishment of its purposes. The General Assembly, the Economic and Social Council, and the Trusteeship Council can only make recommendations but do not have any authority to make binding decisions. The Security Council, of course, can make binding decisions. But it can be paralysed at any moment by any of the permanent members through the veto power. The International Court of Justice, which is the judicial arm of the organization, has no compulsory jurisdiction over disputes among nations. To make the UN an effective international organization, it must take precedence over the member states.

In pursuit of the purposes stated in Article 1 of the Charter, Article 2 prescribes certain principles which may describe the basic rules of international ethics for the Organization and its Members to act.

These principles are:

1. The Organization is based on the principle of the sovereign equality of all its Members.
2. All Members, in order to ensure to all of them the rights and benefits resulting from membership, shall fulfil in good faith the obligations assumed by them in accordance with the present Charter.
3. The members shall settle their international disputes by peaceful means in such a manner that international peace and security, and justice, are not endangered.
4. All Members shall refrain in their international relations from the threat or use of force against the territorial integrity or political independence of any state, or any other manner, inconsistent with the Purposes of the United Nations.
5. All Members shall give the United Nations every assistance in any action it takes in accordance with the present Charter and shall refrain from giving assistance to any state against which the United Nations is taking preventive or enforcement action.
6. The Organization shall ensure that states which are not members of the United Nations act in accordance with these Principles so far as may be necessary for the maintenance of international peace and security.
7. Nothing contained in the present Charter shall authorize the United Nations to intervene in matters which are essentially within the domestic jurisdiction of any state or shall require the Members to submit such matters to settlement under the present Charter; but this principle shall not prejudice the application of enforcement measures under Chapter VII.

Following the first principle of sovereign equality of all states, members have been accorded equal representation in the General Assembly and are entitled to equality of votes. But the preponderant role of the Big Five in the Security Council arising out of their veto power compromises to a great extent the principle of sovereign equality of all states.

The working of the United Nations during the last fifty years has revealed that the commitment of the members to fulfil, in good faith, their obligations as set forth in the Charter has been and often is a pious hope. The Charter has specified particular methods for the pacific settlement of disputes among nations. These are "negotiation, enquiry, mediation, conciliation, arbitration, judicial settlement, resort to regional agencies or arrangements, or other peaceful means of their own choice." (Art. 33.1)

Now, to develop friendly relations among nations, the members must pledge themselves not to use force to settle a dispute in a particular manner. It is also necessary that the members should respect the territorial integrity and political independence of any state. Moreover, friendly relations among nations must have a social and economic base. So it is laid down in Article 55 of the Charter: "With a view to the creation of conditions of stability and well-being which are necessary for peaceful and friendly relations among nations based on respect for the principle of equal rights and self-determination of peoples, the United Nations shall promote:

1 Higher standards of living, full employment, and conditions of economic and social progress and development;
2. Solutions to international economic, social, health, and related problems; and international cultural and educational cooperation; and
3. Universal respect for, and observance of, human rights and fundamental freedoms for all without distinction as to race, sex, language, or religion.

The principle of assistance to the United Nations in any action it takes to maintain peace and security as stated by the Charter is developed in Article 43. Through it, the members "undertake to make available to the Security Council, on its call and in accordance with a special agreement or agreements, armed forces, assistance, and facilities, including rites of passage, necessary for the purpose of maintaining international peace and security."

However, if members follow the third and fourth Principles (Art 2), that is, if they settle their disputes by peaceful means and refrain in their international relations from the use of force, possibly no enforcement action will be necessary.

The next Principle ensures that non-members follow these principles, which indicates the universal and all-embracing character of the organization.

The principle of the UN not to "intervene in matters which are essentially within the domestic jurisdiction of any state" seriously restricts the jurisdiction of the organization. It is difficult to determine when a national development ceases to be a concern of the nation and becomes an issue of the world.

The principle of sovereign equality of all member states and non-intervention by the UN in domestic matters may be viewed as an expression of distrust, for too swift a growth of power in the international organization, and of a determination to provide maximum freedom of external action and the maximum internal control for member states.

The League Covenant and the United Nations Charter: A Comparison

Generally, to draw a comparison between the United Nations and the League of Nations, the differences between them become clear. Moreover, comparisons form the basis of the textual provisions of the League Covenant and those of the UN Charter, not taking into account the actual practice under the Covenant and the Charter. Such a basis of comparison naturally leads to an exaggerated idea of the dissimilarities between the two systems. The favourable comparison of the League and the United Nations must be based on the League system, as it developed under the Covenant. It creates an enormous gap that separates the League of Nations from the United Nations. Many provisions of the United Nations system are taken directly from the Covenant, though usually with changes of names and phraseology. Though some provisions are little more than codifications of League practice as it developed under the Covenant, other provisions represent the logical development of ideas that were in the process of evolution when the League was functioning actively. Of course, there are many exceptions, but scholars need to focus on some important ones; e.g., the United Nations does not represent a break with the past, but rather the continuation of old ideas and methods with some changes deemed necessary in the light of experience.

Let us now turn to some striking similarities between the League of Nations and the United Nations. If one observes the structures of the two organizations at a glance, then these are obvious. Thus, peace and security are the two primary goals for both organizations. They were voluntary associations of sovereign states and constituted the large units of the organizations. Each of these organizations had an Assembly with a universal membership, where members enjoyed equality of voting rights. They also instituted a Council with considerable powers to their members. A secretariat with permanent and non-permanent members headed by a Secretary-General remained the chief executive officer for both the institutions.

We will now turn to some of the differences in the organizational forms of these institutions. Despite their diversities, I will prove later that the core remains the same in both.

The Covenant was a small document with only 26 articles while the United Nations Charter included 111 articles. The League had three principal organs whereas, the UN has six.

With decolonization, the United Nations membership became much larger than that of the League. Membership in all the organs of the two institutions also differed. The League Council consisted of the Principal Allied and Associated powers, in addition to four each permanent and non-permanent member elected by the Assembly for a three-year term. As a result, the League Council had the advantage of flexibility as neither the names nor the number of the Great Powers was mentioned. However, this latter proved to be a disadvantage in practice. It meant that the League Council was never a stable body as powers kept joining and leaving it.

The United Nations Security Council under Article 23 prescribes 15 members, including the names of the five permanent members the Republic of China, France, the Union of Soviet Socialist Republics, the United Kingdom of Great Britain and Northern Ireland, and the United States of America. The General Assembly elects ten non-permanent members for a two-year term. No change in this membership ratio is possible without the revision of the Charter.

The United Nations, unlike the League, had to deal with a world passing through a process of decolonization. The smaller states as a whole, who had not actively participated in the League, participated fully in the UN system. As to the scope of activities of the League and the United Nations, there is a marked difference. The League centred around political disputes alone. In its purview, by guarding political activities alone, League could prevent war and maintain peace. For the United Nations, this was the central concept, but its activities in other areas have also increased substantially. The Charter does not only believe in peacekeeping but also peacebuilding. This meant booming activities in the economic, social, and political spheres. The promotion of human rights became an indispensable part of the Charter, which today constitutes a key area of United Nations activity. The substantive scope of the issues considered by each institution also varies considerably. Apart from the specific conflicts, the League was too preoccupied with just one problem— to form a stable international system in Europe. On the contrary, the United Nations has been confronted with a whole host of problems, such as decolonization, eradication of racism within nation-states, and redistribution of wealth and income from the developed to the developing nations. This reflects a widening of substantive concerns far beyond the scope envisaged by the participants in the League.

The League of Nations operated only in the political field whereas, the United Nations founded 15 specialized agencies operating in diverse professional and technical spheres of administration to encourage multilateral cooperation in education, labour, science, culture, agriculture, and public health.

The League of Nations turned out to be a much more rigid body despite its small Covenant. It stood for the *status quo*, and as a result, it could not keep up with the changing international environment. This rigidity of the League was the root cause of its failure. The United Nations, in contrast, has been able to suit its structure to the changing international scenario. The Uniting for Peace Proposal and the innovative concept of peacekeeping are two examples of the United Nations adapting itself to changes in the global organizational system.

The Working of the League Covenant and the United Nations Charter

The first point that needs special consideration is whether the Charter contains provisions that give the organs of the United Nations greater authority than was vested in the corresponding organs of the League. It places undue emphasis upon the provisions contained in the Charter, regarding voting in the General Assembly and the Security Council. It is, of course, true that under Article 18 of the Charter, decisions of the General Assembly can be taken by a two-thirds majority of the members present and voting, instead of by a unanimous vote of those present, as was the requirement for the League Assembly. However, you must bear in mind while dealing with questions on the policy that the General Assembly can only recommend, and consequently, any decision taken becomes a recommendation. Moreover, it is so unfair to compare these provisions included in the Charter without taking into account the practice of the League Assembly under the Covenant. In many respects, interpreting the rules of the Covenant correctly can bridge the gap between the actual practice of the League and the provisions of the Charter. As provided in the rules of the League Assembly, a state that abstained from voting is not counted as present. As a result, that abstention was a means by which some consequences of the unanimity rule could be avoided. However, the more important, rule established in the first session of the League Assembly, was that a resolution expressing a wish, technically known as a "voeu", might be adopted by a majority vote. Thus, a whole range of League Assembly decisions by majority vote did not differ in any respect from decisions by majority vote in the General Assembly.

When we turn our attention to the Security Council, we admit that a change has been made. Under the League Covenant, the Council was governed by the unanimity rule except in procedural matters that proved a severe handicap particularly, when it acted under Article 11 of the Covenant. It was possible to accuse a member of the Council of threatening or disturbing the peace by exercising its veto power to prevent any effective action under this Article, as happened in the case of Japanese aggression in Manchuria in 1931 and the threat of Italian aggression in Ethiopia in 1935. Under the Charter, a decision may be binding on members of the United Nations (in the case of collective security action) without their consent. Furthermore, this decision may require some specific acts on the part of the members of the United Nations, and it is not to be regarded as a simple recommendation as was the case with decisions taken by the League Council under Articles 10 and 16.

Nevertheless, there are some key points to be kept in mind before we conclude that under the Charter, there is a substantial change. In the first place, a decision by the Security Council can only have the effect of a recommendation when it is engaged in the performance of its functions under Chapter VI, i.e. when it is seeking to achieve the pacific settlement, adjustment of a dispute, or situation. While a decision of the Security Council concerning enforcement action under Chapter VII is binding upon the members of the United Nations, including those not represented on the Security Council, such a decision cannot be taken without the concurrence of all the permanent members of the Security Council. Despite significant changes in the technical provisions of the Charter, one compels to conclude that so far as actual possession of power is concerned, the United Nations has not advanced much beyond the League of Nations. In similar situations, you will anticipate much the same result. Lastly, under either system, success or failure is dependent upon the ability of the more powerful members to cooperate effectively to achieve common ends.

The provisions of the Charter regarding amendments and withdrawal follow in all essential respects those provisions of the Covenant and the practices developed thereunder. Under both the Charter and the Covenant, no amendment recommended by the Assembly can become effective unless ratified by the Great Powers. The Covenant was a little more restrictive than the Charter in one respect, namely, as it requires ratification by all members of the League whose representatives composed the Council, plus a majority of all other members, thereby giving every League member a "veto". On the other hand, the Charter, while limiting the "veto" to permanent members, requires approval by two-thirds of the members of the United Nations. In practice, the Charter provisions do not have substantially different results.

Likewise, regarding withdrawal, the League and the United Nations systems do not differ in any respect. The Covenant of the League generally permitted withdrawal under certain conditions, which were not, however, enforced in practice. The Charter says nothing about withdrawal rights, but one can understand that exercising this right is prevalent. No doubt, the Charter draws influence from the League practice and conforms to it. As decided that exercising this right should neither be subject to legal conditions nor should any attempt be made to force a state to remain a member. It is under a moral obligation to continue as a member and to exercise the withdrawal right only for very good reasons.

The phraseology of the Charter in certain respects undoubtedly represents an improvement over that of the League. For instance, the provision of Article 2, paragraph 4, empowers the members to refrain "from the threat or use of force against the territorial integrity or political independence of any state" represents an advance over the corresponding provisions of the Covenant. It made it possible for members to take refuge in the technicality that an undeclared war in the material sense was no war and, therefore, such use of armed force did not constitute a "resort to war".

The Charter system for the pacific settlement of disputes, while differing from that of the League in many aspects of substance and phraseology, follows it in accepting two basic principles:

1. parties to a dispute are in the first instance to seek a peaceful settlement through their own choice; and
2. the political organs of the international organization are to intervene only when the dispute has become a threat to the peace and when only in a mediatory or conciliatory capacity.

The powers of the United Nations organs for the pacific settlement of disputes are substantially the same as those of the principal organs of the League. Like the Covenant, under the Charter, the functions of political organs in this connection are limited to discussion, inquiry, mediation, and conciliation. The Charter, however, seeks to differentiate between the functions and powers of the General Assembly and the Security Council in a way that the Covenant did not do. More specifically, it makes the Security Council primarily responsible for the maintenance of peace and security; it does not permit a party to a dispute to have the matter transferred at its request to the General

Assembly and limits its power in principle to that of discussion. This constitutes a complete departure from the textual provisions of the League Covenant, which gave the Council and the Assembly the same general competence and allowed a party to dispute, acting under Article 15, paragraph 9, to have a dispute transferred at its request to the Assembly. It is significant, however, that out of some 66 disputes that came before the League, only three were brought before the League Assembly under this provision. It would, thus, appear that actual practice under the Covenant resulted in differentiation of function between the Assembly and the Council. This the Charter seeks to make obligatory.

It is in respect of enforcement action that the provisions of the Charter seem to offer the most marked contrast to the provisions of the Covenant, but here again, when we compare the Charter provisions with how the Covenant provisions were applied, the differences do not appear so great. The League system, as originally conceived, was based on the principle that once a member had resorted to war in violation of its obligations under the Covenant, other members were immediately obligated to apply economic and financial sanctions of broad scope against the offending state. The Council was empowered to recommend military measures which members of the League were technically not required to carry out. The Covenant of the League of Nations left to the members to decide whether or not another member had violated its obligations under the Covenant, and whether or not enforcement measures not involving the use of armed force should be adopted. Those military measures which the League Council could recommend were also strictly non-binding.

The Charter makes the Security Council responsible for deciding what enforcement measures have to be used to maintain the peace. Obligations arise from the members of the United Nations only when they hold such decisions. However, the provisions of the Charter go even further than did the Covenant in providing for obligatory military measures and advance commitments to place specific forces at the disposal of the Security Council. The framers of the Charter sought to provide in little detail for military agreements between the members of the United Nations and the Security Council, as well as the role of the defence staff committee to assist the Security Council to draw up advance plans and implement military measures.

It can, however, be asked whether the Charter system will be more effective than the League system or not regarding the requirement for the unanimity of the permanent members of the Security Council. Like the League, the United Nations is an organization for the enforcement of peace among the smaller states. If the permanent members of the Security Council agree, they will take effective action under the Charter. It is unlikely that such an agreement will be reached to take measures against one of the Great Powers or a protégé of a Great Power. Consequently, the sphere of effective enforcement action by the United Nations is also restricted in advance.

However, there are two significant innovations under the UN Charter that can be mentioned in this context. Firstly, the Covenant of the League did not concede the right of individual or collective self-defence. The UN Charter specifically provides in Art. 51 that "nothing in the present Charter shall impair the inherent right of individual or collective self-defence if an armed attack occurs against a member of the United Nations until the Security Council has taken the measures necessary to maintain international peace and security". Secondly, the UN Charter gives greater recognition to regional arrangements for the maintenance of peace and security. Art. 52 of the Charter enjoins on the members entering regional arrangements "to achieve a pacific settlement of local disputes through such regional arrangements or by such regional agencies before referring them to the Security Council".

Regarding the administration of non-self-governing territories, there are quite a few points in common between the UN Trusteeship system and the Mandates system of the League. However, there are differences too. Chapter XI, "Declaration regarding Non-Self-Governing Territories", is a significant breakthrough in the UN Charter. It embodies in an international document a statement of principles binding upon all states engaged in the administration of non-self-governing territories and empowers such states with the additional obligation to make reports to an international authority.

The machinery for supervision and the lines of responsibility have changed considerably over the years. In trusteeship areas other than strategic areas, the administrative authorities are responsible to the General Assembly and its agent, the Trusteeship Council. However, this change, as compared with the League mandates system, was to an extent, anticipated in League practice by the right which the Assembly asserted and exercised to discuss and make recommendations for the administration of mandated territories. The Charter states the power vested in the United Nations organs, though in a somewhat modified form, which the Council and Mandates Commission of the League lacked and proved a fatal weakness of the League system. I refer to the provision for periodical visits to the trusteeship territories, which should make it possible for the organization to get information on the spot and thereby check upon and supplement the reports of the administrative authorities.

Students of the international organization must recognize the United Nations for what it is, a revised League, no doubt improved in some respects, possibly weaker in others, but a voluntary association of nations closely following the League tradition. The world has witnessed sweeping changes in power distribution, its economic and political structure, and ideologies. These changes create new crises and compel slim chances of success or failure in meeting them, but its mechanism to challenge global issues remain much the same. If anyone wants to know how the United Nations operates or presently what has it achieved, one must delve into its experiences, particularly that of the League of Nations.

Cited Works

Baehr, Peter R. and Leon Gordenker, *The United Nations,* New York: Praeger, 1984.

Eichelberger, Clark M., *Organising for Peace: A Personal History of the Founding of the United Nations,* New York: Harper & Row, 1978.

Goodrich, L.M., Hambro, Edward and A. P. Simons, *Charter of the United Nations: Commentary and Documents*, New York: Columbia University Press, 1969.

Goodrich, Leland M., "From League of Nations to United Nations," *International Organization*, vol. 1, no. 1, [MIT Press, University of Wisconsin Press, Cambridge University Press, International Organization Foundation], 1947, pp. 3–21,

http://www.jstor.org/stable/2703515.

Luard, Evan, *A History of the United Nations*, vol. 1, London: Macmillan, 1982.

Mangone, Gerard J., *A Short History of International Organisation*, New York: McGraw-Hill, 1954.

Russel, Ruth B., *A History of the United Nations Charter*, Washington: Brookings Institution, 1958.

https://history.state.gov/milestones/1937-1945/casablanca

https://history.state.gov/milestones/1937-1945/un

https://legal.un.org/repertory/art23/english/rep_orig_vol2_art23.pdf

https://www.un.org/dppa/decolonization/en/history/international-trusteeship-system-and-trust-territories

https://www.un.org/en/model-united-nations/history-united-nations

PART II
THE STRUCTURE: PRINCIPAL ORGANS

5

THE GENERAL ASSEMBLY

Composition

The UN system is based on six principal organs: the General Assembly, the Security Council, the Economic and Social Council (ECOSOC), the International Court of Justice (ICJ), and the Secretariat. A sixth principal organ, the Trusteeship Council, suspended its operations on 1 November 1994, upon the independence of Palau, the last remaining UN trust territory. Five of the six principal organs are located at UN Headquarters in New York City. The International Court of Justice is located in The Hague in the Netherlands, while other major agencies are based in the UN offices in Geneva, Vienna, and Nairobi.

If the present international society were to be compared with a nation-state, the UN General Assembly could represent a parliament in which the affairs of the world are debated and discussed by the representative of every region.

But the Assembly is not yet a world parliament in any real sense. It has no government. The UN agencies are not ministries, they do not come directly under the General Assembly; they have their assemblies and decide their policies, and the UN General Assembly has only the most transitory power or influence over each. Still less are the member states committed to obeying the Assembly's resolutions. So the Assembly can discuss or recommend but rarely decide.

Again, the General Assembly is not a representative of the people in the way an elected parliament is today supposed to be. It is a representative of governments, which may or may not accurately represent the views of their populations. Thus, governments are represented on a highly uneven basis, with a nation of 50,000 people having equal representation as India with over a billion people.

The General Assembly is the main deliberative organ of the United Nations. It is composed of representatives of all member states, and each has one vote. Decisions are taken on serious questions concerning recommendations on peace and security, admission of new members, and budgetary matters that require a two-thirds majority. Decisions on other questions are taken by a simple majority.

Sessions

The regular session of the General Assembly begins each year on the third Tuesday in September and usually continues until mid-December. At the start of each regular session, the Assembly elects a new President, 21 Vice-Presidents, and the Chairpersons of the Assembly's six main committees. To ensure equitable geographical representation, the presidency of the Assembly rotates each year among five groups of states: African, Asian, Eastern European, Latin American and Caribbean Islands, Western European, and other states.

In addition to its regular sessions, the Assembly may meet in special sessions at the request of the Security Council, a majority of members of the United Nations, or one member of the majority of members concur. Emergency special sessions may be called within 24 hours of a request by the Security Council by the vote of any nine members of the Council, a majority of the United Nations members, or by one member if the majority of members concur.

At the beginning of each regular session, the Assembly holds a general debate in which the member states express their views on a wide range of issues of international concern. Due to a large number of questions for which the Assembly is called upon to consider (there were 154 separate agenda items at the 1988 session of the Assembly), the Assembly allocates most questions to its six main committees:

First Committee (Disarmament and International Security)

Second Committee (Economic and Financial)

Third Committee (Social, Humanitarian, and Cultural)

Fourth Committee (Special Political and Decolonization)

Fifth Committee (Administrative and Budgetary)

Sixth Committee (Legal)

As aforementioned, there is also a General Committee composed of the President and 21 Vice-Presidents of the Assembly and the chairpersons of the six main committees and a Credentials Committee appointed by the General Assembly at each regular session.

Some questions are considered only in plenary meetings, rather than in one of the main committees. All questions are voted in favour of plenary meetings, usually towards the end of the regular session in careful consideration of committees and submitted draft resolutions to the Plenary Assembly.

Voting in committees is by a simple majority. In plenary meetings, resolutions may be adopted by acclamation, without objection, vote, or a vote can be recorded or taken by a roll call.

While the decisions of the Assembly have no legal binding on governments, they bear the burden of world opinions on a range of international issues, as well as the moral authority of the world community.

The work of the United Nations year-round derives largely from the decisions of the General Assembly, that is to say, the will of the majority of the members as expressed in resolutions adopted by the Assembly. Its work is carried out:

1. By committees and other bodies established by the Assembly to study and report on specific issues, such as disarmament, outer space, peacekeeping, decolonization, human rights, and apartheid;
2. In international conferences called by the Assembly; and
3. By the Secretariat of the United Nations, the Secretary-General and his staff of international civil servants.

Agenda

The General Assembly meets annually in regular sessions, intensively from September to December, and resumes in January until all issues on the agenda are addressed – which often is just before the next session starts. Besides the usual items (which differ from year to year), the General Assembly includes the report of the Secretary-General on agenda for discussion in each session as well as the reports of the Secretariat and the ECOSOC. Reports from the various subsidiary organs and specialized agencies also form a part of its agenda as well as anything that has been leftover from the previous session and needs continuous discussion. Any substantive subject proposed by the principal organs, the Secretary-General, and the members are included on the agenda, though the General Assembly has the right to reduce them to five in number. Along with this, a discussion of the budget takes place and any item brought by non-members is also taken into consideration.

The agenda covers a wide, expanding, and increasingly specialized range of topics. In recent years, the items on the agenda have covered subjects ranging from the situation in the Middle-East to the "question of the elderly and the aged", a comprehensive review of peacekeeping operations to the establishment of an international university, the brain drain from developing countries to the question of the human environment, the seabed to the outer space, the punishment of war criminals to international trade law. On the one hand, within the Assembly international issues of this kind are discussed which may not become a full-scale subject for international conferences. On the other hand, a discussion on such an array of subjects, which are often technical, places a considerable strain on the resources of the delegations, especially of the smaller member states. The increasing complexity and technical character of the issues discussed, and the difficulty of the delegates in keeping abreast of them reflect problems similar to those confronting national parliaments. Inevitably, debates lasting two or three days on big issues are inadequate to deal with them. The purpose of the delegates is probably to focus attention on urgent needs or pressing issues, and sometimes they are indeed followed by more expert conferences to obtain even more concrete results.

UNSDG and the 2030 Agenda

United Nations Member States have decided to largely change the development coordination system to help and assist countries to accomplish the 2030 Agenda for Sustainable Development. With a skilful, encouraged, and autonomous resident coordinator (RC) system, as the designated representatives of the Secretary-General to fully control and manage coordination and development activities of UN entities as of 1 January 2019 at the country level. It does not leave behind anyone to ensure sustained social, economic, and environmental gains at the national and local levels. They are also known as the UN Country Teams as they coordinate the UN Sustainable Development Group (UNSDG) agencies, funds, and programmes working on development. The UNSDG guides, supports, tracks, and oversees the coordination of development operations in 162 countries and territories.

Functions and Powers

Under the Charter (Articles 10-17), the functions and powers of the General Assembly include the following important points:

1. The General Assembly may discuss any questions or any matters within the scope of the present Charter or relating to the powers and functions of any organs (except Article 12) and may make recommendations to the Members of the United Nations or the Security Council or both on any such questions or matters.
2. The General Assembly may consider the general principles of co-operation in the maintenance of international peace and security, including the principles governing disarmament and the regulation of armaments, and may make recommendations about such principles to the Members or the Security Council or both.
3. The General Assembly may call the attention of the Security Council to situations that are likely to endanger international peace and security.
4. While the Security Council is exercising in respect of any dispute or situation the functions assigned to it in the present Charter, the General Assembly shall not make any recommendation concerning that dispute or situation unless the Security Council so requests.
5. The General Assembly shall initiate studies and make recommendations for:
   (a) promoting international co-operation in the political field and encouraging the progressive development of international law and its codification;
   (b) promoting international co-operation in the economic, social, cultural, educational, and health fields, and assisting in the realization of human rights and fundamental freedoms for all without distinction as to race, sex, language, or religion.
6. The General Assembly shall receive and consider annual and special reports from the Security Council; these reports shall include an account of the measures that

the Security Council has decided upon or taken to maintain international peace and security.

7. The General Assembly shall receive and consider reports from the other organs of the United Nations.
8. The General Assembly shall perform such functions for the international trusteeship system as are assigned to it under Chapters XII and XIII, including the approval of the trusteeship agreements for areas not designated as strategic.
9. The General Assembly shall consider and approve the budget of the Organization. The expenses of the Organization shall be borne by the Members as apportioned by the General Assembly.
10. The General Assembly shall consider and approve any financial and budgetary arrangements with specialized agencies referred to in Article 57 and shall examine the administrative budgets of such specialized agencies to make recommendations to the agencies concerned.

Uniting for Peace Resolution

One of the outcomes of the Korean crisis of 1950 was the adoption of a 'Uniting for Peace Resolution' by the UN General Assembly on November 3, 1950. The resolution was introduced by the United States on the assumption that in the future the Soviet veto in the Security Council would surely block any action similar to that taken in Korea. The resolution had five main provisions:

1. If the Security Council, because of lack of unanimity among the permanent members, fails to exercise its primary responsibility for the maintenance of international peace and security, in any case where there appears to be a threat to the peace, breach of the peace, or act of aggression, the General Assembly shall consider the matter immediately to make appropriate recommendations to members for collective measures, including, in the case of a breach of the peace or act of aggression, the use of armed forces, when necessary, to maintain or restore international peace and security. If not in session at the time, the General Assembly may meet in emergency special sessions within twenty-four hours of the request thereof. Such emergency special sessions shall be called if requested by the Security Council on the vote of any seven members, or by a majority of the members of the United Nations.
2. It provided for the establishment of a fourteen-nation (China, Colombia, Czechoslovakia, France, India, Iraq, Israel, New Zealand, Pakistan, Sweden, The Union of Soviet Socialist Republic, The United Kingdom of Great Britain and Northern Ireland, The United States of America, and Uruguay) Peace Observation Commission to observe and report on conflict situations in any part of the world that endanger the maintenance of international peace and security.

3. The member states were asked to maintain in their armed forces special elements which could be made available for United Nations service on call of the Security Council or the General Assembly.
4. It provided for the establishment of a fourteen-nation (Australia, Belgium, Brazil, Burma, Canada, Egypt, France, Mexico, Philippines, Turkey, United Kingdom of Great Britain and Northern Ireland, The United States of America, Venezuela, and Yugoslavia.) Collective Measures Committee to study and report on these and other methods for maintaining and strengthening international peace and security.
5. It also urged the members of the UN to renew their fidelity to the world organization, honour its decisions, and promote respect for human rights and the achievement of economic stability and economic progress.

Although the Soviet Union endorsed the contents of the resolution mentioned in paragraphs 2 and 5 above, it contended that certain other parts of the resolution were illegal because the Charter had specifically assigned the responsibility for peace and security to the Security Council. Certain other members of the UN opposed certain parts of the above resolution. They contended that the Charter had limited the power of the Assembly to "discussion and recommendations".

The Uniting for Peace Resolution has greatly strengthened the position of the General Assembly vis-a-vis the Security Council. By virtue of this resolution, the General Assembly has become the ultimate custodian of collective security measures. By a two-thirds majority, the Assembly can now determine when and where a threat to the peace of the world exists and can recommend joint measures that should be taken to counter the threat.

The Role of the General Assembly in World Affairs

The General Assembly deals with three broad areas: the definition of norms that should apply to certain areas of world politics, the commitment of UN resources to various programmes, and the management of conflicts between and among nations.

The Assembly is one of the best forums for discussing general norms of international behaviour since virtually all states of the world are represented in it. It has always devoted considerable time to discussions, and these have greatly influenced the development of norms of international behaviour on many issues. Over the years, the Assembly has played an important role in holding debates on subjects specifically related to the status and implications of self-determination, the principle of non-interference of states in each other's affairs, and decisions regarding participation or non-participation in its activities.

The Assembly is also the best forum for most discussions about efficiently allocating UN resources to various programmes. It can create new UN bodies and controls the allocation of the UN budget, it is committed to the organization for a wide range of activities. The UN activities are viewed as important to the resolution of other issues or the management or pursuit of conflicts, to an extent that member states make great efforts to allocate the organization's resources efficiently. The Assembly has a profound impact on its members since its decisions on the allocation of UN resources are binding on all member states.

The Charter specifies that member states should first try to manage conflicts by recourse to non-UN procedures or institutions, and assigns primary responsibility for UN conflict management efforts to the Security Council. Even so, the Assembly tries to help manage various conflicts. Sometimes, this results from the Security Council's failure to find a course of action due to the veto or member states' decisions to bring the conflict before the Assembly. On a number of occasions, the Assembly has not been an effective manager of conflicts. Despite some noteworthy successes, such as its response to the Suez Crisis of 1956, the Assembly is too large a body to play an effective role and seldom controls enough material resources to do so.

Binding Assembly Decisions

Assembly decisions bind member states mainly in two areas:

1. Determination of who may participate in Assembly and Assembly-sponsored activities,
2. Approval of the regular UN budget and apportionment of assessments among member states. Additionally, member states may agree in advance to accept a particular Assembly resolution as binding.

Questions of participation may arise when two or more delegations claiming to represent the same state, arrive at UN Headquarters. Though traditional international law encourages the acceptance of the *de facto* state, the empirical question is not always easy to decide. The only Third World innovation in this regard is the use of the credentials procedure to deny participation to governments when no rival delegation appears.

Budget questions have always received great attention. Expenditure decisions allocate a small but real set of resources, while assessment decisions determine who has to provide those resources. Arguments about expenditure have usually pitted the majority against the minority, though until the 1970s, these arguments have operated within a context of a realization that no industrial state, from North or South, ever wants the total budget to grow high ceaselessly. After 1973, the struggle intensified as the Third World majority sought to use the regular budget to assure a level of resource transfer to the developing world that most industrial states have refused to support. The old consensus limits the regular budget by placing both peacekeeping and economic activities in voluntary budgets is also being increasingly challenged.

In the 1980s, a financial crisis had threatened to bankrupt and enfeeble the United Nations; it was perhaps the worst crisis the world body had ever faced in its 40-year-old history. The crisis arose from the refusal of the minority of industrialized countries, led by the United States, including the Soviet Union, to accept in budget matters what they called the rule of the "impecunious and often arbitrary and free spending" developing country majority.

In 1986 the United States reacted by withholding more than $100 million in dues.

In the General Assembly, member states acting through consensus approved 71 recommendations contained in the high-level group's report which called for cuts in staff and spending and methods for streamlining and consolidating the inter-governmental machinery of the Secretariat. The Group of High-level Intergovernmental Experts established by the General Assembly on December 18, 1985, through Resolution 40/237, began work in February 1986, at the 121st plenary meeting. Its mandate was not to address the immediate and short-term financial problems of the United Nations but to identify medium and long-term measures to improve its personnel administration to strengthen its effectiveness in dealing with political, economic, and social issues. As a result of the Assembly action on the Group Report, member states have agreed to act by "consensus" on important budget issues which previously had proved highly divisive. If the General Assembly resolution is followed strictly, the programme committee, the CPC, will act by consensus and only proposals agreed to by the major donors will move further for final approval—thus, limiting the capability of the small state's majority to push through expensive projects for the funding to which their contribution was minimal.

Electoral and Constituent Functions

The General Assembly performs two distinct electoral functions, viz., the admission of new members and the choice of members for other organs. As far as the admission of new members is concerned, they are admitted by the General Assembly on the recommendations of the Security Council. Sometimes, certain members have been admitted by the General Assembly even though their cases were not recommended by the Security Council. However, no new member can be admitted without an affirmative vote by the General Assembly. The Assembly can also suspend the rights and privileges or expel a member on the recommendation of the Security Council (Art. 18.2) if he/she persistently violates the principles of the Charter.

As regards the selection of members of other organs of the UN, the General Assembly elects the ten non-permanent members of the Security Council for a term of two years (Art. 23) and the members of the Economic and Social Council (Art. 61). The Secretary-General is also appointed by the General Assembly on the recommendations of the Security Council (Art. 97). The judges of the International Court of Justice are also elected by the General Assembly in collaboration with the Security Council (Art. 93).

The constituent functions of the General Assembly include the power to amend the Charter. Under Article 108, amendments to the Charter can come into force when they have been adopted by a vote of two-thirds of the members of the General Assembly and ratified by their respective constitutional processes by two-thirds of the members of the United Nations, including all the permanent members of the Security Council. It must be noted that amendments to the Charter must be adopted by the General Assembly before they are referred for ratification to the member states. Likewise, a General Conference to review the original Charter can be called by the General Assembly with the concurrence of the Security Council. It must be emphasized once again that the amendments, both proposed by the General Assembly and the Review Conference, become effective only after they have been ratified by two-thirds of the members of the United Nations, including all the permanent members of the Security Council(Art. 109).

The Influence of Assembly Majorities in the UN System

Assembly majorities can influence the UN system in several ways. They can influence the activities of some principal organs through the Assembly's power to elect members. They can also directly control their activities by the Secretariat or subsidiary organs of the Assembly. They can use Assembly authority to carry out a considerable amount of formal and informal restructuring of the UN system. They can try to influence specialized agency activities through recommendations.

Authority over the Secretariat and the Assembly's subsidiary organs provides an effective channel for extending majority control. It can bypass an uncongenial principal organ, as it created UNCTAD rather than using the Economic and Social Council to deal with specialized issues. It can initiate a new area of UN activity, as in the establishment of the UN Industrial Development Organization or the UN Environmental Program. It can alter the definition of particular issues, as in the creation of the Committee of 24 (C-24) to extend the UN role on decolonization or the Division for Palestinian Rights of the Secretariat. The extent to which these UN system activities influence member states' conduct depends on the content and context of the decisions made. Neither the Secretariat nor the Assembly's subsidiary organs have any more direct authority over member states than does the Assembly itself.

Assembly majorities can do other things, like redistributing authority between headquarters and regional or local UN offices, assigning new tasks to the Secretariat, or merging existing aid programmes that have a decisive effect on members.

The majority of the Assembly that exert its power and influence on other principal UN organs differs from organ to organ. The Assembly's influence on the Security Council and the International Court of Justice is low because limitations on the power of election and their relatively small composition prevent it to impose its will on them. The Assembly has a profound influence on the Secretariat because of its control over the budget, and hence over appointments. It also exercises great influence on the Economic and Social Council since all its members are elected and its decisions are taken by a simple majority.

Assembly majorities still have great difficulty in influencing the specialized agencies directly. Assembly resolutions and decisions are not binding on the specialized agencies which take account of them only when their executive councils or governing assemblies adopt them. The lack of hierarchical relation between the General Assembly and the specialized agencies poses a real problem for the Third World majority in the Assembly. The developing countries are not as influential in the specialized agencies as the Assembly. One wishes the agencies could better mobilize to serve their goals.

To the extent that Assembly majorities can guide UN activity, they can influence member states in two ways. Firstly, many UN activities directly impinge upon member states by providing benefits such as aid funds, new information, or access to the expertise they lack at home. It also frames binding rules for particular interactions, such as International Atomic Energy Agency safeguards or International Maritime Organization rules on safe navigation at sea. Secondly, the rest of the UN system can exert indirect influence through appeals and recommendations. This activity can capture the states' attention and encourage negotiations but exerts lesser sway over the outcome than General Assembly recommendations. It rests on the same sorts of symbolic and material incentives to action as Assembly recommendations do.

Evolution of the General Assembly

The history of the General Assembly might be described as a progressive increase in its authority and influence, especially with respect to the Security Council, between 1945 and 1960, followed by a progressive decline.

In the first few years of its life, the role of the Assembly gradually enhanced. Because the Security Council was often annoyed by the free use of the veto, mainly by the Soviet Union, the Western powers resorted to superseding the Council altogether. In 1950, after the outbreak of the Korean War had demonstrated what might then have happened if the Soviet delegation had not been absent from the Council (in protest at its refusal to get a seat for Communist China), a further and more decisive step was taken. As mentioned earlier in this chapter, a resolution, known as the 'Uniting for Peace Resolution', was passed enabling a special Assembly to be called at any time when the Security Council found itself frustrated by a veto from taking effective action, on the affirmative vote of seven members of the Council or by a simple majority of the Assembly. This was done, moreover, to be able to recommend, if necessary, the use of force (this was the real extension of the Assembly's powers). The resolution also created a Peace Observation Commission and a Collective Measures Committee, under the Assembly, to help that body protect international peace and security, though after the first two or three years neither was used.

In the late 1950s, this Uniting for Peace Procedure was used two or three times. It led to the zenith of the Assembly's powers. A special Assembly was called for the stern measure in the Suez and Hungarian crisis in 1956. Over Suez, it led to the creation of the United Nations Emergency Force (UNEF) by the Assembly, and that force was, thus, controlled by the Assembly (in practice through a committee advising the

Secretary-General). Over Hungary, the special Assembly achieved a little, though it served to focus public attention on the crisis and express the verdict of the majority of world opinion against the Soviet action. The Uniting for Peace Procedure was used again during the crisis concerning Jordan and Lebanon in 1958 when a group of observers (the UN Observation Group in Lebanon: UNOGIL) was sent to defuse the crisis and deter foreign infiltration. Finally, during the crisis in the Congo in the early 1960s, though the UN force was authorized and controlled by the Security Council, the Assembly also kept the situation under close supervision and played a dominant role in the next two or three years in influencing UN action in the area.

During the 1950s, therefore, the General Assembly had played an eminent role in determining the UN's response to some world crises. From 1960 onwards, however, the role of the Assembly on war and peace questions began to decline. There were many reasons for this. Firstly, the outright opposition of the Soviet Union and France to attend the previously formed General Assembly, their refusal to contribute to the costs of peacekeeping operations that the General Assembly had authorized, and the prolonged financial crisis due to different constitutional viewpoints served to induce some caution among the other major powers in mobilizing the General Assembly. Secondly, the increasing size of the General Assembly, as well as the change in its composition (Afro-Asian members came to hold more than two-thirds of the votes) meant that it was a less suitable instrument for use in such situations by the US as by the Soviet Union. Thirdly, the far less frequent use of the Soviet veto in the Council reduced the need for an alternative agency. Finally, the desire of the other permanent members to retain the considerable influence which they held in the Security Council encouraged the restoration of the Council's supremacy on questions of security. There were still occasional Special Assemblies: on Rhodesia (1965), South-West Africa (1967), on the June War (1967), and North-South issues in 1974-75. But later, peacekeeping operations in the Congo (1960-64) and Cyprus (1967) were discussed and authorized by the Security Council and not the Assembly. The prolonged discussions on the settlement of the Middle-East crisis from the autumn of 1967 onwards, took place in the Security Council. So was the main debate on Southern Africa in the late 1970s. In times of crises, it was once more the Council, rather than the Assembly, to which conflicting parties looked for redress.

On other questions, however, the Assembly has extended its role. This resulted partly from the change in its membership, both in numbers and in composition. From a membership of 51 in 1945, it has grown to 193 today. This has transformed the regional balance. At the time of the UN's foundation, the largest single group was the Latin American, which had 20 members. There were only 15 West European and other members (including the US, Canada, Czechoslovakia, Greece, and Turkey); five East Europeans; nine Asians; and two Africans. By 1970, the order had been almost reversed. There were over 40 Africans, and more than 30 Asians (again including the Arab countries), while the number of West Europeans and others had only increased to about 20, of the East

Europeans to 10 (including Albania and Mongolia), and the Latin Americans only marginally through the addition of four Caribbean countries. Developing countries now represent well over two-thirds of the total membership.

The advent of new members inevitably meant largely focusing attention on their problems. The primary European problems include the division of Germany, and Berlin, and human rights in East Europe, which had dominated the early years have no relevance today. For a period in the late 1950s and early 1960s, colonial issues dominated the scene beginning with discussions on Morocco, Tunisia, and Algeria in the early 1950s, and culminating in debates, often with great intensity, mainly on African questions in the mid-1960s. In the last decade, questions of Southern Africa have claimed more time of the Assembly than any other single problem.

Today, no single issue receives so much attention as the growing emphasis of the Assembly on the influx of new countries and their development problems. There is an almost uninterrupted series of meetings held by innumerable committees on innumerable subjects associated with ECOSOC, the regional commissions, the UNDP, or other development agencies either in New York or Geneva or elsewhere throughout the year.

The shift in the balance of membership has brought many other changes. The discussion of human rights questions has also come to the forefront. There is increasing emphasis on political rights and racial discrimination. The Third Committee spent many years drafting two Covenants, one on Civil and Political Rights and the other on Economic, Cultural, and Social Rights. A system of periodic reporting on human rights ratified by all members of the Covenant was established, and a committee was appointed to evaluate and comment on each report. With the change in membership of the organization, however, discussions in this field tend to be greatly influenced by political attitudes.

In the First Committee, the character of disarmament discussions has also changed over the years. During the early years, attention had focused on developing nuclear weapons and possible ways to abolish them altogether. For a long time, there were discussions on very ambitious measures designed to bring about "general and complete disarmament", the total abolition of nuclear weapons, or the institution of "measures to prevent surprise attacks" by observation of countries' frontiers. During the 1960s, the United Nations Disarmament Commission made more modest efforts to control arms and submitted proposals to the conference, such as the Nuclear Test Ban Treaty, the Outer Space Treaty, the Non-Proliferation Treaty, etc.

The most significant change in the work of the Assembly in recent years has been the introduction of new kinds of items hardly considered in early Assemblies. These items are technological in character, but political in implication, such as discussions on outer space, the exploitation of the seabed, and the environment (introduced by Sweden in 1968, which after a UN conference in 1972 emerged as a new UN programme in this field) are prominent among them. Other items of this kind are satellite broadcasts, natural resource surveys, population control, application of science for development, sovereignty over natural resources, and so on. The boost in technical interdependence across the world generated a lot of discussion on these issues in the General Assembly, where alone all members are permanently represented.

Before 1960, some States complained about an "automatic majority" of the industrialized countries; after 1960 – with many newly independent States having joined the UN – others complained about a "tyranny of the majority" by the developing countries. Voting patterns tend to vary greatly, depending on the issue at hand. Countries generally vote according to how they perceive the merits of each question. This means that like-minded countries have similar voting patterns on issues of mutual concern. The end of the Cold War has led to a new consensus on major issues. The views of industrialized and developing countries have increasingly converged, and this has been reflected in the voting. Today, no more than 25 per cent of the General Assembly's resolutions are adopted without consensus.

The General Assembly: An Evaluation

Among the five "principal organs" of the UN organization, the Assembly is the foremost. The Secretariat and the Economic and Social Council are principal organs as named by the Charter. These have defined tasks and composition, but they report to and receive direct guidance from the General Assembly. The two other principal organs include the Security Council and the International Court of Justice, which are not subject to Assembly guidance as mandates lack specificity and have little significance. The Security Council deals only with disputes or situations that threaten to lead or have led to an outbreak of war. On the contrary, the International Court of Justice rules on legal questions brought before it voluntarily by states and advises other UN bodies at their request. However, the General Assembly holds discussions and makes decisions on any matters mentioned or implied in the Charter.

The General Assembly predominates many subsidiary UN bodies and organs, as they report it either directly or through the Economic and Social Council. These form a diverse group, including the specialized agencies dealing with international cooperation in defined technical areas, other bodies created to deal with particular global issues (such as the United Nations Development Programme or the UN Environmental Program), and temporary committees studying specific questions (such as the *ad hoc* Committee on International Terrorism), or continuing committees charged with monitoring activities and framing proposals about matters of continuing concern (such as the Committee on Peaceful Uses of Outer Space).

The Assembly predominates the UN as it is the only principal organ in which all member states have equal participation. Each has one vote, and a simple majority takes most of the decisions.. The egalitarian nature of the Assembly also makes it the favourite principal organ of weak states, which have always constituted a majority of UN membership. It gives them the power to exert their influence in making decisions that they lack anywhere else in the international system.

They see it as a place where the weak and developing countries can protect their interests, restrain the strong and promote a more equitable world order. The developing world, which constitutes about three-fourths of UN membership, now enjoys an overwhelming majority in the world body. They can act as a bloc and get any resolution passed by a simple, or if necessary, a two-thirds majority in the General Assembly. They can use this majority to elect members of other principal organs of the UN, restructure the UN system, initiate new areas of activity, assign new tasks to UN organs and commit UN resources to new programmes. The developed countries greatly resent this automatic majority of the developing states, which they use to further their foreign policy and protect their interests. The single-most obsession of the global South is the "development," and these countries utilize the UN to help on a large-scale transfer of resources from the developed to the developing world.

As a deliberative body, the General Assembly is concerned mainly with aggregating interests and making decisions. It also socializes with new governments by intensive interaction with virtually all other states, under a well-developed set of formal and informal rules for transacting business. It affects the articulation of interests and the choice of a place rather than the content, except when it helps governments exchange ideas with one another as expeditiously as possible. Though the application of rules and implementation of decisions are outside its direct purview, the Assembly seeks to influence how to carry out these decisions.

In the ultimate analysis, the General Assembly, like all other international organizations, is one of the elements that affect the processes of world politics by providing the norms within which states and other actors interact in pursuit of their various goals.

Cited Works

Bailey, Sydney D., *The General Assembly of the United Nations*, New York: Praeger, 1964.

Finley, Blanche, *The Structure of the United Nations General Assembly: Its Committees, Commissions and Other Organisations,* 1946-1973. vol. I, II, III. Dobbs Ferry: Oceana, 1977.

Jacobson, Kurt, *The General Assembly of the United Nations: A Quantitative Analysis of Conflict, Inequality and Relevance*, New York: Columbia, University Press, 1978.

Luard, Evan, *The United Nations: How it Works and What it Does*, London: Macmillan, 1979.

Moore, John Allphin, Jr., Jerry, Pubantz. *The New United Nations, International Organization in the Twenty-First Century,* New York and London, Routledge, 2017.

Moore, John Allphin, Jr., and Jerry, Pubantz. *Encyclopedia of the United Nations,* New York, 2008.

Muldoon, James P., Jr., JoAnn Fagot Aviel, Earl Sullivan, and Richard Reitano, eds. *Multilateral Diplomacy and the United Nations Today*, 2nd Edition. Boulder, CO: Westview, 2005.

Peterson, M.J., *The General Assembly in World Politics,* Boston: Allen and Unwin, 1986.

Russel, Ruth B., *The General Assembly, Patterns, Problems and Prospects,* New York: Carnegie Endowment for International Peace, 1970.

Turner, Barry, *The Statesman's Yearbook*, 135th edition, Macmillan Reference Limited, London, 1998.

Weiss, Thomas G., David P. Forsythe, Roger A. Coate, and Kelly-Kate Pease. *The United Nations and Changing World Politics,* 7th Edition. Boulder, CO: Westview, 2014.

Basic Facts about the United Nations, Diane Publishing, New York: UN Department of Public Information, published periodically.

https://www.un.org/en/about-us/trusteeship-council

https://www.un.org/en/model-united-nations/un-structure

https://www.un.org/en/ga/about/index.shtml

https://www.un.org/en/ga/sessions/

https://www.norway.no/en/missions/UN/norway-and-the-un/un-bodies2/the-general-assembly/

https://www.un.org/en/ga/maincommittees/

https://unric.org/en/united-nations-general-assembly-opens-on-15-september-2020/

https://unsdg.un.org/2030-agenda

https://www.un.org/en/about-us/un-charter/chapter-4

https://treaties.un.org/doc/publication/ctc/uncharter.pdf

https://www.un.org/en/ga/sessions/emergency.shtml

http://www.un-documents.net/a5r377.htm

https://undocs.org/en/A/RES/40/237

https://undocs.org/pdf?symbol=en/A/49/100

https://www.un.org/unispal/committee/

https://www.un.org/unispal/about-division-palestinian-rights/

https://www.un.org/unispal/document/division-for-palestinian-rights-ga-resolution-a-res-75-21/

6

THE SECURITY COUNCIL

Composition and Sessions

The Security Council has primary responsibility, under the Charter, for the maintenance of international peace and security. The Council has 15 members: 5 permanent members—(The People's Republic of China[1], The Republic of France[2], the Russian Federation[3], the United Kingdom, and the United States of America) and 10 non-permanent members elected by the General Assembly for two-year terms.

Each member of the Council has only one vote. Decisions on procedural matters require affirmative votes of at least nine of the 15 members. Decisions on substantive matters require nine votes, including the concurring votes of all five permanent members (provided that, in decisions under Chapter VI, and paragraph 3 of Article 52, a party to

---

1. China is an original member of the United Nations, the Charter having been signed and ratified on its behalf, on 26 June and 28 September 1945, respectively, by the Government of the Republic of China, which continued to represent China in the United Nations until 25 October 1971.
   On 25 October 1971, the General Assembly of the United Nations adopted its resolution 2758 (XXVI) *recalling* the principles of the Charter of the United Nations, for the restoration of the lawful rights of the People's Republic of China. It *recognizes* that the representatives of the Government of the People's Republic of China are the only lawful representatives of China to the United Nations and that the People's Republic of China is one of the five permanent members of the Security Council and *decided* to restore all its rights to the People's Republic of China and to recognize the representatives of its Government as the only legitimate representatives of China to the United Nations.
   (courtesy: https://treaties.un.org/Pages/HistoricalInfo.aspx?clang=_en#China)
2. The Republic of France (courtesy: https://unstats.un.org/unsd/geoinfo/ungegn/docs/11th-uncsgn-docs/E_Conf.105_13_CRP.13_15_UNGEGN%20WG%20Country%20Names%20Document.pdf)
3. By a communication dated 24 December 1991, the President of the Russian Federation notified the Secretary-General that membership of the Union of Soviet Socialist Republics (USSR) in the United Nations is being continued by the Russian Federation.
   The Government of the Russian Federation subsequently informed the Secretary-General that as of 24 December 1991, the Russian Federation maintains full responsibility for all the rights and obligations of the USSR under the Charter of the United Nations and multilateral treaties deposited with the Secretary-General and requested that the name "Russian Federation" be used in the United Nations in place of the name "Union of Soviet Socialist Republics". (courtesy: https://treaties.un.org/Pages/HistoricalInfo.aspx?clang=_en#RussianFederation)

a dispute shall abstain from voting). This is the rule of "Great Power unanimity", often referred to as the "veto" power. All the five permanent members have exercised the right of veto at one time or another. If a permanent member does not support a decision but does not wish to block it through a veto, it may abstain from voting.

Under the Charter, all members of the United Nations agree to accept and carry out the decisions of the Security Council. While other organs of the United Nations make recommendations to governments, the Council alone has the power to make decisions that the member states are obligated under the Charter to carry out.

Functions and Powers

Under the Charter, the functions and powers of the Security Council are:

1. to maintain international peace and security following the principles and purposes of the United Nations;
2. to investigate any dispute or situation which might lead to international friction;
3. to recommend methods of adjusting such disputes or the terms of settlement;
4. to formulate plans for the establishment of a system to regulate armaments;
5. to determine the existence of a threat to the peace or act of aggression and to recommend what action should be taken;
6. to call on Members to apply economic sanctions and other measures not involving the use of force to prevent or stop aggression;
7. to take military action against an aggressor;
8. to recommend the admission of new Members;
9. to exercise the trusteeship functions of the United Nations in "strategic areas".
10. to recommend to the General Assembly the appointment of the Secretary-General and, together with the Assembly, to elect the Judges of the International Court.

The Security Council is so organized as to be able to function continuously. A representative of each of its members must be present at all times at the United Nations Headquarters. The Council may meet elsewhere than at its Headquarters if it considers this advisable. In 1972, it held a session in Addis Ababa, Ethiopia, and the following year, it met in Panama City, Panama.

When a complaint concerning a threat to peace is brought before the Council, its first action is usually to recommend that the parties try to reach an agreement by peaceful means. In some cases, the Council itself undertakes investigation and mediation. It may appoint special representatives or request the Secretary-General to do so or to use his good offices. In some cases, it may set forth principles for a peaceful settlement to avert any threat.

When a dispute leads to fighting, the Council's first concern is to bring it to an end, as soon as possible. On many occasions, the Council has issued cease-fire directives which have been instrumental in preventing wider hostilities in many parts of the world. It also sends United Nations peacekeeping forces to help reduce tensions in troubled areas, keep opposing forces apart and create conditions of calm in which peaceful settlements may be sought. The Council may decide on enforcement measures, economic sanctions (such as trade embargoes), or collective military action if the situation worsens.

A Member state, against which preventive or enforcement action has been taken by the Security Council, may be suspended from the exercise of the rights and privileges of membership by the General Assembly upon the recommendation of the Security Council. A Member state that has persistently violated the principles mentioned in the Charter may be expelled from the United Nations by the Assembly on the Council's recommendation.

A State which is a member of the United Nations but not of the Security Council may participate, without a vote, in its discussions when the Council considers that the interests of the members concerned are especially affected. Both, members of the United Nations and non-members, if they are parties to a dispute being considered by the Council, are invited to take part, without a vote, in the Council's discussions. The Council lays down the conditions for participation by a non-member state.

We must also examine how the Council has developed and in what way it operates today.

When the UN was formed, there was a general desire to learn lessons, from the failure of the League of Nations. As it was felt among the intelligentsia, that the League had failed due to four main reasons. Firstly, it lacked armed forces that it could call upon to withstand aggression. Secondly, it lacked the authority, stability, and unity to impose collective decisions to defend a member that was attacked. Thirdly, it was paralyzed in times of crisis by the rule of unanimity. Fourthly, the absence of several major powers – the US throughout its tenure, the Soviet Union, Germany, Italy, and Japan for much of it – had made it unrepresentative and impotent.

The UN Security Council rectified these failings. It wanted to have permanent armed forces at its disposal for use against aggressors. The Council has authority over every member in calling for collective sanctions. The veto is reserved for the five most powerful states. The UN has become a universal body by freely admitting as many members as possible. To enforce the Security Council decisions, all members negotiate with the Council for the allocation of armed forces to the teeth, which may use to keep the peace when such occasion arises. Though having been maintained by the home state, they are available for use by the UN immediately whenever needed.

Moreover, the Council is equipped with powers to make "decisions" which the League Council lacked, that is, powers to command obedience of all UN members. Under Article 25 of the new UN Charter, every member of the organization is under an obligation to "accept and carry out the decisions of the Security Council in accordance with the present Charter". When there is a threat to peace, the Council can first call on all members in certain circumstances either to apply economic sanctions, the severing of communications or diplomatic relations (Art. 41); or, may take such action "by air, sea or land forces as may be necessary to maintain or restore international peace and security" (Art. 42). In this way, the organization possesses the power to act decisively, which the League conspicuously lacked.

The unanimity rule is largely given up. In the Assembly, it is abandoned altogether. In the Council, it is confined to the Big Five, who are enabled to protect themselves through the exercise of the veto; a contrary vote by any of them causes a resolution on substantive issues to fail. Otherwise, a decision on procedural matters can be reached by a majority vote (9 votes out of 15). The granting of the veto power to the five permanent states can represent merely the recognition of the realities of power politics. Even if the veto had not existed in practice, the organization could not have been used wholly against the will of any one of the major powers, without provoking it to leave the organization altogether. The veto can, thus, be regarded as an essential safety valve, which serves to prevent dissension among its leading members. Without it, the organization, if urged to take action against any one of these powers, could have been paralyzed by differences of opinion.

However, the UN never had the armed forces that were expected to be put at its command. A discussion on the establishment of such a force took place in 1946-47 in the Military Staff Committee consisting of representatives of the five permanent members. Differences arose about the size and character of the force. The Soviet Union wished the forces to be stationed only on the territory of those countries which provided them and objected to the use of foreign bases for this purpose. Most of the other members thought bases should be made available for the permanent stationing of the force. The Soviet Union wanted a limited force of not more than 12 divisions' altogether, the US wanted a larger force with at least 20 ground divisions. The Soviet Union wanted an assurance that such forces would be withdrawn after use, within 90 days of the termination of any operation (apparently fearing that they might be used to influence the political situation after such an emergency). The others wanted greater flexibility on this score. The Soviet Union thought that an exactly equal number of forces should be provided by all the permanent members, while the US wanted it to be a negotiable factor.

Thus, the authority of the Council was greatly weakened. Without a special force, it was held, it could no longer call for use of force to resist aggression. Moreover, the Council was hopelessly divided by Cold War disputes. These were reflected in the constant use of the veto by the Soviet Union. All this made it clear that the Council was not going to be the dominant peacekeeping agency in the post-war world that had been originally conceived. It could recommend armed action but not enforce it. The hope that the UN would establish a wholly new "enforcement system" for preserving peace was frustrated.

The voting system, though there was no universal veto, worked a little better than before. The veto, even in its limited form, brought about constant paralysis. All over the world, the East and the West conflicted. Almost at the very beginning of the Council's meetings, the Soviet Union registered its first veto on an issue (foreign forces in Syria and Lebanon) in which none of its vital interests was involved. This foreshadowed a whole series of occasions in the next few years when the Soviet Union exercised its veto on similar questions. It used the veto, in other words, not to protect its vital concerns but to prevent the passage of any resolution with which it happened to disagree: a purpose for which the veto was certainly not intended (later, by the 1970s, the Western powers, then themselves in a minority, vetoed more often than the Soviet Union). In consequence, over innumerable issues decisions could not be taken in the Council. As discussed in chapter 5, it was a sheer chance that this did not affect the Council's response to the Korean War in 1950. Because it had not won its case for the transfer of the China seat to the Chinese People's Republic, the Soviet Union had walked out of the Council at the beginning of 1950. As a result, when the Korean War broke out in June of that year, the Council was able to take prompt and effective action, the day after the hostilities began, solely because the Soviet delegate was not present to cast the veto. Otherwise, he would have surely done it. Even then the Council only "recommended" action by member states to support South Korea, rather than "deciding" on enforcement action under Art. 25.

The effect of all this was that the Council emerged as a far weaker body than many had imagined. Because it had no enforcement powers, it had to rely on negotiations. But it also means that it was inhibited because the Cold War conflicts had soon enveloped the new organization. As a result, to meet the changed situation some amendments began to be made to the UN system by the then ruling majority.

Various measures were introduced to assign a bigger and better role to the Assembly than before, where the veto did not apply. Some steps were also taken to improve the working of the Council. It was generally accepted that an abstention did not represent a veto: in other words, the "concurring" vote of all the permanent members required under Art. 27(3) did not have to be an affirmative vote by each. Later, there emerged the tradition of "consensus" by which a proposal of the statement of the Chairman (comparable to a summing-up by the Prime Minister or chairman of a Cabinet Committee in Britain) was universally accepted for the meeting. This avoided the necessity of taking a vote. More importantly, with the passing of the Uniting for Peace Resolution in the autumn of 1950, it was laid down that a question of peace and security, for which the Council was supposed to have primary responsibility, could be shifted to the Assembly in a situation of crisis (despite the terms of the Charter) if there was a deadlock in the Council. The Assembly then could call for the use of force, if necessary.

During the early 1950s, the Security Council played a passive role. However, from the 1960s, the decline in the powers of the Security Council was arrested, and it once again, started playing a leading role in the settlement of international disputes, as the UN body was primarily responsible for keeping peace and ensuring security. The most important decisions on the Congo Crisis (1960-65), including the dispatch of a force to assist the Congolese government (ONUC), were taken by the Council. Similarly, the Security Council played an important role in the handling of the Cuban crisis. It was the Security Council that held discussions on the Cuban Crisis in October 1962 and the Cyprus Question in the early part of 1964, when clashes broke out between the two communities, and finally decided to send a peacekeeping force to take over responsibility from British forces in the area. The Security Council dealt with many successive African questions concerning South Africa and Southern Rhodesia (Zimbabwe), while Namibia and a series of complaints against Portugal over her African territories. A complaint against Vietnam was filed by The United States to the Security Council on Jan 31, 1966. It was also the Security Council that took the valuable decision on the war in Vietnam on 2 February 1966 (but it was never effectively pursued), the Arab-Israel war in 1967, the India-Pakistan war in 1971, and another Middle-East conflict in 1973. Thus, the improvement in the status of the Security Council was rendered possible because of the deadlock over the Congo in the General Assembly, and the ineffectiveness of the General Assembly to act in the face of the "financial veto" applied by the Security Council. Consequently, once again there was pressure for expansion of membership of the Security Council.

Meanwhile, the composition of the Council had changed. From the beginning of the 1960s, with a substantial increase in the membership of the UN, there had been proposals to enlarge the size of the Council. These were designed partly to allow more members to serve it, and partly to reflect more accurately the composition of the organization's memberships, particularly to provide more seats for Africans and Asians. From the beginning of 1965, total membership increased from 11 to 15, and at the same time, the number of affirmative votes required to pass a resolution was raised from seven to nine (so, marginally reducing the proportion needed for this purpose).

Relations between the General Assembly and the Security Council

Although the primary purpose of the Security Council is to maintain international peace and security, it is obligated to submit annual reports to the General Assembly. The General Assembly is not authorized to comment upon the activities of the Security Council in a manner amounting to an assumption of concurrent jurisdiction in the matter of settling disputes. In other words, the Security Council is not subordinate to the overriding authority of the General Assembly.

The Security Council is composed of diplomats and bureaucrats, while the General Assembly consists of politicians from nation-states. The Security Council holds periodic or monthly sessions, while the General Assembly meets only in annual sessions, special sessions, or emergency sessions (within 24 hours) called by the Secretary-General, at the request of the Security Council or by a majority of its Member States, or of one Member State if the majority of Members concur.

The two organs work together on matters pertaining to the admission and expulsion of members, the appointment of the Secretary-General, and the election of the Judges of the International Court of Justice. There are several procedural situations where the Security Council provides a recommendation to the General Assembly for its action or acts concurrently with the General Assembly. These are the 'Recommendations by the Security Council to the General Assembly' as stated below:

(a) appointment of the Secretary-General,
(b) membership in the Organization,
(c) election of the judges of the International Tribunals for the former Yugoslavia and Rwanda,
(d) conditions on accession to the ICJ Statute, and
(e) conditions under which a State party to the ICJ Statute but not a Member State of the United Nations participates in the election of ICJ judges.

The relationship between the two bodies as originally envisaged by the Charter has been dramatically changed by the passage of the Uniting for Peace Resolution in 1950. Since this Resolution was passed, the General Assembly has been able to wield wide powers when the Security Council is unable to exercise its primary responsibility for the maintenance of international peace and security in any case, due to the lack of unanimity among the permanent members, where there appears to be a threat to the peace, breach of the peace or act of aggression.

The fact is that its mere size and compactness give the Security Council a considerable practical advantage in an organization comprising over 100 members. The General Assembly is usually in session in the last three or four months of the year, but outside these limits, it is an unwieldy body to convoke, compared to a body like the Security Council which is so organized as to be able to function continuously. In a world where unpredictability in international relations seems to be the rule rather than the exception, an agency that can respond quickly, however inadequately, is likely to remain a forum of first resort, and on issues on which the major powers have the last say, often of last resort too.

The Problems of Veto

No provision of the United Nations Charter has attracted more attention and provoked more controversy than the provisions regarding the veto in the Security Council. This controversy has existed since the inception of the UN. To understand this problem, let us examine the relevant provisions of the Charter:

Art. 27, which deals with the voting procedure lays down:

1. Each member of the Security Council shall have one vote;
2. Decisions of the Security Council on procedural matters shall be made by an affirmative vote of nine members.
3. Decisions of the Security Council on all other matters shall be made by an affirmative vote of nine members including the concurring votes of the permanent members, provided that, in decisions under Chapter VI, and Paragraph 3 of Article 52, a party to a dispute shall abstain from voting.

At Dumbarton Oaks Conference, points 1 and 2 of Art. 27 were accepted without any difference of opinion. It included a vote of seven members, which later increased to nine in the UN Charter. Even in the third point, the powers agreed to the general principle as contained in the said provisions. The main controversy ranged over exceptions enumerated in the third point. Whereas the United States took the position, that in voting on a substantive question involving pacific settlement, a party to a dispute should not be allowed to vote, the Russians contended that the principle of big-power unanimity should apply to all substantive matters. However, the differences between the two powers were reconciled and the outcome was the "Yalta formula". This formula was based on the American proposal and excluded a party to a dispute from voting on a matter of pacific settlement, but not when enforcement measures were involved. No enforcement action could be taken without the concurrence of the five permanent members.

Some scholars have justified the principle of unanimity among the permanent members on practical grounds. They observe that the leading industrial powers have almost a monopoly on waging modern global war. Cooperation should exist to a reasonable degree to avoid war. However, if their disagreement reaches a point where using armed force against each other seems the last resort, the obvious result would be a Third World War. Therefore, cooperation among the permanent members is essential if the Security Council needs to perform its functions.

Some of the smaller countries at the San Francisco Conference objected to the proposed voting procedure on the ground that it violated the principle of "sovereign equality" of all members. They expressed the fear that the veto provision would weaken the Security Council by creating the likelihood that it may fail to discharge its duties due to a Council deadlock over the veto.

The Great Powers were opposed to enforcement action against themselves. They argued that if such action became necessary it would mean a general war, breaking the very fabric on which the UN rests. They also held that no enforcement action should be taken against other states without a Great-Power consensus.

A bitter controversy raged between the Great Powers and the small states over the 'veto' provision. However, all the advantages favoured the Great Powers, as the United

Nations Organization could function efficiently only with their support and assistance. With the absence of one or two of the Great Powers, it would have little, if any, value. Before this unalterable fact of international politics, the small states had to bow.

The General Assembly soon became dissatisfied with the "veto" provision. In April 1949, it recommended that the Security Council should consider various questions on procedural matters. Its members should consult among themselves to avoid the veto and must exercise only on issues of vital importance. Except for an agreement to consult in advance, the resolution did not result in any change. However, one important change took place in the original plan whereby abstention is not regarded as veto, despite a clear reference to concurring votes of permanent members in the Charter.

Between 1945 and 1993, a total of 195 resolutions were vetoed, many by more than one permanent member. It may be seen that throughout the history of the UN, a very high number of vetoes were cast either by the Soviet Union (especially during the first two decades) or by the United States and its allies (during the remaining years). Russia resumed using the veto power in 2007. China stands out as the only permanent member that has economically used its veto power.

Conventional wisdom claims that the UN became paralyzed during the Cold War Era, especially after the mid-1970s. During the early years, the West dominated the General Assembly and the Security Council. Thus, the empirical evidence above indicates that the functioning of the Security Council was affected by the vetoes of the Soviet Union But from the mid-1950s, the Western powers extensively used the veto power. The right to veto exercised by erstwhile USSR-Russian accounts for a little less than half the total number. The right to vetoes exercised by the US, the UK, and France combined, account for more than half. In terms of time horizon, 110 out of the total (115 till 1994) Soviet vetoes came in the first 20 years and by 2020 it has vetoed 301 times since 1946. Since 16 February 1946—when the Union of Soviet Socialist Republics (USSR) cast the first veto on a draft resolution regarding the withdrawal of foreign troops from Lebanon and Syria (S/PV.23)—the veto has been recorded 293 times. The highest number of US vetoes (34) in any decade came from 1976 to 1985. This also contributed significantly to the increase in US distrust of the UN. Interestingly, the number of vetoes cast came to its lowest figures in the nineteen-eighties. This was also the period that was being described as the "end of the Cold War". To date, the veto has been used more than 254 times to kill resolutions in the Security Council.

Effects of the Veto

It is very difficult to determine to what extent the "veto" has adversely affected the working of the UN. It has been used by all the major powers with the USSR topping the list. Most of the vetoes were applied to membership applications. From 1946 to 2015, the veto has been used more than 236 times by P5 nations. The frequent exercise of the veto simply demonstrated that there existed a clash of interest between the USA and the USSR, and consequently, there could be no unanimity among the permanent members, which rendered the Security Council less effective. Due to the East-West conflict, the Security Council could not use its enforcement powers effectively in disputes like the Congo, Berlin, Palestine, Indo-China, Hungary, Suez, etc.

The veto has stood in the way of maintaining harmonious relations among the permanent members of the Council, which was a basic prerequisite for peace in the Charter. Due to the existence of this Cold War, certain states have shown reluctance to refer their disputes to the Security Council. It cannot be denied that if there had been no veto, the pacific settlement of disputes might have been expedited.

Because of these complications, sometimes demand is made for doing away with the provision of 'veto' for the privileged Five. But it must be remembered that the real test of the success of the United Nations lies in its ability to influence the actions of states. If the states are unwilling to accept its recommendations or even its decisions, changing the voting procedure will do little or no good. The veto is a symptom of disagreement rather than its cause; its abolition would not alter the causes of conflicts among states.

In conclusion, we may say that the real challenge facing the United Nations is not "abolition of the veto," but the development of a sufficient degree of cooperation among its members, and especially among the Great Powers. The rigours in the 'veto' have been greatly reduced by various measures, but it would certainly be difficult to do away with it because the Big Powers are not likely to agree to its termination.

The Council's Response to Hostilities

Under Chapter VII of the Charter, conceived as a key element of the United Nations system of collective security, the Security Council "shall determine the existence of any threat to the peace, breach of the peace or act of aggression, and shall make recommendations, or decide what measures shall be taken in accordance with Articles 41 and 42, to maintain or restore international peace and security."

During the Korean War in 1950 and the Gulf Crisis in 1991, the United Nations employed force in connection with breaches of the peace, (one of the subjects addressed in Chapter VII), although its attempt failed in the enabling resolutions. On the contrary, for South Africa, the Council invoked Chapter VII, to decide that there was still a threat to peace. Under Article 41, it imposed selective mandatory (1966) and comprehensive economic sanctions (1968) against the white minority regime in Southern Rhodesia (now Zimbabwe) including an embargo on oil and petroleum products (1965) and an arms embargo against the apartheid regime in South Africa (7th August 1963) but the UN-imposed a mandatory arms embargo on 4th November 1977. The sanctions against Southern Rhodesia (Zimbabwe) were terminated in 1979 after agreed steps led to the creation of majority rule in independent Zimbabwe. The arms embargo against South Africa remains in effect.

In addition to imposing economic sanctions under Chapter VII, the Council may, under Article 42, mandate "action by air, sea or land forces as may be necessary to maintain or restore international peace and security." This action may include demonstrations, blockades, and other operations. Under Article 43, member states pledge to make available to the Security Council, if the Council calls for such armed forces, assistance, and facilities necessary to maintain international peace and security, under special agreements to be concluded between them with the Council and subject to their ratification. The Charter envisaged that plans for the use of armed force were to be made by the Security Council with the assistance of its Military Staff Committee. The Committee, consisting of the Chiefs of Staff of the permanent members of the Council or their representatives, was to advise the Council on all questions relating to its military requirements, force employment, and command, the regulation of armaments, and possible disarmament. The Committee was to be responsible for the strategic direction of any armed forces placed at the Council's disposal. To date, however, these provisions of the Charter have not been implemented.

When serious issues of war and conflict (interstate or intrastate) reach the United Nations – as in the case of the Civil War in Libya in 2011, the war in Iraq in 2003, or the problems in Afghanistan in 2002 – they were invariably taken before the Security Council.

More than two dozen Sanctions Committees have also been set up to deal with Security Council-approved sanctions. Since 1990, such bodies have concentrated on Iraq (following the invasion of Kuwait), as well as war-torn states like Afghanistan, Somalia, Angola, Rwanda, Liberia, Sierra Leone, Ethiopia, and Iran. Between 2011 and 2015, the Council imposed sanctions on Libya, Guinea-Bissau, the Central African Republic, and South Sudan. In these cases, "smart sanctions" were targeted at specific individuals and government entities, hoping to avoid imposing hardship on the civilian population. This involved the freezing of assets and blocking the financial transactions of political elites or bodies whose behaviour the Council wanted to change or punish.

The Security Council has also been responsible for the operational war crimes tribunals,—the International Criminal Tribunal for the Former Yugoslavia (ICTY), meeting at The Hague and was established by SC Resolution 808 in 1993, and the International Criminal Tribunal for Rwanda (ICTR), convened at Arusha, Tanzania, and deriving from SC Resolution 955 in 1994.

On balance, the Security Council since the end of the Cold War has taken on an active and productive engagement with world affairs.

Success in East Timor was considered a major triumph for both the United Nations and the Security Council. Other council-authorized operations included the missions in

Bosnia, Kosovo, Afghanistan, and Liberia. By council direction, each of these missions was to be the main institution in stabilizing traumatized postwar societies.

Election-monitoring operations have been very significant. During the 1990s, UN monitors – in groups established by Security Council resolutions – guided elections in Cambodia and various Central American countries. These nations, previously beset by outside interventions and civil war are now living in relative peace. What deserves to be emphasized is that the Council, especially since the end of the Cold War, has performed for the most part with a sense of purpose. At the same time, its resolutions have addressed the tough issues facing the "new" United Nations while taking on the force of legitimacy in world affairs like no unilateral national decision could. Such legitimacy is one reason that even the United States made a genuine effort to elicit SC sanction for its invasion of Iraq and, after the war, sought Council resolutions to bring a UN presence into the war-torn country. Therefore, the Security Council does not appear to be "irrelevant" as we enter the third decade of the twenty-first century.

Although prospects for achieving radical reform of the SC's structural problems seem blocked at this time the Council remains the main UN body that brings legitimacy to world affairs. It is, therefore, the focus of attention when we think of the United Nations.

An Assessment

It is undeniable that the achievements of the Security Council in keeping the peace over the past 77 years have been considerably less impressive than had been hoped at the time of the UN's foundation. One reason for the disappointment often felt at the UN's performance is the unrealistic expectations placed on it. The chief factor contributing to this has been the Charter itself. The machinery proposed in Article 43 of the Charter for a Security Council force raised many hopes but was probably always unworkable. Even if it had been possible to reach an agreement on the composition of a UN force, it would seldom have been possible to use it. One permanent member or another would always have been fearful that this might prove to its disadvantage and so would have used its veto. If there had still been, as occasionally happened in the interwar period, "disputes" that were wholly local, distinct, and unrelated to the global ideological conflict, there might have been a possibility of "great-power unanimity": joint action by the five permanent members acting in concert. But in the post-1945 world, there were virtually no such conflicts. A proposal for UN action in any dispute in whatever part of the world – over Greece, Berlin, Indonesia, Guatemala, Laos, Lebanon, the Dominican Republic, Vietnam, or Angola – inevitably affected the interests of the Great Powers and so invited a veto.

But the fact that the Security Council has not been able to undertake its enforcement role does not mean that it has not had any part to play. It has at least, unlike the League, continued to hold the centre of the stage. The immediate reaction of the victim state when a conflict breaks out is to turn towards the Council and to call for its judgement resolution. Even if it does not resolve the dispute, or puts an immediate halt to fighting that has already broken out, it may at least bear the burden of outside opinion on it. It represents a contribution and certainly an advance in previous times.

Above all, the Security Council should be seen, as a bargaining mechanism, permanently available, for negotiating on agreed courses of action over crises among individual powers and groups of nations, or at least promoting negotiations elsewhere. Every decision is, therefore, a compromise. The Council is not like cabinets within the national states, a unified and single-minded decision-making body comprising ministers who are already close colleagues and committed to a policy. It is rather like an *ad hoc* committee formed by distrustful parties, in which every decision precedes a peaceful negotiation among the adherents having different points of view. Where interests are not too divergent, it may be possible to achieve a consensus on some matters at least (as over Cyprus, the Congo, and the Middle-East). Sometimes, regarding other issues, where there is a direct conflict affecting permanent members (Hungary, Vietnam), this may be impossible, though negotiation may open.

Whether or not the Security Council develops a greater degree of political skill and sophistication is yet to be seen, but over the last 30 years, its primacy within the UN system has been largely restored. It has even begun to reassert itself. It has, over Rhodesia or in the Iraqi annexation of Kuwait, made use of sanctions of a stringent kind that have been almost universally applied. It has set up several peacekeeping forces and may establish more. It has claimed the right to lay down the general terms of a settlement in the Middle-East, something rarely attempted before by an international organization after an armed conflict. It was the focus of pressure for change in Southern Africa.

When the self-renewal matches with a corresponding degree of effectiveness, the Council has to further improvise techniques for peaceful settlement of disputes, with prompt action after the outbreak of hostilities in any part of the world.

The reform issue of Security Council membership is more problematic. A complaint is that the Council is too small and, on the whole, unrepresentative. UN membership grew from 51 members in 1945 to 118 members in 1965, and 193 members a half a century later. In comparison, the size of the Security Council membership increased once in 1965, from 11 to 15 members, through an increase in the number of non-permanent seats. However, the number of permanent members in the Security Council has remained unchanged since its inception. The non-permanent members have risen from 11 members in 1945 to 15 members in 1965. Yet, no new Council seats have been added since 1965. At the same time, the P5 – representing power configurations at the end of World War II – includes neither an African nor a South American state, while two European countries are represented. Further, the European Union contains two permanent members and has a total population and economic wealth more than the United States. Although she aspires to become a single federated union, it has no distinct, legitimate stature on the Security Council. In addition, Germany and Japan, the defeated nations of World War II, are both seen in the new millennium as equally influential, economically and politically, with some other P5 members. Other countries are voicing for expansion and reformation of the Security Council membership, including granting permanent status to countries from overlooked geographic areas, which is justifiably growing.

Therefore, the Security Council must reflect on the changing power composition and roles in today's world. There should be an increase in its permanent members to offer seats to rising and potentially Great Powers like Germany, Japan, Brazil, India, South Africa, etc. A more representative Security Council reflecting present-day international realities is imperative for the UN in the 21st century.

In Hindsight: Challenging the Power of the Veto

The veto power conferred by the UN Charter is, after permanency itself, the most significant distinction between permanent and non-permanent members of the Security Council. The UN would not have been founded without the five permanent members having the power of the veto; indeed, the organization was designed so that all major decisions would require the support, or at least the acquiescence, of the big powers.[4] But from the start, the veto has been a steady source of tension between the permanent members and the wider membership of the UN. Since the end of the Cold War, veto reform has been an element of many initiatives seeking structural reforms in the Council. These initiatives have come from member states that believe that the Council no longer reflects the ways the global order has changed since 1945. Frequently, member states also take up the perceived "abuse" of the veto in discussions of Council working methods, including during the body's annual working methods debate.

On 26 April, the UN General Assembly adopted consensus resolution A/RES/76/262, which calls for the General Assembly to meet whenever a veto is cast in the Security Council. The President of the General Assembly will convene a formal meeting to hold a debate on the vetoed subject within ten working days and, on an exceptional basis, the member or members who have cast a veto will be given precedence in the speakers' list.

The vote was the culmination of an initiative led by Liechtenstein and a core group of countries.[5] Eighty-three members co-sponsored the resolution from every UN regional group, including three permanent members: France, the UK, and the US. Although there have been veto initiatives in the past, this is the first time a UN body has taken action to modify the use of the veto.

---

4. Article 27 (3) of the UN Charter states that decisions on all but procedural matters "shall be made by an affirmative vote of nine members including the concurring votes of the permanent members". In the early years of the UN, a norm developed that has been held to this day whereby "concurring votes" included affirmative votes as well abstentions.
5. Australia, Bulgaria, Costa Rica, Denmark, Estonia, Ireland, Kenya, Kuwait, Latvia, Liechtenstein, Malta, Mexico, New Zealand, Qatar, Sweden, and Turkey.

Such initiatives have a history, though. In the mid-2000s, the deadlock over Syria led member states to search for ways to make veto use more difficult. In August 2015, France, with the support of Mexico, launched the 'Political Declaration on Suspension of Veto Powers in Cases of Mass Atrocity'. The aim was to have the permanent members—the P5—voluntarily pledge not to use the veto in cases of genocide, crimes against humanity, and war crimes on a large scale. Among the veto-wielding permanent members, so far only France and the UK have supported this initiative. As of April 2022, 103 member states and two UN observers had signed the declaration.

This voluntary initiative to suspend veto powers has been dogged by the lack of definition of atrocity crimes. This may also explain why it hasn't come to the fore in connection with the current situation in Ukraine, as some members are wary of describing crimes there as "atrocity crimes" until they have been duly verified.

In a similar vein, in July 2015, the Accountability, Coherence, and Transparency (ACT) group, which consists of 27 small and medium-sized states working to enhance the Council's effectiveness by strengthening its working methods, developed a code of conduct for member states regarding Security Council action against genocide, crimes against humanity and war crimes. The code is meant to encourage timely and decisive action by the Council to prevent or end the commission of genocide, crimes against humanity, and war crimes. As with the later French-Mexican initiative, the code of conduct urges the permanent members to agree to refrain from using their veto in situations involving mass atrocity crimes and also invites current and aspiring elected members to refrain from casting a negative vote in such cases, as it envisions the fight against atrocities as a collective responsibility of all member states. The code of conduct had been signed by 122 member states by 10 February 2022, including eight current elected Council members, two permanent members (France and the UK), and two observers.

The current Liechtenstein-led veto initiative was conceived more than two years ago but was put aside as COVID-19 compelled the UN to work remotely. The return to more normal UN functioning, combined with Council deadlock over Ukraine sparking renewed interest in its reform, created the conditions for the initiative to be revived.

Backers of this initiative may also have been emboldened by the Security Council's referral of the situation in Ukraine to the General Assembly on 27 February. For the first time in 40 years, the Council adopted a "Uniting for Peace" resolution, whereby it refers to the General Assembly as a situation in which its permanent members are deadlocked. This followed Russia's veto, on 25 February, of a resolution condemning Russian aggression against Ukraine. Since then, the General Assembly has adopted three resolutions directly related to the war in Ukraine. The first, which garnered 141 votes, expanded on the failed Council resolution condemning Russia's aggression against Ukraine. The second focused on the humanitarian consequences of Russia's aggression against Ukraine, receiving 140 votes. A third resolution, which had the support of 93 member states, suspended Russia's membership in the UN Human Rights Council.

Since the UN's founding, all five permanent members (China, France, Russia, the UK, and the US) have exercised the right to veto non-procedural decisions of the Council under Article 27 (3) of the UN Charter. They have done so to varying degrees. The USSR/Russia has cast 119 vetoes, with 35 of these related to applications for UN membership in the organization's early years. The US cast the first of its 82 vetoes on a draft resolution on 17 March 1970 (S/9696 and Corr. 1 and 2), at which point the USSR had vetoed 80 draft resolutions. France and the UK have not cast a veto since 23 December 1989 (S/21048) when, in tandem with the US, they prevented the Security Council from condemning the US invasion of Panama. The UK first used its veto on 30 October 1956 (S/3710) during the Suez Crisis and had cast 29 vetoes on draft resolutions before ceasing to use the veto at the end of 1989. France applied its veto for the first time on 26 June 1946 for the Spanish Question (S/PV.49) and cast a total of 18 vetoes on draft resolutions through the end of 1989. Since the People's Republic of China assumed the seat previously held by the Republic of China on 25 October 1971, it has vetoed 16 draft resolutions.[6]

Veto usage since 2000 highlights changes in voting patterns among the permanent members. China has used its veto more actively—13 of its 16 vetoes have been cast since 2000—and, in each of these cases, has done so with Russia. Together with Russia, it vetoed resolutions on Myanmar and Zimbabwe in 2007 and 2008, with its remaining 11 vetoes in this period being on resolutions related to Syria. Since 2000, Russia has vetoed 27 draft resolutions, 16 on Syria and three on Ukraine. It also vetoed resolutions on the 20th anniversary of the genocide in Srebrenica, Georgia, Yemen sanctions, Venezuela, and climate and security. The US is the only member of the P3 (France, UK, and the US) that has continued to use its veto—14 times since 2000, with all but two resolutions related to the Israel-Palestine conflict. It vetoed a resolution on Bosnia and Herzegovina in 2002 and its most recent veto was on a counter-terrorism resolution in 'August 2020'[7].

As these numbers and issues indicate, vetoes affect the Council's ability to address some of the most serious violations of the UN Charter and international law. In Syria, the use of the veto has blocked the Security Council's condemnation of chemical weapons attacks, shut down a chemical weapons investigation mechanism, and prevented a referral to the ICC. In Ukraine, the use of the veto has blocked investigations and the establishment of criminal tribunals, as well as condemnation of Russian aggression against Ukraine.

---

6. Veto statistics are from the Dag Hammarskjöld Library: https://research.un.org/en/docs/sc/quick. These numbers are for vetoes on draft resolutions and do not include vetoes on amendments and other proposals.
7. https://www.securitycouncilreport.org/un_documents_type/other-documents/?ctype=Terrorism&cbtype=terrorism

On "the situation in the Middle-East, including the Palestinian question", the veto has prevented condemnation of the building of illegal settlements, and the use of violence against Palestinians.

The 2020 US veto of a draft resolution on the prosecution, rehabilitation, and reintegration of 'foreign terrorist fighters'[8] and Russia's 2021 veto of a draft resolution on 'climate and security'[9] may portend their new readiness to deploy the veto on thematic issues.

With veto abolition appearing unlikely, as the required Charter amendment needs the support of all permanent members, the General Assembly's 26 April decision is nonetheless a way of imposing greater accountability for veto use. Some analysts think its impact will be minimal: members already offer public explanations of their votes in the Council chamber, and simply having to explain their reasons to the larger membership may not act as a deterrent. As well, the mere threat of veto use can serve to block a Council decision and is nowhere recorded or explained. But the initiative breaks the ice on a long-stalled reform discussion. At a time when questions have been raised about the Council's ability to carry out its mandate according to the Charter and multilateralism is under severe strain, the General Assembly's recent actions may be a much-needed shot in the arm and a reminder of its capacity to take action in the face of Council gridlock.

Cited Works

Basic Facts about the United Nations, Diane Publishing, New York: UN Department of Public Information, published periodically.

Bailey, Sydney D., and Sam Daws. *The Procedure of the UN Security Council*, 3rd Edition. New York: Oxford University Press, 1998.

Boyd, A., *Fifteen Men on a Powder Keg,* New York: Stein & Day, 1971.

Bosco, David L., *Five to Rule Them All: The UN Security Council and the Making of the Modern World,* Oxford: Oxford University Press, 2009.

Davidson, Nicol, *UN Security Council: Towards Greater Effectiveness*, New York: UNITAR, 1990.

Fassbender, Bodo, *UN Security Council Reform and the Right of Veto,* The Hague, The Netherlands: Kluwer Law International, 1998.

Luard, Evan, *The United Nations: How it Works and What it Does,* London: Macmillan, 1979.

---

8. https://www.securitycouncilreport.org/un_documents_type/other-documents/?ctype=Terrorism&cbtype=terrorism
9. https://www.securitycouncilreport.org/un-documents/document/s-2021-990.php

Moore, John Allphin, Jr., and Jerry, Pubantz, *Encyclopedia of the United Nations,* New York, 2008.

Moore, John Allphin, Jr., and Jerry, Pubantz, *The New United Nations: International Organization in the Twenty-First Century,* 2nd edition, New York & London, Routledge, 2017.

https://www.securitycouncilreport.org/atf/cf/%7B65BFCF9B-6D27-4E9C-8CD3-CF6E4FF96FF9%7D/Chap%20VII%20SRES%20277.pdf

https://www.un.org/securitycouncil/sites/www.un.org.securitycouncil/files/en/sc/repertoire/66-68/chapter%208/66-68_08-2-situation%20in%20viet-nam.pdf

https://www.un.org/securitycouncil/content/repertoire/relations-other-un-organs#rel1

https://www.securitycouncilreport.org/monthly-forecast/2022-05/in-hindsight-challenging-the-power-of-the-veto.php

https://www.securitycouncilreport.org/atf/cf/%7B65BFCF9B-6D27-4E9C-8CD3-CF6E4FF96FF9%7D/working_methods_veto.pdf

https://www.securitycouncilreport.org/un-security-council-working-methods/the-veto.php

https://research.un.org/en/docs/sc/quick/veto

https://unesdoc.unesco.org/ark:/48223/pf0000048063

https://www.un.org/en/events/mandeladay/un_against_apartheid.shtml#KeyDates

http://eprints.nottingham.ac.uk/13282/1/383611.pdf

https://www.mofa.go.jp/policy/un/sc/reform.html

7

THE ECONOMIC AND SOCIAL COUNCIL

The Economic and Social Council was established by the Charter as the principal organ to coordinate the economic and social work of the United Nations and the specialized agencies and institutions—known as the "United Nations family" of organizations.

Composition

1. According to Article 61 of the UN Charter, the ECOSOC has 54 members elected by the General Assembly.
2. Subject to the provisions of paragraph 3, 18 members are elected each year for a three-year term. A retiring member is eligible for immediate re-election.
3. At the first election after the increase in the membership of the Economic and Social Council from twenty-seven to fifty-four members, in addition to the members elected in place of the nine members whose term of office expires at the end of that year, twenty-seven additional members shall be elected. Of these twenty-seven additional members, the term of office of nine members so elected shall expire at the end of one year, and of nine other members at the end of two years, in accordance with arrangements made by the General Assembly.
4. Each member of the Economic and Social Council shall have one representative.

Voting

As mentioned in the Article 67-70 of the UN Charter, the voting in ECOSOC is done as follows:

1. Voting in the Economic and Social Council is by simple majority, each member has one vote.
2. Decisions of the Economic and Social Council shall be made by a majority of the members present and voting.

3. The Economic and Social Council shall invite any Member of the United Nations to participate, without a vote, in its deliberations on any matter of particular concern to that Member.
4. The Economic and Social Council may make arrangements for representatives of the specialized agencies to participate, without a vote, in its deliberations and those of the commissions established by it, and for its representatives to participate in the deliberations of the specialized agencies.

Charter Role: Functions and Powers

The functions and powers of the Economic and Social Council (Article 62) are:

1. To make or initiate studies and reports and recommendations on international economic, social, cultural, educational, health and related matters;
2. To promote respect for, and observance of, human rights and fundamental freedoms for all;
3. To call international conferences and prepare draft conventions for submission to the General Assembly on matters falling within its competence;
4. To negotiate agreements with the specialized agencies defining their relationship with the United Nations;
5. To coordinate the activities of the specialized agencies by means of consultations with and recommendations to them, and by means of recommendations to the General Assembly and the Members of the United Nations;
6. To perform services, approved by the Assembly, for Members of the United Nations and, upon request, for the specialized agencies;

Sessions

The Economic and Social Council generally holds two-month long sessions each year, one in New York and the other in Geneva. The year-round work of the Council is carried out in its subsidiary bodies – commissions and committees – which meet at regular intervals and report back to the Council.

Subsidiary Bodies

The Subsidiary machinery of the ECOSOC includes:

Functional Commissions

Statistical Commission

Commission on Population and Development (CPD)

Commission for Social Development (CSD)

United Nations Forum on Forests (UNFF)

Commission on the Status of Women (CSW)

Commission on Narcotic Drugs (CND)

Commission on Crime Prevention and Criminal Justice (CCPCJ)

Commission on Science and Technology for Development

Regional Commissions

Economic Commission for Europe (UNECE)

Economic Commission for Africa (ECA)

Economic and Social Commission for Asia and the Pacific (ESCAP)

Economic and Social Commission for Western Asia (ESCWA)

Economic Commission for Latin America and the Caribbean (ECLAC)

Standing Committees

Committee for Programme and Coordination (CPC)

Committee on Non-Governmental Organizations

Committee on Negotiations with Intergovernmental Agencies

Expert Bodies: Funds and Programmes that Send Reports to ECOSOC

UN International Children's Emergency Fund (UNICEF)

UN Development Programme (UNDP)

UN Environment Programme (UNEP)

Office of the UN High Commissioner for Refugees (UNHCR)

UN Population Fund (UNFPA)

UN Relief and Works Agency for Palestine Refugees in the Near East (UNRWA)

UN Office on Drugs and Crime (UNODC)

World Food Programme (WFP)

UN Human Settlements Programme (UN-HABITAT)

UN Entity for Gender Equality and the Empowerment of Women (UN-Women)

All five Regional Commissions were established according to similar terms of reference to function analogously in their respective regions. Their main objective is to initiate and participate in measures for facilitating concerted action for economic and social development to raise the level of economic activity and advance the levels of living and maintain and strengthen economic relations among their members and other countries of the world. The commissions may, after discussions with any specialized agency functioning in the same general field, and with the approval of the ECOSOC, establish such bodies as they deem appropriate to facilitate the carrying out of their responsibilities.

While the Regional Commissions approve their respective programmes of work, the Functional Commissions and Standing Committees under the decision of the Economic and Social Council, on 10 January 1973, stated their programme objectives so that the Secretary-General can examine, elaborate on the most effective and economic means to achieve the objectives in question, make appropriate recommendations in the biennial programme for budget and the medium-term plan. Some of the Functional Commissions are as follows:

(i) The Statistical Commission promotes the development of national statistics, the coordination of statistical work, and the development of central statistical services; and advises the organs of the United Nations on general questions of statistical information;

(ii) The Population Commission studies and advises on the size and structure of populations, the interplay of demographic factors and policies, designed to influence the size and structure of populations, and changes therein;

(iii) The Commission for Social Development advises on social policies of a general character, vital social problems, and required related measures;

(iv) The Commission on the Status of Women prepares recommendations and reports on the promotion of women's rights in political, economic, civil, social, and educational fields;

(v) The Commission on Narcotic Drugs assists in exercising powers of supervision over the application of international conventions and agreements dealing with narcotic drugs, advises the Council on all matters pertaining to the control of narcotic drugs, and prepares such drafts for international conventions as may be necessary.

Relations with Non-Governmental Organizations

Under the Charter, the Economic and Social Council (ECOSOC) may consult non-governmental organizations which are concerned with matters within its competence. The ECOSOC recognizes that these organizations should have the opportunity to express their views and that they often possess special experience or technical knowledge of value to help them in their work.

Over 5,593 non-governmental organizations have consultative status with the ECOSOC (till April 2021). They have classified into three categories of status:

General Consultative Status is retained for large established international organizations or NGOs with broad outreach which are concerned with most of the activities or issues on the agenda of ECOSOC and its subsidiary bodies;

Special Consultative Status is given to those organizations or smaller new NGOs which have special competence in specific fields of activity of the ECOSOC; and

Organizations or NGOs with narrow and/or technical focus are included on the Roster which can make an occasional contribution to the ECOSOC, its subsidiary organs or other United Nations bodies.

Non-governmental organizations which have been given consultative status may send observers to public meetings of the ECOSOC and its subsidiary bodies and may submit written statements relevant to its work. They may also consult the United Nations Secretariat on matters of mutual concern.

Coordination of the UN System

The Charter assigns to the Economic and Social Council, under the authority of the General Assembly, a central promotional and coordinating role in respect of the whole United Nations System: that is to say, the United Nations *per se*, including UNCTAD, UNIDO, UNDP, UNEP, UNICEF, and other United Nations organs, as well as the specialized agencies and International Atomic Energy Agency (IAEA). The ECOSOC and the General Assembly can provide policy coordination for the entire United Nations System. Firstly, a framework within which each part of the system can play its due role. Secondly, the ECOSOC can best assist the General Assembly in developing the political will and forming the political decisions. It is necessary to launch and maintain broad international actions, which require cooperation within the system.

The ECOSOC's general responsibilities for coordination of the policies and activities of the specialized agencies have links with the General Assembly in Articles 58 and 60; it is a specific authority for negotiation on agreements in coordination with the activities of the specialized agencies in Articles 57 and 63, Article 64 authorizes it to obtain reports from the specialized agencies, and Article 70 arranges for representatives of the specialized agencies to participate without vote in its deliberations.

Unlike the General Assembly, the ECOSOC, 'coordination' from the outset has been a constant and central preoccupation. Negotiation on agreements with the specialized agencies has figured prominently in its early agendas. In late 1946, it has provided for the establishment of an inter-agency coordinating committee under the chairmanship of the Secretary-General. Lately, it has acquired the name of the Administrative Committee on Coordination (ACC). Since the summer session of 1948, a Committee of the Whole on Coordination (known in recent years as its Policy and Programme Coordination Committee) to consider the annual agency reports, the annual reports of ACC, and the ever-increasing range of subjects on the ECOSOC's agenda that affect or call for action of the specialized agencies.

Nevertheless, the ECOSOC as a whole has never been fully reconciled to the autonomous status of the specialized agencies or been happy with its performance as a coordinator. Admittedly, it cannot claim great success for its efforts so far to deal with either the structural developments that have led to lack of coordination or the practical coordination problems themselves. Reasons for its somewhat unimpressive record in this regard are easy to identify if one reflects on the loose and sprawling character of the system, the ECOSOC's lack of financial powers and the history, both the erosion of its authority and the narrowing of its area of responsibility. It can only carry out its coordinating job if the Secretariats of the United Nations and the specialized agencies do the spadework. The ECOSOC's conventional outlook do all the coordinating (ACC merely assisting and making suggestions) combined with its traditionally critical attitude towards ACC, has been a constant handicap, preventing it from more fully mobilizing the resources of the United Nations System. Generally, the Secretariats have much experience working through ACC and also bilaterally. Institutional arrangements within the framework of reasonable decisions taken by intergovernmental organs, where decisions are a source of confusion, the Secretariats can likewise exert a powerful influence to adjust them. If more coherent, purposeful, and better-coordinated arrangements are to be achieved and maintained in the United Nations System, the UN Secretariat's contribution in guiding the General Assembly the ECOSOC becomes essential.

The ECOSOC works through three sessional committees—the Economic Committee, the Social Committee, and the Policy and Programme Coordination Committee.

The Economic and Social Council—an Evaluation

Although afforded the status of a principal organ by the Charter, the Economic and Social Council (ECOSOC) functions under the authority of the General Assembly. As ECOSOC faced criticism for competing with or duplicating the work of the Second (Economic and Financial) and Third (Social) Committees of the Assembly, in many respects, its activities resemble those of the General Assembly committees.

Originally, ECOSOC was established with eighteen members, enlarged to twenty-seven in 1965 and to fifty-four in 1973. Both these enlargements have taken place through Charter amendments. Their implementation has given way to the growing demands by the Third World bloc for voicing and determining economic and social policy. Although all UN members are equally eligible for election, in practice, members representing the industrially developed countries have been elected consistently over the years. A President is elected every year from one of the middle or small powers represented on the ECOSOC.

The failure of so many of ECOSOC's debates to materialize into effective action programmes has produced a mounting frustration among the developing nations, aggravated by present rivalries and deep-rooted antagonisms of the past. Despite having wide discrepancies between the hopes of the framers and the accomplishments of the ECOSOC, still, it has carried on a vast amount of sterling work.

Intense debates on various social and economic questions have raged in ECOSOC, which typify its deliberative role. Recent agenda items, for example, include discussions on housing, human rights, narcotic drug control, water resources, desertification, population problem, trade, industrial development, literacy, refugees, and science and technology.

Two subjects— economic development and human rights stand out in the ECOSOC's deliberations, both in frequency and intensity. Both are popular subjects for the representatives on the ECOSOC from developing world nations. The demands of these representatives for more financial help from the industrial countries, as a rightful legacy of real or imagined exploitations of the past, keep the Western nations on the defensive. Although debates on human rights even touch a tender nerve of participant-nations, they often fail to see the inherent irony of governmental representatives and demand more rights for individuals in the rest of the world than most are willing to grant their citizens.

To undertake studies that help overcome the lack of statistical and other on economic and social conditions in the world is probably the most admirable function performed by the ECOSOC. Here ECOSOC operates as a research agency and clearinghouse, attempting to coordinate the work of numerous committees, commissions, study groups and private or non-governmental organizations. Functional Commissions and Regional Economic Commissions carry out most of the studies for ECOSOC.

Based on its deliberations and extensive studies, the ECOSOC makes appraisals of its findings and, by Charter directive, may make recommendations. Recommendations usually take the form of a draft resolution or declaration. The drafts may merely embody a statement of general principles and require only a favourable vote in the General Assembly for implementation, such as the proclamation of the Universal Declaration of Human Rights of 1948. They may also take the form of conventions requiring affirmative action by the Assembly and subsequent ratification by a stipulated number of member states.

Drafting conventions provide a quasi-legislative role for ECOSOC because it is often involved in the early phases of consensus building for many UN-sponsored treaties. It resembles the national law-making function with the resulting convention that binds consenting states, which often limits governments in their relationship to their citizens, in addition to the international law. While ECOSOC cannot make law, it can reasonably perform a leading role in helping members of the United Nations to develop the law.

The Economic and Social Council has recognized its inadequate impact on UN policies and has repeatedly examined its methods of operation and role within the organization. This concern, coupled with the more broadly representative nature of the fifty-four-member Council, has in most effective ways strengthened ECOSOC's approach to economic and social cooperation. But many problems remain unresolved. Not least are potential conflicts between North and South, developed versus developing and now between and among the least developed and the developing countries themselves. In addition to these conflicts, member states hold diverse views on the role of government, and the types of political, economic, and social systems that should prevail in the world. Finally, the Council ECOSOC itself is a body with limited powers. Although it can only study, discuss, and recommend; and even in this, it is subordinate to the overriding authority of the General Assembly.

Cited Works

Basic Facts about the United Nations, New York: UN Department of Public Information, published periodically.

Cox, R.W., (ed.) *International Organization, World Politics, Studies in Economic and Social Agencies*, London: Macmillan, 1969.

Gregg, Robert W. and Barkun, *The United System and its Functions*, Princeton: Van Nostrand, 1968.

Hill, Martin, *The United Nations System: Coordinating its Economic and Social Work*, Cambridge: Cambridge University Press, 1978.

Moore, John Allphin, Jr., and Jerry, Pubantz, *The New United Nations, International Organization in the Twenty-First Century*, New York and London, Routledge, 2017.

Moore, John Allphin, Jr., and Jerry, Pubantz, *Encyclopedia of the United Nations,* New York, 2008.

Sen, Sudhir, *United Nations in Economic Development, Need for a Strategy,* Dobbs Ferry, N.Y.: Oceana, 1969.

Sharp, Walter R., *The United Nations Economic and Social Council,* New York: Columbia University Press, 1969.

https://www.un.org/en/about-us/un-charter/full-text

https://www.un.org/en/ecosoc/about/subsidiary.shtml

https://www.un.org/ecosoc/en/content/ecosoc-subsidiary-bodies

8

THE INTERNATIONAL COURT OF JUSTICE

After World War I, as was widely hoped that the rule of law might be a substitute for war. All had agreed under the League Covenant to settle "disputes" peacefully. There were three alternative methods for this purpose. Disputes regarded as purely political need to be submitted to the League Council. For partly legal disputes, provision was made for their submission to arbitration through one of the arbitral arrangements already established, or, later, under a less formal legal procedure known as "conciliation." Finally, a wholly new provision known as "judicial settlement" was established for purely legal disputes. The Permanent International Court of Justice set up at The Hague, a new body established for the first time that undertook those provisions.

Many doubted whether anyone could draw a clear distinction between "legal" and "political" disputes. There were two opposite views on this subject. Some ardent believers in international law, mainly lawyers, held that there was no dispute, however "political", which would remain unresolved according to the principles and procedures of international law. Politicians, on the contrary, less firmly convinced, tended to maintain that for many issues, only the traditional methods of diplomacy or the newly established League of Nations could provide solutions. Others held that there were no purely legal questions at all. It was, thus, concluded that the most "important" issues were political rather than legal, and so "unfit for decision by the Court".

As a result, the Court excluded from hearing those issues, disputes, or cases, which most likely lead to wars, or at least, its justification – the treatment of Japanese settlers in Manchuria, the frontier dispute over Wal Wal between Italy and Ethiopia, the demilitarization of the Rhineland, the treatment of German minorities in Czechoslovakia and Poland—never submitted to the Permanent International Court of Justice.

A general belief that law could substitute a war has shaken the established legal machinery. So far proposed that nations need to give a solemn undertaking in all disputes of a legal character. They would accept the jurisdiction of the Court if these were submitted to it by nations that had given a similar undertaking. The opposition of some nations, especially Britain and one or two Commonwealth countries, led to the amendment in this proposal after both the nations concerned needed to have given their prior consent to the Court's "compulsory" jurisdiction. It was the famous Optional Clause to which governments might voluntarily accede. Even then many nations did not accede to it. They also had so many reservations, excluding all disputes of a particular kind, that much of its value was lost.

Jurisdiction

The Court gave its judgement on questions involving the interpretation of international law, treaties and other mutual obligations. It had jurisdiction only over such disputes as members were willing to submit it. However, a few countries agreed in advance to submit all their outstanding disputes to the Court for settlement. Others reserved the right only those cases, which they liked to submit to the Court. The Permanent Court of International Justice was the modest effort made, thus far to establish an international judicial tribunal for the arbitration of controversies between states. It had tried 65 cases and handed down 32 judgements, 23 advisory opinions, 29 contentious cases between States, and several hundred orders during its jurisdiction. Thus, it created a body of legal precedents for resolving future international cases of a justiciable character.

After World War II, an agreement to reconstitute the Court to make it an integral element of the United Nations system was signed. In April 1945, before the end of the war, the US Government invited a Committee of Jurists to meet in Washington and make recommendations for a new statute for the Court. At the San Francisco Conference, all members of the UN had automatically become parties to the promulgation of the new Court. After dropping the adjective, 'Permanent,' was renamed the International Court of Justice. The Court was an organ of the UN (its predecessor had been separate from the League). Its statute became annexed to the Charter.

The statute redrafted adhered to the UN resolution. Every member of the UN had undertaken to comply with the decisions of the International Court of Justice to which it is a party. Article. 94 (1) in the Optional Clause was reproduced in Article 36 of the statute, state parties declared that they would be recognized "as compulsory *ipso facto* and without special agreement, in relation to any other state accepting the same obligation," subject to the Court's jurisdiction over certain types of legal disputes. As laid down in the Charter, the Security Council, could at the request of one party to the suit, "decide upon measures to be taken to give effect to the judgement" of the Court (Art. 94.2).

The jurisdiction of the Court covers all questions which states refer to it, and all matters provided for in the United Nations Charter or treaties or conventions in force. States may bind themselves in advance to accept the jurisdiction of the Court in special cases, either by signing a treaty or convention which provides for referral to the Court or by making a special declaration to that effect. Such declarations accepting compulsory jurisdiction may exclude certain classes of cases.

Under Article 38 of its statute, the Court follows international law in deciding disputes submitted to it, applies:

1. International conventions, whether general or particular, establishing rules expressly recognized by the contesting States;
2. International custom, as evidence of a general practice accepted as law;
3. The general principles of law recognized by civilized nations; and
4. Subject to the provisions of Article 59, judicial decisions and the teachings of the most highly qualified publicists of the various nations, as a subsidiary means for determination of the rules of law.

Composition and Functions

The International Court of Justice is the principal judicial organ of the United Nations. Its statute is an integral part of the UN Charter.

The Court is open to all states which are parties to its statute, and automatically includes all members of the United Nations. A state which is not a member of the UN may become a party to the statute on conditions determined in each case by the General Assembly upon the recommendations of the Security Council.

All countries which are parties to the statute of the Court can be parties to cases before it. Other states can refer cases to it under conditions laid down by the Security Council. In addition, the Security Council may recommend that a legal dispute be referred to the Court.

Both the General Assembly and the Security Council can ask the Court for an advisory opinion on any legal question; other organs of the United Nations and the specialized agencies, when authorized by the General Assembly, can ask for advisory opinions on legal questions within the scope of their activities.

Membership

The Court consists of 15 Judges elected by the General Assembly and the Security Council, voting independently. They are appointed on the basis of their qualifications and high moral character rather than on the nationality, and care is taken to ensure that the principal legal systems of the world are represented in the Court. No two appointed Judges can be of the same nationality. The Judges serve for a term of nine years and may be re-elected. They cannot engage in any other occupation during their term of office.

Generally, the Court sits in a plenary session, but it may also form smaller units called chambers if the parties so request. Judgements given by chambers are considered as rendered by the Full Court.

Judicial Settlement of Disputes

The primary organ of the United Nations for the settlement of disputes is the International Court of Justice. Since its founding in 1946, states have submitted 167 cases to it till-date (2022), and international organizations have requested 27 advisory opinions and 140 contentious cases. Most cases have been dealt with by the Full Court, but since 1981 four cases have been referred to special chambers at the request of the parties.

The World Court, as it is popularly known, has made scores of judgements on international disputes involving economic rights, rites of passage, the non-use of force, non-interference in the internal affairs of states, diplomatic relations, hostage-taking, the right of asylum and nationality. Countries bring such disputes before the Court in search of an impartial solution to their differences. By achieving a peaceful settlement on questions such as land frontiers, maritime boundaries, and territorial sovereignty, the Court has often helped to prevent the escalation of disputes.

In a typical case of territorial rights, the Court in 1999 settled a sensitive frontier dispute between Botswana and Namibia, with a ruling that both countries accepted. In 1994, after Nigerian forces clashed with Cameroonian police, Cameroon instituted proceedings against Nigeria in a sovereignty dispute over the oil-rich Bakassi Peninsula, and then over the whole land and sea boundary. In its Judgement the Court requested Nigeria, expeditiously and without condition, to withdraw its administration and military or police forces from the area of Lake Chad falling within Cameroonian sovereignty and from the Bakassi Peninsula. It also requested Cameroon expeditiously and without condition to withdraw any administration or military or police forces which might be present along the land boundary from Lake Chad to the Bakassi Peninsula on territories which, pursuant to the Judgement, fell within the sovereignty of Nigeria. The latter had the same obligation in regard to territories in that area which fell within the sovereignty of Cameroon. The Court took note of Cameroon's undertaking, given at the hearings, to "continue to afford protection to Nigerians living in the [Bakassi] Peninsula and in the Lake Chad area". Finally, the Court rejected Cameroon's submissions regarding the State responsibility of Nigeria, as well as Nigeria's counter-claims.

In 1992, the Court settled a dispute between El Salvador and Honduras, embroiled in a century-old conflict that had led to a short but bloody war in 1969. The ICJ decided that the legal situation of the waters outside the Gulf is that, the Gulf of Fonseca being an historic bay with three coastal States, the closing line of the Gulf constitutes the baseline of the territorial sea; the territorial sea, continental shelf and exclusive economic zone of El Salvador and those of Nicaragua off the coasts of those two States are also to be measured outwards from a section of the closing line extending 3 miles (1 marine league) along that line from Punta Arnapala (in El Salvador) and 3 miles (1 marine league) from Punta Cosigüina (in Nicaragua) respectively ; but entitlement to territorial sea, continental shelf and exclusive economic zone seaward of the central portion of the closing line appertains to the three States of the Gulf, El Salvador, Honduras and Nicaragua; and that any delimitation of the relevant maritime areas is to be effected by agreement on the basis of international law.

Libyan Arab Jamahiriya clashed with Chad, where each started legal proceedings against the other in the Court. The Court ruled in 1994 that defined the division of territory by a 1955 treaty between Libya and France; Libya then withdrew its forces from an area along its southern border with Chad.

Against the background of conflict or political upheaval, various causes referred to the Court. In 1980, the United States produced a case before the ICJ after its embassy in Tehran was seized and its staff detained. The Court held that Iran must release the hostages, hand back the embassy and pay for its reparations. However, before the Court could set the reparation amount, the US had an agreement with Iran and withdrew the case. In 1989, Iran asked the Court to condemn the shooting down of an Iranian airliner by a United States warship and to find whether the United States was responsible for compensation to Iran or not. The case was closed in 1996 following a compensation settlement.

In 1986, in a case brought by Nicaragua against the United States over the latter's support for Nicaragua's "contras" and laying mines outside Nicaraguan ports – acts that the Court held the United States could not justify on the basis of collective self-defence – had violated its international legal obligations not to intervene in the affairs of another state, not to use force against another state and not to infringe the sovereignty of another state. Accordingly, the Court decided that the United States had to make reparations. However in 1991, before the amount of the reparation had been determined, Nicaragua requested to dismiss that case.

In 1992, Libya brought two cases – one against the United Kingdom and one against the United States – concerning the interpretation or application of the Convention for the Suppression of Unlawful Acts against the Safety of Civil Aviation, arising out of the crash, in 1988, of Pan American flight 103 at Lockerbie, Scotland. In 1992, Libya brought two cases – one against the United Kingdom and one against the United States – concerning the interpretation or application of the Convention for the Suppression of Unlawful Acts against the Safety of Civil Aviation, arising out of the crash, in 1988, of Pan American flight 103 at Lockerbie, Scotland. On 3 March 1992, Libya made two separate requests to the Court to indicate forthwith certain provisional measures, namely : (a) to enjoin the United States and the United Kingdom respectively from taking any action against Libya calculated to coerce or compel it to surrender the accused individuals to any jurisdiction outside Libya; and (b) to ensure that no steps were taken that would prejudice in any way the rights of Libya with respect to the legal proceedings that were the subject of Libya's Applications. On 14 April 1992, the Court read two Orders on those requests for the indication of provisional measures, in which it found that the circumstances of the cases were not such as to require the exercise of its powers to indicate such measures. Within the time-limit fixed for the filing of its Counter-Memorial, each of the respondent States filed preliminary objections: the United States of America filed certain preliminary objections requesting the Court to adjudge and declare that it lacked jurisdiction and could not entertain the case; the United Kingdom filed certain preliminary objections to the jurisdiction of the Court and to the admissibility of the Libyan claims. In accordance with the provisions of Article 79 of the Rules of Court, the proceedings on the merits were suspended in those two cases. By Orders dated 22 September 1995, the Court then fixed 22 December 1995 as the time-limit within which the Libyan Arab Jamahiriya might present, in each case, a written statement of its observations and submissions on the preliminary objections raised, which it did within the prescribed time-limit. On 27 February 1998, the Court delivered two Judgements on the preliminary objections raised by the United Kingdom and the United States of America. It declared that it had jurisdiction on the basis of Article 14, paragraph 1, of that Convention to hear the disputes between Libya and the respondent States concerning the interpretation or application of the provisions of the Convention. The Court then went on to dismiss the objection to admissibility based on Security Council resolutions 748 (1992) and 883 (1993). The President of the Court, on 10 September 2003, made an Order in each case placing on record the discontinuance of the proceedings with prejudice, by agreement of the Parties, and directing the removal of the case from the Court's List.

In 1993, Bosnia and Herzegovina produced a case before the ICJ against the Federal Republic of Yugoslavia, concerning the application of the Convention on the Prevention and Punishment of the Crime of Genocide. The Court called upon the parties to prevent further commission of the crime of genocide and no more aggravating the dispute. In 1996, the Court rejected Yugoslavia's objections to its jurisdiction, the case is still pending before the Court.

The ICJ, in 1996, rejected objections of the United States to its jurisdiction in a case concerning the destruction of Iranian oil platforms by her warships and found that it had jurisdiction to consider some of Iran's claims.

States have often submitted questions of economic rights. For instance, a Chamber of the Court in 1989 rejected a claim for compensation put forward by the United States against Italy for the requisition of an Italian company owned by United States corporations. In 1995, in the context of a dispute over fisheries jurisdiction between Canada and the European Union, Spain instituted a case against Canada after seizing a Spanish fishing trawler on the high seas by Canada.

A case involving claims of environmental protection was brought by Hungary and Slovakia concerning a dispute over the validity of a 1997 treaty that they had concluded on building of a barrage system on the Danube River. In 1997, the Court found both states in breach of their legal obligations and called on them to carry out that treaty.

The International Court of Justice should not be confused with the International Criminal Court (ICC). The ICC was established by the Rome Treaty of 1998 to try war criminals. The Rome Statute then took effect in 2002, upon ratification by 60 States. It applies laws, as authorized by its contracting states, to individuals who are accused of particularly heinous crimes such as genocide. As of summer 2015, 123 nations were States parties to the Rome Statute. Once the ICC went into effect in 2002, the UN's Secretary-General signed a bilateral agreement with it, allowing the referral of cases by the Security Council to the court.

The ICJ hears only cases between states that are voluntarily brought to it by one of the adversaries, or it delivers advisory opinions at the request of UN bodies. States are neither bound to the ICJ's decisions, nor do they become subjects to penalties imposed by the court, whereas convicted defendants are subject to punishment before the ICC.

During its first seventy years, about 150 contentious cases were referred to the ICJ, although several were later removed from the court's list or were considered still pending. Of the approximately seventy-five countries that had been litigants in these cases, the United States was involved most often (about twenty times); the United Kingdom and the former Yugoslavia ranked second and third.

The Security Council created two geographic-specific courts: the International Criminal Tribunal for the Former Yugoslavia and the International Criminal Tribunal for Rwanda. The former was the first institution of international criminal prosecution since the end of World War II. The Rwandan court materialized in late 1994.

Advisory Opinions

Besides these 'contentious cases', the Court has also given some advisory opinions which have in some cases been of far-reaching implications. Some of them related to the UN affairs, particularly relating to the costs of peacekeeping forces. The Court, in its Advisory Opinion of 20 July 1962, replied in the affirmative that these expenditures were expenses of the United Nations. The Court pointed out that under Article 17, paragraph 2, of the Charter, the "expenses of the Organization" are the amounts paid out to defray the costs of carrying out the purposes of the Organization. The Court advised that peacekeeping costs could be reckoned as normal expenses of the organization for Article 19. Though this was overwhelmingly accepted by the Assembly, the UN finally decided not to apply Article 19 as allowed by the advisory opinion. The Court gave an opinion in the early years of the organization on disputes concerning admission into the UN confirming that no admission could be made without a Security Council recommendation. On a case arising out of the death of Count Bernadotte, the UN Mediator in Palestine in 1948, the Court ruled that the UN could bring a claim for reparations for the damage caused to the organization as a whole. The Court also advised during the McCarthy period, when US staff were being dismissed, that the UN was not entitled to refuse to honour awards of compensation made by the UN Administrative

Tribunal to staff whose contracts had been prematurely terminated. Finally, it ruled that Liberia and Panama should be accepted by IMCO (Inter-Governmental Maritime Consultative Organization) for membership of its Council as being among "the largest ship-owning nations".

Possibly, the most famous and important opinion of the Court was that concerning South-West Africa. The Court has given advisory opinions on a number of questions affecting the territory. In 1950, the Court had advised that the Mandate awarded by the League of South Africa over South-West Africa still existed and that, though South Africa need not convert the territory into a Trust Territory, she must submit to the supervision of the Mandate by the UN as the successor to the League (which it never did). In 1960, Ethiopia and Liberia, as former members of the League, brought a contentious case to the Court to the effect that South Africa had failed in its obligations under the Mandate, and asked the Court to rule that South Africa should cease from its present policies and fulfil its obligations. South Africa claimed that the Mandate had lapsed; that in any case, its obligations to report had come to an end; and that it had fulfilled its duties under the Mandate. The Court in 1966 ruled that Liberia and Ethiopia had no legal right or interest enabling them to bring such a contentious case before it. Thus, the long years, and many hours of pleading, on the merits of the case, were wasted, and the matter was dismissed on a procedural point. It remained open to the UN as a whole, as the successor to the League, to revive the proceedings. The Security Council in 1970 invited the Court to give an advisory opinion on "What are the legal consequences for States of the continued presence of South Africa in Namibia notwithstanding Security Council resolution 276 (1970)?"—in defiance of a Security Council 'decision'. On this occasion, the Court did give an opinion to the effect that South Africa's presence in the territory was illegal and that other states were under an obligation to take no action which recognized South Africa's legal authority there.

Limitations of the International Court

The record of the International Court, at first sight is perhaps not impressive. There is only a limited category of cases that are brought before it. Jurisdiction is entirely voluntary: either a nation accepts it for the particular case concerning it, or it enters into a treaty providing for a settlement of disputes by the Court, or it gives a general undertaking to accept the Court's jurisdiction for a particular category of cases concerning other nations which have likewise accepted it. In practice, both the number and importance of cases taken to the Court have diminished rapidly so that now less than one case a year is heard which is often not of major importance. The Court has had to find that it lacks jurisdiction as seen in a number of cases. Over one of the most important cases (the Corfu Channel), the party found responsible for the dispute refused to comply with the Court's judgement. In another important case (the South-West Africa case), the Court originally refused to pass judgement in the form in which it had been presented.

The cases dealing with frequent use of force among nations have never proceeded before the Court. International law can be uncertain or contested that often lead to war. The limits of permissible external intervention in civil war situations, political support for revolutionary movements, the right of nationalization of international waterways or other resources – the rulings of the International Court have not been brought into play at all.

A still more contentious issue concerns the lack of enforcement power available to the Court to secure compliance when it does make judgements. The Security Council can, under Article 94, decide upon measures to be taken to give effect to "the judgements" of the Court, but it has never done so. This leads to a situation where many doubt the utility of bringing disputes to the Court, wondering (for some reason) whether the other disputants involved will accept its jurisdiction, and comply with its judgements.

There is no evidence that even if jurisdiction was guaranteed, governments would be any more willing to move to the Court. The failure to use the Court is not so much the result of inadequate prior commitment as it is due to a lack of agreement among states regarding what the Court can achieve, and to a belief that political remedies may be a better way to pursue political causes.

All this leads some to doubt if the Court has any worthwhile role to play in international relations. Indeed, the international Court has not yet provided the means to establish a wholly new world order based on law and justice. But it would have been foolish to expect this. Although the judgements of the Court, and the conventions were drawn up by the Commission, have been mainly on relatively non-controversial subjects, this does not mean that they have been of no significance. The slow accumulation of international judgements and law can eventually contribute to the establishment of a more lawful world community in which mutual obligations are recognized.

But for this to happen certain conditions have to be fulfilled. The first condition concerns the substance of the law applied. At present, a great deal of international law appears to many governments of the world to be a code made in the first world primarily for itself. The people and governments of other areas have played little part in building it. It can be represented as ideological legitimacy for the *status quo*, designed to uphold the existing distribution of power among states. Some effort has been made to counteract such attitudes. But ultimately the only way in which confidence in the judgements of the Court and the drafting of new conventions can be increased is to make efforts to convince those from developing countries that the law applied provides for change as well as stability, reflects a sense of justice felt in the world as a whole and does not necessarily work against the interests of the have-nots. Like any other law, international law must take account of the changing needs of developing societies if it is to retain the confidence of the world community.

Secondly, this means that the Court in its judgements may be required more often explicitly, to take account of considerations of equity, as well as of prescriptive rights. At present, the court, under Article 38(2) of its statute, cannot take account of equity as against the established law. If the Court is to play an important role in evolving world society, it must be concerned with equity as well as legal rights.

Cited Works

Basic Facts about the United Nations, New York: UN Department of Public Information, published periodically.

Bowett, D.W., *The Law of International Institutions*, London: Stevens, 1963.

Dholakia, R.P., *The Codification of Public International Law*, Manchester: Manchester University Press, 1970.

Luard, Evan, *The United Nations: How it Works and What it Does*, London: Macmillan, 1979.

Moore, John Allphin, Jr., and Jerry, Pubantz, *Encyclopedia of the United Nations*, New York, 2008.

Moore, John Allphin, Jr., and Jerry, Pubantz, *The New United Nations, International Organization in the Twenty-First Century*, New York and London, Routledge, 2017.

Robinson, Jacob, *International Law and Organisation, General Sources of Information*, Leiden: A.W. Sijthoff, 1967.

Roseanne, S., *The World Court: What it is and How it Works*, Dobbs Ferry: Oceana, 1973.

Starke, J.G., *Introduction to International Law*, London: Butterworths, 1977.

https://www.icj-cij.org/en/pcij

https://www.icj-cij.org/en/case/89

https://www.icj-cij.org/public/files/case-related/75/075-19920911-JUD-01-00-EN.pdf

https://www.icc-cpi.int/romestatute20

https://asp.icc-cpi.int/states-parties

https://legal.un.org/repertory/art17/english/rep_supp3_vol1_art17_2.pdf

https://www.icj-cij.org/public/files/case-related/53/5597.pdf

https://www.icj-cij.org/en/case/53

9

THE SECRETARIAT

The United Nations Secretariat is one of the six principal organs of the United Nations, the others organs are the General Assembly, the Security Council, the Economic and Social Council, the Trusteeship Council and the International Court of Justice. It came into being on 1 February 1946, when the first Secretary-General of the UN Mr. Trygve Halvdan Lie was appointed by the General Assembly. He was formally installed by the General Assembly at its 22nd meeting on 2 February 1946. Secretary-General of the UN is appointed by the General Assembly upon the recommendation of the Security Council. Secretary-General is the head of the UN Secretariat and the chief administrative officer of the United Nations (Article 97). The Secretariat performs substantive and administrative work entrusted to it by the organs of the UN, namely, the General Assembly, the Security Council, the Economic and Social Council and the Trusteeship Council, other organs (Article 98). The primary organs adopt resolutions and action programmes for the betterment of many aspects of life, such as the peaceful settlement of disputes between states, achievement of independence, right to self-determination and other human rights of all peoples of the world, improvement of socio-economic conditions in all countries, international cooperation in providing relief to victims of conflict and natural disasters and adoption of regulations for safeguarding of the environment, exploitation of marine resources and promotion of activities in outer space. The resolutions and action programmes are the outcome of deliberations of representatives of member states in those organs and subsidiary bodies. The work of the Secretariat is carried out by the staff of the UN who is appointed by the Secretary-General under regulations established by the General Assembly (Article 101). The Secretary-General prepares an annual report to the General Assembly regarding the work of the organization (Article 98). He/She may bring to the notice of the Security Council any such matter that in his/her viewpoint may threaten the maintenance of international peace and security (Article 99).The resources it requires for carrying out the UN programme of work are provided by the member states. The Secretariat headquarters of the UN is located in New York. It has branch offices in Geneva, Vienna and Nairobi. It also includes the Regional Commissions at Addis Ababa, Bangkok, Beirut, Geneva and Santiago. Its broad functions in various fields with which the United Nations is concerned, vary from field-to-field.

The broad functions of the Secretariat are as follows:

(a) To provide support to the Secretary-General in fulfilling the functions entrusted to him or her under the Charter of the United Nations;

(b) To promote the principles of the Charter and build understanding and public support for the objectives of the United Nations;

(c) To provide advice to the Security Council and the General Assembly, through the Secretary-General, on all matters relating to the maintenance of international peace and security and to carry out activities mandated by these two organs or decided by the Secretary-General in the areas of prevention, control and resolution of conflicts;

(d) To provide humanitarian assistance, in particular to refugees and displaced persons;

(e) To promote economic and social development;

(f) To promote development cooperation;

(g) To promote human rights and international law;

(h) To provide Secretariat and meeting services to the General Assembly, the Security Council and other United Nations bodies;

(i) To conduct studies, promote standards and provide information in various fields that respond to the priority needs of Member States, as mandated by the legislative organs;

(j) To produce and publish statistical publications, information material and analytical studies, as mandated by the legislative organs;

(k) To organize international conferences and other meetings, as authorized by the legislative organs;

(l) To provide technical assistance to the developing countries;

(m) To disseminate information on the activities and decisions of the United Nations to the public;

(n) To cooperate with non-governmental organizations and interact with civil society;

(o) To perform other work as directed by the Secretary-General.

Salient Features of the Organization of the Secretariat

The Secretariat is headed by the Secretary-General who is the Chief Administrative Officer of the United Nations. In the economic and social fields, he is assisted in carrying out his responsibilities as Chief Administrative Officer. The Secretariat is divided into several major units each of which is headed by an Under-Secretary-General, an Assistant Secretary-General or an official of equivalent level. They direct and manage the functions of the major units under the guidance of the Secretary-General and, wherever called for, of the Director-Generals. The major units are variously denominated as "department", "office", "secretariat" or "centre" (henceforth referred to as departments/offices).

There are other Secretariat units, including the Executive Office of the Secretary-General, the Office of Internal Oversight Services, the Office of Legal Affairs, the Department of Political and Peacebuilding Affairs, the Office for Disarmament Affairs, the Department of Peace Operations, the Department of Operational Support, the Office for the Coordination of Humanitarian Affairs, the Office of Counter Terrorism (OCT), the Department of Economic and Social Affairs, the Department for General Assembly and Conference Management, the Development Coordination Office, the Department of Global Communications, the Department of Safety and Security, Internal Justice Bodies, the Department of Management Strategy, Policy and Compliance, other offices and UN Regional Commissions, besides, the Main Headquarters. The Senior Management Group serves as a central policy-planning body to ensure strategic coherence to Secretariat activities and shares an administrative role with the Chief Executives Board for Coordination. In addition, the UN *ombudsman*, although largely independent of outside control, report to and can be removed only by the Secretary-General. In 2015, some forty-four hundred men and women, under the regular budget, made up the staff of the Secretariat.

However, as the new millennium approached, the organization expanded its involvement with the private sector and non-governmental organizations. In development, a new UN engagement with private corporations and NGOs emerged. Secretary-General Kofi Annan launched a "Global Compact" between the United Nations and multinational corporations, administratively housed in the Executive Office of the Secretary-General, to protect human rights, international labour standards, and the global environment. Decreases in donor-state funding made this partnership a necessity.

Speaking on January 31, 1999, to the World Economic Forum in Davos, Switzerland, Annan urged corporations to work with the world body by initiating "a global compact of shared values and principles" based on "human rights, labour standards and environmental practices." This is to fulfil nine principles established in the Rio Declaration of the Earth Summit, the International Labour Organization's Fundamental Principles on Rights at Work, and the Universal Declaration of Human Rights. Subsequently, a tenth principle – to combat corruption – was added to the list in 2004 and commits UN Global Compact participants not only to avoid bribery, extortion and other forms of corruption, but also to proactively develop policies and concrete programmes to address corruption internally and within their supply chains. Companies are also challenged to work collectively and join civil society, the United Nations and governments to realize a more transparent global economy.

With the entry into force of the UN Convention Against Corruption (UNCAC) in 2005, an important global tool to fight corruption was introduced. The UNCAC is the underlying legal instrument for the 10th Principle.

When Secretary-General Ban Ki-moon convened the UN Private Sector Forum in September 2015 to consider how corporations and NGOs could contribute to the implementation of the Sustainable Development Goals, more than 9000 businesses and 3000 non-businesses in over 160 countries and other stakeholders worldwide were members of the Global Compact.

On March 2, 1998, Louise Fréchette became the UN's first Deputy Secretary-General (DSG). The duties of the DSG are to act for the Secretary-General (SG) at UN headquarters when the SG is absent, to enhance coherence and cooperation among UN bodies, to provide leadership in UN economic and social activities, to represent the SG at conferences and official functions, and to "undertake such assignments as may be determined by the Secretary-General."

The Secretariat in the Political Process: Policy through Administration

The administration is the process of implementing the mandate of policy-making bodies. However, all policies leave room for administrative discretion and apply rules to particular cases.

The administration also involves policy decisions indirect ways. Research studies and reports prepared by Secretariat officials add to the information base for government policy. Nearly every international organization can point to a report drafted by expert Secretariat personnel that forms the basis for subsequent action by policy-making bodies.

Successful performance of assigned duties by Secretariat personnel is more demanding. The first UN peacekeeping force in Palestine had to be built almost from scratch when the Suez crisis arose, but that precedent made a peacekeeping force a logical necessity wherever the UN intervened in times of conflict. On the other hand, ineffective administrative performance may lead to modification or abandonment of programmes.

Secretariat Participation in Decision-Making

International officials also participate directly in the decision-making processes of their governing bodies. Among existing international organizations, the greatest influence is probably exercised by the staff of the World Bank, who not only frame the programme for discussion by its Executive Directors and Governing Board but generally secure their approval for what the Bank President and his staff recommend. Governments are, of course, closely consulted in the preparation of the recommendations. The UNESCO Secretariat also fixes the agenda and prepares a programme of action for its governing body. Although the UNESCO General Conference is sometimes disposed to modify the programme, the Director-General is undoubtedly the most important decision-maker in the organization.

The situation is, however, quite different in the UN General Assembly, where most items on the agenda are proposed by member states, or mandated by previous resolutions, and solely compiled by the Secretariat as a preliminary item on the agenda. Although the Secretary-General may suggest additional item, he does not submit a legislative programme, as is done in some other international agencies. However, when legislation involves programmes administered by the Secretariat, the views of the Secretariat may carry weight, especially since the positions of member states are likely to have been solicited in formulating the Secretariat views.

The main functions of the Secretariat are:

- To gather and prepare background information on various issues so that government delegates can study the facts and make recommendations;
- To help carry out the decisions made by the different organs of the United Nations;
- To organize international conferences;
- To translate speeches and distribute documents into the UN official languages;
- To keep the public informed about the work of the United Nations.

The Secretary-General is also responsible for preparing the biennial UN budget. His estimates are based on the amounts required to carry out programmes already authorized by the policy-making bodies. As a result, the final choice of budget figures involves his discretion.

Whether or not the Secretariat of an international agency has a lead role in initiating programme proposals, other avenues of participation in the policy process also exist. Executive heads are usually authorized to participate in formal discussions and debates of agenda items. All UN policy-making organs have provision for hearing the Secretary-General. Other UN officials conduct their lobbying operations with varying degrees of success. The advice of individual civil servants on specific issues holds significance for national officials because of their expertise in a subject. Similarly, suggestions of the Secretary-General are vital for members who seriously consider proposals for new functions or responsibilities for the Secretariat.

The functions of the Secretary-General include:

- Bringing any problem that threatens world peace to the attention of the Security Council;
- Proposing issues to be discussed by the General Assembly or any other organ of the United Nations;
- Acting as a "referee" in disputes between Member States;
- Each Secretary-General also defines his role within the context of his particular time in office.

Secretariat officials also provide their services as storehouses of information on such policy-relevant matters for conducting meetings and drafting resolutions. One of the most vital roles played by the Secretary-General is the use of his "good offices"—steps taken publicly and in private, drawing upon his independence, impartiality and integrity, to prevent international disputes from arising, escalating or spreading. Sometimes, as a result of his mediation, the problems are solved without ever having to go to the Security Council or the General Assembly, or before the problem escalate into open conflict.

The Practice of Diplomacy

International officials also influence organizational policy and world politics through "quiet diplomacy". Here we refer to the Secretariat's role in promoting agreement among states through quiet discussion and reconciliation of differences.

Opportunities for quiet diplomacy are presented in a wide variety of situations. Constant diplomacy is essential for carrying out specific programmes of an organization and to obtain compliance with its resolutions. No peacekeeping mission can be accomplish without the process of negotiations with countries supplying troop contingents and necessary material, as well as with the host country and any other country directly involved. No mission is maintained without continuing negotiation to resolve problems and differences as they arise, the same is true of other operating programmes of the international organization. Every technical assistance project is the product of extensive and detailed interchange among governments and the responsible international agency. When UN resolutions call for government action, rather than to establish operating programmes, Secretariat officials may perform a diplomatic function in seeking compliance from member states.

Another form of diplomatic activity is the resolution of controversies between states. The role of the mediator, conciliator, and consensus-builder often appears in the quiet negotiations that occur behind the scenes of conference diplomacy. While government representatives often fill that role, not a few compromises, later embodied in a resolution, have been forged with the help of a timely suggestion or the mediatory services of a Secretariat official. The expertise, impartiality, and continuity of Secretariats become especially important in negotiating issues that persist over a long period of time within the UN framework, such as arms control or economic development.

The UN Secretary-General and his staff may also mediate particular disputes between countries. Frequently, this involvement comes through a mandate from the Assembly or the Security Council. The diplomatic services of the Secretary-General, acting personally or through his representatives, have been enlisted by the Assembly or the Council in such recent problem areas as the Iran-Iraq war, Afghanistan, Kampuchea (Cambodia), Namibia, the Falkland Islands, Lebanon, the Middle-East, Grenada, and the continuing Greek-Turkish conflict in Cyprus. Sometimes, Secretaries-General have not waited for the Council or the Assembly to act, but have attempted successful mediation on their initiative. Dag Hammarskjold, for example, initiated a successful mediation effort in a 1958 dispute between Cambodia and Thailand. U. Thant attempted, with less success, to be a mediating influence in the Vietnam War, as did Kurt Waldheim in the Soviet invasion of Afghanistan and the Iranian hostage crisis. Perez de Cuellar also attempted independent initiatives in Africa, Central America, the Middle-East and elsewhere, from time to time, during his tenure.

The International Civil Service: Origin and Development

The concept of international civil service is of a comparatively recent origin. It began with the administration of international civil affairs through inter-state treaties in the 19th century. In 1804, an official with the status of an international civil servant was appointed to regulate the navigation of the Rhine by a bilateral treaty between France and the German empire. Similarly, the Paris Treaty of 1856 created a European Commission for Navigation of the Danube with some administrative and engineering staff of international status. In 1874, the Bureau of the Universal Postal Union consisting of a handful of permanent administrative staff was created in Berne. The Congress resulted in the signing of the 1874 Treaty of Berne, which established the first collective Convention governing the international postal service and founded the "General Postal Union". The Treaty went into force on 1 July 1875. Three years later, in view of the numerous accessions which had taken place since the coming into force of the Treaty of Berne, the title "General Postal Union" was changed to "Universal Postal Union". The International Institute of Agriculture was set up in 1889 as a private body called *International Agricultural Commission*. Listed name adopted 7 Jun 1905, when became an intergovernmental organization. Absorbed, 16 Oct 1945, (by B-XB0971 - FAO, since when referred to as *FAO David Lubin Memorial Library)* attended by 70 governments.

The experience of these organizations provided valuable guidance to the later growth and development of international civil service with the establishment in 1920 of the League of Nations Secretariat and the International Labour Office at Geneva, and still later, the UN Secretariat, and the allied agencies of the UN.

1. By resolution of 13 February 1946 (GA/RES/13(I) Section III), the General Assembly of the United Nations decided that "an International Civil Service Commission shall be established by the Secretary-General, after consultation with the heads of the specialized agencies ... to advise on methods of recruitment ... and on the means by which common standards of recruitment in the Secretariat and in the specialized agencies may be ensured".
2. Basic agreements between specialized agencies and UN also provided that they would "consult together concerning the establishing of an International Civil Service Commission to advise on the means by which common standards of recruitment in the Secretariats ... may be ensured".

International Civil Service Advisory Board (ICSAB) was formed in 1948 to advise the Administrative Committee on Coordination (ACC). In 1972, General Assembly (GA) approved the need for an international civil service commission. On 18 December 1974, General Assembly (GA) approves the creation of ICSC in resolution 3357-XXIX, New York made the base for the system and its first session was held in 1975.

Differences between National and International Civil Service

Though national and international administrations may appear to be similar from a specifically functional viewpoint, the two differ considerably in terms of source, nature and application of authority.

The government of a country is representative of its citizens (at least nationally), whereas an international organization is composed of sovereign, independent states which have voluntarily agreed to come together to pursue certain common objectives.

Secondly, national civil servants deal only with the citizens of their respective states, while international civil servants deal with nation-states. Thirdly, on one hand, in a nation-state, the powers of different branches of government are clearly defined in a constitution, its provisions are binding on individual citizens. An international organization, on the other hand, depends on the moral binding of member states for the functioning of its laws virtually to respect its policies as stated in the Charter.

The executive, legislature and the judiciary in an international organization are not equivalent in their powers to their national counterparts. There is no executive in the strict sense in an international organization; superior policy-making organizations, like the General Assembly or the Security Council allocate specific duties to some organizations in certain situations. Most jurists agree that the resolutions and recommendations of the General Assembly (which is the rough equivalent of a national legislature) do not generally impose legal obligations upon member states. Similarly, the jurisdiction of the International Court of Justice is narrowly limited and its opinions are not binding, while the judiciary at the national level has a far more extensive and effective jurisdiction and its opinions are legally binding.

The primary concern of the International Civil Service is to put into effect the deliberations and recommendations of international organizations to promote their stated purposes. The National Civil Service administers national laws undertaking direct administrative responsibility.

A National Civil Servant administers a single political community, while an International Civil Servant administers international organizations which represent a series of contracts between various states.

Finally, the eligibility criteria of International Civil Service are based on contractual relations, rather than be obligatory, as in the case of National Civil Service. The legal relationship between National Civil Servants and their employer, the state, stands on an entirely different footing, that is, it is subject to the sovereignty of the state as compared to the contracting parties in international employment. The International Civil Service lacks many features of its national counterpart, such as a "Central administrative authority, Central recruitment control, Verified service conditions, Central appeals machinery," despite the efforts of the ICSAB (International Civil Service Advisory Board) and ICSC (International Civil Service Commission) established to ensure common service conditions for the various UN bodies.

Characteristics of an International Bureaucracy

While focusing on the above differences, the specific characteristics of an international bureaucracy need to be highlighted. The uneven history of the evolution of the International Civil Service makes a clear definition of international bureaucrats difficult. Suzanne Basdevant has defined international officials in the following manner: "International officials are persons who, on the basis of an international treaty constituting a particular international community, or by an organ of it, and are under its control to exercise, in a continuous way, functions in the interest of this particular international community, and who are subject to a particular personal status." Thus, international civil servants are full-time employees of an international organization, to which they owe their loyalty, and from which they draw their salaries and other benefits.

The League of Nations Staff Regulations stipulated that the officials of the Secretariat of the League of Nations were exclusively international. A similar provision was made in the United Nations Staff Regulations. Under the Convention on Privileges and Immunities of the United Nations, the General Assembly of the United Nations determined that staff members of the UN, other than those who were recruited locally and assigned to hourly rates, were to be considered as UN officials. This definition was subsequently modified to include all regularly employed staff members of the UN, except those under contract. A similar definition is used in the Specialized Agencies of the UN.

By its very nature, and because Iris Claude has described "it is a bureaucracy without a government, without a country," standing alone in an international vacuum, "lacking the appropriate institutional envelopment and political allegiance." The international civil service will be plagued by difficulties of a unique type. Therefore, it has to develop its framework and norms specifically suited to its requirements.

Apart from the above distinguishing features, there are others that characterize international officials as a civil service. The first is the international character and loyalty of the personnel. Members of the UN Secretariat and other UN bodies are international civil servants. They exist not to carry out the instructions of any individual state but to implement the joint policies of all states, enunciated through a constitutional process by the policy forming organs of the United Nations. The staff of international civil service are servants of all the states belonging to the organization, not the servants of the states of which they are citizens.

The international civil service is not a multinational institution, and it is not intended that several National Civil Service systems shall coexist in an international Secretariat, nor is it supranational since it has no authority over any state. Though the members of the international civil service are nationals of particular countries and are often seconded by their respective governments, they have to give up their nationalistic and partisan loyalties and develop an entirely international outlook, an attitude defined by Wilfred Jenks thus: "The international outlook required of the international civil servant is an awareness made instructive by the habit of the needs, emotions and prejudices of the differently circumstances countries, as they felt and expressed by the people concerned, accompanied by a capacity for weighing these frequently imponderable elements in a manner before reaching any decision judicious to which they are relevant." Yet, however, desirable the inculcation of an international outlook may be, the question arises whether it is possible to develop this outlook in the absence of a concept of international citizenship or not. The answer is that it is possible though difficult.

The loyalty required of an International Civil Servant does not derogate his nationalism but is a necessary fulfilment of it. The Executive Committee of the Preparatory Commission of the United Nations held the same view: "Loyalty to the organization is in no way incompatible with an official's attachment to his own country, whose higher interest he is serving in serving the United Nations. It clearly involves, however, a broad international outlook and a detachment from national prejudices and narrow national interests." The ICSAB in its report on standards of conduct in the International Civil Service took a similar stand. Maheu, former Director-General of UNESCO, speaking to his staff on this subject said: "It is a grave error to believe that the international service required you to forget, or worse, to repudiate, your respective countries. If we are international, it is not because of the effects of a particular nature, but it is because of our work, our function, our approach to problems in our field. Our work, our function, our point of view are far from being incompatible with what we are by our nationality, and it is our privilege to proclaim here all that is universal in our different cultures and our national histories. Far from being without a country, we belong, on the contrary, to all countries."

The second characteristic of the International Civil Servant is independence. To safeguard this independence, the United Nations Charter provides that "In the performance of their duties, the Secretary-General and the staff shall not seek or receive instructions from any Government or any other country external to the organization. They will refrain from any action which might reflect on their position as international officials responsible only to the organization." To facilitate the adoption of such an independent attitude, the Charter also expects the respective member states to pledge "to respect the exclusively international character of the responsibilities of the Secretary-General and the Staff, and not to seek to influence them in the discharge of their responsibilities." A further injunction to UN officials is the prohibition on the acceptance of any honour, decoration, favour, gift or remuneration from any government, except for war service, or from any source external to the organization without first obtaining the approval of the Secretary-General.

The third important requirement of UN officials is political neutrality. The only concession given in this matter is that they are not deprived of the right to vote in national elections. The United Nations Staff Regulations provide that "staff members may exercise the right to vote but shall not engage in any political activity which is inconsistent with, or might reflect upon, the independence and impartiality required by their status as international civil servants." The regulations debar the international civil servants from indulging in any political activity, including public pronouncements or open expression of their opinions, on issues of a political nature. The argument put forward for this bar on political activity was that since there were great differences in the political systems of the member states, political activities and propagandizing on the part of officials may result in an international organization being mired in national politics.

UN officials can perform to the optimum level only if they abstain from bringing issues of national politics into international bodies.

A corollary to his special status as an international office is the presence of safeguards to ensure his independent functioning and are generally known as legal immunity. These are:

1. Inviolability of his person, domicile, private property and his private correspondence;
2. Immunity from all legal proceedings;
3. Immunity from measures of attachment and requisition of residence, goods in the residence and means of transport;
4. Repatriation facilities in time of international crises are equivalent to those accorded to diplomatic agents.

Reforms

In the last few years, the UN has enacted major Secretariat reforms to enhance its efficiency and effectiveness. These have included appointing an Under-Secretary-General for Internal Oversight Services, reducing operating expenses, cutting high-level posts and eliminating some 1,000 positions. The 1998-1999 budget of $2.53 billion reflects a reduction of $76 million, or about 3 per cent, over 1996-1997—the first-ever reduction in absolute terms.

The pace of reforms accelerated dramatically with the appointment of Mr Kofi Annan as Secretary-General. Mr. Annan had put in motion the most far-reaching set of reforms ever proposed to the General Assembly. Among the measures enacted were:

- reducing administrative costs, and using the savings for development activities;
- organizing the UN's work programme into four core areas – peace and security, development, economic and social affairs and humanitarian affairs – with human rights as a cross-cutting issue;
- appointing a Deputy Secretary-General to oversee the day-to-day work of the UN and coordinate its reform efforts;
- establishing a cabinet comprising the UN senior managers to speed up decision-making and enhance coordination;
- establishing a UN Development Group comprising the heads of the UN development programmes and funds, to facilitate joint decision-making on development activities;
- consolidating into a single department the work of the UN Secretariat in economic and social affairs;

- combining the programmes on human rights into a single Office;
- combining the programmes on fighting crime, drug trafficking, money laundering and terrorism into a single Office;
- placing the country operations of the different UN funds and programmes under a single UN office ("UN House") under a Resident Coordinator, thus, establishing common premises for all operations, increasing coordination and reducing costs;
- undertaking a major reform of personnel aimed at improving the management of staff at all levels.

Cited Works

Basic Facts about the United Nations, New York: UN Department of Public Information, published periodically.

Bailey, Sydney, *The Secretariat of the UN*, London: Carnegie Endowment, 1962.

Jacobson, Harold Karen, *Networks of Interdependence: International Organisations and the Global Political System*, New York: Knopf, 1979.

Langford, G., *The International Civil Service*, N.Y.: Oceana, 1963.

Luard, Evan, *International Agencies, The Emerging Framework of Interdependence*, London: Macmillan, 1977.

Meron, Theodore, *The United Nations Secretariat,* Lexington: Lexington Books, 1977.

Moore, John Allphin, Jr., and Jerry, Pubantz, *Encyclopedia of the United Nations*, New York, 2008.

Moore, John Allphin, Jr., and Jerry, Pubantz, *The New United Nations, International Organization in the Twenty-First Century*, New York and London, Routledge, 2017.

Weiss, Thomas George, *International Bureaucracy: An Analysis of the Operations of a Functional and Global International Secretariat*, Lexington: Lexington Books, 1975.

https://undocs.org/pdf?symbol=en/ST/SGB/1997/5

https://www.unglobalcompact.org/what-is-gc/mission/principles/principle-10

https://globalcompact.ca/about/ungc-10-principles/

https://www.un.org/en/model-united-nations/secretariat

https://icsc.un.org/home/history

https://www.un.org/depts/dhl/dag/docs/internationalcivilservant.pdf

https://www.upu.int/upu/media/upu/files/aboutupu/acts/manualsinthreevolumes/actinthreevolumesconstitutionandgeneralregulationsen.pdf

https://www.ungeneva.org/en/history/before-the-league

https://uia.org/s/or/en/1100035539

https://unsceb.org/international-civil-service-commission

PART III
GLOBAL CONFLICTS AND THE UNITED NATIONS

10

PREVENTIVE DIPLOMACY

The Concept of War and Security: Transformations

War has been a recurring and intractable problem in international politics and the main rationale behind the creation of Intergovernmental Organizations, from the Concert of Europe in the nineteenth century to the League of Nations and the UN in the twentieth century. Underlying Rationalist International Relations Theory is the premise for interstate cooperation in solving practical problems of world politics that will create the conditions for lasting peace. International law was seen as providing the rules that would help build order in interstate relations, and international courts or diplomatic procedures would provide the means to settle disputes peacefully. So despite the two World Wars and the gradual increase of the nuclear club of nations in 20th-century history, it was also the period when various approaches to war and disarmament surfaced in the study of International Relations.

Yet the nature of wars and conflicts has changed significantly since the end of the 20th-century and newer concepts of security have also evolved. World history has shown a sharp decline in the incidence of interstate war and none between major powers since 1945. Since 1980, the major ones have been the Iran-Iraq War (1980-1988), the Ethiopia-Eritrea War (1998-2000), and the Russo-Georgia War (2008). In contrast, the number of intrastate (internal) armed conflicts rose exponentially from the mid-1970s to the mid-1990s and reduced thereafter. This trend is evident in struggles for self-determination, such as those of the Tamils in Sri Lanka, the Muslims in Indian-administered Kashmir, the ethnic conflicts in Somalia, civil wars in the former Yugoslavia and Rwanda, the north-south civil war in Sudan (1983-2005) and between Nigeria and Boko Haram (since 2009). Some civil wars, such as in the Democratic Republic of Congo (1996-2001) and Libya (since 2011), have been internationalized with "foreign" intervention in support of either one or the other combatant in these states Afghanistan is a case in point. Although data shows a decline in the number of active conflicts of all types since the mid-1990s, war and the use of force has never been given up as an option to settle disputes in world politics.

Whether the declining trend in active conflicts shows fewer new conflicts or a growing efficacy in resolving old ones is yet to be debated seriously. Many post-Cold War intrastate wars have been accompanied by humanitarian disasters resulting from recurring conflicts, ethnic cleansing or genocide, famine and disease in 'failed' states. Traditionally, security in Realist Theory has symbolized state security – the security of borders, control over the citizenry and freedom from interference in the government's sovereignty over its internal matters. With the volume of internationally recognized human rights norms steadily increasing after World War II, the balance between the rights of "sovereign" states and the rights of "people" began to be defined sometimes in opposition to one another. Increasingly, it was argued that human (citizen) security should take precedence over the security of governments or states. This paradigm shift has provided support for the emerging norm of a "Responsibility to Protect" and legitimacy for armed intervention to protect citizens within states against the violence of governments, paramilitary forces, militias, and the internal police.

International Organizations and Security

The idea of a global organization to promote security among states was born in the early years of the twentieth century and promoted by prominent statesmen and peace groups during World Wars I and II, who argued that the conventional balance of power approach to dealing with international conflict had failed to keep the peace and, therefore, new pacifist approaches were needed.

Both the League of Nations and the UN were products of deep convictions that a permanent universal international organization could prevent future wars. The League of Nations Covenant and the UN Charter focused extensively on basic principles for preventing war, on mechanisms for peaceful settlement of disputes, and on provisions for enforcement actions in case war broke out. Both recognized the special prerogatives of major powers with respect to peace and security and the necessity of a small decision making body with authority to take action on behalf of all members. A key difference was the League's requirement for unanimity among Council members, in contrast to the UN Security Council's requirement for a majority of the non-permanent members, coupled with no opposition from any permanent member (the veto power).

Both the UN and the League of Nations were also based on the concept of collective security, articulated by US President Woodrow Wilson, as an alternative to the traditional balance-of-power politics that had frequently led to the use of force by states. Regional security arrangements established during the Cold War were either traditional alliances-formal or informal commitments for mutual aid in case of attack-or collective defence organizations, such as NATO. The ASEAN Regional Forum, established in the mid-1990s, represents a very different approach in its focus on confidence-building and conflict prevention through increased communication. The EU's Rapid Reaction Force has been deployed in several conflict zones since 2003. Both the Economic Community of West African States (ECOWAS) and the Southern Africa Development Community

(SADC) have taken on security obligations when the UN and OAU or AU have been unable to act. The Shanghai Cooperation Organization was established on 15 June 2000 in part to mainly address the growing threat of terrorism, regional security issues, ethnic separatism and religious extremism. To date, the SCO's priorities also include regional development in Central Asia since 2001. The cooperation activities focus on security developments in the region and key issues related to counterterrorism and prevention of violent extremism. Since 2017, DPPA has deployed a Liaison Officer to the SCO in Beijing.

The UN Charter provisions have indicated a sharing of responsibility between the UN and regional organizations. This only became important after the Cold War ended, when the UN undertook more peace operations than it did before and regional organizations took a number of initiatives to address the upsurge in violent conflicts. In 1992, Secretary-General Boutros Boutros-Ghali's *An Agenda for Peace* called for more regional action and cooperation with the UN to share the responsibilities of keeping, making and building peace. Since then, there have been numerous cases of peacekeeping and enforcement activity by regional and sub-regional organizations sometimes delegated under Security Council authorization with retroactive approval, in collaboration or partnership.

UN efforts have included different types of peaceful settlement approaches such as mediation and good offices until after the Cold War, peacekeeping operations were largely used in lieu of the enforcement. Since 1990, the UN has undertaken many new peace operations with mandates ranging from enforcement to post-conflict peacebuilding along with sanctions and other measures. The UN also has a long record in the field of disarmament and seeks to address terrorism, primarily through establishing international law.

Peaceful Settlement of Disputes: Varying Patterns

The international norm of peaceful settlement of disputes as outlined in Article 2, Paragraph 3 of the UN Charter which states: "All Members shall settle their international disputes by peaceful means in such a manner that international peace and security, and justice, are not endangered".

Most of the common procedures for peaceful settlement of international disputes are catalogued in Article 33, Paragraph 1, of the Charter:

"The parties to any dispute, the continuance of which is likely to endanger the maintenance of international peace and security, shall, first of all, seek a solution by negotiation, enquiry, mediation, conciliation, arbitration, judicial settlement, resort to regional agencies or arrangements, or other peaceful means of their own choice."

All of these techniques of dispute resolution were embodied in international law and practice well before the advent of the United Nations. The Charter merely recognizes their existence and encourages their use. The procedure of "good offices" is another time-honoured approach to dispute settlement. Unlike the procedures listed in Article 33, which parties to a dispute are urged to use, "good offices" (not mentioned in Article 33) depends entirely on the initiative of third parties.

Except for negotiations, each of the procedures requires the assistance of third parties, that is, representatives of states or organizations not directly involved in the dispute. Most are also political rather than judicial modes of settlement, in the sense that parties are left free to accept or reject proposed settlements, as their interests dictate and their capacities permit. Third-party assistance is concerned primarily with finding some common ground where agreement can be reached. Arbitration and judicial settlement, however, are in the judicial mode because:

(1) the basis of the decision is supposed to be international law rather than national interest and power, and
(2) the decisions are legally binding on the parties that accept these settlement procedures in a particular case.

Negotiation among parties to a dispute is as old as the state system and is the most common method of settlement. It involves direct discussion by diplomatic representatives of the states concerned, reach agreement on matters at issue.

Good offices (not mentioned in Article 33) is the name given to friendly assistance rendered by a third party to bring disputants together so that they may negotiate a settlement. Good offices may be tendered by a state, a group of states, or even by an individual of international standing such as the UN Secretary-General.

Mediation occurs when the third-party actively participates in the discussion of substantive issues and offers proposals for settlement. If the disputants are not on speaking terms the mediator may also tender his good offices as a prelude to mediation. A mediator may meet with the parties either separately or jointly and is expected to maintain an attitude of impartiality throughout.

Enquiry, or inquiry, may be used when the disputing parties are unable or unwilling to agree on points of fact relating to a controversy but are willing to let an impartial commission investigate and report on the facts.

Conciliation is a procedure for settling a dispute by referring it to a commission, or, occasionally, a single conciliator, charged to examine the facts and recommend a solution that the parties are free to accept or reject. Conciliation is more formal and less flexible than mediation. On the contrary, mediation is a continuing process of assisting negotiations among parties to a dispute, conciliation involves formal submission of the dispute to a conciliation body in anticipation of a final report containing the conciliator's findings and recommendations for settlement.

Arbitration is a procedure by which disputants agree to submit a controversy to judges of their own choice, who render a legally binding decision based on principles of international law. Generally, each side names one or two arbitrators, and those two or four designate one additional arbitrator to complete the panel. The essential characteristics of arbitration are:

(1) free choice of judges (arbitrators),

(2) respect for international law, and

(3) obligation to comply with the award.

Judicial settlement or adjudication, like arbitration, produces legally binding awards or judgement based on rules of international law. Unlike arbitration, however, the judges are not chosen by the parties for their particular cases but are members of a reconstituted international court and are based on voluntary acceptance by the parties, either through advance agreement to accept the jurisdiction of the court in special types of cases or through agreement at the time the dispute is submitted. The same is generally true of arbitration. The International Court of Justice (ICJ) and its predecessor from the League of Nations days, the Permanent Court of International Justice, provide the principal examples of judicial settlement at the global level.

In a conflict situation, determining who can most effectively intervene, through which tools and what negotiating goals for ending the conflict should be set, are key issues. What constitutes success needs to be defined. Is it a permanent end to a conflict (Liberia's Civil War) a freeze on active fighting (in Cyprus) a short-to-medium-term end to violence (independence for South Sudan) getting parties who previously would not speak to each other to meet face-to-face (Israeli-Palestinian) or building the foundations for long-term peace (Kosovo, East Timor, and Burundi)? Answers to these questions depend upon the stage of the conflict at which intervention occurs. Dealing with a conflict before the level of armed violence escalates rapidly or trying to find a peaceful solution to a conflict with already high levels of violence requires different types of intervention. Long-standing, intractable conflicts (Kashmir, Northern Ireland, Cyprus) seem to defy many efforts at peaceful settlement, conflicts such as Somalia in the late 1990s, or others such as that between the Tamil Tigers and the government of Sri Lanka, due to their long-drawn conflict.

The record of the UN in dispute settlement cases has not been very impressive. By one assessment, 191 disputes that involved fighting were referred to the UN between 1945 and 1990. Only 47 of these (representing 24.6 per cent) were successfully resolved. The success rate during the first four decades was even lower at 23 per cent. Overall, the success rate kept declining from over 30 per cent in the early 1950s to the very low figure of around 15 per cent during the decade starting around 1972. However, the number of disputes differ from one organ or specialized agency to another. It is generally believed that the UN has become more effective after the Cold War ended. The number of disputes referred to the UN and the success rate in resolving the referred disputes rose notably after 1985. But this appears to be more due to the significant increase in the number of less intense/insignificant disputes referred to the UN since 1985 as compared to 36 per cent of the referred disputes being insignificant later during the forty-year period. During this period, the United States was the target of complaints no less than nine times, followed by Israel (five times) and South Africa (four times). The United States also used the veto more frequently than any other permanent member of the UN Security Council to ward off complaints against it and protect Israel.

Partly because of the low success rate in the resolution of disputes by the UN, and substantively because states have sought to retain their autonomy in decision-making, the number of disputes and armed conflicts which have not been referred, to the UN has been substantial. This is particularly so in respect of intra-state conflicts with or without external intervention.

Between 1985 and 1990, more than 43 intra-state armed conflicts (with external intervention in the majority of cases) had came before the UN.

Since 1988, a large number of conflicts have been ended at least temporarily through negotiation, many of them through mediation. This trend has encouraged still more efforts at mediation, even of intractable conflicts, by the UN and a host of other regional intergovernmental organizations.

The first such *ad hoc* group was the Contact Group for Namibia, formed in 1978 by the United States, Canada the United Kingdom, France and Germany. It was able to negotiate an agreement for Namibia's independence from South Africa in part because of the relationships the countries had with the different parties, including the South West Africa People's Organization (SWAPO). The group was unable, however, to persuade South Africa to implement the agreement until more than a decade later. The Contact Group idea was later adopted by two groups of Latin American countries to mediate in the Central American conflicts of the 1980s. It has been employed in a number of other situations thus, including to address the problem of piracy off the coast of Somalia and the violence between pro-Russian separatists and the government in eastern Ukraine. In addition, numerous "friend" groups have been formed to aid the UN Secretary-General in addressing conflicts in Haiti, Angola, Iraq and elsewhere. Since 2003, the Middle-East Quartet, made up of senior UN, EU, US, and Russian officials has endeavoured to support the Israeli-Palestinian peace process. The Department of Political and Peacebuilding Affairs (DPPA) supports UN peacemaking efforts by advising and assisting the Secretary-General in his Middle-East diplomacy and by overseeing UN political activities in the region by peace efforts, coordinating humanitarian aid and development assistance, and supporting Palestinian state-building efforts. The Secretary-General also works to ensure close cooperation in international peacemaking efforts with the League of Arab States and the broader international community. DPPA also assists the Secretary-General's crisis management activities, which included his direct involvement in efforts to bring about a stop to the fighting in Gaza, in July-August 2014. Senior officials of the Department of Political Affairs provide regular briefings to the Security Council on the situation in the Middle-East and the state of peace initiatives in the region. The Office of the United Nations Special Coordinator for the Middle-East Peace Process (UNSCO), based in Jerusalem, Ramallah and Gaza, is a field mission of the

Department of Political and Peacebuilding Affairs that supports peace negotiations and the implementation of political agreements between Israel and the Palestinians. Special Coordinator, Tor Wennesland, is the focal point on the ground for UN support to peace initiatives – including the work of the Middle-East Quartet. UNSCO is also responsible for coordinating the activities of more than twenty UN agencies, funds and programmes on humanitarian and development assistance to the Palestinians.

The United Nations would have done better if it had the legal right and the potentiality of enforcement. In this respect, it reflects the limitations of the larger international system, which lacks a sufficient sense of community to support international coercive action.

The Charter framers at San Francisco never hoped that the United Nations would abolish differences of interest among states. They did believe that international conflicts should be kept within peaceful bounds and that the United Nations had been a helpful adjunct to other settlement techniques. No war of global extent, no conflict severe enough to threaten the system of independent states has emerged since the United Nations was established. To this conflict containment, the UN has made a significant contribution.

Preventive diplomacy has received significant attention since the publication in 1992 of *An Agenda for Peace*, in which then-UN Secretary-General Boutros Boutros-Ghali (1992) defined preventive diplomacy as "action to prevent disputes from arising between parties, to prevent existing disputes from escalating into conflicts and to limit the spread of the latter when they occur". Most often, this takes the form of diplomatic efforts sometimes coupled with sanctions of some sort. From late 1992 until 2001, however, the UN deployed a thousand peacekeeping troops to prevent the spread of violence from other regions of the former Yugoslavia into Macedonia—an important innovation.

The UN has created three regional offices for preventive diplomacy, in Central Asia, West Africa, and Central Africa. NGOs have created the Global Partnership for the Prevention of Armed Conflict, for example, and a variety of other non-governmental, private actors including local civil society groups are active in preventive activities.

The tools for preventive activities include early warning, fact-finding missions, political missions, special envoys, early response systems, good offices, mediation, conciliation, and locally-based "infrastructures for peace". Multilateral political missions are at the heart of the UN's preventive activities. In 2013, there were thirty-seven such missions, ranging from large ones in Iraq and Afghanistan to small ones in Nepal and Sierra Leone. Some staff may focus on human rights or legal issues, others may emphasise constitutional failure, while still others may provide technical support for managing elections. These political missions have a track record of helping fragile states avoid full-scale conflict. At all phases of the conflict cycle, missions can facilitate political processes, but they cannot do so unless the potential parties to a conflict permit their assistance. In addition to political missions, the UN established the Standby Team of Mediation Experts in 2008, consisting of eight individuals experienced in mediation and peacebuilding who brought in specialized skills such as expertise in natural resources, property rights, and constitution-making. The team was deployed more than seventy times in 2012 to over thirty countries. DPPA provides backing to the High-Level Advisory Board (HLAB) on Mediation, established by Secretary-General António Guterres in September 2017. The 18 members of the HLAB -- current and former global leaders, senior officials and renowned experts -- back specific mediation efforts around the world. In 2020, the practice of remote or virtual deployments of the Standby Team was substantially expanded so as to meet the evolving needs of mediation actors. With support from donors, the Department has also established a rapid response fund to start up mediation processes at short notice. Advance planning and ready resources are a key to effective early mediation when crises are brewing.

In 2020, the United Nations Special Political Missions have been established earlier by the United Nations Security Council at various parts of the continents. These missions are discussed below:

1. The United Nations Integrated Peacebuilding Support Office in Guinea-Bissau (UNIOGBIS) stabilizes peace, enhances cooperation and assists in multidimensional engagement.
2. The United Nations Support Mission in Libya (UNSMIL) is mandated to conduct human rights monitoring and reporting, support key Libyan institutions and efforts to secure uncontrolled arms, support the Libyan transition process, including the constitutional process and the organization of elections, provide essential services and deliver humanitarian assistance, support ceasefire monitoring, and coordinate international assistance. UNSMIL would monitor and report abuses and violations of human rights and violations of international humanitarian law, including sexual violence in conflict, notably through the effective deployment of women and child protection advisers. The Security Council requested the Secretary-General to include in his regular reporting the efforts of the United Nations to address the COVID-19 pandemic and the impact of the pandemic on the ability of UNSMIL to deliver its mandated tasks.
3. The United Nations Assistance Mission in Somalia (UNSOM) has been mandated to provide good offices functions supporting the peace and reconciliation process of the Federal Government of Somalia, including coordinating international donor support, in particular on security sector assistance and maritime security, and to help build its capacity in the areas of protection of human rights and rule of law; to provide support for the delivery of elections which were free, fair, timely, peaceful, transparent, credible and inclusive, incorporating a direct voting component enabling as many citizens as possible to vote; also support Somali commitments to ensure that women filled at least 30 percent of the seats in both houses of Parliament, and increasing participation and empowerment of women, minority communities and

other marginalized groups at all decision-making levels. UNSOM would provide strategic advice to institutional capacity building, collaborate with the international financial institutions to support the mobilization of economic and development assistance, and ensure effective and integrated cooperation of the United Nations agencies, funds and programmes and promote cooperation with relevant partners, with a view to making maximum use of development financing in Somalia, including in response to flooding, locusts and the COVID-19 pandemic; to enable Somalia to strengthen revenue mobilization, resource allocation, budget execution, and anti-corruption measures. UNSOM was requested to focus its human rights-related technical advice and capacity-building support on protecting women and girls from sexual and gender based violence, promoting accountability for human rights violations and abuses, including through working with civil society, reinforcing and aligning human rights across the security related and humanitarian agendas, and monitoring and including information on the human rights situation in the reporting of the Secretary-General.

4. UN Integrated Transition Assistance Mission in Sudan, (UNITAMS) has led to the establishment of a civilian-led transitional Government and transitional institutions, by resolution 2524 (2020), after signing the Constitutional Document in the Sudan on 17 August 2019 to assist the political transition, support peace processes, assist peacebuilding, and support the mobilization of economic and development assistance and coordination of humanitarian assistance.
5. The United Nations Regional Office for Central Africa (UNOCA) provides assistance to support preventive diplomacy and mediation in situations of tension or potential conflict. It also works closely with UN entities on the ground, governments, regional and sub-regional organizations to address cross-border challenges such as arms trafficking, organized crime and the presence of armed groups; incorporate gender perspectives in the implementation of its mandate, and to take into consideration in its activities climate and ecological change and natural disasters on the stability of the Central African region.
6. The United Nations Office for West Africa and the Sahel (UNOWAS) has merged the United Nations Office for West Africa and the Office of the Special Envoy for the Sahel into a single entity with the mandate to support the consolidation of peace and democratic governance in the region. UNOWAS assists in peacebuilding, sustaining peace efforts and enhancing subregional capacities for conflict prevention and mediation; helps prevent cross-border and cross-cutting threats to peace and security; human rights and gender mainstreaming into conflict prevention and management initiatives. UNOWAS focuses on social cohesion and effective and meaningful participation of women, youth and other relevant stakeholders and improving electoral processes at local and national level. It also takes into consideration the adverse implications of climate change, energy, poverty, ecological changes and natural disasters on the stability of West Africa and the Sahel region.

7. The United Nations Integrated Office in Haiti (BINUH) supports the Government of Haiti in promoting and strengthening political stability and good governance, preserving and advancing a peaceful and stable environment, and promoting and protecting human rights. BINUH also assist the Haitian Government in planning and executing free, fair and transparent elections; reinforcing the capacity of the Haitian National Police; developing an inclusive approach to reduce community violence; addressing human rights abuses and violations; improving penitentiary administration management and oversight of prison facilities; and strengthening the justice sector.
8. The United Nations Assistance Mission in Afghanistan (UNAMA) provides political good offices in Afghanistan; to work with and support the government; to support the process of peace and reconciliation; to monitor and to promote human rights and the protection of civilians in armed conflict; to promote good governance; and to encourage regional cooperation. By resolution 2543 (2020), the Council reiterated the priorities of UNAMA to support the Afghan-led and Afghan-owned peace process, transparent and inclusive Afghan elections; support regional cooperation, with a view to promoting stability and peace; cooperate with and strengthen the capacity of Afghan institutions and civil society in the protection and promotion of human rights; support the importance of gender equality and the empowerment of women and girls, as well as to ensure the protection of civilians, especially women, children, displaced persons, as well as the return of internally displaced persons and refugee populations to their homes or local integration or resettlement and, in this instance, adding minorities; and promote enhanced cooperation with the United Nations Office on Drugs and Crime. The resolution requests UNAMA to strengthen capacity to report on violations and abuses against children and to support efforts to strengthen the protection of children, including through engagement with all parties to the conflict to undertake specific commitments and measures to end and prevent violations and abuses against children and sustained dialogue with the Government on the swift and full implementation of the Action Plan and Road Map to End and Prevent Child Recruitment. The Mission's priority to coordinate and facilitate the delivery of humanitarian assistance to the needy.
9. The United Nations Regional Centre for Preventive Diplomacy for Central Asia (UNRCCA) with the initiative of the governments of the five Central Asian countries consider the multiple threats that face Central Asia, including international terrorism and extremism, drug trafficking, organized crime and environmental degradation. With a view to strengthening the United Nations capacity for conflict prevention in Central Asia, the Centre was assigned a number of tasks, including liaising with the Governments of the region on issues relevant to preventive diplomacy; monitoring and analysing the situation on the ground; and maintaining contact with regional organizations such as the Organization for Security and Cooperation in Europe and the Shanghai Cooperation Organization. The Centre was established with an open-ended mandate.

10. United Nations Assistance Mission for Iraq (UNAMI) is responsible for coordinating activities of the United Nations in post-conflict processes in Iraq and humanitarian and reconstruction assistance; promoting the return of refugees and displaced persons, economic reconstruction and the conditions for sustainable development; and supporting efforts to restore and establish national and local institutions. By resolution 2522 (2020), the Special Representative of the Secretary-General for Iraq and UNAMI to provide advice, support, and assistance to the Government and the people of Iraq on advancing inclusive, political dialogue and national and community-level reconciliation. UNAMI was also requested to advise, support and assist the Government on facilitating regional dialogue and cooperation on issues of infrastructure and public health, in addition to border security, energy, trade, environment, water, and refugees. According to the Resolution 2522 (2020) added the improvement of governance as one of the objectives of the Mission's mandate to promote accountability and the protection of human rights and also requested it to mainstream gender throughout the mandate and to assist the Government in ensuring the full, equal and meaningful participation, involvement and representation of women at all levels.
11. The United Nations Special Coordinator for Lebanon was also responsible to ensure that the activities of the United Nations country team in Lebanon were well coordinated with the Government of Lebanon, donors and international financial institutions.

The UN has sought to increase its capacity in early warning and preventive diplomacy since the mid-1990s. Both member states and UN officials have long been reluctant to provide the UN with intelligence-gathering capability, fearing that the UN's impartiality would be impaired. But in 2000, the high-level panel chaired by Lakhdar Brahimi recommended the enhancement of UN intelligence capabilities. In 2005, the Joint Mission Analysis Centre was created within the Department of Peacekeeping Operation (DPKO) and in 2007 and 2010 additional intelligence-gathering apparatus was established to provide more strategic-level analysis. Efforts continue to improve the UN's tools for preventive diplomacy and coordination with other actors.

Chapter VI of the Charter is devoted to the "pacific settlement of disputes" and the role of the Security Council. Article 33 provides that the parties to a dispute "shall, first of all, seek a solution by negotiation, enquiry, mediation, conciliation, arbitration, judicial settlement, resort to regional agencies or arrangements, or other peaceful means of their own choice". When the Security Council deems it necessary, it may "call upon the parties to settle their dispute by such means".

Moreover, at any stage of a dispute "likely to endanger the maintenance of international peace and security", the Security Council may "recommend appropriate procedures or methods of adjustment" Article 36 (1). The Security Council further has the right by Article 37(1) to take charge of a dispute dangerous to peace if the parties fail to settle it by peaceful means, and by Article 38, may make recommendations with a view to the pacific settlement of a dispute if the parties request it to do so. In addition, Article 99 gives the Secretary-General the power to use his initiative in settling disputes by bringing them before the Security Council or by using his good offices or those of his representatives in helping to settle disputes either at the request of UN organs or the parties concerned or on his initiative.

When, in January 1946, Iran complained that the presence of Soviet troops on its soil threatened her peace, the Security Council, after discussion, took note of the readiness of the parties to negotiate and asked them to report on the result of their negotiations. In May, Iran reported to the Council, the withdrawal of the Soviet troops from her region. Thereupon, the Security Council adjourned its discussion of the case.

In 1947, the United Kingdom brought to the Security Council its dispute with Albania over the damage to British warships and injuries to naval personnel caused by mines in the Corfu Channel during October 1946. The United Kingdom held Albania responsible for it. Albania denied the claim and accused the United Kingdom of violating its territorial waters. Upon the recommendation of the Council, the parties took the case to the International Court of Justice. A similar recommendation was issued by the Security Council in 1976 with regard to a complaint by Greece against Turkey concerning rights in the Aegean Sea continental shelf.

The Security Council has to constantly recommend that parties to disputes and other situations which might lead to international friction must pursue a peaceful settlement of their conflicts. Such recommendations or appeals, under Chapter VI of the Charter, were issued in connection with the situation in the Middle-East in 1967, when the Council adopted a framework for a settlement (resolution 242 [1967]) and requested "the Secretary-General to designate a Special Representative to proceed to the Middle-East to establish and maintain contacts with the States concerned". This request aimed "to promote agreement and assist efforts to achieve a peaceful and accepted settlement in accordance with the provisions and principles" outlined in the resolution. In 1973, also in connection with the situation in the Middle-East, the Council issued a specific call to the parties concerned to start comprehensive negotiations "aimed at establishing a just and durable peace" in the region (resolution 338 [1973]). Similarly, the Security Council has urged the Greek and Turkish Cypriot communities in the Republic of Cyprus to seek a solution to their differences through negotiations, with the help of the Secretary-General's good offices. (Since 4 March 1964 the Council has adopted resolutions 353 and 354 amplifying this provision from 23 July 1974.)

In many cases, the Council requested the Secretary-General to make his good offices available in the search for peaceful solutions: of the question relating to the frontier between Yemen and the Federation of Saudi Arabia (1966); of the situation in the India-Pakistan subcontinent (1971); of a complaint by Iraq concerning incidents on its frontier with Iran (1974); of the situation in Cyprus (1975 and thereafter); of the situation of American hostages in Iran (1979); and the case of the Falkland Islands (1982).

In the case of the situation between Iran and Iraq, the Council expressed support for the Secretary-General's offer of good offices (made first in 1980, and reiterated in subsequent years). It also called on Iran and Iraq to cooperate with him in efforts to achieve a comprehensive, just and honourable settlement, acceptable to both sides, of all outstanding issues, in accordance with the principles contained in the Charter of the United Nations.

On some occasions, the Council authorized the Secretary-General to name Special Representatives in connection with efforts to promote the resolution of conflict situations, for example, in the Middle-East, as indicated above (1967 and 1968); the India-Pakistan subcontinent (1971); Timor or East Timor is now Timor-Leste (1974, 1975); Southern Rhodesia (Zimbabwe) (1977); Namibia (1972-1978); and Western Sahara (1988).

The Security Council has also requested the Secretary-General to undertake missions or become involved in international crises, to seek peaceful solutions. Such assignments were made in connection with the situation in Namibia (1974); the complaint by Iraq concerning incidents on its frontier with Iran (1974); the situation concerning Western Sahara (1975); the situation in the region of the Falkland Islands (Islas Malvinas, 1982); and complaints by Lesotho (1982) and Botswana (1985) against South Africa.

Under Article 34 of the Charter, "the Security Council may investigate any dispute or any situation which might lead to international friction or give rise to a dispute". The Security Council has employed this instrument of fact-finding and inquiry throughout its history. In the early years, the Security Council undertook investigations of a dispute between Indonesia and the Netherlands by establishing a Consular Commission and then a Committee of Good Offices (1947). In the dispute between India and Pakistan over Kashmir, it established a five-member United Nations Commission for India and Pakistan for investigation and mediation (1948) and later appointed a UN Representative to help the two sides in their search for an agreement. When Lebanon complained of interference by the United Arab Republic in its internal affairs (1958), the Council dispatched an observer group to Lebanon to report on the situation. In 1959, the Council set up a sub-committee to look into allegations by Laos of North Vietnamese intervention and participation in the activities of the rebels in Laos.

In fulfilment of its obligations under Chapter VI of the Charter, the Security Council has also used other approaches, as exemplified by its approval of the Geneva Peace Conference on the Middle-East, arrangements involving joint chairmanship (The former USSR and the United States), and the role of the Secretary-General in the conference procedure (1973).

In many cases, when the Council was convened urgently to consider the outbreak of an armed conflict, it has called for an immediate ceasefire. Such calls, in a few cases directed at only one party, have been issued in connection with the situation in the Middle-East (1948, 1956, 1967, 1969, 1970, 1973, 1978, 1981, 1982, 1983); the India-Pakistan subcontinent (1948, 1971); Cyprus (1964, 1974); the region of the Falkland Islands (Islas Malvinas, 1982); and the situation between Iran and Iraq (1980, 1982,

1983, 1986, 1987). The Council also demanded the cessation of an armed attack against Guinea (1970) and an end to colonial wars against Angola, Mozambique, Cape Verde and Guinea (Bissau) by the Portuguese authorities (1972). There have been a number of other instances where the Council sought to secure a ceasefire and take other immediate measures to reduce the tension between warring parties. Frequently, it has had to reiterate its calls for a ceasefire and to deplore the continued fighting or the resumption of hostilities as in Afghanistan after the US pullout of its troops was completed by September 2021.

The UN Role: An Evaluation

The question of how effective UN intervention has been in the actual resolution of international disputes is far more complex and likely to be even more subjective than the question of the degree or extent of the UN's participation in the handling of international disputes. The balance sheet of the UN's effectiveness in resolving international disputes presents a mixed picture of positive achievement, deadlock, and outright failure.

In several cases, definite and permanent settlements were reached. For example, the Soviet Union withdrew its troops from Iran in 1946 and later again (by UN negotiated Geneva Accords) from Afghanistan in 1988. The Indonesian Crisis was ultimately resolved with the establishment of an independent state of Indonesia in 1945 and similarly, the Namibian dispute was finally resolved by the establishment of an independent Namibian state in 1990. British and French troops were withdrawn from Syria, Lebanon and in the Suez Crisis largely due to UN intervention. In 1948 the Berlin Crisis was finally resolved by direct negotiations outside the United Nations but its mediation paved the way for an agreement. Similar was the case in the Balkan conflict between Greece and its neighbours. Some disputes were brought before the International Court of Justice largely due to Security Council efforts as the Corfu Channel dispute in 1946.

In such cases as Palestine and Kashmir, hostilities were brought to a stop and the basis laid for negotiations to settle the outstanding issues but the UN's efforts have been short of the final settlement.

In several cases, the United Nations has, in effect, defaulted. Major failures of the UN's action were in Korea in 1950 and the Gulf War in 1991. Whatever the outcome of the UN action, its efforts were completely ineffective even in establishing a line of contact between the opposing sides before the UN operations were undertaken. No real process of peaceful settlement was established in the case of both these conflicts after the termination of the collective security operations. Instead, the UN's action resulted in its virtual identification with one of the parties to the dispute.

Several factors have influenced the United Nations' effectiveness as a dispute-settling agency. In the first place, the promptness with which the UN has acted has added a lot to its success. Where the UN reacted vigorously and quickly, its mediation commanded respect.

Secondly, the responsibilities and nature of personnel chosen for mediation have profoundly affected the results of UN actions. The Kashmir, Korea, Palestine, and Balkan commissions were slow, ponderous, indecisive and sometimes inept. The skill and experience of personnel chosen by the Secretariat at the service of the commissions and mediators are of basic importance to the success of the UN's efforts to resolve disputes. Personnel should be chosen on the basis of their unquestioned integrity, impartiality and discretion in the discharge of their responsibilities.

Thirdly, the "internationalization" of disputes through the UN has had the effect of constantly drawing attention towards the state's conflicts agitating the international system. Public debates in the UN's various forums can be substantially influential in moulding world public opinion and this should have a wholesome effect on the rational handling of sources of international friction.

Fourthly, an outstanding characteristic of the UN's contribution to the resolution of international disputes has been its pragmatic approach. Various techniques have been employed. Each situation has been handled keeping in view to discover a basis upon which the disputing parties would be willing to negotiate with regard to the issues in dispute. If initial recommendations were disregarded by one or more of the parties, UN organs willingly reconsidered the problem and sought to devise another and more acceptable approach. For example, an appeal for direct negotiations was sufficient in the Iranian and Syrian-Lebanese cases but it had no effect in the Suez Crisis or at one stage of the Kashmir dispute. UN fact-finding contributed to the settlement of the Indonesian Crisis, but had a little appreciable effect in the Balkans.

Fifthly, in the resolution of international disputes, the effectiveness of the Security Council has been more than that of the General Assembly, thus, confirming the original expectations of the UN Charter. Most of the cases ultimately settled were handled by the Security Council and many of the "deadlocked" cases were handled exclusively by the General Assembly or by both the General Assembly and the Security Council. The processes of conciliation have not suffered badly because of the veto in the Security Council. As a matter of fact, the veto has rarely kept the Security Council away from some kind of action under its peaceful settlement responsibilities; its effect has been to block a particular course of action and force the Security Council to look for a more generally acceptable approach.

However, the UN is circumspect in maintaining its impartiality and skilfully organizes and conducts its mediation. It depends on the measure of support it receives from the Great Powers to effectively resolve international disputes.. It has not been, nor will it ever be, in a position to force an unacceptable solution on a Great Power.

We may, therefore, conclude that the UN's record, both in resolving disputes by agreement and in helping them become dormant, has been by no means unimpressive. Many disputes are referred to the UN simply because, at a particular point in time, there is no other way in which they can be resolved. The mere ventilation of a dispute before UN organs provides an opportunity for exploring all possible means for resolving it.

Cited Works

Annan, Kofi, *We the Peoples: A UN for the 21st Century*, Boulder, CO: Paradigm, 2014.

Basic Facts about the United Nations, New York: UN Department of Public Information, published periodically.

Goodrich, L. M. & A. P. Simons, *The United Nations and the Maintenance of International Peace and Security*, Washington, D.C.: The Brookings Institution, 1955.

Raman, K. Venkata, *The Ways of the Peacemaker: A Study of UN Intermediary Assistance in the Peaceful Settlement of Disputes,* New York: UNITAR, 1975.

Ramcharan, Bertrand G., *Preventive Diplomacy at the UN,* Bloomington: Indiana University Press, 2008.

UN and the Maintenance of International Peace and Security, New York: UNITAR, 1987.

Ghali Boutros Boutros, *An Agenda for Peace*, UN document A/47/277-S/2411, New York: United Nations, June 17, 1992.

https://unsco.unmissions.org/middle-east-peace-process

https://www.un.org/securitycouncil/content/repertoire/political-missions-and-offices

*http://dppa.un.org.951846395.proxy.jingzhou.gov.cn/en/prevention-and-mediation?proxy=https_*

https://www.un.org/securitycouncil/content/repertoire/political-missions-and-offices

https://www.un.org/securitycouncil/sites/www.un.org.securitycouncil/files/en/sc/repertoire/72-74/Chapter%208/72-74_08-2-Consideration%20of%20questions%20relating%20to%20Africa%20with%20which%20the%20Security%20Council%20is%20currently%20seized%20and%20the%20implementation%20of%20the%20Council's%20relevant%20resolutions.pdf

https://www.un.org/securitycouncil/sites/www.un.org.securitycouncil/files/en/sc/repertoire/72-74/Chapter%208/72-74_08-9-Question%20concerning%20the%20situation%20in%20territories%20under%20Portuguese%20Administration.pdf

https://dppa.un.org/en/shanghai-cooperation-organization

https://unsco.unmissions.org/sites/default/files/quartet_report_and_statement_1_july_2016.pdf

https://unsco.unmissions.org/sites/default/files/security_council_briefing_-_23_february_2022_0.pdf

https://unsco.unmissions.org/

https://reliefweb.int/report/occupied-palestinian-territory/joint-press-statement-middle-east-quartet-envoys

https://www.un.org/securitycouncil/sites/www.un.org.securitycouncil/files/en/sc/repertoire/72-74/Chapter%208/72-74_08-6-The%20situation%20in%20Cyprus.pdf

11

COLLECTIVE SECURITY

The primary reason for the establishment of the United Nations in 1945 was the maintenance of peace and security in the world. But the frequency of wars – big and small since then – testifies to the oft-repeated assertion that the UN security system has not worked as expected under the Charter. The search for security remains the primary concern of all states. Most of them do not seriously rely on the UN for their security requirements. Even today, they depend mostly on their strength of arms or that of their allies in times of need. This does not, however, reduce the UN to utter impotence. The UN has by various devices reduced the intensity of conflicts in various regions of the world. Its role in dispute settlement, arms control and "peace-building" through the promotion of international cooperation in socio-economic fields will be discussed in the succeeding chapters.

The UN's war prevention role as envisaged under the Charter has been called "collective-security". The most common security arrangement since ancient times among independent states has been the military alliance. Balance of power refers to a system in which states rely on military alliances to further their security requirements. The concept of "balance" refers to such a distribution of power among states that no state is powerful enough to disturb the *status quo* through the force of arms. Governments whose individual national interests are threatened by a common enemy form alliances to deter prospective aggressors. Such combinations generally have limited goals, are temporary, and vary in composition. The result might be deterrence through strength, compromise through bargaining or war through the collapse of the system.

The outbreak of World War I revealed all the serious limitations of the balance of power system as a peacekeeping device. It was a system in which peace depended on the convergence of particular national interests, rather than on the recognition of a common interest in keeping the peace, which should be the only real foundation of any permanent system of peacekeeping.

The need to find a viable substitute to "balance of power" as a system of guaranteeing peace was a major preoccupation of the Versailles Conference in 1919 and a serious concern of President Woodrow Wilson of the USA. The experiences of earlier "security umbrellas" had not been encouraging. The principal historical precedents were conquests, political federations, and military alliances. The conquest was morally indefensible and the creation of a voluntary world federation also seemed utopian given the deep-seated sentiments of nationalism and jealousies among nation-states. The military alliance system had in any case become discredited after World War I.

Another institutional legacy of the 19th century was the Concert of Europe, a system of Great Power consultation succeeding the Napoleonic Wars, which continued sporadically till the outbreak of World War I. Though the Concert prevented a few wars, it was not an organized security system nor was it uniformly effective in preventing wars.

Therefore, the statesmen at Versailles were forced to create a new set-up. The result was the world's first attempt at "collective security" through the League of Nations. The League collapsed with the outbreak of World War II, but the concept of collective security was again revived with the formation of the United Nations.

Collective security refers to an interstate arrangement by which all states are committed to helping any country threatened with armed aggression by any other state. The idea is to deter aggression with the power of collective force. There are no predetermined allies or foes among states in a collective security system.

Charter Provisions

The Charter by Art. 1 calls for security through "effective collective measures for the prevention and removal of threats to the peace, and for the suppression of acts of aggression or other breaches of the peace". These collective measures are elaborated, in Chapter VII (Articles 39 to 51) of the UN Charter. Under these provisions, the Security Council has been authorized to "determine the existence of threats to the peace, breaches of peace, or acts of aggression" and can make recommendations, or decide what measures should be taken "to maintain or restore international peace and security" (Art. 39). However, "to prevent an aggravation of the situation, the Security Council may, before making recommendations or deciding upon measures ...call upon the parties concerned to comply with such provisional measures as it deems necessary or desirable". Such provisional measures are taken "without prejudice to the rights, claims, or position of the parties concerned. The Security Council" is expected to take due "account of the failure to comply with such provisional measures" (Art. 40). The Security Council can call upon the members of the UN to apply measures like the complete or partial interruption of economic relations and of rail, sea, air, postal, telegraphic, radio and other means of communication and severance of diplomatic relations to give effect to its decisions (Art. 41). In case, the measures so recommended by the Security Council are considered inadequate or prove inadequate, the Security Council can take such action by air, sea, or land forces as may be necessary to maintain or restore international peace and security. Such action can include demonstrations, blockades, etc. (Art. 42).

Article 43 (1) imposes an obligation on all the members of the UN "to make available to the Security Council, on its call and in accordance with a special agreement or agreements, armed forces, assistance and facilities, including rights of passage necessary for the purpose of maintaining international peace and security". The agreement(s) mentioned in Art. 43 (1) have to be negotiated, on the initiative of the Security Council, between members and the Security Council (Art.43[3]). Under Art. 45, the members have to provide to the United Nations national air force contingents for combined international enforcement action. To advise and assist the Security Council, on all matters regarding military requirements for maintenance of international peace and security, the employment and command of force placed at its disposal, the regulations of armaments and possible disarmament, a Military Staff Committee has been provided. The members of the Military Staff Committee consist of the Chiefs of Staff of permanent members of the Security Council or their representatives (Articles 46-47).

The responsibility for the implementation of the Security Council's decisions can be entrusted by it to all members of the UN or some of them (Art. 48). Members are expected to afford mutual assistance in carrying out the measures decided by the Security Council (Art.49).

Another important provision regarding collective security is Article 51 of the Charter. It lays down that "nothing in the present Charter shall impair the inherent right of individual or collective self-defence if an armed attack occurs against a member of the United Nations, until the Security Council has taken the measures necessary to maintain international peace and security. Measures taken by members in the exercise of this right of self-defence shall be immediately reported to the Security Council and shall not in any way affect the authority and responsibility of the Security Council under the present Charter to take at any time such action as it deems necessary in order to maintain or restore international peace and security".

A survey of provisions of the UN Charter (Articles 39 to 51) shows that these were intended to avoid the shortcomings of the League regarding provisions about collective security. The UN Charter is clear about the formal commitments to collective security. Art. 2, para 5 lays down that the members promise to "give the United Nations every assistance in any action it takes in accordance with the present Charter, and shall refrain from giving assistance to any state against which the United Nations is taking preventive or enforcement action."

Prerequisites of a Collective Security System and the UN

The essential elements of an effective collective security system are the prohibition of the use of force under all circumstances by all states in principle, collective guarantees of security by all for all states, collective force as deterrence to end aggression anywhere, the automatism of collective action in case of aggression anywhere, use of the system without any partiality towards the aggressor or victim by any state, quick assignability of guilt to an aggressor and permanence and generality of the system. How far the UN security system as provided in the Charter stands the test of these six points will be examined now.

1. Prohibition Against Force

UN Charter is indeed emphatic against the arbitrary use of force by states. But there are two major loopholes in the prohibition on the use of force: the first, under Art. 106 and the second under Art. 51 of the Charter. Art. 106 permits the Big Five (pending the creation of a UN force based on national contingents supplied through agreements referred to in Art. 43) to take any kind of joint action for maintaining world peace and security. So far, Art. 43 has not been implemented, and the possibility of close military collaboration among the five powers has also remained a distant possibility.

The second loophole is the right of self-defence (individual/collective) provided under Art. 51 that undermines the UN prohibition on the use of force. It is the right of collective self-defence that has been invoked in the framing of all the Cold War military alliances. Acts of aggression have always been committed in the name of national self-defence. Under Art. 51, the UN members can resort to force on the basis of their own judgement and initiative. The right to self-defence, in particular, is antithetical to collective security.

2. Collective Guarantees

The UN Charter not only accepts the concept of collective protection, but also makes specific provisions on collective determination of a crisis (Articles 24 and 39), on collectivized forces (Arts. 43-45), and on collective, military policy and command (Arts. 45-47).

But these provisions have been undermined by other provisions or by actual practices of the UN. The veto available to the five Permanent Members simply means that:

(a) no action can be taken by the Security Council against any Permanent Member state without its consent;

(b) the Security Council can be debarred from taking any action; and

(c) by accentuating bloc antagonisms, the veto undermines collective guarantees.

The "special agreements on the supply of national contingents" envisaged under Art. 43 are purely voluntary. So far no agreements have been reached and no permanent force at the disposal of the UN has been raised. The Charter does not make any specific provisions about raising an independent force for the UN through direct recruitment.

Further, under Arts. 51, 106 and 107, the Charter nullifies the provisions on collective guarantees by permitting coalitional war rather than collectivized security.

3. Collective Deterrence

Deterrence can be achieved only when collective power is overwhelming and irresistible. Overwhelming power for the UN can be built in two alternate ways—either by building power in a way that no single or even a combination of states can challenge; or by reducing the military strength of all the states in such a way that they are not in a position to challenge the UN force. The Charter pays little attention to the question of disarmament or armament control. The UN force is to be based on national contingents placed under the world body. Obviously, this force cannot be expected to possess overwhelming power. The possibility of organizing preponderant power against the superpowers seems remote. In short, theoretically and practically, the UN security system is far from possessing the power of collective deterrence.

4. Automatism of Response

Under the Covenant of the League of Nations, any Member "resort to war" was *ipso facto* a "war against all other members of the League" which were obliged to "immediately" enforce economic and diplomatic sanctions against the warring state (Art. 16). This is not the situation in the UN. The Security Council has to determine the crisis and decide the measures, without any obligation to act quickly or automatically. The Security Council's response may start with provisional measures (Art. 40), and may escalate to economic and diplomatic sanctions (Art. 41) and may ultimately reach the stage of military sanctions (Art. 42). In short, automatism is not a built-in feature of the UN security scheme.

5. Anonymity of Aggressor and Victim

In theory, the UN is expected to act against any aggressor to protect any victim anywhere in the world and at any time. But the UN cannot act against the Big Five, who can thwart any action of the Security Council by exercising their veto in their own favour. The Permanent Members can and do use their veto in support of their military allies. Sometimes, a Big Power may use its veto to support the position of a non-aligned state. Such exercises of the veto may be purely political and subjective rather than legalistic or objective. Thus, the principle of anonymity is least available under the UN security system.

6. Assign ability of Guilt

One of the serious defects in the UN security system is the absence of a definition of "aggression" or armed attack. Under the UN Charter, the Security Council is expected to determine the nature of a crisis (Art. 39). Without an objective definition of "aggression" the issue of determining a crisis often becomes a matter of political controversy.

The UN Charter envisaged a stable and permanent security system that could be operationalized to meet any aggression or threat to peace, anywhere at any time. The

UN measures in Korea and the Gulf and other police operations were organized to meet particular situations on an *ad hoc* basis. In short, constitutionally and operationally the UN security system has evolved as a hybrid of principles, approaches and arrangements, far from the requirements of what an ideal collective security system should be.

Neither the UN Charter provisions nor the precedents facilitated to the transformation of the action of the UN security system into a full-fledged collective security system. The implementation of even the limited scheme of security that is envisaged in the Charter has not been politically feasible.

The reasons why the Charter framers did not create a full-fledged collective security system or why the UN practices did not attempt to transform the security system into a fully operational collective system may be explained in two ways. One, neither the Charter makers nor the UN politicians had a clear concept of collective security or a consistent policy on the establishment of a genuine system of collective security. Two, the world is not yet ready for a system of collective security, i.e., the prerequisites for a fully workable system of collective security are not yet present in the world.

Collective Security and Korea

Korea was the first test of the collective security system envisaged under the UN. There an act of aggression was met with armed force under the aegis of international authority. Even though all the conditions of the UN Charter were not complied with (especially the condition of concerted action by all the five Great Powers), the defence of the Republic of Korea was undertaken by armed forces drawn from 16 nations. Let us examine the role of the UN in Korea to make a proper assessment of the collective security system.

On 25 June 1950, North Korea attacked South Korea. Communist China later joined hands with North Korea in this aggression. The Security Council, in the absence of the Soviet Union, passed a resolution (9 to nil), fixing the responsibility for the armed attack on North Korea and called for an immediate cessation of hostilities and withdrawal of North Korean forces to the 38th Parallel. As the North Korean authorities failed to comply with these directives, police action by the UN to repeal the attack was sanctioned by the Security Council. Thus, the Security Council demonstrated that even though the UN had no armed forces at its disposal, it was not impotent in the face of open aggression. However, it is also true that the Council was able to agree on positive action—only due to a series of self-imposed absences from the Council by the representative of the Soviet Union, and the presence of substantial units of American air, land and naval forces in Japan and adjacent areas.

Though the war dragged on, the Chinese intervention, the military stalemate, and the growing concern about a Third World War breaking out brought about dissension in the United Nations. Nearly all members breathed a sigh of relief when the Korean Armistice was arranged in July 1953.

The UN action helped preserve the independence of the Republic of Korea, but it brought no renewed enthusiasm for collective security on a voluntary basis or otherwise. At first, seen as the rebirth of collective military action, the Korean War proved to be its requiem. The reasons for this are well known and discussed below.

One of the reasons why collective security is so rarely operationalized is the ambiguous form in which armed conflicts have occurred since Korean War. Civil wars, revolutions, guerrilla warfare, and subversion are common forms of violence that have erupted time and again in various parts of the world. This new dimension of conflict brings into question the appropriateness of a collective military response which increases the already difficult task of singling out an aggressor. Should the United Nations support the rebels, or should it weigh in on the side of the *status quo*? Should enforcement action be taken against the foreign sponsor or a better? The probability that the Korean experience may have encouraged the subsequent use of more covert forms of aggression rather than overt military invasion, does little to enhance the value of collective military sanctions in meeting the kinds of threats that do exist.

The Korean War also highlighted the basic defects of the United Nations as an instrument for launching collective security operations. Its decision-making apparatus was shown to be unsuited to decisive action in times of crisis. Only the absence of the Soviet delegate had made the initial Security Council action possible in Korea in 1950 though the Soviet Union insisted that Security Council resolutions adopted in its absence were void. Other members argued that an absence was the equivalent of an abstention, which, by precedent, was not a veto. Whatever the legal merits of the issue, the Security Council was immobilized by the Soviet return. Responsibility for decisions was then shifted to the General Assembly though that body proved too large, too unwieldy, and too much divided between counsels to direct a military operation effectively.

Korea further revealed the disadvantages of dependence on the voluntary commitment of forces in times of crisis. The United States contributed over half of the ground forces, 85 per cent of the naval forces, and nearly 95 per cent of air force contingents, with South Korea providing most of the remaining personnel. Less than 10 per cent came from other contributors. This means that the Korean War was largely an American operation. It was directed by a United Command, a euphemism generally understood to mean US command. The United Nations undoubtedly provided a valuable political cover for US operations in Korea, but a collective response so heavily dependent on a single Great Power, and so closely tied to its national interests, is a questionable kind of collective security.

One enduring institutional legacy of the Korean conflict is the Uniting for Peace Resolution, adopted by the Assembly in early November 1950. The resolution was a US proposal intended to make the United Nations more efficient in dealing with future threats to the peace.

The resolution formally affirmed the responsibility of the General Assembly for dealing with international violence when the Security Council was unable to act, including the right to recommend collective military action.

The Gulf Crisis (1990-91) and the UN

On August 2, 1990, Iraq's army annexed Kuwait following Iraqi grievances over its oil pricing, Kuwaiti loans to Iraq and Iraqi claims on Kuwaiti territory. Between August 2 and November 20, 1990, the Security Council passed 12 resolutions on the Gulf crisis, beginning with Resolution 660 condemning the Iraqi invasion of Kuwait. On August 6, 1990, the Security Council imposed mandatory economic sanctions on Iraq, following which US President George Bush ordered the deployment of American troops in the Gulf. On August 25, 1990, the Security Council by another resolution invested the United States and other western powers, which had assembled a naval armada in the Gulf, to use "necessary measures" to enforce the economic embargo on Iraq. The Security Council at the same time activated the Military Staff Committee and asked the western naval powers in the Gulf to coordinate with it and periodically submit reports to facilitate Security Council monitoring of what would, in effect, be a blockade.

Later, on 29 November 1990, the UN Security Council passed a resolution (resolution 678) authorizing "all necessary means" including force to drive the invading Iraqi troops out of Kuwait, if Iraq failed to act by 15 January 1991, to comply with the UN's earlier calls for withdrawal from Kuwait. The vote in the 15-member Security Council was 12 to 2 in favour, with China abstaining and Cuba and Yemen voting against the Resolution. The vote was a triumph for the US which had intensely lobbied for it. On 17 August 1990, after Iraq refused to comply with the deadline set by the UN, the United States launched air attacks against Iraq and started a war that had a US-led coalition of forces from 30 countries fighting Iraq for 42 days. On 27 February 1991, Kuwait was "liberated" from Iraq and the US-led coalition forces suspended their offensive combat operations against Iraq after it agreed to honour all UN resolutions. Subsequently, on April 4, the Security Council passed Resolution 687 with a large majority ordering Iraq to destroy its chemical, biological and ballistic weapons and accept its current border with Kuwait, besides agreeing to let a portion of its future oil earnings compensate Kuwait in return for a formal end to the Gulf War, the withdrawal of US forces from Southern Iraq and lifting of much of the trade embargo against Iraq. On April 10, the Security Council unanimously voted to establish a 300-military observer for the UN Iraq-Kuwait Observation Mission (UNIKOM) to monitor a demilitarized zone between Iraq and Kuwait. On 11 April the Chairman of the U.N. Security Council handed a letter declaring the cease-fire on the Iraqi Ambassador to the United Nations, and the cease-fire based on Resolution 687 of the U.N. Security Council was officially established. Thus the Gulf Crisis came to an end.

However, the collective security operation in the Gulf leaves a lot to ponder about. It would be interesting to draw parallels with the earlier Korean operations in 1950. This was the second time in the history of the UN that the use of force was authorized. In Korea, troops of the various countries involved fought under the UN banner. In the Gulf operation, each country acted on its own in coordination with others under an umbrella sanction by the UN. Both the operations were authorized by the Security Council. In 1950, despite the Cold War, this had been made possible by the Soviet abstention on the day of voting (in all certainty the Soviets would have used the veto if they had been present). In 1990, this became possible due to the changing climate of cooperation between the US and the Soviet Union. The US had intensely lobbied to get the Security Council to authorize the use of force against Iraq. Both the Soviet Union and China did not use the veto due to their domestic compulsions, which necessitated the continuance of US aid and cooperation to deal with their internal problems. Hence, due to this unprecedented consensus, collective action against Iraq became possible during the Gulf crisis. The Korean operation dragged on for months though it managed to ultimately succeed in its limited goal of repelling the North Korean attack against South Korea. In the Gulf crisis, the war was short and decisive and was entirely successful in its aim to "liberate" Kuwait. In both the operations, it was the US, which dominated the entire conduct of the security operations. It was also the US, which lobbied to get the Security Council to authorize the use of force, which was essentially in its interests. The Security Council was not even kept informed of what was happening in the Gulf in terms of para 4 of Resolution 678. Nor could it meet during the four weeks of the war. The UN during the Gulf War was reduced to a hapless witness to its own delegated authority extended beyond the letter and spirit of its resolution. People all over the world were left to wonder whether the real aim of the US-led coalition forces was the total destruction of Iraq's military and nuclear capability or the "liberation of Kuwait" as mandated by Resolution 678.

With hindsight it can be said that the US in both the collective security operations acted more in furtherance of its foreign policy interests than in the interests of international law or of the world body.

Post-Cold War Collective Security: An Assessment

The provisions of collective security under the UN system have been subjected to much criticism. Critics point out that collective security is not only unworkable but also an unwise and dangerous principle, mainly because under it no war could be localized; in fact every war would rather become a world war.

Under the UN Charter, a state can either be a disruptor of peaceful order or a member of the collective enforcement body. There is no room for neutrals under the system of collective security. However, to accommodate the practice of neutrality in the recent times, the states have been permitted to become members of the UN, even if they refrain from supporting the positive measures undertaken by the organization to enforce peace.

In the second place, the notion of collective responsibility had to be reconciled with the right of self-defence conceded to the member states. If the UN had been given full authority to determine when a state is or is not acting in legitimate self-defence, it would have eliminated the right of collective self-defence. The UN Charter concedes the right of collective self-defence under Article 51. However, this right has been circumscribed by many restrictions, viz. if an armed attack takes place against a member of the UN the right to self-defence cannot be exercised until the Security Council acts to maintain peace and security. If a state takes any action in self-defence pending the fulfilment of the above two conditions, it has to report the measures taken to the Security Council.

As collective security measures can be undertaken only if the Security Council approves them by seven votes, including the votes of the permanent members, such actions are rendered impossible without a consensus amongst the permanent members. It was due to this difficulty that collective security action could be taken only twice during the long history of the UN. However, after the passage of the Uniting for Peace Resolution of 1950, the General Assembly was authorized to take action for the preservation of peace and security in the world, if the Security Council was not able to form a decision due to the exercise of 'veto power'.

In the fourth place, it is pointed out that one of the basic principles of collective security is that all the states should have equal say in arriving at collective decisions. In fact, the small states should have a greater say in collective security because they are more dependent on collective security than the larger states. The success or failure of collective security efforts largely depends on the support of powerful states, but normally they are reluctant to act unless their national interests are affected.

The cases of Korea and the Gulf have also raised some important questions. First, they demonstrated that it was extremely difficult to draw a line of distinction between the collective purposes of international police action and the strictly national interests of those participating in it. Second, the operations could not maintain a truly collective character because many states contributed little material support to the UN. The direction of both the operations was virtually monopolized by the United States. Third, members of the United Nations shirked the responsibility of exercising independent judgement in making vital decisions and strategies of the operation. Fourth, the more the sense of power available to enforce collective security is overwhelming, the greater the danger of its improper exercise becomes rampant. Fifth, the use of force even under collective authorization runs a grave risk of triggering a chain reaction of ever-widening violence. Sixth, to stop an enforcement action is a more complex than to start it. The necessary procedure to terminate enforcement action is also a serious omission in the Charter.

Since the beginning of the 21st century, in practical terms, the United Nations "subcontracted" – authorizing a state or group of states to act on behalf of the world community to restore peace and stability – this became a regular feature of Security Council action at the turn of the millennium. It had been frequently used in Somalia, Rwanda, Bosnia, Kosovo, Timor-Leste, Libya, and the Central African Republic.

Immediately affected by the new understanding of collective security was the forty-year-old practice of peacekeeping. As a result of Secretary-General Boutros Boutros-Ghali's *An Agenda for Peace*, three new terms – preventive diplomacy, peacemaking, and post-conflict peacebuilding – entered the UN lexicon. Preventive diplomacy attempts either to resolve intra- and interstate conflicts before violence erupts or to limit the spread of violence, it is intended to be a proactive peacekeeping approach. Peacemaking seeks to bring hostile parties to an agreement through negotiation and mediation before or after the intervention of UN peacekeeping forces. Peacebuilding aims to construct an environment that sustains durable peace, often by UN administration or facilitation of domestic political functions. It also includes addressing the economic, social, cultural, and humanitarian problems that underpin violent conflicts. Taken together and coupled with the long-standing UN policy of peacekeeping, preventive diplomacy, peacemaking and peacebuilding, which amount to the UN effort of sustaining and rebuilding nations torn apart by internal violence or governmental collapse. Collectively, they represent a theoretical foundation for subsequent UN efforts into nation-building. This promotes the idea that the international community has the "responsibility to protect" domestic populations from the egregious violation of their human rights by their governments. Critics of Boutros Boutros-Ghali's report suggested that an expansion of the UN role in these ways was first and foremost beyond the UN's financial and political capabilities and second, a form of international neocolonialism reminiscent of the League's old mandate system.

The Politics of UN Sanctions

The UN Charter provides for the imposition of economic and other sanctions like arms embargo, severing of diplomatic ties, trade embargo, etc., against any state that defies the resolutions of the UN and, hence of the majoritarian wishes of the international community. The UN sanctions were imposed in recent times against South Africa, Zimbabwe, former Yugoslavia, Angola, Haiti, Iraq, Somalia and Libya. In some of these cases, although the countries specifically the citizens concerned suffered, the basic purpose of the sanction was never achieved. There has been no case in which the directly hit country somersaulted, abandoned the stand it had taken in defiance of the UN, or to be more precise, Security Council's directives due to the sanctions.

The experience of recent events in Angola, Haiti, and Somalia have clearly shown that the purpose of the UN sanctions had been defeated because of the counter-threats by certain governments and armed opponents. The worst experience in recent times has been in Somalia where a strong and popular tribal warlord, M.F. Hasan Aidid, not only defied the UN resolutions but waged a regular, determined war against UN troops and also inflicted casualties on military personnel of several nations.

Whenever the UN imposes sanctions, there are in almost all cases, differences of opinion among the Great Powers. The former Soviet Union and France have often differed from the USA, whose President has in many cases pressurized the Security Council members to impose sanctions to serve certain American political objectives, short and long-terms. To the extent that two major powers did not (and were not willing to) extend wholehearted cooperation in this matter, the sanctions were weakened and not fully effective.

In Haiti, a tiny country, dominated by drug traffickers virtually humiliated the UN Security Council and bulldozed it with threats of violence. Haiti was the first country to prompt the UN to impose economic sanctions on the ground that a democratically elected regime was ousted by a military coup. Haiti has also the dubious distinction of being the only country against which the UN sanctions were imposed, suspended and then re-imposed. The reason for the re-imposition of sanctions was that Haiti violated the agreement reached through international consultations.

A similar occurrence in Angola, where a solemn accord was violated by a guerrilla group, UNITA (backed by South Africa and the CIA of the USA) showed the futility of such UN action. The rebel group defied the United Nations by disregarding the results of an election that the UN had described after investigation to be free and fair. The protracted conflict, in violation of international law and a large-scale war, resulted in the deaths of about 1,000 people every day.

Economic sanctions are a potent weapon having much deterrent value and the erring countries generally fear the consequences. Since the loss of life involved in sending armed forces to a war-afflicted country is heavy, economic sanctions are the only way out if the UN is to assert itself in cases calling for enforcement of peace, due regard for human rights and preventing massacres of innocent men, women and children by politically motivated gangs and other lawless elements.

Economic sanctions, coupled with a general boycott and restrictions on the supply of weapons, oil and other commodities may partially prove effective in bringing defiant regimes to compliance. South Africa is one such example. Although other factors, too, led to ending apartheid, the embargo on the supply of certain commodities finally showed results. When the international community decided to lift sanctions, including those on oil and arms supplies, imposed on South Africa early in October 1993, as Dr. Nelson Mandela confirmed the sanctions had caused considerable damage to the economy of that country for years. The UN General Assembly lifted economic sanctions against South Africa and urged all nations to repeal boycott legislation, saying that the transition to democracy was well underway.

In the case of South Africa, Rhodesia (Zimbabwe) and Iraq, certain Great Powers such as the UK, France and the USA, had much stake in the ostracized country, was a notable factor. A decision to impose sanctions against an erring nation is never unanimous as it does not detract from the validity or desirability of enforcing restrictions through international consensus, in deserving cases.

Sanctions have now become a key enforcement instrument, particularly for the UN, serving one or more purposes to coerce a change of behaviour, to constrain access to critical goods and funds and thereby raise costs and force changes in a target's behaviour, or to signal and stigmatize targets in support of international norms. Beginning with the sanctions imposed on Iraq in 1990, the Security Council utilized different forms of sanctions in fourteen situations over the next eleven years. Over the twenty-year period from 1992 to 2012, the Council imposed sanctions in twenty-two situations. Fourteen of the cases involved peace enforcement, all but one in interstate conflicts, four related to terrorism, three related to the proliferation of nuclear weapons four related to upholding democratically elected governments and one related to the Right to Protect (R2P).

A study of UN sanctions would reveal the imposition of the following norms on the states through sanctions: prohibition of war and armed conflict (Angola, Sierra Leone, Ethiopia, Eritrea, DRC), human rights (Former Yugoslavia, Rwanda, Afghanistan, Sudan), counterterrorism (Libya, Sudan, the Taliban/al-Qaeda), no constitutional changes in government (Haiti, Guinea- Bissau, Cote d'lvoire), nuclear non-proliferation (Iran and North Korea), the authority of the Security Council and protecting civilian populations under the R2P norm (Darfur, Central African Republic, Côte d'Ivoire, Democratic Republic of the Congo, Liberia, Libya, Mali, Somalia, South Sudan, Syria, and Yemen).

When Iraq invaded Kuwait in August 1990, the Security Council immediately invoked Chapter VII to condemn the invasion and demand withdrawal. Subsequent resolutions imposed mandatory economic and transport sanctions against Iraq and established a sanctions committee to monitor implementation. Following the Gulf War's end, in April 1991, Resolution 687 enumerated terms of the cease-fire agreement and a far-reaching plan for the destruction, under international supervision, of Iraq's chemical and biological weapons and ballistic missiles, the renunciation of nuclear weapons, and the placement of all nuclear-usable material (such as for power plants) under international control. The comprehensive sanctions were to continue until all the provisions were carried out to the Security Council's satisfaction, except for oil sales authorized under the 1995 Oil-for-Food Programme, which allowed the Iraqi regime to sell a limited amount of oil on international markets to pay for food and medical supplies.

By the late 1990s, the Iraq sanctions had become controversial and malnutrition, contaminated water supplies, increased infectious disease, and higher infant and child mortality rates had produced a humanitarian crisis that generated widespread sympathy and calls for ending sanctions. Resentment against sanctions among neighbouring and other nations that relied on trade with Iraq grew, and compliance was nosedived as unauthorized trade and transport links multiplied.

In 2001 and 2002, NGOs, human rights groups, and independent think tanks initiated proposals for "smart sanctions" intended to keep the pressure on Iraq to comply with the disarmament provisions by targeting the ruling elite where it would hurt but to lift most restrictions on civilian imports.

The Iraq experience demonstrated three problems with comprehensive sanctions. The first involved the large-scale negative civilian impacts, especially of general trade sanctions, this changed many people's perception of the pain/gain trade-offs in sanctions. The second problem was that devastating a target state's economy did not necessarily impose any economic pain on the government elite in terms of their private wealth and resources, and prospects for compliance were low unless sanctions affected them directly. Third, in interstate conflicts and failed states, sanctions were largely ineffective in an environment where governmental controls over taxation, documentation of imports and exports, or borders were loose or mostly absent.

In short, a major lesson was that sanctions must be tailored to the specific situation if they are to be effective. Since 1994, no new comprehensive sanctions have been initiated by either the Security Council or regional organizations except against Russia in 2022 during. The Ukrainian conflict instead, targeted sanctions have been used, including arms embargoes (the most common) diplomatic sanctions (suspensions from IGO membership, limiting diplomats' travel) financial sanctions (notably freezing assets of governments and individuals, investment banks, limits on banking services) travel bans and aviation sanctions (prohibiting international transit by air and naval carriers) and commodity sanctions (e.g. trade in oil, timber, and diamonds). Targets have included entire governments, government leaders, rebel factions, terrorist groups and specific individuals.

Cited Works

Biersteker, Thomas, Sue Eckert, and Marcos Tourinho, eds., *Targeting Sanctions: The Impacts and Effectiveness of UN Action*, New York: Cambridge University Press 2015.

Center on International Cooperation, New York University, *Annual Review of Global Peace Operations,* Boulder: Lynne Rienner, 2013.

Cortright, David & George A. Lopez, *The Sanctions Decade: Assessing UN Strategies in the 1990s*, Boulder, CO: Lynne Rienner, 2000.

Gordenker, Leon, *The United Nations and Peaceful Unification of Korea,* The Hague: Nijloff, 1969.

Lal, Nand, *From Collective Security to Peacekeeping,* New Delhi, 1975.

Lepgold, Joseph, and Thomas G. Weiss, eds., *Collective Conflict Management and Changing World Politics,* Albany: State University of New York Press, 1998.

Moore, John Allphin, Jr., and Jerry Pubantz, *The New United Nations, International Organization in the Twenty-First Century*, New York and London, Routledge, 2017.

Naidu, M.V., *Collective Security and the United Nations*, Delhi: Macmillan, 1974.

Saksena, K.P., *The UN and Collective Security: A Historical Analysis*,. Delhi: D.K. Publishing House, 1974.

Thakur, Ramesh, *The United Nations, Peace and Security: From Collective Security to the Responsibility to Protect,* Cambridge: Cambridge University Press, 2006.

http://erepository.uonbi.ac.ke/bitstream/handle/11295/17972/Kwake_Obstacles%20to%20the%20united%20nations%20as%20a%20collective%20security%20mechanism%20during%20the%20Iraq%20war%2C%202002-2005.pdf?sequence=3&isAllowed=y .

https://www.mofa.go.jp/policy/other/bluebook/1991/1991-2-1.htm#:~:text=

https://www.globalr2p.org/what-is-r2p/

12

PEACEKEEPING, PEACEMAKING AND PEACEBUILDING

Peacekeeping is one of the major ways in which the United Nations helps to maintain international peace and security. In the UN context, peacekeeping has been defined as the use of multinational forces, under UN command, to help contain and resolve a conflict between hostile states, and sometimes between antagonistic forces within a single state. It is a technique pioneered by the UN—the soldier as a catalyst for peace rather than as an instrument of war.

Around the world, respect for the UN's peacekeeping activities is growing. As the tensions of the Cold War receded, the international community is increasingly relying on UN peacekeepers to help resolve regional crises. In 1988 and 1989, there were five new UN peacekeeping operations. The number of operations in the field doubled in two years, a striking increase when it is remembered that only 13 such operations had been established during the previous 40 years. In September 1988, the Norwegian Nobel Committee awarded the Peace Prize to the peacekeeping forces of the United Nations. There is a growing demand for peacekeeping forces to perform an increasing variety of functions, which require new combinations of defence, police and civilian personnel.

United Nations peacekeepers can be sent as unarmed observers or as a lightly-armed peacekeeping force. They might be dispatched to observe a situation and report to the Secretary-General, to supervise troop withdrawals or help ensure compliance with treaties or other agreements. They might be asked to enquire into ceasefire violations or patrol buffer zones. Or they could be assigned to help supervise elections, monitor maintenance of law and order situations and ensure the transition of territory towards independence. In addition, they often provide much needed medical services, assist in the resettlement of refugees, and work to restore normal civilian activities in areas torn apart by strife. Last but not the least, they serve to remind warring parties that the whole world is watching what they do.

How Peacekeeping Operations are Established

When a UN member state or group of states, or the Secretary-General, proposes the establishment of a peacekeeping operation, three basic conditions have to be met. Firstly, there must be a consent of the country or countries involved. Secondly, the proposal must enjoy broad support from the international community—specifically, it must attract the necessary votes for adoption by the Security Council. Thirdly, the member states must be ready to volunteer personnel.

The UN has an impartial role. The success of a peacekeeping operation depends not only, on the parties' consent but also on their full cooperation, especially regarding the freedom of movement of the UN personnel within their territories and the facilities necessary to carry out the mandate.

For the 15-member Security Council to adopt a proposal for a peacekeeping operation, there should not be any negative vote from any of its five permanent members (China, France, the Former Soviet Union (Russia), the United Kingdom, the United States). The Secretary-General reports to the Council on how the operation can be launched and executed. Being subject to the Council's approval, he must then make the required arrangements—chooses the supply of military or other civilian personnel, supplies and equipment, transportation and logistic support to the UN.

In approving the Secretary-General's report on the establishment of a peacekeeping operation, the Council also decides how to fund it: on a voluntary basis, or as usual, on an obligatory basis in conformity with the expenses of the world organization as stated in the provisions of the Charter. In the latter case, the General Assembly decides how the expenses are apportioned among the member-states.

The UN troops may use force only in exceptional circumstances. They carry light arms and may employ them only if they are attacked, or if they are stopped by force from carrying out their mandate.

The effectiveness of peacekeeping forces derives from a combination of factors—the physical presence of military personnel who will return fire if they are fired upon, the moral authority of the UN and the pressure of world public opinion. Together, they deter the hostile parties from using force in the presence of UN peace-keepers.

At the beginning of 1990, some 20,000 personnel were serving in 10 UN peacekeeping operations. In addition to more the 14,000 troops and military observers, there were also civilian police monitors and civilian support staff contributed by governments, staff members from the UN Secretariat and locally recruited civilians. By May 2010, UN Peacekeeping had entered a phase of consolidation. The numbers had, for the first time in a decade, begun to decline slightly.

Today, a little more than 110,000 military, police and civilian staff currently serve in 14 peacekeeping missions, representing a decrease in both personnel and peacekeeping missions, as a result of peaceful transitions and the rebuilding of functioning states.

United Nations soldiers work under the UN commander, who takes orders from the Secretary-General (who is himself responsible to the Security Council), but they remain under national command in matters of pay, discipline and promotion.

The United Nations Concept of Peacekeeping

The main responsibility for peacekeeping lies with the Security Council. The UN Charter states that when the Security Council determines the existence of any threat to the peace, breach of the peace, or act of aggression, it shall decide what the UN should do to maintain or restore international peace and security. The Security Council looks first for peaceful settlement of the dispute. If its recommendations are not followed by the parties involved, it can call for action by the international community, which might include asking member states to make armed forces available to enforce its wishes.

Since the UN was founded, there have been only two military enforcement actions—in 1950 and 1990 when the Security Council, in a series of resolutions, recommended member states to collectively deter aggression by use of force against an identified aggressor. These two operations differed from peacekeeping operations, which are based on the consent of the parties, are not permitted to use force except in self-defence, and are under the command of the Secretary-General.

Peacekeeping as a concept is not specifically described in the UN Charter, but it has evolved over the years as an internationally acceptable way of controlling conflicts. Since the advent of UN peacekeeping, for the first time, military forces have been used not to wage war, establish domination, serve the interests of any power or group of powers but rather to control and resolve conflicts between states or communities within states.

Of these peacekeeping operations, some have been peacekeeping forces and the others were military observer missions. This distinction is not, however, absolute. Unarmed military observers are often attached to peacekeeping forces, and specialist military units, sometimes armed, can be attached to observer missions. In the past, several operations included major civilian elements, the UNTAG operation in Namibia being the most recent example. At UNTAG's maximum strength, there were 4,500 military personnel, 3 infantry battalions, 1500 police, 300 military monitors, 945 election supervisors provided by Governments and 1651 UN employees, 2000 civilians including local employees and international personnel from 124 nationalities and many observers in all. Future operations may require other combinations of personnel performing an increasing variety of functions.

Peacekeeping represents an improvised addition to the original framework of the UN Charter like the Uniting for Peace Resolution of 1950. Peacekeeping forces grew out of the Suez crisis of 1956. We will now examine some varying patterns of major UN peace operations hitherto undertaken in various parts of the world.

Peacekeeping in the Middle-East

Repeated violations of the UN-arranged truce between Israel and its Arab neighbours occurred almost from the day it was signed in 1948, in spite of the presence of the UN Truce Supervision Organization (UNTSO in Palestine) set up in 1948. In 1955 and 1956, Arab commandos (called "fedayeen") repeatedly raided Israeli territory from bases in Egypt to which Israel retaliated. This escalated the situation and set the stage for the Suez Crisis of 1956, from which the UN Emergency Force emerged as a hurried innovation for the maintenance of world peace.

The main factor in the crisis in the Middle-East was the nationalization of the Suez Canal Company by President Gamal Abdel Nasser's Egyptian Government on July 26, 1956. This aroused the antagonism of France and the Britain, whose governments believed that their interests were severely hurt by this unilateral action by Egypt.

The signal of the breakdown of the fragile truce came on October 29, 1956, with the advance of Israeli military forces across the Egyptian border. Two days later, Britain and France bombed Egyptian military bases. On October 30, Britain and France presented an ultimatum to Egypt and Israel: within 12 hours all troops must withdraw 10 miles from the Suez Canal. To guarantee free shipping in the Canal, Egypt was told to permit a temporary British-French occupation of the Egyptian towns of Port Said, Ismailia and Suez. Egypt immediately rejected the ultimatum, while Israel accepted it.

Meanwhile, the United States asked for a meeting of the Security Council. The United States and the Former Soviet Union introduced conciliatory draft resolutions seeking to avoid further fighting, but the representatives of France and the United Kingdom used the veto. The Council thereupon decided under the Uniting for Peace Resolution, to call an emergency special session of the General Assembly.

The General Assembly adopted a resolution urging an immediate ceasefire by all states taking part in the hostilities. Behind the scenes and outside the United Nations, the United States and the Former Soviet Union increased pressure, especially on the British and French governments, to stop the fighting. At the same time, French and British troops landed near the Suez Canal. It took several days before the ceasefire sought by the General Assembly was accepted by the belligerents, but soon after it came into effect, a new United Nations presence supervised it.

This new presence was the United Nations Emergency Force (UNEF). On November 5, the General Assembly approved a proposal by Foreign Minister Lester Pearson of Canada to set up an international force to guarantee and supervise the ceasefire. Secretary-General Dag Hammarskjold was instructed to take the necessary measures to create the force. After 24 hours of consultation with his aides and representatives of member governments, Hammarskjold produced a seminal report, laying down the following principles for a peacekeeping force:

(a) It would be temporary
(b) Its function would be strictly neutral;
(c) It would not alter the military balance of power; it would maintain law and order; supervise the truce, patrol along the truce line, and supervise the observation of UN resolutions.
(d) It would comprise military units from UN members, but the Great Powers would be excluded.
(e) Its commander would be appointed by the United Nations and would be accountable to the General Assembly or the Security Council.
(f) Its withdrawal would require the consent of the conflicting parties.

Hammarskjold's report was adopted by the General Assembly on 7 November. The Communist states and Egypt and Israel abstained. The Soviet Union was of the view that the creation of such a force was the prerogative of the Security Council. Britain and France, as well as the United States, voted in favour.

The Secretary-General had the responsibility for actually organizing the new force. Hammarskjold and his staff negotiated with member governments about their contributions to the force and the conditions under which these could be used. He helped the military commander appointed by the Assembly to get the new force in shape and to set out regulations for its operation. In all, his role encompassed practical activities that went beyond his rights, mentioned in Article 99 of the Charter, to bring to the attention of the Security Council any matter that threatened peace and security.

In less than ten days, the first UNEF units landed in Egypt. At its maximum, UNEF included some 6,000 men, dispatched to the area in national units of about 500 officers and soldiers. This was no international army in which soldiers of one nationality were commanded by officers of another. But UNEF did include contingents from Canada, Denmark, Finland, Norway, Sweden, Brazil, Colombia, India, Indonesia, and Yugoslavia, who were chosen from among offers by 24 governments. Each of the contributors was considered more or less neutral in the Middle-East conflict.

UNEF operations proceeded in two distinct phases. The first – in the area of the Suez Canal – saw the relatively smooth formation of a buffer zone between the Anglo-French and Egyptian forces. As the European troops withdrew in December 1956, UNEF filled the vacuum and then restored the territory to Egyptian control. The second phase – in the Sinai Peninsula – was more difficult. It required heavy political and diplomatic pressure, mainly from the United States, to overcome Israeli reluctance to leave. Finally, Israel evacuated the entire Sinai area and the Gaza Strip. UNEF soldiers manned the fortress of Sharm-el-Sheikh at the entrance of the Gulf of Aqaba, an access point for southern Israel. Elsewhere along the 273 kilometre long border between Israel and Egypt, UNEF patrolled but solely on the Egyptian side of the line.

The UNEF operation ended abruptly in May 1967 following the maneuvering that preceded the next Arab-Israeli War. The Egyptian government ordered Hammarskjold's successor, U. Thant, to withdraw the force. U. Thant consulted his advisory committee, made up of the contributors to the force, and found that only one would risk staying in the face of Egyptian threats to surround and overrun UNEF. Under these circumstances, he believed that he had no alternative but to agree on withdrawal, pointing out that the consent of the conflicting parties to the entry of UNEF was a precondition of its deployment. In May and June 1967, UNEF withdrew, leaving only the UN Truce Supervision Organization in the area.

As a means of preserving the ceasefire that suspended the October War of 1973 between Israel, Egypt, and Syria, a second UNEF was created by the Security Council. This time UNEF was stationed on both sides of the Egyptian-Israeli line. This force served as a buffer between Egypt and Israel in the Sinai Peninsula for the next six years, but in July 1979, the members of the Security Council decided in informal consultations that the force should be given no additional extension of time. This decision reflected growing tension between the United States and the Soviet Union over their roles in the area and the unlikelihood of the Council adopting a resolution to continue the force.

In the northern sector of the 1973 war, Israeli forces captured the Golan Heights from Syria, dominating the route to Damascus. As part of the ceasefire agreement, the parties accepted the presence of the UN Disengagement Observer Force, attached to the UN Truce Supervision Organization. This observer team, consisting of about 1,200 men, has been regularly renewed, every six months and has had a substantial effect in checking tensions at a key military site.

A much larger peacekeeping group, modeled on UNEF, was put in place by the Security Council in southern Lebanon following Israeli occupation of that area in 1978. The United Nations Interim Force in Lebanon (UNIFIL) had the difficult assignment of supervising the withdrawal of Israeli troops from the area, ensuring the restoration of international peace and security, aiding the Lebanese government to restore its authority, to prevent renewed fighting, and to guarantee that its operations would not be used for hostilities of any kind. UNIFIL obviously reflected earlier UN experience in its emphasis on contributions from states that were not engaged in the area and had no Great Power contributors. It included both units never before seen in the area, such as those from Nigeria and Fiji, and more familiar Europeans, such as a group from the Netherlands. Until 1982, UNIFIL achieved moderate success in keeping law and order in its territory. It never did achieve control of the whole territory assigned to it in southern Lebanon because of opposition from the Israeli-supported units commanded by Major Haddad and from Israel itself. In June 1982, Israeli forces on their way north to Beirut in pursuit of the Palestine Liberation Organization simply cut through UNIFIL, which following its mandate, could offer no effective armed resistance. Since then, UNIFIL has remained in position, its mandate extended, but its role in the territory has been opposed by Israel and has been very limited.

Since 1985, the situation in the UNIFIL area of operation has remained essentially unchanged. Israel has maintained its presence in Lebanon, on the grounds that this is necessary to ensure Israel's security so long as the Lebanese Government is not able to exercise effective authority and prevent its territory from being used to launch attacks against northern Israel. The Israeli authorities have held that UNIFIL, as a peacekeeping force, is not capable of assuming this responsibility.

The Secretary-General has made every effort, at all levels, to convince the Israeli authorities to complete the withdrawal of their forces from Lebanon. However, with the exception of the withdrawal of the SLA from two positions near Yatar in October 1987, Israel has insisted on maintaining, and indeed strengthening, its control in southern Lebanon.

UNIFIL has been prevented from implementing the mandate given to it by the Security Council. In these circumstances, the Force has used its best efforts to keep the area, where it is deployed, free from hostilities and to shield its inhabitants from the worst effects of violence that nevertheless occurs. It has also provided humanitarian assistance. Despite the continuing impasse, the Security Council has repeatedly extended the mandate of the Force at the request of the Government of Lebanon and on the recommendation of the Secretary-General.

United Nations Operation in the Congo

The Republic of the Congo (Leopoldville) (now the Republic of Zaire), a former Belgian colony, became independent on 30 June 1960. In the days that followed, disorder broke out, and Belgium sent its troops to the Congo, stating that its aim was to protect and evacuate Europeans.

One 12 July 1960, the Congolese Government asked for United Nations military assistance to protect the national territory of the Congo against external aggression. Two days later, the Security Council called upon Belgium to withdraw its troops from the Congo and authorized the Secretary-General to provide the Congolese Government with such military assistance as might be necessary until, through the efforts of the Government with the technical assistance of the United Nations, the national security forces might be able, in the Government's opinion, to meet their tasks fully.

In less than 48 hours, contingents of a United Nations Force, provided by a number of countries including Asian and African states, began to arrive in the Congo. At the same time, United Nations civilian experts were rushed to the Congo to help ensure the continued operation of essential public services.

Over the next four years, the task of the United Nations operation in the Congo was to help the Congolese Government restore and maintain the political independence and territorial integrity of the Congo, to help it maintain law and order throughout the country, and to put into effect a wide and long-term programme of training and technical assistance programmes.

To meet the complex tasks before it, the United Nations had to assemble a large team. At its peak strength, the United Nations Force totalled nearly 20,000 officers and men. The instructions of the Security Council to this Force were strengthened early in 1961 after the assassination in Katanga province of former Prime Minister Patrice Lumumba. The Force was to protect the Congo from outside interference, particularly by evacuating foreign mercenaries, and advisors from Katanga and preventing clashes and civil strife by force, if necessary, as a last resort.

Following the reconvening of Parliament in August 1961 under United Nations auspices, the main problem was the attempted secession, led and financed by foreign elements, of the province of Katanga. Just as in September and December 1961, in December 1962, too the secessionist forces under the command of foreign mercenaries clashed with the United Nations Forces. Secretary-General Dag Hammarskjold lost his life on 17 September 1961, in the crash of his aeroplane on his way to Ndola (in what is now Zambia) where talks were to be held for the cessation of hostilities.

In February 1963, after Katanga had been reintegrated into the national territory of the Congo, a phasing out of the Force was begun, aimed at its termination by the end of that year. At the request of the Congolese Government, however, the General Assembly authorized the stay of a reduced number of troops for a further six months. The Force was completely withdrawn by 30 June 1964.

In the 1990s, UN forces would return to the Congo with a different type of mission, reflecting novel post-Cold War requirements. The initial Congo mission raised constitutional questions about peacekeeping and military enforcement under Chapters VI and VII of the UN Charter as well as about the role of the Secretary-General in peace and security issues. The mission was generally perceived as a UN failure because it entangled the United Nations in the Cold War rivalry of the time, cost far too much, and was too ambitious in its goals. This mission turned into an early experiment in nation-building – an undertaking that went beyond the existing understanding of the Charter. Nonetheless, the effort did introduce some elements of future peacekeeping missions, many of which remained dormant until the Cold War hostilities receded. For instance, for the first time, UN civilian police contingents were introduced into a peacekeeping mission. The pre-eminent role of the Secretary-General and his staff, challenged by the Soviet Bloc at the time, increasingly became a hallmark of later missions, and the insertion of UN forces in a domestic conflict became an accepted mechanism by the 1990s.

United Nations Peacekeeping in Cyprus

Cyprus became independent in 1960 with a Constitution that was intended to balance the interests of the island's Greek Cypriot and Turkish Cypriot communities. A treaty of August 1960, entered into by Cyprus, Greece, Turkey and the United Kingdom, guaranteed the basic provisions of the Constitution and the territorial integrity and sovereignty of Cyprus.

Following the outbreak of fighting on the island in December 1963, the Security Council met to consider a complaint by Cyprus charging intervention in its internal affairs and aggression by Turkey. Cyprus declared that the root of the problem lay in the divisive provisions of the Constitution, which had split the people into hostile camps. Turkey maintained that Greek Cypriot leaders had tried for more than two years to nullify the rights of the Turkish Cypriot community denying all charges of aggression.

On 4 March 1964, the Security Council unanimously recommended the establishment of a United Nations Peacekeeping Force in Cyprus (UNFICYP) with a mandate to prevent the recurrence of fighting, help maintain law and order, and promote a return to normal conditions. Since 1964, the Council has periodically extended UNFICYP's mandate, usually for periods of six months at a time.

Concurrently, within the functioning of UNFICYP, the United Nations has been active in promoting the settlement of the Cyprus problem. This task, first entrusted to a mediator, has since 1968 been carried out through the good offices of the Secretary-General. Within this framework, inter-communal talks between representatives of the Greek Cypriot and Turkish Cypriot communities, as well as high-level meetings, have been held in an effort to reach a just and lasting solution to the problem.

In November 1974, the General Assembly unanimously called on all states to respect the sovereignty, territorial integrity, independence and non-alignment of Cyprus. It urged the speedy withdrawal of all foreign interference, and safe return of all refugees to their homes. The Assembly said it was up to the Greek Cypriot and Turkish Cypriot communities to resolve the constitutional issues. It urged the continuation of the contacts which were taking place between representatives of the two communities with the help of the Secretary-General.

The Secretary-General reviewed the situation again in September 1986. Two high-level members of his staff undertook a mission to Cyprus, Turkey and Greece in November to explore ways of moving forward; another mission was sent to Cyprus in February 1987 for the same reason. Although efforts have been made by the Secretary-General to resume the negotiating process, both sides have maintained their positions and the impasse remains.

In the meantime, UNFICYP continued to carry out its daily task of supervising the ceasefire and maintaining close surveillance over the buffer area between the ceasefire lines, as well as making efforts to discharge its functions with regard to the security and well-being of the Greek Cypriots in the north.

On 29 May 1987, the force had the strength of 2,328, made up of contingents from Austria, Australia, Canada, Denmark, Finland, Ireland, Sweden and the United Kingdom. Costs are met by those governments and the Government of Cyprus, and by voluntary contributors. Contributions, however, have not been sufficient to meet the cost of the Force. In May 1987, the Secretary-General reported the accumulated deficit as being more than $150 million, which, he said, placed an unfair share of the cost on the troop-contributing countries. He hoped that the Security Council would agree that the United Nations' share of cost should be financed from assessed contributions. The Security Council has constantly extended the mandate of the United Nations Peacekeeping Force, urging all the sides, and all involved parties to respect UNFICYP's mandated authority in, and the delineation of, the buffer zone separating Greek and Turkish communities in the northern and southern regions of the Mediterranean island since 1974.

The Council reaffirmed the importance of the 2018 United Nations *aide-memoire* to ensure peace and security in the buffer zone. The Council called on both sides to respect the integrity of the buffer zone, remove all unauthorized constructions and prevent unauthorized military or civilian activities within and along the cease-fire lines and take "all appropriate measures" to ensure the safety and security of UNFICYP personnel.

To reduce existing barriers to intercommunal contact, the crossing points were reopened on 4 June 2020 to the operating status that existed prior to 29 February 2020.

The resolution 2587 (2021), the Council urged the sides—and all involved parties—to respect UNFICYP's mandated authority in, and delineation of, the buffer zone separating Greek and Turkish communities in the northern and southern regions of the Mediterranean island since 1974.

The Security Council extended the mandate of the United Nations Peacekeeping Force in Cyprus (UNFICYP) for six months—until 31 January 2022—expressing serious concern over violations of the military *status quo* along the cease-fire lines, reported encroachment by both sides into the buffer zone and increase in unauthorized construction—all of which pose challenges to the Force's operations.

Multitasking Peacekeeping Operations

Today, peacekeeping involves more troops, often more heavily armed than traditional peacekeepers, and with mandates that permit the use of force other than in self-defence. The line between peacekeeping and peace enforcement often gets blurred in practice, with no peace to keep, no cease-fire to monitor, and no consent for the mission from local regimes or perhaps failed states, such as in Somalia and the Democratic Republic of Congo (DRC). The resolutions for most peace operations now invoke Chapter VII not only to provide the legal basis for a range of actions but also to remind member states' of their obligations to give effect to Council decisions. Most operations since 1990 have a blend of a police and civilian personnel to carry out various parts of hybrid and complicated tasks.

Beginning with Somalia in 1992, subsequent missions further transformed the practice of peacekeeping as the UN and its members confronted intrastate conflicts, accompanied by humanitarian crises and also includes the case of the Democratic Republic of Congo (DRC), the collapse of state institutions. The Security Council responses vary with on a case-by-case basis to the different situations. As a result, peace operations stretch beyond the traditional principles of consent, impartiality, and limited use of force. All UN Secretaries-General since 1990 have contributed their ideas and initiatives to this new approach to peacekeeping, as did the 2000 report on UN peacekeeping reform by a high-level Panel on United Nations Peace Operations, known as the Brahimi Report, and a number of subsequent reports within and outside the UN.

Multidimensional peacekeeping operations comprise a mix of military, police and civilian components working together to lay the foundations of sustainable peace. While troop contingents may engage in observer activities characteristic of traditional operations, they are more likely to be monitoring the cantonment, disarmament, and demobilization of military forces and clearing landmines. Other military personnel, civilians and police, along with NGOs and UN agencies such as the UNHCR, UNICEF, and the UNDP, are normally involved in restoring law and order repatriating and resettling refugees organizing and supervising democratic elections, human rights monitoring and promotion and rebuilding the police and judiciary-tasks that are variously characterized as peacebuilding or state-building. In four post-Cold War situations (Namibia, Cambodia, Kosovo and East Timor), the UN also provided interim or transitional civil administration.

Of the fifty-six peacekeeping operations, the UN has undertaken between 1988 and 2014, the majority have involved Peacebuilding tasks, some of which the UN and other actors initiated even before the conflict terminated. Peace operations whose mandate includes Peacebuilding depend on the nature of the conflict situation as well as the political will in the Security Council, because such operations typically include various UN agencies, regional IGOs and NGOs, coordinating the military and civilian components. Case studies of the former Yugoslavia and Democratic Republic of Congo, where there were large humanitarian crises but there was no peace to be kept, illustrate the new challenges faced by Peacekeepers in new missions today.

The UN's experience in Somalia in 1993 demonstrated that targeting "an enemy" is particularly problematic if the UN wishes to maintain its impartiality. The authorization to use force other than to protect civilians for a limited time looks more like war than keeping peace and jeopardizes the safety of peacemakers themselves as well as civilian and humanitarian UN workers.

Post-conflict Peacebuilding and State-building

The basic idea here is to prevent renewed hostilities and aid countries in building the foundations for long-term stability and initiating the process of democratization. When the UN first undertook some of these tasks, however, there were serious questions regarding its authority for doing so, given Article 2(7) of the UN Charter—long seen as marking the line between states' sovereignty and UN authority.

"Peacebuilding" is the recognition that prevention and rebuilding are inextricably linked, a formal agreement ending a civil war is meaningless unless coupled with long-term programs of rehabilitation. Peacebuilding operations are complex and multifaceted, including military and civilian tasks associated with such operations. Peacebuilding is more than promoting stability, it is designed to create a positive peace, eliminate root causes of conflict, to allow states and societies to develop stable expectations of peaceful change. In some cases, such as Kosovo and East Timor, the UN has gone beyond Peacebuilding to state-building i.e., working with local actors to create the foundations and institutions of a government. To examine the evolution of post-conflict peacebuilding and state-building operations, we look at the first two such missions in Namibia and Cambodia, then at the later operations in Kosovo and East Timor.

United Nations Transition Assistance Group in Namibia

The United Nations operation in Namibia marked the culmination of 70 years of pressure by the organized international community – through the League of Nations and then the United Nations – to enable the people of the Territory to live in peace, freedom and independence. Its climax came shortly after midnight on 21 March 1990, when the South African flag was lowered, the Namibian flag was raised, and the Secretary-General of the United Nations, Mr Javier Perez de Cuellar, administered the oath of office to Mr Sam Nujoma as President of the newly independent state.

Namibia had been the particular concern of the United Nations from its earliest days in 1946. In 1966, the General Assembly terminated the mandate of South Africa to administer the Territory and placed it under the direct responsibility of the United Nations. From that time onwards, the pace of negotiation quickened, and led, though still at tortuous length and with great complexity, to the Security Council's decision on 16 February 1989, to implement a settlement proposal which had first been agreed to in 1978.

The agreed settlement was a negotiated compromise and led to a most unusual, indeed *sui generis*, United Nations operation: the *de facto* but illegal occupying power. South Africa, and the United Nations, in which *de jure* authority reposed, but which had not previously been able to establish effective administration in Namibia, were to work together to enable the Namibian people to exercise their right of self-determination. The central objective of the United Nations operation was to create conditions for the holding of free and fair elections for a Constituent Assembly which would draw up a constitution under which Namibia would proceed to independence as a free and sovereign state.

On 21 November 1989, the newly elected Constituent Assembly convened, under the Settlement Plan and with a Constituent Assembly Proclamation. The Constituent Assembly quickly elected officials and proceeded, initially in committees, to draw up a Constitution. The Constitution was adopted by consensus on 9 February 1990. It provided for independence six weeks later, on 21 March 1990. In his report to the Security Council of 16 March 1990, the Secretary-General reported that the constitution was to enter into force on independence and that it reflected the "principles concerning the Constituent Assembly and the constitution for an independent Namibia" adopted by all the parties concerned in 1982.

In the period between the elections and independence, the Administrator-General remained responsible for the administration of the Territory, and his activities continued to be monitored by UNTAG. After the elections, UNTAG closed some of its centres, and reduced staffing in others, and all of them were closed at independence. UNTAG's police monitors continued with their tasks until independence and there was no reduction in their strength until just before that time.

The military component of UNTAG was gradually wound up in the early months of 1990, with certain logistic elements, and many monitors and observers, leaving during January and February. Meanwhile, however, a Tripartite Military Integration Committee was established, with UNTAG in the chair, to develop a concept for an integrated Namibian army. The Committee was to plan the integration of Namibian armed personnel who had fought on both sides of the war and develop a military structure for a future Namibian army.

The independence ceremony, which took place just after midnight on 21 March was attended by the Secretary-General, who administered the oath of office to President Sam Nujoma, following the terms of the Constitution, and by many leaders from around the world. In his final report to the Security Council, on 28 March 1990, the Secretary-General reported: "Thus was achieved, in dignity and with great rejoicing, the goal of independence for Namibia which the United Nations and its member states have striven for so long".

In his report of 23 January 1989, the Secretary-General recommended to the Security Council that the costs of UNTAG should be considered as expenses of the Organization to be borne by members under Article 17, Paragraph 2, of the Charter. He also expressed his intention to recommend to the General Assembly that the assessments to be levied on member states be credited to a special account, which would be established for this purpose. This recommendation was duly accepted by the General Assembly in Resolution 43/232 of 3 March 1989.

The UNTAG operation had many novel features and constituted an evolutionary step beyond the United Nations' traditional role of peacekeeping and monitoring of self-determination processes. This was because of the far-reaching mandate given to the Secretary-General by the Security Council. UNTAG's principal function was to create conditions for the holding of free and fair elections. This meant that it was required to be, and was deeply involved in the whole political process of Namibia's transition from an illegally occupied colony to a sovereign and independent State. UNTAG thus had to play its part in monitoring and implementing a ceasefire, withdrawal and demobilization of troops, monitoring a local police force, managing a political "normalization" process, supervising and controlling the resultant elections and assisting in the transition to independence. Because of the vast international interest in Namibia, a territory with a unique status under international law, each step was taken under a searchlight of public scrutiny and comment. The mandate made it one of the most political of United Nations operations, and the logistical dimensions, together with the strict timetable involved, caused it to be one of the most demanding, in practical terms, to be put in the field.

The internal lessons to be drawn for the United Nations are far-reaching. The UNTAG experience can be of great value in the planning and execution of United Nations operations in future. The foundation for the success of such operations remains, as ever, the full cooperation of the parties, the continuing support of the Security Council, and the timely provision of the necessary financial resources. If these are forthcoming, UNTAG showed how much the United Nations could achieve by making full use of all its resources, including the diverse skills, and the commitment, of its staff. On 21 March 1990, Namibia achieved independence and UNTAG left the country. UNTAG was seen as a harbinger of a new and vital role for the UN in a world of disintegrating states.

United Nations Transition Authority in Cambodia

The Security Council on 28 February 1992, voted unanimously to authorize the establishment of a United Nations Transition Authority in Cambodia (UNTAC) and asked the Secretary-General to begin the deployment of the force "as rapidly as possible in the most efficient and cost-effective way".

By its resolution, the Council approved the Secretary-General's plan for the deployment of UNTAC and his preliminary estimate of some $2 billion for the cost of the force for approximately 15 months. The Council said it was vital that elections be held in Cambodia by May 1993 at the latest and called on all the parties concerned to comply scrupulously with the Paris Agreements signed in October 1991.

The Council further urged the Cambodian parties to agree to the complete demobilization of their military forces before the end of the registration for the elections, as well as to the destruction of weapons and ammunition.

UNTAC was a delicate and difficult mission for it aimed to put an end to two decades of war, destruction and suffering, to create the conditions for lasting peace and to lead the Cambodian people to free and democratic elections.

UNTAC was headed by a Special Representative for Cambodia and comprises more than 70,000 United Nations personnel, including human rights, civil, administrative and military components as well as a police component of some 3,359 civilian police monitors operating throughout the territory.

The electoral component consisted of 1,614 international personnel operating from headquarters in Phnom Penh and another 900 personnel covering many centres throughout the country.

The operation covered seven major areas: promotion of human rights, free and fair elections scheduled for spring 1993, military arrangements, civil administration, maintenance of law and order, repatriation of Cambodian refugees and displaced persons, and rehabilitation of the infrastructure during the transitional period.

The total budget of UNTAC is expected to be $1.6 billion. It is the largest operation undertaken by the United Nations in the past three decades, but the deployment of its various components has been planned to keep in view the Organization's serious financial situation.

The successful elections notwithstanding the boycott by the Khmer Rouge were a feather in the UN cap. The UN operation in Cambodia has no peer in history. They constitute the most ambitious project ever undertaken by the United Nations in the interest of bringing peace and democracy to a nation and combining it with a phenomenal programme of rehabilitation and reconstruction.

For this purpose, UNTAC was equipped with a 22,000-strong establishment taking its military and civil components together. India contributed some 2,000 of them. In about a year, UNTAC has repatriated nearly four million refugees, a gigantic task by any definition. It also established an entire network of roads and communications. The election work entailed the registration of five and a half million voters and 1,500 polling booths throughout the country except the territory controlled by the Khmer Rouge. Some of these were established in areas bordering on the territory it controls. In protecting them, several UN personnel, including those from India, have suffered damage but UNTAC had remained undaunted. The UNTAC could register an impressively large number of voters and enable over four million of them to vote, despite disturbing conditions is a tribute as much as to UNTAC's tenacity of purpose as to the determination of the people of Cambodia to grab this unique opportunity for peace.

Despite these stupendous difficulties, the UN Security Council decided that the elections should be held on schedule. Given the intimidation and violence that marked the run-up to the election, there were doubts about whether free and fair elections would be held or not. When Mr Akashi, the Japanese Chief of UNTAC, certified that they have been so, the UN accepted that verdict.

Welcoming thc installation on 21 September 1993 of the new government of Cambodia, Secretary-General Boutros Boutros-Ghali, congratulated the Cambodian people on their historic achievement. He said in a statement that under the guidance of Prince Norodom Sihanouk (who was elected to be the head of Cambodia government) they had overcome two decades of strife and devastation and had laid a sound foundation for rebuilding a peaceful and democratic country.

The United Nations Transitional Authority in Cambodia (UNTAC) thus ended its mandate on 26 September 1993. The successful conclusion showed what the international community could achieve when it was united and determined in pursuit of a worthy goal, and when the people concerned were willing to make mutual concessions. The Cambodian people and their government would continue to need the assistance of the international community in the years ahead what the Secretary-General said and the United Nations would remain committed to supporting Cambodia as it faced the challenge of post-conflict nation-building.

Kosovo and East Timor

The UN built on its experience in Namibia and Cambodia to face the new challenges in both Kosovo and East Timor in the late 1990s with even more extensive multidimensional responsibilities. In neither case, however, there was a prior peace agreement or an existing state, both were provinces of other countries. (Yugoslavia/ Serbia and Indonesia) Both cases involved the initial use of force by a coalition of the United States and NATO in the case of Kosovo, and a UN-authorized Australian-led force in the case of East Timor. In the case of Kosovo, international legal status was among the questions to be determined in East Timor, as in Namibia, the outcome was to be independent statehood.

Following NATO bombing of Serbia and intervention to protect Kosovo Albanians in 1999 from ethnic cleansing by Serbian/Yugoslav military forces that displaced more than a million people, Security Council Resolution 1244 (1999) authorized the UN Mission in Kosovo (UNMIK) to undertake wide-ranging civilian administrative functions, in conjunction with a NATO peacekeeping force (KFOR). These duties included maintaining civil law and order, aiding in the return of refugees, coordinating humanitarian relief, supporting the reconstruction of key infrastructure, promoting Kosovo's autonomy and self-government and helping to determine Kosovo's future legal status. The head of UNMIK, a Special Representative of the Secretary-General (SRSG), was expected to coordinate the work of several non-UN organizations, among which various functions were divided, but over which he had little power. The Kosovo mission was the first UN mission designed with other IGOs as full partners. The UN had chief responsibility for civil administration, police and justice, the OSCE handled democratization and institution building, the EU was responsible for reconstruction and development and the UNHCR was responsible for all humanitarian matters. A contact group (United States, United Kingdom, France, Germany, Italy, and Russia) originally formed in the early 1990s to address Yugoslavia's breakup provided a political mechanism to ensure the support of key powers for UNMIK.

However, there have been some problems with the Kosovo mission. First, the Albanian Kosovars sought independence, but the mandate called for respecting Yugoslavia's sovereignty and the protection of Serbs living in Kosovo who wanted to be part of Yugoslavia (now Serbia). Thus, it wasn't clear when and how independence could be achieved given Serbia's strong opposition, supported by Russia and others, and the absence of any international agreement. Second, it proved particularly difficult to recruit adequate numbers of police for UNMIK. Third, coordination among the partner organizations has been hampered by different organizational objectives and cultures, and the UN has no authority to impose coordination. Fourth, Kosovo's economy has become extensively criminalized, with little done by UNMIK to curb transnational drug, organ and human trafficking. Despite the difficulties, the international state-building efforts supported by various actors did succeed in collaboration with local actors in building two effective state bureaucracies-the police and customs services.

In 2006, the UN's Special Envoy for Kosovo, Martti Ahtisaari, initiated a diplomatic process to determine Kosovo's final status, which led to a proposal for self-government under EU supervision-thus continuing indefinite international supervision and leaving Kosovo's legal status undetermined. In 2008, Kosovo's Provisional Self-Government Assembly declared the country's independence and received recognition from sixty-nine UN members, including the United States and many European countries, but strong opposition from Russia and Serbia. Responsibility for policing and rule of law were transferred from UNMIK to the EU in 2008, with the EU Rule of Law Mission in Kosovo (EULEX) becoming the EU's largest civilian mission, UNMIK retains responsibility for promoting security, stability and respect for human rights, there is an EU-appointed special representative in Kosovo and 5,000 NATO KFOR troops remain in place. In 2010, the ICJ issued a ruling that Kosovo's declaration of independence did not violate international law with Kosovo itself declaring the end of "supervised independence" in 2012 since Kosovo's declaration of independence, the objective of the mission has been the promotion of security, stability and respect for human rights through multi-community engagement in the country and with leaders in both Kosovo and Serbia.

The difficulties of state-building in Kosovo have been reinforced by the experience in East Timor (now Timor-Leste), where the transition to independence under UN auspices initially seemed peaceful, but the newly independent government proved to have little capacity beyond its capital and the UN was forced to return in 2006 when riots and political instability resurfaced. This mission was undertaken in 1999 after almost fifteen years of UN-mediated efforts to resolve the status of East Timor-a former Portuguese colony seized by Indonesia in the mid-1970s-when after an UN-organized vote endorsed independence, violence broke out, Indonesian troops failed to restore order, and almost half a million East Timorese were displaced from their homes. The Security Council initially authorized the Australian-led multinational force to restore order and then created the UN Transitional Administration in East Timor (UNTAET) with an ambitious and wide-ranging mission ranging from exercising all judicial, legislative and executive powers to assisting in the development of state services and humanitarian aid, promoting sustainable development, and building the foundation for stable liberal democracy.

As in Kosovo, the UN's role in East Timor involved collaboration with other international organizations-both IFOs and NGOs-and a very ambitious mandate with a short timeline. But East Timor faced a far greater problem-total destruction wrought by the Indonesia-backed militias and the departure of all civilian administrations. Unlike in Kosovo, however, the UN's charge was unequivocal UNTAET was to lead the territory to statehood. Still, there was no roadmap to follow and little knowledge of the situation.

Despite Timorese complaints of delay and insufficient empowerment, in 2002, after just three years, elections were held and an independent Timor-Leste was recognized. A small UN operation continued to provide support for stability, democracy, justice, law enforcement, and external security until 2005 when it was terminated despite Timor's lack of economic development and still shaky political institutions. Grievances within the armed forces led to intercommunal violence and political tensions, producing a crisis in 2006. The Security Council authorized the new UN Integrated Mission in Timor (UNMIT) with a mandate very similar to that of UNTAET to support the government and relevant institutions to consolidate political stability and ensure security (Resolution 1704), but with fewer personnel and resources. The 2006 crisis, however, had revealed the weakness of government institutions, the police and the military as well as rivalries among leaders, regional differences, and a culture of violence. Timor-Leste seemed a classic example of a "failed state". One of the major problems with the UN administration had been its failure to share power sufficiently with Timorese counterparts. There was also a presumption that Timor lacked institutions, and therefore, UN staff sought to create them rather than working with indigenous judicial institutions, in other words, a failure to understand local conditions. Whether the earlier UN mission had failed in its mandate, or underlying local factors were responsible for the 2006 crisis, continues to be a matter of debate.

UNMIT terminated its mission in December 2012, following a two-year transition process that included national elections, the formation of a new government and working with the parliament, civil society and media to create a resilient state.

New Role for Regional Organizations

Regional intergovernmental organizations have also played an important role in post-cold war collective security operations. They have been a part of peacekeeping operations, delivered humanitarian assistance, provided mediation and negotiation services to intra state conflicting parties and organized collective responses to threats in their regions. Both the Millennium Summit in 2000 and the 2005 World Summit endorsed an active involvement of regional organizations in cooperation with the Security Council on critical issues such as the "responsibility to protect" populations in their respective regions from genocide and crimes against humanity.

Regional organizations offer an alternative to direct UN peacekeeping, share costs in peacekeeping and other activities with the world organization, and have a better knowledge of the issues involved in a regional conflict. The African Union (AU) is a good example of a regional organization that has played a serviceable role in cooperating with the United Nations in addressing civil and international conflicts on the African continent. For example, it intervened with troops in the Darfur region of Sudan in April 2004. The AU committed an initial force of 3,200 troops to Darfur, with the number rising eventually to 7,000. Limited in resources and finances, the AU indicated it would remain only until a UN peacekeeping operation replaced it. In June 2007, the Sudanese government gave its initial approval to a joint AU-UN force but insisted that the majority of peacekeepers be Africans. The joint operation continued to face hostile enemy forces well into 2015.

Also in Africa, the Economic Community of West African States (ECOWAS) undertook its own joint peacekeeping operations. During the 1990s, the United Nations engaged in co-deployments and joint peacekeeping operations with the AU and ECOWAS in Sierra Leone and Liberia. In the Liberian case, the Security Council endorsed the ECOWAS intervention. Leaders praised the organization as an example of the emerging importance of such action in the restoration of peace in "failed states". In 2003, ECOWAS peacekeepers joined the familiar UN blue helmet as the regional operation became a UN peacekeeping effort.

Secretaries-General Kofi Annan and Ban Ki-moon were strong advocates for the engagement of regional organizations in UN activities especially, peacekeeping. Of particular note at the time Ban Ki-moon spoke to the Council was the European Union's active engagement in strike-torn Mali and in the Central African Republic, and its involvement along with the Organization for Security and Cooperation in Europe (OSCE) in addressing the conflict in Ukraine.

Peace Operations: The Challenges

Given the evolution from traditional peacekeeping to complex peacekeeping, to Peacebuilding and state-building, organizing these various peace operations has become very problematic. When a new UN mission is approved or a mission mandate expanded by the Security Council, the UN's Department of Peacekeeping Operations and Department of Field Support are responsible for determining the exact logistics support, seeking the necessary military and civilian contingents to service the operation. The UNSG appoints a force commander from the top officer core of a member country and for major operations also appoints a special representative to oversee the entire mission. When a peace operation includes the organization and supervision of elections, the UN's Electoral Assistance Division, established in 1992 is also involved.

The size of peace operations-whether UN, regional, hybrid or partnering-has varied widely from small monitoring missions, numbering less than a hundred to major operations in the Congo in the 1960s. Cambodia, Somalia and Bosnia in the early 1990s and the DRC, Somalia and Darfur required over 15,000 troops. For example, the joint UN-AU mission in Darfur, authorized in 2007, was at barely 75 per cent of strength at the beginning of 2009. In 2012, it still had fewer troops and police than authorized.

Since the permanent UN military forces envisioned by the Charter (Articles 43-45) were never created, the UN has relied on *ad hoc* military, civilian or police units volunteered by member states to create multinational operations. During the Cold War, these were drawn almost exclusively from the armed forces of states other than the P-5 (often middle powers and nonaligned members such as Canada, India, Sweden, Ghana and Nepal) to keep the two superpowers out of regional conflicts.

Major powers including the United States, Great Britain, France and Russia have also contributed forces since the end of the Cold War and especially with much larger peace operations. Top troop contributors to UN missions in 2004 were Pakistan, Bangladesh, India, Ethiopia, and Nigeria, top police contributors were Bangladesh, Jordan and India. China first made personnel (civilian police) available for the UN mission in Haiti in 2004, in 2014 it had about 2,200 military and police deployed in nine UN operations. Overall, in 2014, the UN had more than 104,000 troops, police and military observers deployed in sixteen missions, with 128 member states making contributors ranging from 3 to 10,000 persons.

An important innovation in personnel followed Security Council Resolution 1325 (2000), which called for greater participation of women in peacekeeping and protection activities. As of early 2015, there were more than 500 women in four all-female police units and over 4,000 women in total UN peace operations. The impetus for adding women came both from the advocacy of women's NGOs prompted by sexual violence in conflicts and from gender-based violence committed by peacekeepers themselves.

Different countries have important goals to be served by contributing to peacekeeping operations. The difference between poorer countries' military salary levels and UN troop wages make the services rendered economically attractive. Small states such as Chile and Nepal gain prestige, valuable training and field experience by participating in UN peacekeeping. Canada and the Nordic countries long saw peacekeeping contributions as a way to reiterate their commitment to multilateralism and UN objectives. Brazil, Japan and Germany's contributions reflect their long-pending interest to secure permanent seats on the Security Council. China's participation reflects its national ambitions and hegemonic role in global governance. There has been a steady decline, however, in peacekeepers from Western developed countries hence the heavy UN reliance on personnel from African and South Asian countries.

The sheer number of new operations (fifteen) that the UN undertook between 1989 and 1993 taxed its capacity to organize and supervise missions. The failure of the Security Council to act in a timely fashion regarding conflicts in several African countries, including Liberia, Sierra Leone and Sudan, led Secretary-General Boutros Boutros-Ghali (1992) to call for greater participation by regional organizations to share the burden and "contribute to a deeper sense of participation and democratization in international affairs". By the late 1990s, there were more regional IGO peace operations than UN operations, a trend that has shifted since 2003 with more efforts involving both the UN and regional IGOs in addressing threats to peace and security, particularly in Africa.

Regional and sub-regional IGOs vary widely in their organizational capacities. Resource constraints particularly afflict all of the African organizations. As a result, capacity-building efforts have been under way since the mid-2000s, supported by the G-8's Global Peace Operations Initiative and the EU's African Peace Facility. NATO is the exception to the general rule that IGOs do not have any military capabilities except those that their members commit for action on an *ad hoc* basis, but the earlier discussion of its role in Afghanistan showed the difficulties even it has encountered in getting members to commit troops and not limit their use. The EU's rapid reaction force is relatively recent. That capability proved vital on three occasions in the DRC and has been utilized more recently in a number of situations.

With the absence of a multilateral force, a few countries, notably Canada and the Scandinavian countries, have earmarked portions of their military forces specifically for peacekeeping assignments and trained them accordingly. International peacekeeping centres have now been established in many countries and on all continents to train military, police and civilians.

With currently peacebuilding activities an integral part of virtually all multidimensional UN peace operations now, they have also become part of the activities of many UN agencies and other organizations. Given the number of non-UN actors involved, there has been a continuing call for better coordination and sustained international efforts. The establishment of the UN Peacekeeping Commission (PBC) in 2006, bringing together all the relevant actors to develop integrated strategies and sustained attention for post-conflict peacebuilding and recovery is the focus of all capacity building activities.

The PBC is composed of thirty-one UN member states, including the P-5. It forms what are known as "country-specific configurations" for each of the countries in which it is involved, these include the thirty-one PBC members for the World Bank, IMF and regional banks, top providers of financial aid, military personnel and civilian police in the country relevant regional and sub-regional organizations, the senior UN representative in the field and other relevant UN staff. In short, the PBC itself and particularly the country groupings are expected to serve as an intergovernmental advisory body to bring together all relevant actors, muster resources and advise on strategies with a permanent representative of a member state serving as an advocate for the country. The UN General Assembly created the Peacebuilding Fund for post-conflict reconstruction, to be financed by voluntary contributions, and the Peacebuilding Support Office within the Secretariat. The three institutions together constitute what is now called the UN's "peacebuilding architecture".

The first two countries referred to the PBC by the Security Council were Burundi and Sierra Leone. Later the Central African Republic, Guinea, Liberia, and Guinea-Bissau have been added. In each of the countries on its agenda, consultations between the PBC and government identify critical areas for consolidating peace, such as strengthening the rule of law, security sector reform, promoting good governance, and youth employment and specific peacebuilding projects for funding by the UN and international and national donors. The fund also supports projects in non-PBC countries to avert the risk of relapse into conflict, help implement peace agreements or strengthen peacebuilding efforts.

United Nations Peacekeeping: Some Observations

Experience of the United Nations' peacekeeping operations discussed here suggests certain potentials and limitations that can be traced to foreign policies determined outside the United Nations and the actions of the Secretary-General. These potentials and limitations can be described as follows:

Peacekeeping operations make up part of what Hammarskjold called "preventive diplomacy" keeping involved intervention by the United Nations in conflicts that were marginal to the Cold War. The explicit aim was to keep them outside of the East-West power conflict. For preventive diplomacy to succeed, the two most powerful UN members, the erstwhile Soviet Union and the United States had to agree or at least keep hands off the UN military actions. In other words, they had to regard the prevention of any extension of conflicts as important enough so that they were prepared to accept the neutralization of large territories outside of the real centres of power.

In the case of UNEF, a minimum degree of understanding between the Soviet Union and the United States made possible the creation and execution of the plan. In the case of ONUC, the situation was somewhat different. The Soviet Union soon withdrew its original acceptance of the operation. This change is related to the complicated character of the operation in the Congo. What began as an action to reverse foreign (Belgian) intervention and to maintain law and order, gradually developed into attempts to curb internal chaos and civil war. At least indirectly, both the United States and the Soviet Union encouraged the breakdown. The same would apply, on a more limited scale, to the role of UNIFIL.

If the United Nations is to employ military action, the force acting on its behalf must be strong enough to accomplish its stated purpose. Anything less will mean a fatal loss of prestige and the end of any effective UN role. Furthermore, a force employed for its military capacity must be authorized to do more than shoot in self-defence. Such a force requires a leader – presumably the Secretary-General – who can persuade either the Security Council or the General Assembly to adopt the required resolutions to guide policy. Alternatively, the Secretary-General must be prepared to interpret existing resolutions feasibly and face the consequences.

A Secretary-General who undertakes such ventures must enjoy a great deal of confidence from the member governments. Hammarskjold had such general confidence, although he had to endure personal attacks from the Soviet Union that eroded his political position. It was his proposals and confidence-building that provided the foundations for UNEF and ONUC. He expanded the office of the Secretary-General so that its occupant could sometimes develop extensive powers within his formal mandate.

Hammarskjold's successors have added little to the principles that have operated since his time. These led to such initiatives as:

(a) obtaining military contributions from national governments;

(b) securing permission for free passage through national territories;

(c) getting permissions from host states where operations must take place; and

(d) negotiating with governments about financial contributions.

All of these initiatives require extensive diplomatic discussion and formal agreement with concerned governments. They offer opportunities for creative diplomacy but also include the perils of failure and diminished prestige.

If the United Nations is to employ troops, whether, for peacekeeping or military operations, they must be subject to a process of selection. Which governments should be asked to do so and what will be its political and financial consequences? Generally, the permanent members of the Security Council are excluded, although, in the case of Cyprus and Lebanon the United Kingdom has contributed troops, French soldiers have served in UNIFIL.

Despite all these years of peacekeeping, a series of legal questions remain unanswered:

(a) To what extent are members legally bound to contribute contingents to a peacekeeping force set up by the Security Council or the General Assembly?

(b) May a government withdraw its contingent without the explicit permission of a UN deliberative organ?

(c) What are the rights of states on whose territory operations take place? Under what circumstances may they legally require withdrawal? How can legal obligations regarding the operation of a force be made politically effective?

In a divided world permanently threatened by the possibility of a nuclear holocaust, UN peacekeeping operations can limit and localize the scope of international conflicts. UN forces try to keep an armed conflict at a low level while efforts to secure a political settlement of the problem are on.

The presence of United Nations forces has prevented the aggravation of various conflicts and maintenance of international peace. UN forces by forming a buffer zone separate the warring parties. The rival states resist attacking the UN force because these represent the international community. Their presence encourages the parties to the dispute to settle issues through negotiation rather than violence.

The financial feasibility of such forces remains another critical problem. Considering the apparent contribution of UNEF I and ONUC to peace and stability, their combined cost was relatively small—some $15 million to $20 million a year for the latter. Nevertheless, the unwillingness of some members to pay the costs of peacekeeping brought the United Nations to the verge of bankruptcy. The financial impact of the Congo crisis was temporarily cushioned by the issuance of UN bonds, but ONUC had to be disbanded and withdrawn from the Congo in 1964 because of the financial drain on the organization, not because its usefulness had ended.

The financial problem, while a serious one, was symptomatic of a more fundamental political problem—disagreement over the establishment and control of peacekeeping operations. Both France and the Soviet Union maintain that the sole control of UN forces should rest with the Security Council, where each of the five permanent members holds the veto. They object to the deployment of the UN forces without their consent, and to the principle that a state can be required to pay for any UN security function that a majority of the Assembly decides to make chargeable to the organization as a whole.

The assessment issue was sidestepped in the creation of the UN Cyprus force (1964) by making it dependent on voluntary contributions, and nine years passed before another UN peacekeeping force was created. The UN forces established since then have all been authorized and controlled by the Security Council and financed by an Assembly-approved mandatory assessment formula that minimizes the contributions of developing countries. Although the Soviet Union initially voted for UNEF II and UNDOF and abstained on the UNIFIL authorization, it now pays assessments only for UNDOF. Along with some 20 East European and Arab states, it refuses to support UNIFIL on the ground that Israel as the "aggressor" in Lebanon should pay the costs of peacekeeping. Soviet contributions to UNEF II ceased after 1976 because the Israeli-Egyptian disengagement agreement was negotiated under American rather than UN auspices.

Although the UN peacekeeping presence has proved its worth in the field, its future is problematic. A Special Committee on Peacekeeping Operations, established during the financial crisis of 1964-65, has laboured for more than 20 years without resolving the thorny issues of finance and control. Apart from the merits of particular operations, the United States has favoured an active supervising role for the Secretary-General, while the Soviet Union would confer sole power on the Security Council. In practice, since 1973 peacekeepers have followed guidelines prepared by the Secretary-General and approved by the Council. The expertise of the Secretariat and a small cadre of peacekeepers in the field is an international asset of great potential value in future operations. Several middle powers have been willing to supply needed troops and have also accumulated valuable experience in the process.

It can be said that though the efforts of UN forces have not yielded effective results in all cases, it cannot be denied that most of them did a creditable job. The success of UN peacekeeping efforts depends on the consent of the host states, cooperation of the

Great Powers, and the suppliers of forces, whether military, police or civilian. Withdrawal of consent by the host state can lead either to the termination of the operations or to a period of severe disturbances. Similarly, without the cooperation of the big powers, UN peacekeeping measures are bound to fail. Finally, unless the states contributing forces and finances come forward with necessary forces and finances, UN peacekeeping cannot succeed.

The United Nations is getting increasingly drawn into internal conflicts, resolving, which is a much more treacherous undertaking than monitoring peace on international borders, according to Michael Renner, senior researcher at the Worldwatch Institute in Washington.

Renner was releasing the Worldwatch report Critical Juncture, the Future of Peacekeeping, authored by him.

"One of the problems in Bosnia is the continued unwillingness to make available to the UN the kind of resources and political wherewithal necessary to play a constructive role," Renner says. Under such conditions, improvisation compromised timely response, and the explosion of responsibilities threatened to overwhelm peacekeeping and communication abilities.

There were only 15 persons in the UN headquarters in New York to supervise 60,000 peacekeepers in the field, Renner pointed out. And very often a larger and more extended UN presence was required than what the Security Council members were willing to authorize.

The UN and the international community will have to discuss and define a set of criteria, which will trigger appropriate peacekeeping action if the UN is to be turned into peacemaker of first recourse, rather than peacekeeper of last resort, the report said. To bring that about, the report suggests:-

- Establishment of an early warning office that continuously monitors potential trouble spots around the world.
- Setting up permanent conflict resolution committees in each region of the world to defuse tensions before violence erupts.
- Deploying peacekeepers proactively to prevent aggression, when warranted by an early warning alert or when requested by a Government.
- Creation of a two-tier UN peace force consisting of a permanent, individually-recruited, non-combat force, as well as a specially trained backup army made up of troops of contingents available to the Security Council on short notice.
- Establishing a regular annual peacekeeping budget, with a reserve fund to cover unforeseen expenses.

It would also help, the report pointed out, if Governments paid off the $645 million of arrears they owed the UN on peacekeeping assessments.

How Important is UN Peacekeeping Today

By late 1998, 16 operations were deploying about 14,347 UN military and civilian police personnel. The number of personnel was down considerably from the peak of 80,000 reached in 1993. At that time, of 14 operations, 3 (in Cambodia, Somalia and the former Yugoslavia) accounted for some 63,000 uniformed personnel or 80 per cent of the total.

In contrast, the number of operations has remained relatively steady over some years, varying between 14 and 17 at any one time. These include several long-running operations, such as those in Cyprus and in Jammu and Kashmir, whose presence is seen as essential despite the seemingly intractable nature of the conflicts. In 1998, new operations were established in the Central African Republic and Sierra Leone. The number of countries volunteering uniformed personnel has also remained steady at about 75. In total, some 118 countries have provided military and civilian police personnel to UN peacekeeping operations.

Member states, regional organizations and the UN Secretariat are working to improve overall preparedness, standby capacity, logistical support and training.

Today, 80 member states have officially expressed their willingness to enter into standby arrangements with the UN. Sixty of these have specified the resources they could make available if they decided to participate in an operation, and 20 have signed standby agreements. Within this framework, a group of member states had established a Standby Forces High Readiness Brigade to enhance the capacity of their troops to serve together in a peacekeeping context.

The international community has drawn lessons from past operations and is working to strengthen the United Nations peacekeeping capacity in some areas. A blueprint of reform was provided by the Secretary-General's Panel on Peace Operations, chaired by Ambassador Lakhdar Brahimi, which issued its report in 2000.

The Security Council and other bodies are now tackling the major issues at stake, which include:

- enhancing preparedness;
- speeding up deployment;
- strengthening the deterrent capacities of peacekeepers; and
- ensuring full political and financial support by the Member States.

Operations can take many forms and are constantly evolving in the light of the changing circumstances. Among the tasks discharged by peacekeeping operations over the years are:

- **Maintenance of Ceasefires and Separation of Forces:** By providing "breathing space," an operation based on a limited agreement between parties can foster an atmosphere conducive to negotiations.

- **Preventive Deployment:** Deployed before conflict breaks out, an operation provide a reassuring presence and a degree of transparency, which favour political progress.
- **Protection of Humanitarian Operations:** In many conflicts, civilian populations have been deliberately targeted as a means to gain political ends. In such situations, peacekeepers have been asked to provide protection and support for humanitarian operations. However, such tasks can place peacekeepers in difficult political positions and can lead to threats to their security.
- **Implementation of a Comprehensive Peace Settlement:** Complex, multi-dimensional operations, deployed based on comprehensive peace agreements, can assist in such diverse tasks as providing humanitarian assistance, monitoring human rights, observing elections and coordinating support for economic reconstruction.

Currently, there are 13 UN Peacekeeping operations across 3 continents. Over 120 countries contribute troops, police and civilian personnel to UN Peacekeeping, the personnel engaged are over lakh persons. The UN Peacekeeping budget at $7.3 billion is still less than 0.5 per cent of global military expenditure.

Cited Works

Basic Facts about the United Nations, Diane Publishing, New York: UN Department of Public Information, published periodically.

Boulden, Jane, *The United Nations Experience in Congo, Somalia, and Bosnia,* Westport, CT: Praeger, 2001.

Boutros-Ghali, Boutros, *Supplement to an Agenda for Peace*, New York: United Nations, 1995.

Boyd, James M., *United Nations Peacekeeping Operations: A Military and Political Appraisal*, New York: Praeger, 1971.

Chandra, Satish, Chandra, Mala, *International Conflicts and Peace Making Processs: Role of the United Nations*, Mittal Publications, 2006.

Cox, Arthur M., *Prospects for Peacekeeping*, Washington: Brookings Institution, 1967.

Diehl, Paul F., and Alexandru, Balas, *Peace Operations*, 2nd ed. Malden, MA: Polity, 2014.

Fabian, Larry L., *Soldiers without Enemies: Preparing the United Nations for Peacekeeping*, Washington D.C.: Brooking Institution, 1971.

Higgins, Rosalyn, *United Nations Peacekeeping: 1946-1967*, New York: Oxford University Press, 1980.

James, Alan, *The Politics of Peacekeeping*, New York: Praeger, 1969.

Jenkins, Rob. *Peacebuilding: From Concept to Commission*, New York: Routledge, 2013.

Ki-moon, Ban, *Report of the Secretary-General on Peacebuilding in the Aftermath of Conflict*, 23 September 2014. A/69/399-S/2014/694.

Mingst, Karen A., Karns, Margaret P., and Lyon Alynna J, *The United Nations in the 21st Century*, Fiftieth edn., New York, Routledge, 2016-2018.

Moore, John Allphin, Jr., and Jerry Pubantz, *The New United Nations, International Organization in the Twenty-First Century*, New York and London, Routledge, 2017.

Oestreich, Joel E., *International Organizations as Self-directed Actors: A Framework for Analysis,* vol. 64, London, Routledge, 2012.

Paris, Roland, and Timothy D. Sisk, eds., *The Dilemmas of Statebuilding: Confronting the Contradictions of Postwar Peace Operations*. New York: Routledge, 2009.

Report of the Panel on UN Peace Operations, A/55/305-S/2000/809 21 Aug, 2000.

Rikhye, Inderjit, *The Blue Line: International Peacekeeping and its Future,* New Haven: Yale University Press, 1974.

The Blue Helmets: A Review of United Nations Peacekeeping, UN Publications DPI/850, 1990.

UN Department of Public Information, *The Blue Helmets: A Review of United Nations Peacekeeping*. 3rd Edition, New York: United Nations, 1996.

UN Department of Public Information, *UN Peacekeeping: 50 Years*, 1948-1998. New York: United Nations, 1998.

White, N.D., *The United Nations and the Maintenance of International Peace and Security,* Manchester University Press, 1990.

https://peacekeeping.un.org/en/our-history

https://peacekeeping.un.org/sites/default/files/past/untagFT.htm

https://peacekeeping.un.org/sites/default/files/past/unef1backgr2.html

https://peacekeeping.un.org/sites/default/files/past/onucB.htm

https://cdn.peaceopstraining.org/theses/baudouin.pdf

https://media.un.org/en/taxonomy/term/101501

https://www.un.org/press/en/2021/sc14589.doc.htm

https://undocs.org/pdf?symbol=en/S/RES/745(1992)

https://peacekeeping.un.org/sites/default/files/past/untacfacts.html

13

HUMANITARIAN INTERVENTION

Most post-1990 conflicts in "failed" states have been characterized by major humanitarian crises, genocide, crimes against humanity, widespread human rights violations and the presence of a huge number of refugees and Internally Displaced Persons within states. UN peace operations and the UNHRC, the Office for the Coordination of Humanitarian Affairs (UNOCHA), and humanitarian NGOs have been challenged as never before. The very fact that the Security Council during the 1990s repeatedly referred to "humanitarian crises" as threats to international peace and security under Chapter VII signalled the change.

UN responses to these humanitarian crises have been varied, inconsistent and selective. The creation of "safe havens" and "no-fly zones" in northern and southern Iraq in April 1991 protected Iraqi Kurds and Shiites without the consent of state authorities. The UN intervened in Somalia and through NATO in Kosovo, but responded only partially to the genocide in Rwanda, belatedly to that in Darfur and decided not to intervene after the Taliban takeover of Kabul in 2021. Differing great power interests in the Security Council, as well as persistent media attention also play a role in the UN's selective decisions to intervene or not to intervene.

Two major changes in global conflicts in the 1990s brought in the debate over the Responsibility to Protect (R2P) norm and the Protection of Civilians (POC) mandate now included in many peace operations. While R2P and POC are similar in some ways they differ in other respects. R2P applies to genocide or mass atrocities and involves all types of war crimes, a narrower scope than POC which applies to only those war crimes that involve civilians. Where POC applies to all parties in a conflict (state and non-state actors), R2P applies only to states. Altogether, between 2006 and late 2014, the Security Council approved twenty-six resolutions referring to R2P and/or POC.

R2P, however, is not essentially about military intervention. R2P may involve taking on a whole series of measures like diplomatic persuasion, imposition of sanctions, use of the International Criminal Court process, and only in exceptional cases undertaking of military action. Primary responsibility lies with sovereign states to protect their citizens, secondary to the international community. When prevention fails and a state is not protecting its people, then the UN has responsibility for acting under the Charter.

Since the 2011 intervention in Libya, there has been recurring debate about the UN's failure to intervene in Syria. However, no one can deny that these conflict situations were not directly comparable. The UN-sanctioned intervention in Libya had strong endorsements from four regional organizations-the Arab League, GCC, OIC, and AU. Additionally, the United States, Britain and France were willing to act and believed that they could foil Qaddafi's threat of mass atrocities by timely intervention. Despite no clear references to R2P in Security Council debates, critics have concluded that states consensually agreed to intervene, or not to block intervention (in Libya), in large part because of the power of ideas and norms of human protection related to R2P.

The NATO intervention evolved to include regime change, however, Russia, China, Brazil, India, and others had quickly turned hostile, creating a "Libya" effect over Security Council discussions of possible action in Syria. The humanitarian crisis in Syria had been far greater than any imagined in Libya, but the problems are due not only to the Assad regime but also to various rebel groups. There had been no call from the Arab League, GCC or OIC for intervention, the Arab states were divided. Most importantly, Russia and China exercised their veto power to present intervention against the Assad regime in the Security Council and the United States has been unwilling to act.

Since 2014, there have been ten UN operations with POC mandates. The Security Council has held regular meetings on the subject since 1999 and along with the Security-General has issued both country-specific and thematic resolutions on both genocide and protection of civilians in armed conflict. There are now senior advisors to the UNSG on both genocide and protection of civilians in armed conflicts, the UN's High Commissioners for Human Rights and Humanitarian Affairs who have regularly pleaded for UN intervention.

There is no doubt that the Security Council's inability to act in the Syrian crisis-even to condemn the use of force against civilians by the Syrian government and the humanitarian crisis has been disappointing. In fact, in August 2012 the General Assembly, by a vote of 133 in favour with 12 opposed and 31 abstentions, deplored the Council's failure to respond to the crisis and condemned the "widespread and systematic gross violations of human rights" by the Syrian government and pro-government militias (Resolution 66/253B). Secretary-General Ban Ki-moon called the P-5 "incapable of taking collective action" and spoke of an "exponential rise in war crimes" as an impact. However one must understand that international military intervention has not generally been considered the appropriate, the right response, particularly prior to the Syrian government's chemical weapons attack that killed 1,400 civilians in August 2013. An important lesson is that many states remain wary of approving an outside intervention in an interstate conflict without that state's consent when the interests of several great powers oppose intervention. That could be a reason for a lack of UN response to any kind of intervention in Afghanistan after the US troop pull-out in 2021.

The debate about the future of R2P and humanitarian intervention will continue. Almost simultaneously with the intervention in Libya and the beginning of Syria's civil war, the Security Council authorized the UN Operation in cote d'Ivoire (UNOCI) to use "all necessary means" to protect civilians (Resolution 1975) and, in effect, help oust Laurent Gbagbo, who had refused to leave office after losing the presidential election in 2010. Both the AU and ECOWAS had recognized his opponent, Alassane Ouattara, as president-elect, there were warnings from the special advisers to the UNSG on genocide and R2P of the possibility of mass atrocities. UN and French forces turned the tide, blurring the line between POC and regime change and raising concerns about compromising the UN's impartiality in the situation. As in the Libyan case, however, in Syria regional IGOs played a major "gatekeeping" role in justifications of UN intervention.

Even if humanitarian intervention is to take place, there is still the need for early warning, preventive action, and peacebuilding once interventions have taken place, as the chaos that has engulfed Libya since the fall of Qaddafi is an ample example. In the future, however coalitions or partnerships involving the UN and regional IGOs, boosted perhaps by a coalition of powerful states, are likely to signify international humanitarian interventions. The UN-AU Hybrid Mission in Darfur (UNAMID) demonstrates the problems a "humanitarian" intervention can encounter, especially, if it lacks sufficient support from major powers, is faced with opposition from both government and rebel forces and lacks good visionary leadership. Given the problems in Darfur, Syria and elsewhere the future of R2P and humanitarian interventions in global conflicts is likely to continue to be marked by selective and *ad hoc* interventions.

In the 21st century failed states will continue to present the most serious threat to global security. For three decades, major international organizations, led by the United Nations, have attempted to address this threat through direct intervention and the promotion of democratic nation-building. The effort has extended from Namibia and Angola to Timor-Leste, Cambodia, Kosovo, Bosnia, Afghanistan, Somalia, Haiti, Rwanda, Liberia, South Sudan, and Libya, among other hot spots. In 2009, UN Secretary-General Ban Ki-moon spelt out this conception of democracy in his notable "Guidance Note on Democracy". Secretary Ban's framework accepted the internationally agreed "normative content" of the global democratization project as it had emerged in the post-Cold War era, and asserted that the world organization "advocated a concept of democracy that is holistic". Holistic democracy promotion has become the strategy not only of the UN but also of the European Union, the Organization for Economic Cooperation and Development, the Association of East Asian Nations, the African Union, other regional organizations, and regional development banks.

The "Responsibility to Protect" doctrine was ratified at the World Summit in 2005. By its logic, the principle reinforces the commitment to holistic democracy. It requires intervention in the domestic affairs of states not just to bar immediate threats to individuals' survival, but also on behalf of perceived legitimate ends: security, human rights, democracy, and development. The establishment of R2P, according to Secretary-General Ban Ki-moon, "affirmed the role of the international community in assisting States to protect their populations from these crimes, including by assisting those which are under stress, before crises and conflicts break out". In his view, peacekeeping and nation-building built on the global democratization movement are critical components of the humanitarian intervention principle. He cited as success stories Sierra Leone, Guinea, and Tunisia.

Humanitarian Crisis in Afghanistan

After the US forces withdrew from Afghanistan by 31 August 2021, Afghanistan was taken over by a Taliban ruled government. The US president feared that the longer US forces would stay, there would be a growing risk of an attack by a terrorist group known as ISIS-K, which is an ISIS affiliate in Afghanistan. China and Russia projected a united front on the Taliban's takeover in Afghanistan with the top leadership of the two countries pledging to enhance cooperation in handling the aftermath. In a call to Russian President Vladimir Putin, Chinese President Xi Jinping reiterated China's position of non-interference and respecting Afghanistan's sovereignty. The wave of brutality – the latest in 40 years of conflict in that country has forced more than half a million people from their homes so far. The crisis is taking the heaviest toll on women and children, who make up 80 per cent of Afghanistan's refugees and internally displaced people. Alongside homelessness and the threat of violence, they're facing drought, food scarcity, COVID-19 and a health system at breaking point. UNHCR, the UN Refugee Agency, is providing Afghans with emergency shelter, food, water, and healthcare, but their supplies are running dangerously low.

Within twenty-four hours of 11 September 2001, terrorist attacks on the United States, the UN Security Council had approved Resolution 1368, which, among other things, recognized the US right to self-defence under Article 51 of the UN Charter. The United States interpreted the resolution as providing an international legal basis for its military action against the Taliban regime and al-Qaeda camps in Afghanistan one month later, with the private approval of the Security Council. Following the December 2001 Boon Conference, which established the Afghan Interim Authority, Security Council Resolution 1386 authorized the British-led International Security Assistance Force (ISAF) with enforcement power under Chapter VII, to help the Afghan transitional authority maintain security.

In 2003, NATO took control of ISAF, with the United States continuing combat operations against al-Qaeda and the Taliban under Operation Enduring Freedom. NATO's

ISAF mandate envisioned the operation as limited to peacekeeping and peacebuilding, but the weakness of the Afghan government and the resurgence of the Taliban turned it into something more. Security Council Resolution 1776 (2007) mandated ISAF to disarm militias, reform the justice system, train a national police force and army, provide security for elections, and combat the narcotics industry. From 2006 onward, the distinction between US-led combat operations and NATO/ISAF actions blurred as the latter took on more offensive operations. At its height in 2008, ISAF had over 50,000 troops from forty countries, but NATO commanders faced significant difficulties persuading European members to contribute troops and not to impose restrictions on how those forces could be used.

NATO's enforcement action in Afghanistan was seen as a major test of its ability to operate outside Europe—a test of both military capabilities and political will. Like the United Nations, NATO was established to deal with traditional interstate security threats. Afghanistan, however, exemplifies the complexity of security governance challenges in the twenty-first century, when "extreme belief systems unstable and intolerant societies, strategic crime and the globalization of commodities and communications combine to create a multidimensional threat transcending geography, function and capability".

Cited Works

Ki-moon, Ban, *Guidance Note of the Secretary-General on Democracy,* New York: United Nations, 2009.

Weiss, Thomas G., *Humanitarian Intervention: Ideas in Action,* Malden, MA: Polity, 2007.

Weiss, Thomas G., *The Responsibility to Protect. E-International Relations*, 2011. Found at *http://www.e-ir.info/wp-content/uploads/R2P.pdf*

PART IV
DEVELOPMENT AND FUNCTIONAL COOPERATION

14

DEVELOPMENT COOPERATION IN THE UN SYSTEM

North-South Politics

The political struggle between the rich (North) and the poor (South) group of nations for the establishment of a more egalitarian world economic order plays a much more dominant role in the United Nations today than it did in the 1940s and 1950s, though it began to emerge almost from the beginning of the UN's existence. However, North-South politics in the UN has certain distinctive features which make it different from other political struggles in the world body. It is not a power struggle between any two nations (like the Cold War which was essentially between the two superpowers), but a bloc struggle between two major economic groups in the UN. It is not associated with strategic issues (like problems of peace and war) nor is it in the real sense a contest for supremacy between two ideological viewpoints since it is rather a difference of economic interests represented by two broad economic groups of nations—the rich and the poor. Strictly speaking, it is not a race for votes or converts, since all members *ipso facto* (from the very fact of their existing economic status at one point of time) belong to one camp or the other.

Some important results follow from the above premises. Since North-South politics is not a power struggle, it takes the form not of bitter personal antagonism between the major contestants, but confrontation between two opposing groups of nations for a radical redistribution of the world's resources. Since it is not a confrontation on strategic issues, it is less characterized with the fear and hysteria which, say, the cold-war politics evoked in its heyday. Moreover, since North-South issues reflect a divergence of economic interests rather than political ones, it cuts across traditional ideological divisions and arises mainly in the economic rather than in the political debates and institutions of the UN. Finally, since it is not a contest for votes, the strategies are also different. It is not a question of cajoling and canvassing to win support among nations but one of confrontation and negotiations between large organized groups that cut across the whole membership of the UN.

The first signs of "groupism" on an economic basis started crystallizing from the very inception of the UN, when about half its members were from developing countries, mainly from Latin America. It was largely at Latin American insistence that at San Francisco, the Economic and Social Council was given an equal role with the Security and Trusteeship Councils among the "Principal" organs of the UN. It was in response to their demands that in 1948 the Technical Assistance Programme was initiated. The Latin Americans were soon joined by other newly independent developing countries (e.g., India) in such efforts.

One of the first strategies adopted (since votes were difficult to muster) was the periodic mobilization of reports and resolutions. In 1950 an ECOSOC report on "National and International Measures for Full Employment" proposed an expansion of the activities of the World Bank and better commodity schemes. In 1951, another ECOSOC report on "Measures for the Economic Development of Underdeveloped Countries" proposed the establishment of "an international" development authority to assist underdeveloped countries in preparing, coordinating and implementing their programmes for economic development and to distribute to underdeveloped countries grants-in-aid for specific purposes. In 1952, ECOSOC was authorized to prepare a detailed plan for setting up a special fund for grants-in-aid and low-interest, long-term loans to underdeveloped countries. In 1953, a Committee of Nine produced a further report recommending the establishment of a Special UN Fund for Economic Development (SUNFED).

The rich, developed countries reacted with their counter-proposals. In 1953, the US proposed that development assistance should be linked to disarmament, that the savings accrued from a scheme of internationally supervised disarmament could be diverted to a fund for assistance to developing countries. The US, therefore, made it clear that large-scale assistance was not to be made available without disarmament. It also blamed the Soviet Union for refusing to accept international inspection for disarmament. The rich countries right from the beginning showed great reluctance to get down to a particular framework for the transfer of resources from the rich to the poor, saying they wanted to keep all their options open. And when ECOSOC finally voted in favour of a fund with only three (including the US and Britain) voting against it, the rich countries made it obvious that they were not yet ready to contribute to it.

Although SUNFED never came into existence, the continued pressures by the Third World eventually forced the West to put forth other alternatives. The result was the setting up of a Special Fund, (proposed by the US) to be financed entirely by voluntary contributions, and devoted to pre-investment surveys and training. The World Bank, which had previously been hostile to an independent fund on the lines proposed by ECOSOC, put forward ideas of its own for an International Development Association, which would be under its auspices (and therefore subject to the voting system used within the Bank). Thus, the sustained campaign by the developing countries did not achieve its original objective but it was at least successful in getting the developed world to agree to other compromise alternatives.

However, later events in the UN proved that the North could not be bulldozed into giving concessions beyond a point. The developing countries, not content with the Special Fund and the IDA, continued their efforts to establish a Capital Development Fund. As the entire developed world *en bloc* resisted the idea, they finally had to rest content with the establishment of a fund with only voluntary contributions. However, at subsequent pledging conferences for a Capital Development Fund only nominal sums were hesitantly offered. This has convinced the Third World that on economic issues, it is better to negotiate for an agreed solution, however, modest than to force through proposals to which the developed world is hostile. Without the voluntary cooperation of the rich, the poor are not likely to go very far in implementing proposals where the former are the major contributors.

Therefore, when UNCTAD (United Nations Conference on Trade and Development) was set up in 1964, negotiations and consensus were stressed for achieving progress in North-South dialogues. Several conciliation procedures have been used by UNCTAD to reach compromises on vexed economic negotiations. Informal meetings of the developed and the developing countries usually succeed in achieving agreement on a text where necessary. On issues where the North shows great reluctance to agree with the South, voting is delayed till an agreement is hammered out. It was only after protracted negotiations that agreements were reached on a system for generalized preferences for developing countries and some movement towards acceptance of the common fund idea was made at UNCTAD conferences.

Economic questions are the only ones, which have actively promoted bloc politics for a very long time. They are thus the ones on which regional groups consistently vote together. Though there are exceptions, such countries as the Scandinavian ones, the Netherlands, Ireland and France quite often have voted apart from other rich states. Similarly, among the developing countries, there are divergences between the less and the least developed ones. However, an identity of economic interests will remain the base for a fundamental political divide among nations for years to come till efforts by the developing world, for the establishment of a more egalitarian international economic order ultimately succeeds.

Economic Development and the UN

Most newly independent Third World nations since the end of World War II have shown two main priorities —nation-building and socioeconomic progress in the shortest possible time. But these nations embarking on the path of modernization lack the experience and knowledge needed to avoid costly mistakes and choose the most adequate model of development from a host of others. One of the greatest contributions of the UN has been to create opportunities for a meaningful dialogue between the developed and developing countries and among the developing countries themselves. The dialogue has been carried on for years now and has covered almost all possible aspects of development—objectives, strategies and evaluation of results. The principal forums for carrying on the dialogue have been the Economic and Social Council (ECOSOC), the General Assembly in regular and special sessions, the Second (Economic and Financial) Committee of the Assembly, the informal forum of UN headquarters, and innumerable conferences, committees, commissions and agencies of the UN system.

The dialogue has had an educative experience for both the North (developed) and the South (developing) countries. For the world at large, the dialogue has been equally enlightening since the deliberations have stressed the urgency of economic development, the causes and cures for poverty, and the responsibilities of the more fortunate to alleviate poverty through resource transfers from the developed to the developing world. The main divide between the developed and the developing world has been on the strategies of development, with the Western states advocating gradualist policies and the adoption by long-term strategies for development and the developing states demanding rapid progress through short-term measures and massive technical and capital transfers from the First World to the Third.

These debates have generated increased knowledge and understanding of the approaches and problems of development. But the search for shortcuts to development and new approaches based on ground realities continues while the attitude of the developing countries appears to be getting more aggressive towards the developed countries, which are forced to be on the defensive.

The Regional Commissions

Between 1947 and 1974, ECOSOC set up five regional commissions. They are Economic Commission for Europe (ECE), Economic Commission for Asia and the Far East (ESCAP), Economic Commission for Latin America (ECLA), Economic Commission for Africa (ECA), Economic Commission for Western Asia (ECWA).

The main objective of the commissions has been to provide research and planning facilities that can stimulate a spirit of self-help in meeting regional problems through increasing regional integration. Cooperation within each of the regions has been fostered by numerous conferences, regular exchanges of information, the development of personal and official contacts, and an atmosphere of unity created and fostered mainly by the work of each commission's secretariat. Each of the commissions sends annual and special reports to ECOSOC on the progress achieved within its area and makes recommendations to increase the pace of development.

The Development Decades

Four major campaigns to speed Third World development have taken the form of Development Decades for the 1960s, 1970s, 1980s and the 1990s. The First Development decade call was given in 1961 when the 16th General Assembly proclaimed the need to mobilize and sustain support for the measures required on the part of both developed and developing societies to accelerate progress towards self-sustaining growth of the economy of individual nations and their social advancement. The target set by the

Assembly was to raise the annual rate of growth in the developing countries to a minimum of 5 per cent. All UN member states were urged to pursue policies and adopt measures aimed at achieving this goal.

The first Development Decade suffered from a lack of proper planning and weak implementation of UN recommendations. The Second and Third Development Decades benefited from improved planning, but major development goals were not achieved. One major problem was the failure of many developing countries to carry out economic, political and social reforms. Another was the flow of development capital which had not been as targeted, hence leaving the developing countries in a fix. For each decade the goal of a transfer of 1 per cent of total GNP from each of the developed states to the developing states was established as the primary objective. Actual assistance fell from 0.51 per cent of GNP in 1960 to below 0.40 per cent in the 1970s and 1980s. Growing population growth further negated programme goals by diverting attention within the developing countries to increasing food production to avert famines.

In the Third Development Decade, the United Nations adopted a New International Development Strategy (NIDS) and established a Substantial New Programme of Action (SNPA) for the Least Developed Countries. NIDS aims at getting each developed country to transfer 0.7 per cent of its GNP each year to Third World development assistance. The global recession of the early 1980s added to the drying up of sources of capital, and inflation has reduced the buying power of aid funds.

SNPA requested that donor countries contribute an additional 0.15 per cent of GNP each year during the 1980s for the benefit of the poorest or least developed countries. It is also strongly recommended that the industrialized countries convert their public loans given to the poorest countries to outright grants. The UN General Assembly proclaimed 1991-2000, as the Fourth Development Decade and called for wide-ranging national and international measures for rapid development, especially in the least developed countries.

The new 10-year strategy, adopted after the Assembly admitted that the Third Development Decade had failed to attain most of its aims, made recommendations in many areas including external debt, development finance, international trade, commodities and agriculture.

To help speed up the economies of developing nations, the strategy urges the developed nations to at least reach, if not surpass, the targets fixed for official assistance (ODA), divert some of the funds released following disarmament to the needy countries and recycle part of the huge surpluses built up by some industrialized nations to the developing ones.

The strategy asks the developing countries to liberalize trade regimes, create trade opportunities, foster regional and sub-regional market arrangements among themselves and promote faster industrialization, particularly by implementing the global system of trade preferences, a multilateral trading system among themselves.

Emphasizing the need for industrial development, it calls for attaining a target of eight to ten per cent growth in industrialization.

This means it says, restoring the manufacturing sectors in many developing countries whose industries have stagnated in the eighties and making greater use of their underutilized capacities.

On the deteriorating debt situation of the developing countries, it says finding a solution is the responsibility of both debtor and creditor countries, of commercial banks and international financial institutions. It urges the creditor countries to review their tax policies, regulations and accounting practices to make it easier for debtor nations to reduce commercial debts and debt servicing obligations. Financial institutions should continue to support schemes for this purpose applying their guidelines with flexibility.

To supplement these efforts the General Assembly in 1967 established the UN Industrial Development Organization (UNIDO). Its main objective is "to promote the industrial development... and accelerate the industrialization of the developing countries, with particular emphasis on the manufacturing sector." UNIDO, however, has not received strong financial support from industrialized countries. It functioned as an autonomous organization within the United Nations till 1986, when it became a UN specialized agency. Its oft-proclaimed goal is to have the Third World account for 25 per cent of the world's industrial output by the year 2000 (it accounts for only 11 per cent now) with the active assistance of the industrialized countries. Unfortunately, this assistance has not been forthcoming.

Though the overall goals of these decades have not been achieved so far, the idea behind them has succeeded in stimulating new approaches and new programmes of development. Countrywide economic planning for development has been almost universally accepted and implemented, technical assistance programmes have been hastened and new research institutes and planning agencies have become functional in many parts of the world.

Most UN efforts to finance economic development have taken the form of loan programmes carried on by the World Bank group—the International Bank for Reconstruction and Development (IBRD), the International Finance Corporation (IFC), the International Development Association (IDA) and also indirectly, the International Monetary Fund (IMF). Although all of them are specialized agencies that function within the framework of the UN system, each is involved in its fund-raising operations. Developing states have not given up their attempts to establish an effective capital grants type of international organization, but they have really turned to the World Bank Group and the IMF for capital aid in the form of loans to supplement loans from national, regional and private sources.

Technical Assistance Programmes

Technical assistance, which involves the teaching of skills and new technologies, is a vital instrument of development programmes. It has occupied a sizeable portion of the energies and funds of the advanced countries and UN development programmes. In 1949 President Harry Truman urged Americans to adopt a bold new programme, for making the benefits of scientific advances and industrial progress available for the improvement and growth of underdeveloped areas. The Americans in 1949 offered the underdeveloped world a large-scale technical assistance programme, led the General Assembly to adopt an Expanded Programme of Technical Assistance (EPTA). It went beyond the then-existing meagre UN programme and was financed through voluntary contributions rather than through the regular budget. Nine years later, in October 1958, the Assembly complemented the EPTA by establishing a Special Fund to lay the groundwork for encouraging capital flows into developing states. In November 1965, the Assembly combined the EPTA and the Special Fund into a new UN Development Programme (UNDP) to secure a unified approach. The EPTA had incorporated three main forms of assistance:

(1) providing experts, including some from the underdeveloped countries themselves, to train cadres of technicians,
(2) awarding fellowships for technical training in advanced countries, and
(3) supplying limited amounts of equipment for training and demonstration purposes. Funds for the EPTA came from voluntary contributions offered at annual pledging conferences, a system continued by the Development Programme. Although the EPTA and the Special Fund were to be coordinated from the start, the latter functioned independently in allocating money and determining priorities. The amalgamation of the two in 1966 in the UN Development Programme (UNDP) held out some assurance that both programmes would thereafter operate under a single source of direction. The UNDP is the world's largest agency for technical cooperation currently supporting several thousand development projects.

The diversity of needs in the developing world has led to the inauguration of a variety of special UN projects, each devoted to a particular aspect of economic development, not covered by the general assistance programme. To fill the need for senior administrators in developing societies a new Operational Executive and Administrative (OPEX) personnel service was established in 1958 by the General Assembly. Another complementary personnel programme emerged in 1963 when the General Assembly established the UN Institute for Training and Research (UNITAR) in 1966. This body specializes in conducting seminars for new members of government delegations and their staffs and individuals in UN-related bureaucratic posts.

A World Food Programme was undertaken jointly in 1963 by the United Nations and the FAO to provide food for economic and social development projects and to supply food aid in emergencies. The World Bank has become active in the field of technical assistance through project preparation, development programming and training of senior development officials. The United Nations University in Tokyo carries on a fellowship programme that is linked with organizations in over 60 countries. Its objective is to supply scholars, scientists and government officials to help fill some of the knowledge gaps in the areas of poverty, famine and resource management.

There has been little criticism of the principle of technical assistance but there have been serious problems in practice. Duplication and overlapping of jurisdiction have plagued UN programmes, and between these and bilateral and regional programmes have sometimes aroused petty jealousies and conflicts. Efforts within the United Nations to coordinate programmes have been only partially effective, and future consolidations and partnership arrangements, such as those carried out by the EPTA and the Special Fund through the UN Development Programme resources, are needed to put to optimum use the limited resources and personnel that are available.

Most developing states prefer to receive multilateral aid through UN agencies which are usually given without strings attached. However, despite large-scale efforts by the UN, where on balance do the developing states stand today? Where do they stand in terms of economic development when the Fourth Development Decade started in 1991? What are the prospects for development in the coming decades? Although more has been done to promote world economic development during the last two decades than in all the past ages in history much more is needed and expected. Progress, defined as an improvement in mass standards of living, has failed to measure up to aspirations. Large pockets of poverty dot the globe where the basic necessities of life are not available to the poor. Agricultural production, while increasing substantially in many developing states, has been outstripped by population growth and millions remain undernourished. Africa continues to be plagued by recurrent famines. Housing remains a serious problem in developing countries where large sections of the poor are homeless. Despite extensive UN and national programmes, it will take years to wipe out illiteracy from this world. Unemployment and underemployment also pose serious problems in most countries of the Third World.

While it was once thought that gradual development of the poorer countries would lead to a narrowing of the gap between them and the more developed regions, the opposite has been the case. Average per capita incomes, in the industrialized nations are now about 50 times those of the least developed countries. The annual increase alone in per capita incomes in the richer nations (about $300) exceeds the total annual per capita incomes of scores of developing countries.

In 1971 the United Nations identified 24 countries as "least developed", based on their particularly low levels of per capita incomes and their highly fragile economies. Not one of them has since risen above this status. Rather, more and more have fallen into it. The remainder of the 1970s saw six more countries classified as least developed, and the 1980s another 12, bringing the total by the end of 2002 to 50.

The developing countries' persistent economic difficulties and the austerity measures adopted to deal with them have had severe social repercussions, bringing an erosion of the gains of previous decades. Throughout the developing world, the numbers of poor people are rising and reaching an estimated 2 billion people as stated in the Millennium Declaration.

There is still great diversity in approaches to development among the developed and developing countries. The industrialized West would like to see a greater measure of political and economic freedom, freer trade, reduced restrictions on investment opportunities, internal reforms, free exchange of currencies—these they feel would do much to hasten desirable economic changes in developing states. For the West more capital lending organizations are not necessary since they would tend to spread capital more unfairly, and ineffectively. But the main objective of the great majority of Third World states to obtain the full support of the developed states for a large-scale capital grants programme has not been realized. Although the developing states scored a voting victory in setting up the UN Capital Development Fund, the refusal of capital-surplus states to volunteer large contributions made it impossible for the Fund to serve its intended purpose. Without it, or some other similar programme, other UN development programmes have remained useful and desirable, but not central to development. This is the view of most of the leaders of the Third World. Future progress in the development and modernization of Third World societies will depend on a reconciliation of the interests and approaches of the developed and developing countries. It would be unrealistic to expect the leading capitalistic states of the world to promote industrial growth and lend capital to the public sector in Third World countries. Conversely, very poor countries cannot be expected to generate the savings needed for private investment on a large scale or to tamely allow the domination of their economies by huge multinational corporations. A major challenge for the United Nations is to try to reduce the levels of conflict between the two groups and to somehow get them to work together for mutual advantage.

The UN feels compelled to step up its direct involvement in resolving the world's most troublesome economic and financial issues for several reasons. One is its concern that these economic maladies may undermine global peace and political stability. As Secretary-General Javier Perez de Cuellar told the Economic and Social Council in early July 1989, "Gains made on the political level risk becoming illusory if we cannot respond to the aspirations for well-being of the big majority of the world's population".

Another reason is the evident weakening of the existing mechanisms for managing the world economy. The financial institutions and systems established in the wake of World War II have been unable to adequately or rapidly adapt to changing times. The decades since then have seen the emergence of a growing assertiveness on the part of the developing countries, the rise of new global economic and financial powers like Japan and Germany and a greater orientation to privatize and adopt market economies by the Soviet Union and other centrally planned economies of Eastern Europe and even China.

The issues facing the international economy have become more complex. The Third World debt alone is of such magnitude – and is so intertwined with other issues like trade and financial flows – that the approaches of the past are inadequate. No single country or group of countries can hope to find an effective and lasting solution. No isolated, case-by-case strategies have yet shown much promise of success.

The United Nations, because it is representative of all the regions of the world, is uniquely placed to approach economic and development issues from a broad perspective, one that takes into account the views of both the developed and the developing countries, including the poorest and the most vulnerable. Its aim should be to spur new methods of international cooperation that can promote economic stability and equitable development.

In 1980, industrialized countries pledged at the General Assembly to devote 0.7 per cent of their Gross National Product (GNP) for Official Development Assistance (ODA) to developing countries. But that target has been reached by only a few countries—currently Denmark, Finland, Norway, and Sweden. On average, ODA has remained at less than half of the targeted level, or about 0.3 per cent of industrialized countries' GNP, falling in real terms with the end of the Cold War. In 1999, ODA, at $56 billion, represented a mere 0.24 per cent of the GNP of the 21 main donor countries. The largest donor continued to be Japan, followed by the United States, France and Germany.

In the past, official development finance from northern governments represented the bulk of the financial resources going into developing countries. But in the last few years, private investment in developing countries has increased dramatically, and private investments and loans now far outweigh official flows. Of total net resource flows of $240 billion to developing countries in 1998, $147 billion was private flows, and only $88 billion was official flows including non-ODA funds.

The Right to Development and the Least Developed Countries

UNCTAD and UNDP were significant victories for states of the South but they did not produce immediate changes in the development policies of donor states. Developed nations often criticized UN development efforts for the New International Economic Order violated free trade principles, or seemed to be politicized by the overlapping confrontation between the capitalist West and the socialist bloc. In the view of major Western nations, any moral claim to resources from the industrialized North by the postcolonial world was presumption stating that economic development could best be achieved by full participation in the world trade system and the creation of free-market economies at home. Some Western European states also expressed concern that unfettered industrial development in the Third World could do irreversible damage to the environment.

In December 1986 the General Assembly declared development to be an inalienable human right by which each person and all peoples are entitled to participate in, contribute to and enjoy economic, social, cultural and political development in which all human rights and fundamental freedoms can be fully realized. Several world conferences subsequently reaffirmed the principle in their final documents. Among them, the most important were the Rio Declaration of the 1992 Earth Summit, the 1993 Vienna Declaration and Programme of Action at the World Conference on Human Rights, and the Declaration of the Third UN Conference on the Latest Developed Countries in 2001. The Right to Development has also been highlighted in the Millennium Declaration (2000), the 2002 Monterrey Consensus, the 2005 World Summit Outcome Document, and the 2007 Declaration on the Rights of Indigenous Peoples.

Declared principles require policy initiatives to make them meaningful. After four years of deliberation, the General Assembly, in June 1997, adopted the Agenda for Development. The idea for an agenda emerged in 1992 in response to Secretary-General Boutros Boutros-Ghali's elaboration of *An Agenda for Peace.* At that time, many nations in the global South worried that the international community was downgrading development concerns in favour of concentrating on the traditional issues of peace and security. Poorer nations believed in a continued need to assert the UN's primacy in the area of economic progress for less privileged peoples. Fearing that UN agencies had become marginalized by the Bretton Woods institutions, they saw the core thrust of the agenda as reaffirming the importance of development and reinventing the world organization's central role in that process. The agenda addressed the familiar components of development-such as economic growth, trade, finance, science and technology, poverty eradication, employment, and human resource development – but also placed new emphasis on the role of democracy, human rights, popular participation, good governance, and the empowerment of women.

Between 1980 and 2011, the United Nations convened four world conferences on the plight of least developed countries, acknowledging at each meeting that the many international efforts to lift impoverished countries out of the depths of privation had largely failed. Conference declarations noted that the world economy marginalized poor countries in fact, in many cases these countries' per capita incomes were decreasing, even in absolute terms. The growing international debt crisis of the 1980s aggravated their plight. Each conference called for new types of aid and for economic reforms in LDCs that would make these states more competitive in world trade and more efficient at home.

The first UN Conference on Latest Developed Countries (UNLDC-I) occurred in Paris in 1981. The conference adopted the "Substantial New Programme of Action" noted previously which emphasized the decentralization of LDCs' economies, political democratization, and financial transparency. The one hundred fifty governments attending the second world conference established as its basic principle "shared responsibility and strengthened partnership" between LDCs and all other groups-developed states, NGOs, other developing states, international financial institutions, and the private sector.

Although economic conditions did not improve noticeably in the least developed states during the 1990s (only one LDC – Botswana – "graduated" from the official list of forty-nine nations in this category), signs could be seen that the UN's attention had generated new international and domestic initiatives to solve their problems. Lending states evinced a new interest in debt relief, as evidenced by the World Bank's and IMF's creation of the Heavily Indebted Poor Country (HIPC) Initiative in 1996. HIPC efforts have been reinforced by additional funding and concessions from the major economic powers, known as the G-8. Assistance was given to more than two dozen states, with long-term commitments of more than $35 billion. In April 2002, the International Monetary Fund added another $2 billion to HIPC resources. In June 2005, the G-8 reached an agreement on a $40 billion write-off of debt owed by eighteen of the world's poorest countries and owed mostly to the International Monetary Fund, the World Bank, and the African Development Bank.

In addition to the World Bank Group institutions, the four UN regional development banks contribute financial support and expertise to economic development activities in the developing world. Along with the World Bank, sub-regional banks, and Multilateral Financial Institutions (MFIs), these banks make up a complex lending structure directed at development. They are the African Development Bank, created in 1964 the Asian Development Bank (1966) the Inter-American Development Bank (1959) and the newest of the four, the European Bank for Reconstruction and Development, established in 1991.

Despite the new sense of cooperation among the various actors in the development effort, between 1990 and 1998 the GDP in the least developed countries grew by only 3.2 per cent, compared with 3.4 per cent for the more fortunate developing countries. Much of the LDC growth by the turn of the century was explained by one state's progress-namely, Bangladesh. According to successive annual Human Development Report editions issued by UNDP, this growth rate was insufficient for LDCs to make any headway on ending crushing poverty and its attendant social problems. In this context, Secretary-General Kofi Annan opened the third UN Conference on Least Developed Countries on May 14, 2001, in Brussels. Charged with developing "measures for the sustainable development of the least developed countries and their progressive integration into the world economy", the conference set a goal of having rich countries provide development assistance equal to 0.15-0.20 per cent of their Gross National Income (GNI), the United Nations later endorsed this goal as part of the Millennium Development Goals.

This collection of recommendations reflected the merger of an evolving policy consensus on two fronts-economic development strategy and a global environmental policy that had been gestating for nearly thirty years. Secretary-General Annan highlighted the development strategy at the Millennium Summit. Noting that in the new century the United Nations must serve not only the states that are its members but the world's people as well, Annan called on the summit participants to end extreme poverty wherever it existed, calling such poverty "an affront to our common humanity". He laid out an ambitious set of Millennium Development Goals (MDGs) and targets to be achieved by 2015. These goals were updated to Sustainable Development Goals, to be adopted and implemented by 193 countries by the year 2030.

Cited Works

Ki-moon, Ban, *Guidance Note of the Secretary-General on Democracy,* New York: United Nations, 2009.

Bhagwati, Jagdish, *Economics and World Order—From the 1970s to the 1990s*, New York: Macmillan, 1972.

Brandt, Willy, *et. al.*, 'North-South: A Programme for Survival,' *The Report of the Independent Commission on International Development Issues*, London: Pan Books, 1980.

Collier, Paul, *The Bottom Billion: Why the Poorest Countries Are Failing and What Can Be Done about it*, New York: Oxford University Press, 2008.

Harrison, Paul, *The Third World Tomorrow,* Harmondsworth: Penguin, 1980.

Human Development Reports—2000-2020, UNDP Publications.

Kim, Samuel, *The Quest for a Just World Order,* Boulder, Colorado: Westview Press, 1984.

Lall, Sanjaya and Paul Streeten, *Foreign Investment, Transnationals and Developing Countries,* London: Macmillan, 1977.

Meier, Geral M., *Emerging from Poverty: The Economics that Really Matter,* New York: Oxford University Press, 1984.

Moore, John Allphin, Jr., and Jerry, Pubantz, *The New United Nations, International Organization in the Twenty-First Century*, New York and London, Routledge, 2017.

Nafziger, E. Wayne, *The Economics of Developing Countries,* Elmont, California: Wordsworth Publishing, 1984.

Nicholas, H.G., *North-South Programmes for Survival*, London: Pan Books, 1980.

Weiss, Thomas G. & Anthony Jenning, *More for the Least? Prospects for Poorest Countries in the Eighties,* Lexington, Mass: D.C. Heath, 1983.

15

ROLE OF THE SPECIALIZED AGENCIES

Although the United Nations is a part of the UN system which has many organs, specialized agencies, programmes, funds, financial institutions, councils, entities, etc. It coordinates its work with these separate UN system entities, which cooperate with the Organization to help it achieve its goals. The UN specialized agencies are autonomous international organizations working with the United Nations. All were brought into an association with the UN through negotiated agreements. Some existed before the First World War. Some were associated with the League of Nations. Others were created almost simultaneously with the UN. Others were created by the UN to meet emerging needs. According to the Article 55 of the Charter, it promotes:

(a) higher standards of living, full employment, and conditions of economic and social progress and development;

(b) solutions of international economic, social, health, and related problems, and international cultural and educational cooperation; and

(c) universal respect for, and observance of, human rights and fundamental freedoms for all without distinction as to race, sex, language, or religion. The UN Charter only makes passing reference to them under Articles 57, 58, 59, 62, 63, 64, 66, 70, 73, 91, and 96.

The specialized agencies can be broadly classified into three categories;

1. The first category consists of Specialized Agencies concerned with technical matters, viz. International Civil Aviation Organization (ICAO) was formed in 1944 with headquarters in Montreal, Canada.

The Convention on International Civil Aviation, drafted in 1944 by 54 nations, was established to promote cooperation and "create and preserve friendship and understanding among the nations and peoples of the world."

Generally, it is known as the 'Chicago Convention', permitted international transport by air, and led to the creation of the specialized agency better known as– the International Civil Aviation Organization (ICAO).

The World Meteorological Organization (WMO) is an intergovernmental organization with a membership of 193 Member States and Territories. It originated from the International Meteorological Organization (IMO), the roots of which were planted at the 1873 Vienna International Meteorological Congress. The World Meteorological Convention was signed on 11 October 1947 and came into force on 23 March 1950. In the interim, the work of the International Meteorological Committee continued – in particular by making sure the many resolutions and recommendations of the Washington meeting were implemented. The Committee also secured recognition for itself by the United Nations as the preparatory body for the new organization and accordingly took part in relevant UN activities. The last meeting of the IMO Conference of Directors was held in Paris in March 1951 and IMO formally became the World Meteorological Organization on 17 March 1951. Thus, WMO became the specialised agency in 1951 of the United Nations for meteorology (weather and climate), operational hydrology and related geophysical sciences a year later. The Secretariat, headquartered in Geneva, is headed by the Secretary-General. Its supreme body is the World Meteorological Congress.

The history of the successful modern postal system began with the efforts of Heinrich von Stephan, a senior postal official from the North German Confederation, who drew up a plan for an international postal union, and upon his recommendation, the Swiss Government convened an international conference in Berne on 15 September 1874 to promote the organization and improvement of world postal services in a spirit of international cooperation. Representatives from 22 nations attended the conference, and on 9 October – a day now celebrated as World Post Day – the Treaty of Bern established the General Postal Union, signed which came into force on 1 July 1875. This treaty succeeded in unifying a confusing international maze of postal services and regulations into a single postal territory for the reciprocal exchange of mail and removed the barriers and frontiers that hampered the free flow and growth of international mail. Membership in the Union grew so quickly that its name was changed to the Universal Postal Union in 1878. The organization became a United Nations specialized agency for postal services in 1948. The fundamental rules introduced by the 1874 Treaty of Berne were as follows:

- The UPU was created in Berne on 9 October 1874 in what is today the Empire-Saal at the restaurant Zum Äusseren Stand in downtown Berne.
- The UPU is one of the oldest international organizations in the world and the only United Nations specialized agency in the Swiss capital.
- The formation among all member countries of a single postal territory for the reciprocal exchange of letter-post items.
- It guaranteed freedom of transit within the territory of the Union;
- The standardization of the charges to be collected by each country for letter-post items addressed to any part of the Union's territory (a principle changed by the

1989 Washington Congress, which gave countries the option of increasing or reducing the basic charges. These charges are, therefore, now guideline charges);

- The abolition of the sharing of charges for letter-post items between the country of origin and the country of destination, each administration retaining the entire amount of the charges which it collects, subject to remuneration, at the established rates, of intermediate administrations ensuring the transit of such items. (Since the 1969 Tokyo Congress, which adopted the system of terminal dues, the UPU has allowed administrations of destination to demand a lump-sum remuneration from dispatching administrations as compensation for the amount of mail received in excess of the mail dispatched);
- The institution of an arbitration procedure to settle disputes between administrations;
- The creation of a central office, called the International Bureau, the cost of which is borne by all contracting countries;
- The periodical meetings of a Congress of plenipotentiaries of the member countries to revise the basic Acts of the Union and discuss questions of common interest.

Today, these rules appear in the UPU Constitution adopted in Vienna in 1964 and the Convention, adopted at successive Congresses up to the 26th Congress.

1. On 17 May 1865, the first International Telegraph Convention was signed in Paris by its twenty founding members, and the International Telegraph Union (the first incarnation of ITU) was established to supervise subsequent amendments to the agreement. That significant date – 17 May – eventually became World Telecommunication and Information Society Day. The International Telegraph Conference held in Vienna in 1868, decided the ITU established its headquarters at Berne, Switzerland. The new name International Telecommunication Union (ITU) was adopted at a conference in Madrid in 1932 and came into effect on 1 January 1934. In 1948, the headquarters of ITU was shifted from Berne to Geneva. On 15 November 1947, an agreement between ITU and the newly created United Nations recognized ITU as the specialized agency for telecommunications. The agreement formally entered into force on 1 January 1949.
2. The second category consists of organizations engaged in social and humanitarian activities, viz. International Labour Organization (ILO) was formed in 1919 with Geneva as its headquarters and in 1946, the ILO became a specialized agency of the newly formed United Nations; United Nations Educational, Scientific and Cultural Organization (UNESCO) was formed on 16 November 1945 with Paris as its headquarters and became an agency of the United Nations in 1946; the International Health Conference was held in New York City between 19 June and 22 July 1946, where the Constitution of the World Health Organization was adopted and signed on 22 July 1946 by representatives of 51 Members of the UN and 10 other nations,

but WHO's Constitution came into force on 7 April 1948, celebrated every year as World Health Day. WHO headquarters is in Geneva. The preamble and Article 69 of the Constitution of WHO provide that WHO should be a specialized agency of the UN.

3. The third category comprises a group of organizations designed to tackle international financial problems, especially those concerning economic development. It includes the International Bank for Reconstruction and Development (The World Bank) was founded in 1944 with Washington D.C. as its headquarters; International Development Association (IDA) formed in 1960; International Finance Corporation (IFC) formed in 1956 with its headquarters in Washington.

Before we undertake a detailed examination of some of the important Specialized Agencies, it should be noted that their membership is very large. Some of them, like the Universal Postal Union, have more members than the United Nations itself. These agencies normally work through a "Central Bureau". They also have an assembly composed of representatives of all the member states. In addition, they have a Secretariat which performs routine office and maintenance functions.

International Labour Organization

Rendering social justice to the working people of the world is the surest means for durable world peace. Realizing this, an International Labour Organization (ILO) was established on 11 April 1919 and was associated with the League of Nations. The organization was dedicated to the work of improving the living and working conditions of workers throughout the world. Although the first session of ILO was held in Washington in October 1919, the US did not become its member till 1934. During the period intervening in the two World Wars, ILO conducted thousands of studies and held hundreds of conferences. The chief achievements of ILO during this period were the adoption of Conventions for an eight-hour day and a forty-eight-hour week, holidays with pay, sickness and old-age insurance, freedom of association, forbidding night-work for women and their employment in mines, forbidding the employment of children under fifteen years of age, etc. In 1946, it became the first Specialized Agency of the United Nations.

The main organs through which ILO works are given below.

The International Labour Conference

Like most other international organizations, ILO has a General Conference to which four delegates are deputed by each member-state. These four delegates from each state include two representatives of the government, one of the workers and one of the employers. Except for the government representatives, the delegates vote as individuals. All conventions and recommendations are adopted by a two-thirds vote of the members. The chief function of the International Conference is to lay down the minimum international standards of working and living conditions. It is also responsible for the election of members of the governing body. The annual budget of the organization is also approved by the conference. Finally, it also examines reports received from member states regarding the implementation of conventions and recommendations adopted by the conference.

The Governing Body

The Governing Body is the executive organ of ILO. It consists of 56 members. It elects its own Chairman and Vice-Chairman for one year. The Governing Body normally holds three meetings in a year but special meetings can also be convened at the request of the members. The chief responsibility of the Governing Body consists of :

(a) selecting items for the agenda,

(b) appointment of the Director-General,

(c) supervising the work of the International Labour Office, and

(d) drafting budget proposals. It also determines general policy.

The International Labour Office

The International Labour Office is a combination of the Secretariat, a World Information Centre and a Publishing House. The Labour Office is headed by the Director-General, who is appointed by the Governing Body. The Office is staffed by experts drawn from different countries of the world. Although ILO has its permanent headquarters in Geneva, it has branch offices in certain other countries, including India. The chief responsibility of the International Labour Office is to prepare documents and bring out periodical publications. The office also constantly engages in research and studies on the problems connected with labour.

Objectives of ILO: The objectives of ILO have been stated in very clear terms in Article 2 of the Philadelphia Declaration thus:

"Believing that experience has fully demonstrated the truth of the statement in the constitution of the International Labour Organization that lasting peace can be established only if it is based on social justice, the conference affirms that:

1. All human beings, irrespective of race, creed or sex, have the right to pursue both their material well-being and their spiritual development in conditions of freedom and dignity, of economic security and equal opportunity.
2. The attainment of conditions in which this shall be possible must constitute the central aim of national and international policy.
3. All national and international policies and measures, in particular those of an economic and financial character, should be judged in this light and accepted only in so far as they may be held to promote and not hinder the achievement of this fundamental objective.

4. It is the responsibility of the International Labour Organization to examine and consider all international economic and financial policies and measures in the light of this fundamental objective.
5. In discharging the tasks entrusted to it the International Labour Organization, having considered all the relevant economic and financial factors, may include in its decisions and recommendations any provision that it considers appropriate.

The Working Methods of ILO: ILO uses three complementary methods to carry out its tasks: standard-setting, which has grown for half a century into a true International Labour Code; technical cooperation, notably in industrialising countries; and information, education and research in matters concerning labour.

The International Labour Code

From its start, ILO has set as a prime task the definition of minimum international standards for certain aspects of working conditions, social well-being and fundamental human rights. The introduction of new techniques in the industry, as well as the increasing number of newly independent countries, makes the setting of such standards more necessary than ever. The standard setting thus remains one of the essential tasks of the International Labour Conference. The conventions and recommendations, that the conference has so far adopted (e.g., 160 conventions and 170 recommendations up to 1985) make up the International Labour Code.

Conventions are juridical instruments similar to national treaties. Member states of ILO are obliged to submit them to their parliaments or other competent legislative authority. These authorities remain free, however, to decide whether or not the convention should be put into effect. A state which ratifies a convention pledges to make its provisions effective.

Although ILO cannot enforce acceptance of its standards, it can and does keep watch over the way conventions are applied in the countries which have ratified them. Governments make regular reports to ILO concerning, first, the submission of the newly adopted standards to their parliaments and, second, how the ratified conventions are put into effect. ILO may call upon governments to present reports indicating how their legislation and national practice meet the standards or, if they do not, setting forth the difficulties encountered in their application. Such reports are regularly requested for certain groups of standards, in particular those relating to human rights.

A committee of independent experts and a tripartite committee of the conference study these reports, while special procedures have been devised to examine complaints concerning alleged non-observance of ratified conventions or violations of trade union rights.

The conventions and recommendations of ILO bear upon a broad spectrum of subjects, ranging from hours of work to equal pay, from sickness insurance to the abolition of forced labour, from social security for migrant workers to trade union rights.

By the end of 1970, ILO conventions had received nearly 3,700 ratifications, but their effects are not limited to the countries which have ratified them. Even when a country has not ratified a convention, the standards set can still serve as a milestone on the road to social justice. The International Labour Code has exercised a significant influence on the evolution of labour legislation and social policy in the world. Moreover, the standards provide guidelines for the implementation of ILO's operational and educational activities.

The misery, ruin and insecurity which were the legacy of World War II made it obvious that social progress and economic development are interdependent. Even before the end of the hostilities, ILO affirmed in Philadelphia in 1944 that "poverty anywhere is a threat to prosperity everywhere". It recognized that better use of the world's productive resources was indispensable to attain the goal of social justice.

At first, ILO's technical assistance programmes were of limited importance because of a lack of financial resources, but great strides have been made during the last ten years, largely due to an increase in the sums allocated to it by the United Nations Development Programmes (UNDP). Between 1960 and 1970, UNDP entrusted ILO with carrying out more than 150 major projects throughout the world.

ILO's technical cooperation activities are carried out in such fields as organization of employment services, training and vocational rehabilitation, social security, productivity and management development co-operatives, handicrafts and small industries, labour administration and inspection, labour management relations, industrial safety and health, labour statistics, worker's education and rural development. Technical cooperation efforts are carried out principally by sending experts to work on field projects.

Technical cooperation programmes are guided by the principles and standards set by the International Labour Conference and specialized ILO committees. Conversely, the experience gained in the field is useful in guiding ILO's standard-setting work and educational and research activities.

Standard-setting and technical assistance both depend upon research and studies carried out by the International Labour Office. The Office is not only a centre of reference, information and research; it is also a laboratory of ideas.

One important part of this work is the preparation of reports for a variety of purposes.

ILO is also a publishing house, printing a large number of periodicals, texts of labour laws and regulations, studies, technical works and manuals in different languages. It is an information centre which answers thousands of inquiries each year.

ILO has also established two institutions of advanced training: the International Institute for Labour Studies in Geneva and the International Centre for Advanced and Vocational Training in Turin.

Therefore, the three main fields of ILO activity are the Development of human resources, which has the twofold objective of first improving the job capabilities of each individual by appropriate training and then making the best use of the manpower available in each particular country; development of social institutions, that is, establishment or strengthening of the administrative bodies, professional or cooperative organizations, and channels of participation and communication which are the framework of society, and improvement of living and working conditions among the population in general, as well as among particular job categories and sub-groupings of society.

ILO makes these three major programmes effective by its activities in standard-setting technical cooperation, research and dissemination of information.

Despite its technical and functional orientation, ILO has not been immune from the world of power politics outside it. In 1977, the United States withdrew from the organization accusing it of political bias. The United States saw the tripartite principle threatened by delegations from the Soviet bloc and some other states whose employer and labour representatives were, for practical purposes, government representatives under a different label. It was also unhappy at what is referred to as selective concern for human rights, especially as reflected in the actions of the International Labour Conference, which antagonized friends of the US and ignored violations in some other countries. Excessive politicization was also alleged, particularly in penalizing Israel for actions that had little to do with labour standards and in granting observer status to the Palestine Liberation Organization in 1975. The US however again returned to ILO in 1980 after extracting from it verbal guarantees that it would behave more "impartially" in the future.

UNESCO for Education, Science and Culture

The United Nations Educational, Scientific and Cultural Organization (UNESCO) came into existence on 4 November 1946. Its constitution, drafted earlier by the governments of the UK and France, was later adopted by 43 members of the UN. By an agreement of 14 December 1946, UNESCO was recognized as a Specialized Agency of the World Organization. The organization has 193 members.

The purpose of UNESCO has been eloquently expressed in the preamble to its constitution which reads: "The governments of the states, parties of this constitution, on behalf of their peoples declare that since wars begin in the minds of men, it is in the minds of men that the defences of peace must be constructed; that ignorance of each other's ways and lives has been a common cause, throughout the history of mankind, of that suspicion and mistrust between the peoples of the world through which their differences have all too often broken into war..."

Organization

The organization of UNESCO consists of three organs:

1. General Conference,

2. Executive Board, and
3. Secretariat.

The General Conference: The General Conference is the governing body of UNESCO and is composed of representatives from member states. Each member state can appoint not more than five delegates but has only one vote. The Conference meets every 2 years. However, an extraordinary session can be called by the Executive Board. The General Conference determines the main lines of the work of the organization. It can summon international conferences on education, the sciences and humanities and the dissemination of knowledge. The Conference also considers the annual reports submitted by the member states. The General Conference elects the members of the Executive Board, and with their consent appoints the Director-General of the Secretariat.

The Executive Board: The Executive Board consists of 58 members elected by the General Conference from amongst the delegates appointed by the member states. While electing the members of the Executive Board, the General Conference considers persons competent in the arts, the humanities, the sciences and education, who are qualified by their experience and capacity to fulfil the administrative and executive duties of the Board. Due consideration is also given to the geographical factors as well as the diversity of cultures. At any one time, not more than one member from any member-state can be represented on the Board. The members of the Executive Board are elected for a term of three years and are eligible for re-election.

The Executive Board is responsible for the execution of programmes adopted by the Conference. The Board recommends to the General Conference cases for the admission of new members. The reports of the Director-General are examined by the Executive Board before submission to the General Conference.

The Secretariat: The Secretariat consists of a Director-General and other staff as may be required. The Director-General is appointed by the General Conference on the recommendation of the Executive Board for six years. The other members of the staff are appointed by the Director-General following the regulations approved by the General Conference. The Director-General, or a deputy designated by him, participates in the meetings of the General Conference and the Executive Board but has no right to participate in voting.

Functions

As the very name of the organization suggests, it is concerned with a broad range of programmes and activities in the fields of education, science and culture. About the objectives of the organization Article 1 provides that it shall "contribute to peace and security by promoting collaboration among the nations through education, science and culture to further universal respect for justice, for the rule of law and for the human rights and fundamental freedoms which are affirmed by the peoples of the world, without distinction of race, sex, language or religion by the Charter of the United Nations". Thus the functions of UNESCO broadly fall into three categories: (i) education, (ii) natural sciences, and (iii) social and human sciences and culture. Let us examine the functions under each category below:

Educational Functions: Education is now recognized as a fundamental human right as well as an indispensable factor in social and economic development. At present, at least half of the world's population cannot read or write. UNESCO, therefore, attaches top priority to the imparting of education to children as well as adults. During World War II, thousands of schools, museums and libraries were destroyed, UNESCO planned worldwide campaigns to obtain voluntary assistance for the war-devastated countries in the form of educational materials, books, fellowships and study grants. UNESCO also made direct grants, though on a smaller scale, for books and periodicals, sound projectors and radio sets for schools, microfilm equipment and museum and laboratory supplies. Though these grants were very meagre, they stimulated voluntary contributions and action on a much larger scale.

UNESCO helps its members in the educational field by furnishing advice and expert assistance on matters like teacher training, school construction, school finance, preparation of curricula and textbooks and other teaching materials. To improve the status of teachers it collaborates with ILO. In addition, UNESCO has established Regional Research and Training Centres and an International Institute of Educational Planning in Paris.

Natural Science: UNESCO also helps its members to improve the teaching of basic sciences at all levels. The Source Book for Science Teaching was a major contribution of UNESCO in this regard. It also encourages basic research in fields like mathematics, physics, geology, hydrology, oceanography and seismology. An International Indian Ocean Expedition was arranged in which research vessels of more than 20 nations took part. Again, in 1965, scientists from all over the world were invited to participate in research on the problems relating to water resources.

UNESCO also makes efforts to apply science and technology to development. Through advisory missions, regional conferences and Special Fund projects, it helps to fulfil the needs of developing countries in training scientists and technologists and developing scientific and technological research.

UNESCO emphasizes the essential unity of all human knowledge and has devoted considerable attention to the social implications of technological change and the problems of racial tensions. Thus, for the last few years, it has been emphasizing the problem of human rights, and the economic and social consequences of disarmament.

UNESCO also attached great importance to the encouragement of original artistic creations as well as the preservation, and protection of mankind's cultural heritage. For this purpose, it has sponsored extensive cultural programmes in the arts, literature and philosophy. It helped to establish the International Theatre Institute. A project has been launched to promote translations of the most important works of literature from every country. A system of book coupons has been developed to enable countries with weak foreign exchange positions to procure books from other countries. In other words, UNESCO helps in solving the foreign exchange problem in the purchase of books by acting as a banker, exchanging the currency of one country for that of another.

UNESCO has helped in programmes of international exchange of knowledge. It collects and publishes information about the availability and conditions of fellowships and scholarships. It plays an active role in disseminating knowledge about the Universal Declaration of Human Rights through exhibitions and other methods.

Criticism against UNESCO has come from both the East and the West. It is stated that UNESCO is a Western organization trying to impose its ideas on the orient and does not take sufficient cognizance of the civilizations of the East. It is said to be "atheistic and anti-religious". The educational programmes of UNESCO are stated to be too radical with a distinct bias towards the teaching of science and international affairs.

UNESCO has also been criticized on the ground that it is run by government officials. Its Executive Board is not considered to be representative. It is said to be too centralized. There is also overlapping of its activities with other specialized agencies.

As regards UNESCO's projects, it is said that these are too vast and too ambitious. There are far too many conferences and seminars, many of which result in no action.

The original aim of UNESCO was to help create conditions favourable for world peace through the promotion of international understanding. The Cold War frustrated this ambition. Having come to realize the impossibility of its playing any significant or direct role in the establishment of peace, UNESCO redefined its task as "peace-building", which covers almost all constructive activities in the field of economic and social development. Although the idea of "peace-building" or "peace construction" was made explicit in the Preamble of the Constitution of UNESCO, it was given practical content for the first time in 1965.

Another aspect, of UNESCO's role as a "peace-building agency of the UN system" has been to study the problems posed by nuclear armament. UNESCO has shown a keen interest in promoting peace through disarmament from its very early years. It stood for peaceful uses of atomic energy. But it was precluded by the prevailing political climate and by its Constitution from taking an active interest in the political aspects of disarmament.

UNESCO has been aware of the close relationship between disarmament and development. Although it cannot take any direct interest in disarmament, the consequences of disarmament for development form "a legitimate sphere of its concern". In other words, UNESCO can entail a study of disarmament in its technical, if not political, sense.

The role of UNESCO in the promotion of development has been significant. But the lack of an effective policy seems to minimize the impact of UNESCO. The main reason for this seems to lie in the fact that much of the knowledge and information available in the field of economic and social change has yet to be exploited systematically.

Moreover, the East-West split and the cleavage between the "haves" and the have-nots" has become a constant refrain in most international meetings, limiting the usefulness of UNESCO. It should be pointed out here that social science programmes do not tend to elicit practical support from member-states. Further, although UNESCO has aroused a considerable amount of interest in the study of techniques for the promotion of international cooperation between different nations, it has not been successful in bridging the psychological divisions between the rich and the poor nations.

Following new developments in international relations, UNESCO has found it difficult to cope with the problems assigned to it. Nations, divided by ideology, separated by culture and distinguished by vast economic and technological differences, have added to the difficulties of UNESCO in implementing the objectives of its Constitution. Its resources are extremely scarce and invariably the programmes selected tend to reinforce the position of those countries which provide the maximum of its resources. The competing demands made on UNESCO can hardly satisfy any nation or group of nations.

The diversity of the objectives of UNESCO has often stretched its capacities to the limit. Its mandate is too broad. Education, science and culture can be constructed to embrace almost anything. UNESCO has undoubtedly promoted the production and exchange of information in its various fields of activity, and its technical assistance programme has added something to national resources for education and development. Critics have pointed out that its impact would have been greater if it had a narrower field of operation. Lastly, the governments of developed countries that pay most of the bills, including both the United States and the Soviet Union, have from time to time protested at the inflated budgets and bloated bureaucracy of UNESCO. In 1984, the US Congress report gave details of mismanagement in UNESCO's personnel programme and financial activities. From the mid-1970s the US repeatedly objected to the "politicization" of UNESCO—particularly as expressed in Arab-sponsored resolutions criticizing Israel for its educational policies in the West Bank and the attempted exclusion of Israel from participation in UNESCO. Still more objectionable to the West has been the Third World's demand for a New International Information Order, whose declared purpose is to redress the imbalance in the flow of world information alleged to result from the control of world news and information channels by the developed states. Correcting these distortions is considered essential to development, but the West, led by the US, views this as an attempt to legitimize government control over news leading to restrictions on the freedom of journalists and the media. In December 1984, America's dissatisfaction with UNESCO finally prompted it to withdraw from UNESCO. It was followed by the UK and Singapore in 1985. Since the US paid 25 per cent of UNESCO's regular budget and Britain nearly 5 per cent this has led to the severe curtailment of many programmes. However, the US rejoined the organization in October 2003 to again withdraw in 2019.

World Health Organization (WHO)

The World Health Organization (WHO) came into being on 7 April 1948, when 26 United Nations member-states had ratified its constitution. The date is observed annually as World Health Day.

The governing body of WHO is the World Health Assembly, on which all 194 member states are represented as the WHO team that works to improve everyone's ability to enjoy good health and well-being. It meets annually to review the organization's work and decide on policy, programme, and budget. The Executive Board has 34 members, who are technically qualified in the field of health, each designated by a Member State that has been elected to serve by the World Health Assembly; it acts as the executive arm of the Assembly. Member States are elected for three-year terms.

WHO's objective is the attainment by all people of the highest possible level of health. Since 1977, when the World Health Assembly set "Health for All by the Year 2000" as WHO's overriding priority, a global strategy has been worked out to reach this goal. The strategy, which requires the combined efforts of governments and people for its implementation, is based on the primary healthcare approach, involving eight essential elements: education concerning prevailing health problems; proper food supply and nutrition; safe water and sanitation; maternal and child health, including family planning; immunization against major infectious diseases; prevention and control of local diseases; appropriate treatment of common diseases and injuries; and provision of essential drugs.

WHO helps countries reinforce their health systems by building up infrastructures, particularly health manpower and including services for the individual, family and community, health institutions, systems for referring complex problems to more specialized services, and provision of essential drugs and other supplies and equipment.

WHO also promotes the research required to develop appropriate technologies relating to all aspects of health, including nutrition, maternal and child care, environmental safety, mental health, control of specific diseases, accident prevention, medical care and rehabilitation.

The provision of safe drinking water and adequate waste disposal for all were objectives of the International Drinking Water Supply and Sanitation Decade (1981-1990), in which WHO played a major role. The International Drinking Water Supply and Sanitation Decade, 1981-1990, was launched at a special session of the United Nations General Assembly on 10 November 1980. The idea of establishing the Decade was first discussed at Habitat: United Nations Conference on Human Settlements (Vancouver, 1976) and was endorsed by the United Nations Water Conference (Mar del Plata, Argentina, 1977).

WHO is leading a worldwide campaign to provide effective immunization for all children by 2000 to prevent the six major communicable diseases of childhood—diphtheria, measles, poliomyelitis, tetanus, tuberculosis and whooping cough. It is also active in international efforts to combat diarrhoeal diseases and killers of infants and young children.

Global research programmes administered by WHO include a special programme, in collaboration with the United Nations Development Programme (UNDP) and the World Bank, of research and training in tropical diseases (malaria, leprosy, schistosomiasis, filariasis, trypanosomiasis and leishmaniasis). Working in cooperation with the World Bank, the Food and Agriculture Organization, UNDP and several donor countries, WHO is engaged in a massive programme to combat onchocerciasis or river blindness, in western Africa. It also directs and coordinates a special programme and a global strategy to prevent and control AIDS (Acquired Immuno-Deficiency Syndrome), first identified in 1981, through public information and education about the modes of its transmission. However, lack of funds is a persistent problem for WHO. As pressures for expanding the functions of the organization have increased, the financial problem has become acute. Lack of funds has also given rise to serious policy-making difficulties. The available resources have to be spread among the multitude of objectives and functions and priorities have to be assigned to specific programmes and projects. The secretariat and policy-making organs have to spend much time finalizing programmes. It becomes difficult to reconcile the different viewpoints and demands.

WHO's constitution makes provisions for regional offices. This has led to several problems for the organization, such as the problem of coordination. These have tended to lead to duplication of efforts. With the increase in the number of new nations and the growing concern for development, new patterns of cooperation have emerged and WHO has been confronted with the problem of evolving a suitable approach. As a functional organization, WHO has profited all countries and has as its objective good health for everyone, everywhere. Accordingly, the types of programmes chosen require centralization. On the other hand, the goal of good health can also be attained through effective national health programmes, which involve cooperation with several agencies within a country. It also makes coordination and cooperation among various agencies necessary. Thus, there has been a split between supporters of the two approaches within WHO.

Furthermore, like other international organizations, WHO has not been completely free from politics. Since health problems affect everyone, the membership of the organization should be universal. But certain states have been excluded from or have refused to participate in it for political reasons. The establishment of a regional office in the Middle-East and a proposal to include the Arab states and Israel in the same region could not be executed.

Cited Works

Ayres, Robert L., *Banking on the Poor: The World Bank and World Poverty*, Princeton: Princeton University Press, 1983.

Bennet, Ale Ray, *International Organisations: Principles and Issues,* New Jersey: Englewood Cliffs, 1984.

Corrigan, Peter, *The World Health Organisation,* Hove: Wayland Publishers, 1979.

Cox, Robert (ed.), *International Organisation and World Politics: Studies in Economic and Social Agencies*, London: Macmillan, 1969.

Elmandjra, Mahdi, *The United Nations System: An Analysis*, London: Faber and Faber, 1973.

Gardner, Richard N. & Marx F. Millikan, (eds.) *The Global Partnership: International Agencies and Economic Development*, New York: Praeger, 1968.

Hass, E.B., *Beyond the Nation-State,* Stanford: Stanford University Press, California, 1964.

Hill, Martin, *The United Nations System: Coordinating its Economic and Social Work,* Cambridge: Cambridge University Press, 1978.

Horse, David A., *The Origin and Evolution of the ILO and its Role in the World Community*, Ithaca, N.Y.: Cornell University Press, 1969.

Jackson, Sir Robert, *Study of the Capacity of the United Nations System*, vol. 2, Geneva: UN, 1969.

Jacobson, Harold Karen, *Networks of Interdependence: International Organisations and the Global Political System*, New York: Knopf, 1979.

Luard, Evan, *International Agencies: The Emerging Framework of Interdependence*, London: Macmillan, 1977.

Moore, John Allphin, Jr., and Jerry, Pubantz, *The New United Nations, International Organization in the Twenty-First Century*, New York and London, Routledge, 2017.

Rothstein, Robert L., *Global Bargaining: UNCTAD and the Quest for a New International Economic Order*, Princeton: N.J. Princeton University Press, 1976.

Satyamurthy, T.V., *The Politics of International Corporation, Contrasting Conceptions of UNESCO*, Geneva: Librairie Droz, 1964.

Sewell, James P., *UNESCO and World Politics*, Princeton: Princeton University Press, 1975.

Spaull H., *The Agencies of the UN: A Survey of Economic and Social Achievements,* London: Ampersand, 1967.

http://apps.who.int/iris/bitstream/handle/10665/170492/EB89_24_eng.pdf?sequence=1

https://public.wmo.int/en/about-us/who-we-are/history-IMO

https://public.wmo.int/en/about-us/who-we-are/history-of-wmo

https://www.itu.int/en/history/documents/itu-history-overview.pdf

https://applications.icao.int/postalhistory/the_air_post_conferences.htm

https://www.icao.int/about-icao/history/pages/default.aspx

https://www.upu.int/en/News/2014/10/Universal-Postal-Union-marks-140-years-as-part-of-Berne-community

https://www.un.org/youthenvoy/2013/08/ilo-international-labour-organization/

http://www.dagdok.org/un-system/un-specialized-agencies/unesco/

https://documents1.worldbank.org/curated/en/729441468325246298/pdf/271450REVISED010WB0Revised01PUBLIC1.pdf

https://www.upu.int/UPU/media/upu/files/aboutUpu/acts/manualsInThreeVolumes/actInThreeVolumesConstitutionAndGeneralRegulationsEn.pdf

16

PROGRAMMES AND FUNDS

Economic and technological change, population trends, urbanization, and closer contacts among countries are some of the factors influencing profound social change and pushing social questions to the forefront of government concerns. In many developing countries, economic stagnation or decline has caused the ranks of the poor to swell, forced cutbacks in public services and aggravated social problems.

The United Nations has responded to these trends by giving greater prominence in its activities to social development. A range of programmes is carried out by the UN, particularly through its office in Vienna, which is the nucleus of UN social policy activities designed to help developing countries strengthen their national and local capacity for social analysis, policy planning and design, and project implementation.

Increasing priority is being given in the UN to programmes dealing with social implications of structural adjustment, human resource development, population activities, advancement of women, drug abuse control, crime prevention, application of science and technology to development, exploitation of new and renewable sources of energy and protection of the environment. This is shown by the Secretary-General's decision to concentrate on issues relating to social policy and development, in one office—the United Nations Office in Vienna. The UN helps governments investigate and make maximum use of natural resources, modernize and expand transport and communication facilities, meet their housing needs, and promote urban planning and rural development. The UN family is also helping developing countries to improve their national statistical, budgetary, and public administration services.

The United Nations has major programmes geared to target groups—children, youth, the elderly, the disabled, migrants, and refugees. It created a Research Institute for Social Development (UNRISD) in 1963 as an autonomous UN agency. The institute conducts research into problems and policies relating to the social aspects of development and economic change. UNRISD's work is guided by two underlying concerns: to improve the living standards of the world's poor, and to increase their participation in development. Its work is usually carried out in collaboration with national research institutions.

Current activities focus on food policy in a period of world recession; the social impact of economic crises; the social situation of refugees and returnees; measurement and analysis of social and economic development; economic reform and social participation; sustainable development and people's participation; ethnic conflicts; development and political violence.

The Institute, which is based in Geneva, is financed by voluntary contributions.

One of the commissions set up under ECOSOC, when the UN was founded, was the Commission on Narcotic Drugs. It eventually drafted and brought into force the 1961 Single Convention on Narcotic Drugs, which unified the previous separate instruments in this field and established a single system of drug inspection and control.

A few years later the UN established a Programme for Control of Drug Abuse which was financed by voluntary contributions. This grew to substantial proportions because of a large financial contribution made by the US, then becoming increasingly concerned about the problem of drug abuse among its population. A far more vigorous programme was undertaken to control of production and trade of drugs. Finally, in 1972 amendments to the 1961 Convention were introduced giving greater powers to the International Narcotic Control Board to limit the production and traffic of drugs.

The UN also established programmes to help the hundreds of thousands of refugees left stranded by World War II and subsequent events. At the end of the war there was founded an International Refugee Organization to assist these people in resettling themselves elsewhere (usually for political or other reasons they could not return to their own countries). It succeeded in the settlement of about a million refugees by persuading governments to receive them, and by providing them with temporary accommodation and transport. The office of the United Nations High Commissioner for Refugees (UNHCR) was created in 1950, during the aftermath of the Second World War, to help millions of Europeans who had fled or lost their homes. We had three years to complete our work and then disband. In 1961, International Refugee Organization was replaced by a High Commissioner for Refugees (UNHCR) based in Geneva, with a far smaller staff and a more limited budget. The administrative budget of the High Commissioner was provided by the UN itself but relief funds came from voluntary contributions by governments.

Another area in which the UN has become increasingly involved in the protection of the world environment. Some work in this field had been done for some time by some specialized agencies, for example, WHO, which for long has had an interest in atmospheric pollution, and IMCO, concerned with marine pollution. In 1968, at the initiative of Sweden, it was decided to hold a major UN conference on environmental protection. This took place in Stockholm in 1972 whose principal purpose was "to serve as a practical means to encourage, and to provide guidelines … to protect and improve the human environment and to remedy and prevent its impairment". It covered a wide range of subjects, including protection of certain wildlife species, preservation of archaeological treasures, conservation of the earth's resources, protection of arid areas such as the Sahara, and problems of humans to record the changes in the world's environment. Eventually, it was decided to establish a large-scale UN Environmental Programme (UNEP) to be voluntarily financed, but assured of $100 million over the first five years. This was to set up an Earth Watch Programme designed to monitor changes in the World's environment in all its aspects. It was to include a Global Environmental Monitoring System and an International Referral System for storing all relevant information concerning the state of the world's environment, and some specialized studies, for example, on soil erosion and desertification. There was also to be an international register for toxic chemicals. The programme was to assist developing countries in organizing their environmental work and seek to guide and coordinate national policies in this field. Its headquarters was established in Nairobi, where most of these programmes have now been launched though, sadly, some of the initial impacts now seem to have been lost.

This represents only a small sample of the activities of the UN in the social field. The UN has had a long-standing interest in housing matters, which have been discussed endlessly in a Committee on Housing, Building and Planning. There is also a permanent centre for the same purpose within the Secretariat.

The UN also takes an interest in the problems of women. The Commission on the Status of Women has prepared conventions relating to women's rights, for example, on the political rights of women and marriage. It has generally sought to secure more equal employment opportunities for women and to remedy some of the legal disabilities from which women suffer in many countries.

All these subjects and many others are discussed annually in the Third Committee of the General Assembly. The agenda is inevitably something of a hotchpotch of diverse matters, none of which can ever be treated in more than a superficial way. Discussion is dispersed in many organizations and committees and activity, too, is on a small scale. Nonetheless, it lends an international dimension to a type of discussion which is normally conducted only within a narrow national framework. At least social problems are now looked at sometimes from an international as well as a national perspective. So they seem sometimes to demand both international and national remedies.

The World Summit for Social Development (Copenhagen, 1995) was part of a series of global conferences convened by the United Nations, to enrich the international agenda and raise awareness of major issues, through the cooperation of member states and the participation, of other development actors. Some 117 heads of state and government, supported by delegates representing 186 countries, adopted the Copenhagen Declaration on Social Development and the Programme of Action.

Governments pledged to confront the profound social problems of the world by addressing three core issues common to all countries: the eradication of poverty, promotion of full employment, and promotion of social integration, particularly of the disadvantaged groups. The Summit signalled the emergence of a collective determination to treat social development as one of the highest priorities of national and international policies and to place the human/person at the centre of development.

Five years later, a special session of the General Assembly (Geneva, 2000) reaffirmed the centrality of more equitable, socially just and people-centred societies. It agreed on new initiatives, including creating a coordinated international strategy on employment, developing innovative sources of public and private funding for social development and poverty eradication programmes, and setting for the first time a global target for poverty reduction—halving the proportion of people living in extreme poverty by 2015. Globally, the number of people living in extreme poverty declined from 36 per cent in 1990 to 10 per cent in 2015.

Women

Women's groups and political parties the world over have approached the cause of women's rights in two ways. First, maintaining that civil and political rights apply to men and women equally. Secondly, securing the same access to the same opportunities as men and recognizing that economic, social and cultural rights as listed in the 1948 Universal Declaration of Human Rights must be granted to women fully and unconditionally.

The Declaration was adopted by the UN General Assembly in Paris on 10 December 1948 during its 183rd plenary meeting. Here we survey the work the UN has done for women's rights first by outlining some of the general principles emanating from the 1948 Universal Declaration of Human Rights and then briefly referring to the disadvantage of women in employment, education and suffrage. The function of the Commission on the Status of Women and its Covenant and Declaration are looked at in some detail. The achievements of three great International Women's Conferences are described, in the UN Decade for Women, which resulted from conference recommendations.

The objective of early UN legislative work was for women to seek their freedom from, among other things, arranged marriage, serfdom, prostitution, ineligibility in voting and professional entry, and unequal remuneration. Much more firmly the UN now requires member states to declare and pursue national policies promoting, for instance, equal access to education and equality of treatment in occupation and employment.

One in three of the world is female. Many of them are drudges working in general for two-thirds of human working hours. For this, they earn only 10 per cent of the world's income and they own 1 per cent of the world's property. Domestic work, heavy and lasting long hours, is usually regarded as a duty and is unpaid. Many women are in low-paid, part-time or temporary employment where job insecurity is marked.

Of the 800 million illiterates in the World, 500 million are women. In 1945, women were denied to vote in one in three of the UN's 51 member states. Today, they are eligible to vote in 150 of the 191 member states. Yet the percentage of women in policy-making positions at local, national and international levels is still remarkably small, and this is reflected in the balance of representation in the General Assembly and the Security Council.

On 11th June 1946, the Economic and Social Council established the Commission on the Status of Women. Meeting each year the Commission carries out a watchdog function observing the statutory rights enunciated by the rulings of the General Assembly, such as that in 1952 regarding women's entitlement to vote and hold public office on equal terms with men; On 20 February 1957 Convention safeguarding a wife's nationality on marriage, and the Declarations in 1962 and 1965 upholding the principle of free consent to marriage. In 1963, efforts to consolidate standards on women's rights led the UN General Assembly to request the Commission to draft a Declaration on the Elimination of Discrimination against Women, which the Assembly ultimately adopted in 1967. The legally binding Convention on the Elimination of All Forms of Discrimination against Women (CEDAW), also drafted by the Commission, followed in 1979. In 1999, the Optional Protocol to the Convention introduced the right of petitioning for women victims of discrimination. Many of the Conventions mentioned above were brought together in one Declaration on the Elimination of Discrimination against Women in 1975. Drafting work within the Commission was encouraged by the World Plan of Action for the Implementation of the Objectives of International Women's Year, adopted by the World Conference of International Women's Year, held in Mexico City in 1975, which called for a convention on the elimination of discrimination against women, with effective procedures for its implementation. After the Declaration was accepted by the General Assembly in 1976, the work began on drafting a single Convention that included what the Declaration said but was not limited to it. This was the Convention against All Forms of Discrimination against Women. The text of the Convention on the Elimination of All Forms of Discrimination against Women was prepared by working groups within the Commission in 1976 and extensive deliberations by a working group of the Third Committee of the General Assembly from 1977 to 1979. The General Assembly adopted it in 1979 and after its resolution 34/180, at the Copenhagen Conference on 17 July 1980, 64 States signed the Convention and two States submitted their instruments of ratification. It came into force on 3 September 1981, when the required number of states had ratified it. This brought to a climax the United Nations'efforts to comprehensively codify international legal standards for women.[1]

1. From: Progress Achieved in the Implementation of the Convention on the Elimination of All Forms of Discrimination against Women: *Report by the Committee on the Elimination of Discrimination against Women (A/CONF.177/7).*
   Published by the United Nations Department of Public Information C DPI/2044 C May 1999
   https://www.un.org/womenwatch/daw/cedaw/cedaw20/history.htm

The Convention requires signatories to submit reports on the measures they adopt to improve the status of women. Members of the General Assembly, earnestly framing a Resolution and seeing it embodied in a Convention such as this, are well aware that ratification permits 100 or so states to adopt and interpret that Convention in ways suited to their culture, and economic and social structures.

Each year the General Assembly hears the Commission on the Status of Women submit a progress report. With the clauses of the 1981 Convention in mind, the Assembly can then judge the advancement made in this direction and how much remains unrealized.

Another UN body, the Committee on the Elimination of Discrimination Against Women, complements the work of the Commission. Made up of 23 members (CEDAW), who are lawyers, experts on women's matters, teachers, and diplomats, sitting in their capacity, the Committee spends two weeks in New York each year at an investigative workshop sifting the reports governments are required to submit and interviewing their authors. These discussions help the Committee to appreciate what (and how) governments think, and they bring home to government ministers what the outside world thinks of them. This ongoing monitoring process attempts to bridge the gap between equality *de jure* and equality *de facto* by increasing awareness of women's legal rights.

The UN has taken a bold lead in advancing the cause of women's rights in the last 20 years. It was the General Assembly that voted for the 1975 International Women's Year. There would be three commanding aims, equality, development, and peace. Marking 100 years of struggle for women's liberation, the year was not seen as a global extension of a movement spearheaded merely by the world's richest states. All states, rich and poor, would campaign not simply for "equality" but prepare women for equal roles in partnership "freeing them to share both the tasks and the fulfillments that are the birthright of all humankind". The hub of activity was Mexico City in 1975 with the first international conference on women to be sponsored by the UN. Eight thousand women from 133 states and 113 NGOs were there. The presence of 1,200 journalists attested to its significance. Several days of intensive discussion saw two measures adopted: The Mexico Declaration on Equality of Women and Their Contribution to Development and Peace and a World Plan of Action for the implementation of the objectives agreed. Once more the agenda for action was moving from protection to promotion: equal educational access, a greater emphasis on literacy and civic education, coeducational training in industry and agriculture; in employment, less discrimination in conditions and terms for female workers and improved welfare services for women and their families, explicit recognition of the value of women's work in the home and other unpaid activities; and eligibility to vote and hold office and greater participation in policy-making.

This tremendous list of points in the World Plan of Action was endorsed by the General Assembly who then declared the years 1976-85 to be a UN Decade for Women. In brief, the objectives of the Decade were to "transform fundamental relationships within society to ensure a system which excludes the possibility of exploitation", a system with "set targets and priorities ... for equitable representation of women at all levels of policy and decision-making". Two practical steps followed. A Voluntary Fund for the Decade was instituted, to continue as a UN Development Fund for Women as part of the UN Development Programme (UNDP), in itself the world's largest multichannel programme for economic and social development, active in 150 countries. Also created was an International Research and Training Institute for the Advancement of Women (INSTRAW). Here research and training would be done in collaboration with UN Specialized Agencies, Governments and NGOs with the central idea of promoting the role of women as key agents of development.

Copenhagen was the venue for the second international meeting in 1980. There was disappointment with progress in emancipation at this halfway point in the Decade of Women. There was some dissent, too, over the universality of women's rights when representatives of certain Socialist states pinpointed women as a political vanguard, where 93 per cent of them in the workforce were "active builders of Communism". Yet delegates reported that in nations where ideology conferred egalitarian status it was the male intentions and attainments and prerogatives that were given priority. Apart from this, the main task of the conference was to decide how to channel into action the objectives of improved provision for education, employment, and health.

With the end of the UN Decade for Women in 1985, there had to be a major review exercise. The third international women's meeting took place in 1985 in Nairobi, where over 2,000 workshops discussed every topic of interest to women. As at all other international conferences organized for women by the UN, a great number of NGOs actively participated, representing women's and youth groups, trade unions, religious groups, political parties and community groups. Many radical views were expressed from Islamic fundamentalism to advance positions on women's liberation. An exhibition of tools and technology from many parts of the world demonstrated how women's lives could be improved at little cost and with some elementary skills.

A set of guidelines was adopted, termed Forward-looking Strategies for the Advancement of Women to the Year 2000. Taking up the movement in the UNESCO medium-term plans the aims as twofold: to enumerate obstacles still needing removal if the goals of the decade were to be overcome, and to concentrate on priorities. It was agreed that issues needing urgent attention were the inadequate remuneration of female labour and the position of women who were elderly, young destitute, rural, immigrants or refugees. Women should have a greater say in decision-making. Special attention was given to the problem of violence against women and general questions of women's vulnerability. These strategies were to be reappraised every five years.

The Nairobi Conference featured particularly a long and detailed look at the economic issues relating to women's emancipation. The case of Africa afforded a useful lesson. In that continent, between 60 and 90 per cent of all food production, processing and marketing were in the hands of women. Therefore, the crisis of food in Africa should be addressed through women and they should be involved up to the highest level. Mobilization of women in the fullest sense was related to three main areas of concern. Firstly, there was the capacity of women to participate in development. Significant factors here were literacy, care of children and facilities in the home. Secondly, there was an opportunity to participate, dependent to a large extent on what the local culture preferred, allowed or denied women. Thirdly, there was the will of women to participate, which depended on an increasing sense of their worth and dignity.

Physical and mental violence against women has preoccupied the 45 members of the Commission on the Status of Women. European recession has made women often the first victims. Armed conflict in Bosnia, Sri Lanka, South Africa, and Central America has caught them up in vicious turmoil. The UN Committee on the Elimination of Discrimination against Women in 1993 dispatched a team of medical experts to former Yugoslavia to investigate rape allegations and they reported strong evidence that Muslim women especially had been victims. Elsewhere, in such countries as Saudi Arabia, Kuwait, and Iraq, conflict is not alone responsible for the lack of esteem in which women are held.

The Commission currently has launched enquiries into four major areas: the education of women as to their legal rights; the structural causes of extreme poverty among women in affluent states; the concept of women-at-risk (social and cultural discrimination); and women's involvement in peacekeeping operations. Women at risk are now highly visible in the media. They are half of the world's 20 million refugees. They are deprived of normal family and community support. Widowed, evicted, abused, such gravely traumatized individuals may need special resettlement opportunities.

Meanwhile, women's lobbies from around the world, including India, had become vocal and agitated on this whole question of women and development. They had almost entirely rejected the welfare approach to women needing some supportive assistance only to those in distress or (moral) danger. Likewise, they were not fully satisfied with the women in development at various levels. Now they were thinking of altogether a complete shift in the paradigm of development which had, according to them, entirely ignored the gender perspectives so far. Women now believed that the very objectives of development, the strategies to achieve them and the programme content had to be revamped from a new gender perspective. That alone will make development meaningful for women and in turn make women a tremendous force to boost the entire process of development.

Recently, the World Bank has prepared a separate report on gender disparity in India with special reference to family planning, maternal health, nutrition, and education.

One of the significant developments in this context has recently taken place in India. By amending the Constitution, a third tier of the federal structure has been created in the form of panchayats (village councils) and local municipal bodies. At this level, a provision has been made in the law for reserving 30 per cent of the seats for women. It is believed that with this statutory instrument women will be empowered in decision-making on development at local levels.

The UNDP's Human Development Report, 1995, has done qualitatively innovative work in evolving a Gender Development Index (GDI) to supplement their earlier Human Development Index (HDI). They also devised a Gender Empowerment Measure (GEM) to assess the extent of decision-making powers given to women in various aspects of a nation's life.

The report has outlined a five-point far-reaching programme to achieve a breakthrough in the status of women. These five points are:

1. Setting a firm timetable, say, the next 10 years, to end legal discrimination against women and establish a framework for the promotion of legal equality, under the UN Convention on the Elimination of All Forms of Discrimination Against Women, 1979;
2. Taking concrete action to restructure social and institutional norms;
3. Initiating specific measures to move towards the 30 per cent threshold as a minimum share of decision-making positions held by women at the national level, to reach an ultimate target of 50 per cent;
4. Implementing key programmes for universal family education, improved reproductive health and more financial credit for women;
5. Mobilizing national and international efforts to target programmes that enable women to gain greater access to economic and political opportunities.

United Nations conferences, combined with the energy of national women's movements, have galvanized understanding, interest and action concerning the advancement of women around the world.

Three world conferences – Mexico City, 1975; Copenhagen, 1980; and Nairobi, 1985 – greatly enhanced international awareness of the concerns of women and created invaluable links between national women's movements and the international community.

At the Fourth World Conference on Women (Beijing, 1995), representatives of 189 governments adopted the Beijing Declaration and Platform for Action, aimed at removing obstacles to women's participation in all spheres of public and private life. The Platform identifies 12 critical areas of concern:

- The persistent and increasing burden of poverty on women;
- Unequal access to and inadequate educational opportunities;
- Inequalities in health status, and unequal access to and inadequate healthcare services;
- Violence against women;

- Effects of conflict on women;
- Inequality in women's participation in the definition of economic structures and policies and in the production process itself;
- Inequality in the sharing of power and decision-making;
- Insufficient mechanisms to promote the advancement of women;
- Lack of awareness of, and commitment to, internationally and nationally recognized women's human rights;
- Insufficient mobilization of mass media to promote women's contribution to society;
- Lack of adequate recognition and support for women's contribution to managing natural resources and safeguarding the environment;
- The girl child.

At the special session of the General Assembly in 2000 to follow up on the conference, countries pledged additional initiatives–such as strengthening legislation against all forms of domestic violence and enacting laws and policies to eradicate practices such as early and forced marriage and female genital mutilation. Targets were set to ensure free compulsory primary education for both girls and boys, and to improve women's health through wider access to healthcare and prevention programmes. Both MDGs and SDGs had specific targets for women's rights and welfare mandating all signatory states to implement them by 2030.

Children

Although UNICEF is not regarded as one of the specialized agencies of the UN, it is the one devoted exclusively to the needs of children and works in over 190 countries. Established right in the first session of the General Assembly in 1946, UNICEF has come a long way. From being regarded merely as a supply agency, distributing milk and vitamin tablets to war-affected children in postwar Europe and China, it is now like a global guardian of children everywhere.

Through its extensive network in developing countries linked with the counterpart national development agencies, UNICEF works with governments, non-government organizations (NGOs) and local communities. The programmes it now sponsors or supports range from sanitation, water, health, nutrition, education, and environment to 'women as mothers' and 'families as nurseries for children'. It emphasizes need-based programmes and has an extensive programme for the training of personnel needed for these various services.

More than the programmes, it assists with funds or with personnel, material, and equipment. It is one of the most powerful advocates of the rights of children. With that kind of record, it was not surprising that it should be awarded in the year 1995 the Nobel

Prize for its monumental work. UNICEF collects millions of dollars annually as voluntary contributions from public and member governments. For instance, in 1991 more than a quarter of its total income of over US $800 million came in the form of voluntary donations. With this, it supports programmes for children in 128 countries.

India has been a close collaborator with UNICEF both in the planning of its global programmes and implementation of its national counterpart in India. This is made possible by the constitution of the Executive Board of UNICEF on which member countries are represented and which approve the UNICEF-sponsored programmes annually. Very often, Indians have been elected as Chairmen of the Executive Board. At a momentous conference held in Lake Como in Italy in 1964, UNICEF turned fully and finally to the path of development strategy. At that conference, it was a member of the Indian Planning Commission (Prof. V.K.R.V. Rao) was elected Chairman. His presidential address gave a lead in changing over from an ameliorative agency to the one committed to planned development.

Over the years UNICEF has worked out its priorities scientifically. It tries to balance between those children who run a high risk for survival and those who have a high potential for development. It is concentrating on children in the age groups 0-6, regarded as foundational years, which make or mar the life of an individual. The best example of responsive cooperation between India and UNICEF is India's programme called "Integrated Child Development Scheme" (ICDS) which is the largest single programme for that age group.

The highlight of the UNICEF endeavour came in the year 1990 when it held the World Summit for Children at the UN Headquarters when more than 70 Heads of Government or State and representatives from 152 countries endorsed UNICEF policies. The Resulting Declaration and Plan of Action recommend the rights of the young as the "First Call" on nations' resources.

The World Summit for Children was a landmark event for the United Nations, the United Nations Children's Emergency Fund (UNICEF), and most importantly, for the world's children. It was the first time in history when a Summit-level meeting was held exclusively to address children's issues. Specific actions for child survival, protection and development were suggested by the World Declaration and Plan of Action, in the areas of :

- Child health
- Food and nutrition
- Role of women, maternal health and family planning
- Role of the family
- Basic education and literacy
- Children in especially difficult circumstances

- Protection of children during armed conflicts
- Children and the environment
- Alleviation of poverty and revitalization of economic growth

In addition, the Action Plan set specific goals for the decade that was to follow the Summit (the 1990s). The goals had been formulated before the Summit began, in consultation with Governments, UN agencies, including WHO, UNICEF, UNFPA, UNESCO, UNDP and the IBRD, and many NGOs.

The goals set were in the areas of child survival, development and protection, supporting sectoral goals such as women's health and education, nutrition, child health, water and sanitation, basic education, and children in difficult circumstances (the goal of which was to 'provide improved protection of children in especially difficult circumstances, and tackle the root causes leading to such situations'.

The Summit Plan of Action had set the following goals for the year 2000, taking the year 1990 as the base:

1. Reduction of infant mortality and under-five child mortality rates by one-third;
2. Reduction of maternal mortality rate by half;
3. Reduction by half of the rate of malnutrition among children under five;
4. Universal access to safe drinking water and sanitary means of excreta disposal;
5. Universal access to basic education and completion of primary education by at least 80 per cent of children of that age group. (UNICEF co-sponsored with UNESCO the World Conference on 'Education for All' in the year 1990 in Thailand).

As has been already noted, in cooperation with WHO, UNICEF has successfully assisted the universal immunization programme for children exceeding 90 per cent coverage in most places.

By far the most important single achievement of UNICEF is the adoption of the Convention on the Rights of the Child by the General Assembly in November 1989. This is the most comprehensive mandate on the status and the rights of children and the obligations of the state and society towards them. UNICEF also goes on the credit for mobilizing world opinion against discrimination against the girl-child in all forms.

Within three years of this adoption, as many as 120 member states had ratified or acceded to the Convention. They have to periodically report the progress made by them in honouring/applying the various regulations and clauses of the Convention in their respective countries. A committee on the Rights of the Child has been established under the Convention to monitor the progress made by member states.

It is worthy of mention here that the UNICEF style of functioning is somewhat different from other specialized agencies of the UN. That is why one can see in concrete terms the progress of the programmes made on various fronts. The main strategies behind UNICEF achievements are: breaking down aims into 'doable' propositions, securing public support, mobilization of new communication capacities, and deployment of UN/UNICEF expertise and course close monitoring of the programmes.

The good news since the 1990 Children's Summit is that

- A one-third cut in mortality among children under the age of five was achieved over the last ten years by 63 countries.
- Deaths of young children from diarrhoeal diseases were cut in half, saving as many as 1 million lives.
- There were 3,000,000 fewer child deaths per year at the end of the decade than at the beginning.
- There has been a 99 per cent reduction in the number of reported polio cases in the world.
- More children than ever before are now in school, one result being a rise in the adult literacy rate, from 75 per cent in 1990 to 79 per cent in 2000.
- An estimated 90,000,000 newborns are protected every year from iodine deficiency, the major cause of mental retardation.
- By 2050, 70 per cent of the world's adolescents will live in cities, more exposed to the marketing of unhealthy foods and more vulnerable to diet-related diseases than ever before.
- Moreover, thanks to the heightened awareness of child rights stirred by the Convention on the Rights of the Child, which has been almost universally ratified, egregious violations of children's rights are being more systematically exposed, and action is being taken to overcome them. NGOs and the mass media are also playing an increasingly active role in drawing public attention to the need for children to be protected. They now have a much higher profile on the national and global political agendas. The Security Council itself has taken up their issues particularly that of children affected by cough.

Impact of COVID-19 on Children

Children are the biggest victims of the COVID-19 pandemic as they risk their lives in profound ways. All the world's children are being affected, in particular by the socio-economic impact, and in some cases, by mitigation measures that may inadvertently do more harm than good. Moreover, the harmful effects of the pandemic are distributed unequally. They are most damaging for children in the poorest countries, in the poorest neighbourhoods, and those in already disadvantaged or vulnerable situations. UNICEF, thus, has estimated, the level, breadth, and severity of child poverty, based on shortcomings in six dimensions (all of which are rights constitutive of poverty). These dimensions are education, health, housing, nutrition, sanitation, and water.

Using severe thresholds of deprivation in each of these dimensions, about 45-50 per cent of children in developing countries suffer at least one severe deprivation. This number is about 75-80 per cent of children if "moderate" deprivations are used and are even higher if all dimensions are characterized by more stringent standards. Moreover, on average, children suffer 0.7 of deprivation at the severe threshold and 1.4 deprivations at the moderate threshold.

The ongoing crisis could increase the number of children living in monetary poor households by up to 117 million by the end of 2020, according to the latest analysis from UNICEF and Save the Children. Immediate loss of income often means families are less able to afford basics, including food and water, are less likely to access healthcare or education and are more at risk of violence, exploitation, and abuse.

The impact of COVID-19 (and the lockdown-type initiatives to control and contain it) in the short run, only the dimensions that are affected quickly are analyzed. The two dimensions that are affected most rapidly are education (due to the immediate effect of school closures) and health (due to the disruption of health services). Moreover, deprivation in these dimensions might change differently in the first year of a pandemic than in the subsequent years (e.g. at a different pace and even in the opposite direction).

Education

The changes in other dimensions that react more slowly for which the impact accumulates through time, school closures do not automatically translate into education deprivation. 188 countries have imposed countrywide school closures, affecting more than 1.6 billion children and youth. The potential losses in learning for today's young generation are hard to fathom. More than two-thirds of countries have introduced a national distance learning platform, but among low-income countries, the share is only 30 per cent. Before this crisis, almost one-third of the world's young people were already digitally excluded. For children to be able to participate in distance learning, they need to have access to these elements. Most countries use a combination of them (e.g. Radio and TV). If children have none of the ones used in their country, they are excluded from distance learning and could be counted as severely deprived of education as they live in overcrowded conditions, and they will not be able to benefit from the distance learning system very well. Thus, they can be said to be partially excluded and to fall under moderate deprivation in the education dimension.

If schools were closed, as was the case in the majority of countries for most of 2020. Thus, the procedure to assess education deprivation (severely or moderately, as explained above) is only applied when schools have been closed for more than 10 per cent of the academic year (otherwise, no additional children are projected to be deprived of education). For instance, if schools are expected to be open for 40 weeks, we have included, for modelling as deprived children, school systems that had closures of at least 4 weeks. Deprivation in education, given the information about school closures and re-opening, is expected to recover during the second year of the pandemic – at least partially. Thus, the projection model incorporates a recovery in education deprivation during 2021.

First-year (2020) Severely deprived: Children who were severely deprived before COVID-19 + children who did not access school for more than 10 per cent of the academic year in 2020 and who do not have access to technologies at home, which allowed them to participate in distance learning programmes.

Moderately deprived: Children who were moderately deprived before COVID19 + children who did not access school for more than 10 per cent of the academic year in 2020 and who could not participate properly in distance learning due to overcrowded conditions in the household.

[Data on school closures in 2020: UNESCO Data on available distance learning programmes: COVID-19 Global Education Recovery Tracker]

Second-year (2021) Severely deprived: Children who were severely deprived before COVID-19 + children who did not access school for more than 10 per cent of the academic year in 2021 and who do not have access to technologies at home, which allowed them to participate in distance learning programmes.

Moderately deprived: Children who were moderately deprived before COVID19 + children who did not access school for more than 10 per cent of the academic year in 2021 and who could not participate properly in distance learning due to overcrowded conditions in the household

[Data on school closures in 2021: UNESCO Data on available distance learning programmes: COVID-19 Global Education Recovery Tracker]

Health

Health services (whether they are immunization, preventive, or curative) have been disrupted to varying degrees in different countries. We have information on this from periodic country office reporting against an evolving questionnaire to assess the socio-economic impact of the pandemic as well as disruption of social services. For instance, if services declined by 10 per cent, the immunization rate (nationally) would also decline and the incidence of deprivation in health due to immunization would go up.

The effect of the pandemic is on children who are newly born or were still too young to be vaccinated before the onset of COVID, and who miss out on their vaccines due to the health services closure described above. Firstly, this requires establishing a ranking of children, from the least likely to the most likely to be vaccinated. The baseline is determined by the pre-COVID lack of immunization rates. Secondly, an additional group of children is added to them. This second group is made up of children who would likely have been vaccinated if pre-COVID rates had prevailed, but whose likelihood of being vaccinated is close to those with the lowest chances of being vaccinated. For instance, let us assume that 50 per cent of children were not vaccinated before COVID and immunization services declined by 10 per cent. Then, due to COVID, the percentage of unvaccinated children would become 55 per cent. They can be considered the "newly" deprived in health (i.e. who would have been vaccinated were it not for the disruption in health services due to COVID). A similar logic is applied for deprivation in Acute Respiratory Illness treatment and access to Reproductive Health Services. However, this means that the pool from which additional children can be found to fall into poverty is small as the former only applies to children 3-5 years old and the latter to children 15-17 years old. These groups represent a small fraction of all children.

As during 2021 many health services throughout the world started to revert to some degree of normalcy (at least avoiding operating at full capacity) the model captures the likelihood of a reduction in health deprivation. This is done by taking the 2019 situation as a baseline and repeating the process with the new data on health services disruption.

First-year (2020) Severely deprived: Children who were severely deprived before COVID-19 + children who are at highest risk of not receiving any vaccination/are not treated by any health service when affected by high fever and heavy coughing/do not have access to any contraception methods.

Moderately deprived: Children who were moderately deprived before COVID19 + children who are at highest risk of not receiving all four vaccinations/are not treated by a professional health service when affected by high fever and heavy coughing/do not have access to modern methods for contraception.

[Data on service disruption in health in 2020: UNICEF Socio-economic impact of the pandemic Second- year (2021)]

Second-year (2021) Severely deprived: Children who were severely deprived before COVID-19 + children who are at highest risk of not receiving any vaccination/ are not treated by any health service when affected by high fever and heavy coughing/ do not have access to any contraception methods. These indicators are used for children of different ages (e.g. immunization for infants and reproductive health for older adolescents)

Moderately deprived: Children who were moderately deprived before COVID19 + children who are at highest risk of not receiving all four vaccinations/are not treated by a professional health service when affected by high fever and heavy coughing/do not have access to modern methods for contraception.

[Data on service disruption in health in 2021: UNICEF Socio-economic impact of the pandemic]

While the available evidence indicates the direct impact of COVID-19 on child and adolescent mortality to be very limited, the indirect effects on child survival stemming from strained health systems, household income loss, and disruptions to care-seeking and preventative interventions like vaccination may be substantial and widespread.

Presently, more vulnerable children are becoming malnourished due to the deteriorating quality of their diets and the multiple shocks created by the pandemic and its containment measures. Efforts to mitigate the transmission of COVID-19 are disrupting food systems, upending health and nutrition services, devastating livelihoods, and threatening food security.

The COVID-19 crisis could lead to the first rise in child labour after 20 years of progress. Child labour decreased by 94 million since 2000, but that gain is now at risk. Among other impacts, COVID-19 could result in a rise in poverty, and therefore, an increase in child labour as households use every available means to survive. A one percentage point rise in poverty could lead to at least a 0.7 per cent increase in child labour in certain countries. Lockdowns and shelter in place measures come with a heightened risk of children witnessing or suffering violence and abuse.

Refugee Rights

The root causes of refugee displacement are invariably linked to conflict, persecution and the denial of human rights. Torture, political killings and forced displacements related to ethnic and other differences have become commonplace occurrences, resulting in over 23 million people of concern to UNHCR across the world, including over 13 million refugees, nearly 5 million Internally Displaced Persons (IDPs) (of a total of nearly 30 million), 3.3 million returnees and 1.3 million others. UNHCR provides international protection to refugees, ensuring respect for their basic human rights, particularly to see that no refugee is forcibly returned to a country or territory where he or she fears persecution or danger to life and liberty. Refugees, particularly women and children, are easy victims of human rights abuses.

One of the major challenges UNHCR faces today is a general trend by some States to veer away from a legal or rights-based approach to refugee protection.

Increasingly, refugees have to face closed borders or interdiction on the high seas. Even if granted asylum they could often face prejudice, rejection and hostility. Worse, their humanitarian plight often gets mired in issues of security and social tensions, and sometimes, plain politics. The 1951 Convention Relating to the Status of Refugees, the main international instrument for the protection of refugees, is a direct descendent of the UN Charter and the Universal Declaration in its first preambular paragraph. Article 33(1) of 1951 shall expel or return a refugee in any manner whatsoever to the frontiers of territories where his life or freedom would be threatened on account of his race, religion, nationality, membership of a particular social group or political opinion.

The principle of equality and no discrimination – whose violation creates refugees – forms the core of the human rights vision of the UN Charter, which states that human rights and fundamental freedom should be available to all human beings without discrimination. Article 14, Universal Declaration of Human Rights states, that everyone has the right to seek and enjoy other countries' asylum from persecution. A human rights approach to the protection of refugees is about the fundamental entitlement of all human beings to live in dignity. Refugee concerns, when conceived of as a claim of human rights, are elevated from the realm of State and international good faith to a level of legal entitlement requiring a specific national and international response.

Gross human rights violations against refugees may constitute persecution in the home country, as defined in the refugee definition. Their identification thus becomes important not only in the context of preventive measures in asylum countries but also in countries where refugee status determination takes place. Analyzing human rights violations of refugees, therefore, has a dual role to play in their protection. Recognizing such violations as persecution is of paramount importance when interviews of asylum-seekers are undertaken.

The detention of asylum-seekers is another concern of UNHCR in some developed countries. In several countries, detention is in prison-like environments. A UNHCR guideline has constantly urged that detention should be used only as a last resort measure. Family reunification is another area of concern. Respect for the family unit – recognized in the UDHR – may be violated when family reunification is not facilitated by States. During repatriation, when refugees return home, human rights programming and approaches are equally important. The reintegration of refugees into their home communities often has its own set of complications. During repatriation, UNHCR collaborates with other UN agencies such as WTP, UNICEF, UNDP and NGOs, providing a rights-based approach in its programmes.

Throughout 1999, the Office of the United Nations High Commissioner for Refugees (UNHCR) provided international protection and assistance to some 22 million people who had fled war or persecution. Of these, some 17 million were refugees and returnees, and some 4.6 million were Internally Displaced Persons. Internal conflicts have become the main cause of refugee crises.

UNHCR has been the lead humanitarian agency during the conflicts in the Balkans, which produced the largest refugee flows in Europe since the Second World War. It was the lead agency in addressing the massive exoduses out of Kosovo and East Timor in 1999. It has also been assisting refugees, displaced people and returnees in Africa's Great Lakes region and other parts of the continent, and southwest Asia.

Refugees are defined as those who have fled their countries because of a well-founded fear of persecution for reasons of their race, religion, nationality, political opinion or membership in a particular social group, and who cannot or do not want to return.

Internally Displaced Persons (IDPs) are people who have been forced to flee their homes to escape war, generalized violence, human rights violations or natural and man-made disasters, and who have not crossed an international border. Civil wars have created large groups of internally displaced all over the world. Today, there are an estimated 20 to 25 million internally displaced—more than the number of refugees.

The needs of Internally Displaced Persons are similar to those of refugees: they need immediate protection and assistance, as well as long-term solutions, such as return or resettlement.

UNHCR has been called to assist an estimated 4.6 million internally displaced in various regions. Increasingly – in the former Yugoslavia, East Timor, Colombia, and

Chechnya – UNHCR has decided to assist all uprooted people based on humanitarian needs, rather than refugee status. According to UNHCR, around 2.6 million Afghan refugees abroad (at the end of 2020) hadn't yet entered or completed asylum processes. Around 85 per cent of them can be found in Afghanistan's neighbouring countries, Iran and Pakistan while Germany comes third.

UNHCR's most important function is international protection—trying to ensure respect for refugees' basic human rights, including their ability to seek asylum, and ensure that no one is returned involuntarily to a country where he or she has reason to fear persecution. Other types of assistance include:

- Help during major emergencies involving the movement of large numbers of refugees;
- Regular programmes in such fields as education, health, and shelter;
- Assistance to promote the self-sufficiency of refugees and their integration into host countries;
- Voluntary repatriation;
- Resettlement in third countries for refugees who cannot return to their homes and who face protection problems in the country where they first sought asylum.

However, the sudden return of large numbers of people can quickly overwhelm fragile economic and social infrastructures. To ensure that returnees can rebuild their lives after they go back home, UNHCR works with a range of organizations to facilitate reintegration. This requires emergency assistance for those in need, development programmes for the areas that have been devastated and job-creation schemes.

The links between peace, stability, security, respect for human rights and sustainable development are increasingly seen as crucial in the search for durable solutions to the refugee problem.

UN Development Programme (UNDP)

In 1965 the General Assembly replaced the Special UN Fund for Economic Development and the Expanded Programme of Technical Assistance with a new organization – the UN Development Programme (UNDP). UNDP is an outcome of the First Development Decade and a subsidiary organ of the General Assembly, with Headquarters in New York. It is today the lead agency for all UN development activities. It maintains a network of national and regional offices in more than 170 countries and territories. About 90 per cent of UNDP's resources – derived primarily from voluntary contributions and amounting to the largest item in the UN budget – go to about sixty-five nations with nearly 90 per cent of the world's poorest people. More than 80 per cent of all UNDP staff serves in local offices in developing countries. Among its many publications, the annual Human Development Report is the most rated one. This report is a compilation of statistics based on comparative country data that provides human development-related information on specific countries as well as on world and regional trends.

Following the 1992 Earth Summit (the UN Conference on Environment and Development), UNDP took on expanded responsibilities for implementing many of the new UN initiatives directed at sustainable development. The conference's Agenda 21 called for UNDP to join with the UN Environment Programme, the World Bank, UNCTAD, the Global Environment Facility (GEF), the International Development Association (IDA), and regional development banks to carry out more than one thousand specific recommendations. In fulfilling its new tasks, related to Agenda 21, UNDP has come to play a coordinating role among these UN agencies, and particularly between recipient nations and the Bretton Woods financial institutions. It distributes most of the technical assistance resources provided by the UN System.

With its new responsibilities, UNDP expanded its mission statement in the early 1990s to encompass humanitarian assistance and social development. To attain the larger goal of sustainable human development, UNDP has focused on poverty eradication, democratic governance projects, information and communications technology, and energy and environmental disaster management to support elections in failed states. To move the development process forward as smoothly as possible, UNDP has sponsored a process that brings together governments that receive assistance from the donor community to address the priority items on the agency's agenda. UNDP actively associates with developing countries advancing the Sustainable Development Goals (SDGs) approved by world leaders in 2015. On 1 January 2016, the 17 Sustainable Development Goals (SDGs) of the 2030 Agenda for Sustainable Development — adopted by world leaders in September 2015 at a historic UN Summit — officially came into force. Over the next fifteen years, with these new Goals that universally apply to all, countries will mobilize efforts to end all forms of poverty, fight inequalities and tackle climate change, while ensuring that no one is left behind.

Seeking to promote these goals in all parts of its work, UNDP engages in, for example, with member states in any collaborative venture that likes women's empowerment for example.

It joined with UNIFEM and UNCTAD in July 2003 to create a special UN task force on "gender and trade", hoping to "sensitize" policymakers to issues of international trade that affect women's lives and their roles in the development process. The task force found that increased trade and investment in the labour-intensive sectors of developing countries expand work opportunities for women. It also warned that economic liberalization, particularly of a country's service sector, worsen inequities in women's access to basic resources and services. It called for global attention to the needs of women in the workplace and to the creation of employment conditions that ensure gender equality.

UNDP is also responsible for the UN Volunteers (UNV), the UN Capital Development Fund (UNCDF), which provides credit for the poor in LDCs and encourages sustainable uses of natural resources and the Drylands Development Centre (UNDP-DDC), which spearheads efforts to reverse the spread of desertification and drought. UNDP has formed partnerships with other UN programs and specialized agencies to address specific issues such as HIV/AIDS and environmental degradation.

UN and the Environment

In December 1972, the General Assembly created the UN Environment Programme (UNEP). Its expenses were to be paid through a voluntary fund, and its headquarters was located in Nairobi to ease concerns in the developing world that UNDP might represent Northern nations' desire to limit development policies. During its first decade, UNDP became an effective and visible actor in promoting environmental awareness and in attracting major contributions from the industrialized states to international awareness and attracting major contributions from the industrialized states to international environmental projects.

On several occasions, UN conferences and meetings have identified UNDP as the lead agency for international efforts to save the environment. However, unlike UNDP, which plays an equivalent role in the area of development, UNDP vies for leadership with other organizations and faces more limited funding in its endeavours to affect global environmental policy. Its success has been due in part to:

(a) the political talents of its successive directors-five during its first forty-five years of existence: Maurice Strong (Canada), Mostapha Tolba (Egypt), Elizabeth Dowdeswell (Canada), Klaus Topfer (Germany), and Achim Steiner (dual citizenship-Germany and Brazil)
(b) the organization's mobilization of scientists, civil society organizations, and environmental NGOs on behalf of particular environmental initiatives and
(c) the scientific expertise it has developed in several monitoring and information-sharing programs.

UNDP also serves as the secretariat for several of the international environmental conventions member states have signed since its inception, including both the Basel Convention on the Movement of Hazardous Wastes and the Montreal Protocol on substances that deplete the ozone in our atmosphere. This latter agreement grew out of the 1985 Vienna Convention for the Protection of the Ozone Layer, itself the culmination of four years of negotiation initiated by UNEP. In 1983, the General Assembly established the World Commission on Environment and Development (WCED), with Norwegian Prime Minister Gro Harlem Brundtland as the commission's chairperson. Secretary-General Javier Perez de Cuellar charged the commission with establishing "a global agenda for change".

The twenty-one-member commission and its panel of experts held hearings and interviewed thousands of individuals and groups during the two years. The commission's final report, titled Our Common Future, proved to be one of the UN's most widely read and influential publications. It concluded that further progress could be made only if the legitimate claims of both camps were recognized. Our Common Future encouraged the world community to develop legally binding rights and obligations for states that recognized the direct links between development and the environment. It introduced the concept of sustainable development, defined as "development that meets the needs of the present without compromising the ability of future generations to meet their own needs". Sustainable development became the popular mantra for all future UN efforts to address global environmental challenges, culminating nearly thirty years later in a set of eighteen UN-approved Sustainable Development Goals (SDGs). The United Nations created new agencies and reformed old ones to enshrine this concept as a central responsibility of national governments and international organizations.

The WCED called on the United Nations to convene another world conference, this one with the expressed purpose of drafting an international convention on the rights and duties of states in terms of sustainable development. The result was the UN Conference on Environment and Development (UNCED), also known as the Earth Summit, which convened in Rio de Janeiro in 1992. UNCED was the largest, most expensive, and most widely covered UN meeting at that time in history. One hundred seventy-eight national delegations and two-thirds of the world's heads of government attended. More than one hundred forty Non-Governmental Organizations, with UN blessing, staged a Global Forum in tandem with the conference that attracted thirty thousand participants.

UNCED produced three important international agreements-the Rio Declaration, the Agenda work of United Nations Framework Convention on Climate Change (UNFCCC) and the Convention on Biological Diversity (CBD). These documents attempted to balance the concerns of developed states for greater environmental protection-and their desire to avoid huge new financial responsibilities associated with the proposed global commitments-with the developing countries' desire to protect their sovereignty and pursue unrestrained national economic policies.

The Rio Declaration asserted twenty-seven "principles" that reflected the existing consensus on sustainable development. The first principle proclaimed, "human beings are at the centre of concerns for sustainable development", shifting the emphasis away from the prior (Stockholm's) emphasis on "nature" and environmental conservation. It elevated the right of development to equal status with environmental protection. It called on development states to increase aid to poor nations to support the latter's efforts to meet the goals of the declaration, which, as operationalized on August 21, were likely to impose huge new costs on involved governments. The declaration reasserted Stockholm's "Polluter Pays Principle" as well as Principle 21 of the Stockholm Declaration, which stated that governments, although free to develop their domestic resources as they wanted, were accountable for practices that injured the environment beyond their borders.

Agenda 21, an eight-hundred-page document, was filled with more than one thousand specific recommendations to achieve a "comprehensive plan for global action and all areas of sustainable development". It set international and national objectives and provided programmatic suggestions on how to fulfil the objectives. The areas designated for remedial progress included world trade, poverty eradication, population, cities, atmospheric pollution, deforestation, drought, desertification, marine resource management, waste management, agriculture, biodiversity, and the transfer of technology. Agenda 21 identified many UN agencies, including UNEP, UNDP, the World Bank and its Global Environment Facility (GEF), the regional development banks, and UNCTAD, as actors with central responsibility for making sustainable development a reality. It encouraged broad participation by NGOs, individuals, subnational jurisdictions, businesses, labour, and the intellectual community. While reasserting sovereignty as an element of sustainable development. Agenda 21 sought to democratize diplomacy and remove it from the sole purview of national governments.

UNCED also issued the Statement of Forest Principles. This document fell far short of the world convention on forests that developed states and NGOs sought. Developing states that profited from the export of lumber products (such as Brazil and Indonesia) resisted international restrictions on the use of forests. With no possibility of an agreement between developing and developed states, the statement simply called for the protection of forests but recognized the right of states to use their forests as they wanted. After the Earth Summit, international negotiations continued within UN-sponsored bodies, culminating in the creation of the UN Forum on Forests (UNFF) by ECOSOC in October 2000. The new forum became a "subsidiary body" of ECOSOC, convening yearly after that, regularly recommending steps governments could take to protect their forests. It planned its twelfth session for mid-2017, at which time it hoped to approve a strategic plan through 2030.

More than one hundred fifty nations and the European Union took the occasion of the Earth Summit to sign the UN Framework Convention on Climate Change (UNFCCC) and the Convention on Biological Diversity (CBD), which provided much of the perceived "success" of the Rio Conference.

The most lasting product of UNCED's work was the establishment of the Commission on Sustainable Development (CSD) as a functional body of the Economic and Social Council. With its membership of fifty-three states dominated by developing states, it was expected to pressure rich nations for the resources needed to cover extra costs in the Third World imposed by environmental-friendly development policies. Emphasizing the importance of the CSD, the General Assembly directed Non-Governmental Organizations, other UN bodies, and intergovernmental economic organizations, on both global and regional levels, to participate in the commission's work. NGOs could submit written reports and address the commission, as well as to conduct "consultations" with its members at the invitation of the chair or the UN Secretary-General. More than one thousand NGOs gained accreditation to CSD. In

1997, the Earth Summit +5 Special Session of the General Assembly directed CSD to begin work on identifying "indicators of sustainable development" that could be used to measure progress towards the goals established at Rio, which it thereafter completed.

Although the commission had the primary responsibility for ensuring sustainable development, all UN agencies after 1992 premised their activities on its attainment. The World Bank's Global Environment Facility, the WTO, and UNCTAD took on primary responsibility for enhancing financial and trade assistance to the Third World to help states reach self-sustaining development. As part of this effort, UNCTAD decided to make sustainable development the central theme of its third Conference on Least Developed Countries. At the national and subnational levels, UNDP and Habitat assisted with the capacity building and infrastructure necessary for a social and economic order that could maintain the principle. UNDP launched a sustainable development network (SDN) to foster dialogue among citizens and policymakers and to provide the latest technical information related to the topic. Even relatively independent agencies such as the World Health Organization (WHO) undertook its promotion. WHO underwent a structural reorganization to make "sustainable development and healthy environment" one of its primary "clusters" of activity after Gro Harlem Brundtland, the former chair of the World Commission on Environment and Development, took over as WHO's Director-General in July 1998.

The WHO experience demonstrated that by the turn of the century sustainable development had metamorphosed to solely a development and environmental construct. The UN had adapted it to other areas of concern. UNEP executive director Klaus Topfer expanded the concepts reached in July 2000 by asserting that "the most toxic element in the environment is poverty". He and other UN officials began talking about sustainable human development (SHD).

While sustainable development was enshrined at the 1992 Earth Summit as the overarching aspiration for all UN environmental activities and merged with all UN development efforts at the Millennium Summit in 2000, the Rio gathering additionally gave impetus to five areas of environmental policy that would then be pursued in UN and other IGO settings. They were as follows:

- The atmosphere and climate change
- Water pollution and marine resources
- Biodiversity and natural resources
- Deforestation and desertification
- International financing of environmental initiatives

Climate Change Refugees

As the climate changes, it is changing peoples' lives. Global warming is now impacting the ecosystem worldwide. With ecological collapse intensified by storms, droughts, wildfires, soil desertification, landslides and sea-level rise, people are being pushed to the brink, forced to leave their homes to seek shelter elsewhere. The World Economic Forum finds that between 2008 to 2016, extreme weather events forced over 20 million people each year to become climate refugees. The World Bank estimates that by 2050, 1.2 billion people could become environmental refugees – 143 million are predicted in sub-Saharan Africa, Latin America and South Asia. Over 40 million climate migrants are expected in South Asia alone.

- From 2008 to 2018, 253 million people were displaced by natural disasters – climate events now displace up to 10 times more people globally than wars;
- 3.3 million climate-related displacements occurred in South Asia in 2018 – India saw over 2.7 million people displaced by increasing storms and floods;
- 1.2 billion people could be displaced by climate events by 2050 – the most vulnerable countries include Mozambique, Zimbabwe, the Bahamas, Japan, Malawi and Afghanistan;
- Climate change is a major conflict multiplier – water access fuelled intense conflicts across 45 countries through 2017; and
- 1 billion children (nearly half the world's kids) live in one of 33 'extremely high-risk' countries, climate shocks impacting their education, healthcare, nutrition, water provision and safety.

I would describe climate migration today as a crisis that has an emergency element in some parts of the world and a long-term dimension that will only deepen. We need a legal definition that protects these people. At the moment, those seeking refuge in other countries are governed by the Refugee Convention of 1951. The standards for being recognized as a refugee were persecution over race, religion, nationality, social group or political opinion. This was mainly designed to help refugees fleeing their countries due to war or persecution. That criterion has been further broadened but it still doesn't include persons whose farms have disappeared in a drought or whose island faces a rising sea because of climate change. But, that said, there will still be people forced out of their homes due to the ecological crisis who will need legal protection.

Cited Works

Acker, S., J. Megarry, S. Nisbet, E. Hoyle, *World Year Book of Education: Women and Education*, London: Kogan Page, 1984.

Braidotti, R., E Charkiewicz, S. Hausler, S. Wieringa, *Women, the Environment and Sustainable Development: Towards a Theoretical Synthesis*, London: Zed Books (for INSTRAW), 1994.

Basic Facts about the United Nations, New York: UN Department of Public Information, published periodically.

Grant, J.P., *The State of the World's Children*, Oxford: Oxford University Press (for UNICEF), 1994.

Kumar, Satish (ed.), *The United Nations at 50: An Indian View*, New Delhi, UBSPD, 1995.

Luard, Evan, *The United Nations: How it Works and What it Does*, London: Macmillan, 1979.

Moore, John Allphin, Jr., and Jerry, Pubantz, *The New United Nations, International Organization in the Twenty-First Century*, New York and London, Routledge, 2017.

Sen, Samar, *United Nations and the Global Challenge*, New Delhi, Kanishka, 1996.

Sulivan, D. J., *In Brief: Human Rights at the UN*, New York: UN, 1990.

United Nations, *The World's Women: 1970-1990, Trends and Statistics*, New York: UN Department of International Economic and Social Affairs, 1991.

United Nations, *The Progress of Nations*, New York: UNICEF, 1994.

Whittaker David J., *United Nations in Action*, M.E. Sharpe, UCL Press Limited in 1995.

https://books.google.co.in/books

Relevant Web Sites:

UN Climate Change Conference 2015 *(www.documentcloud.org/documents/2646001-Final-COP21-draft.html)*

UN Development Programme (www.undp.org)

UN Environment Programme (www.unep.org)

UN Framework Convention on Climate Change (UNFCCC) and Kyoto Protocol *(www.unfccc.int/2860.php)*

https://www.unhcr.org/history-of-unhcr.html

https://www.unglobalcompact.org/what-is-gc/our-work/sustainable-development

https://www.un.org/en/conferences/children

https://data.unicef.org/resources/impact-of-covid-19-on-children-living-in-poverty/

https://www.un.org/en/conferences/children/newyork1990

https://www.un.org/womenwatch/daw/cedaw/committee.htm

https://www.ohchr.org/en/universal-declaration-of-human-rights

https://www.un.org/sustainabledevelopment/poverty/

https://legal.un.org/avl/ha/dunche/dunche.html

17

THE UNITED NATIONS AND HUMAN RIGHTS

From time immemorial the guarantee and protection of human rights were considered to be the exclusive concern of individual states. The concept of international protection of citizen's rights is a relatively new idea and until World War II such protection was limited to special groups – primarily diplomatic representatives and aliens – whose status had to be protected in foreign states. From time to time, states have also undertaken treaty obligations concerning their nationals, as seen in the various European treaties from the 16th century onwards, guaranteeing freedom of worship to religious minorities, or the 1890 treaty providing effective measures to end the slave trade.

In the 20th century, the victorious powers after World War I, wanted new states and the defeated countries of Eastern Europe to assume treaty guarantees of the linguistic, educational and other rights of ethnic minority groups incorporated within their territories. The League Covenant went a bit further in making the "well-being and development" of subject peoples in mandated territories [Article 22 (1)] a matter of international concern, and in committing members to "secure just treatment of the native inhabitants of all their dependent territories" [Article 23(b)]. Viewed against this backdrop, the UN Charter's emphasis on the promotion of human rights which was to a great extent a reaction to Nazi atrocities constitutes a sharp break with tradition. No less than seven references to human rights are found in the Charter—the Preamble, Article 1 (purposes and principles), Article 13 (responsibilities of the Assembly), Article 55 (objectives of economic and social cooperation), Article 62 (functions and powers of ECOSOC), Article 68 (a commission to promote human rights) Article 76 (objective of the Trusteeship system). The new approach did not take the form of specific legal obligations, but it did assert an international interest in the promotion of individual human rights.

The UN record in dealing with human rights must be assessed to the in-built limitations of international organizations to affect the conduct of states in this sensitive area. The difficulty is worsened by disagreement among states on the nature of the rights to be protected and on the priorities among them. Western democracies have emphasized political and civil rights, such as freedom of speech, religion and press and freedom from arbitrary arrest and imprisonment. Socialist and Third World states give priority to economic, social and cultural guarantees—the right to food, clothing, decent housing, humane working conditions and education. Some rights, for example, equal rights for women, may challenge old social customs and mores in various societies. Different societies have different values (democracy may be preferable to some, socialism to others), different priorities (the right to food may seem more important to poor states than the right to freedom of speech)—different resources and organizational capacities (some states lack the institutional and resource capacity to guarantee certain rights). For these reasons, states guard their sovereign authority to define individual rights and decide what protection shall be given. The UN's relevant activities over the years fall into four distinct categories: defining and clarifying the rights of individuals (standard setting); studying particular human rights, or human rights in particular places, and recommending measures for their fuller realization, (promotional activities); providing assistance directly to victims of human rights violations (the humanitarian function); and protecting violations in specific cases (the implementation aspect).

Standard Setting

Voluntary norms are commonly set by an international forum through the declaration of generally applicable rules of behaviour. The most celebrated such statement in the field of human rights is the Universal Declaration of Human Rights approved by the General Assembly on 10 December 1948, a statement of the individual rights which it was felt signatory states should see protected within their own countries. Its 30 articles encompass a broad range of civil, political, economic, social and cultural rights and reflect the different aspirations and values that had to be reconciled to secure wide agreement for its adoption. The political and civil rights of the old liberal school are joined with the economic and social ideals of the new socialist school while all are hedged with the right of the sovereign state to limit individual rights and freedoms as necessary to meet the just requirements of morality, public order and the general welfare in a democratic society. Although the practical application of some of the enumerated economic and social rights might require more state control than is consistent with some of the political rights, and others depend on the availability of adequate economic resources, the Declaration as a whole is admirable and appealing human rights document.

Other human rights declarations since approved by the Assembly include the Declaration of the Rights of the Child (1959 and later 1990), the Declaration on the Granting of Independence to Colonial Countries and Peoples (1960), the Declaration on the Elimination of All Forms of Racial Discrimination (1963), the Declaration on the Elimination of Discrimination against Women (1967), the Declaration on the Protection of All Persons from Being Subjected to Torture and other Cruel, Inhuman or Degrading Treatment or Punishment (1975), the Declaration on the Elimination of All Forms of Intolerance and Discrimination-Based on Religion or Belief (1981), and the Declaration on the Right of All Peoples to Peace (1984).

In addition to declarations which are formal statements of principles, the UN General Assembly every year adopts many resolutions dealing with some aspects of human rights. Many deals with economic and social conditions, but some are addressed to particular violations of civil and political rights. South Africa and Israel have been the most frequent targets in recent years, although Afghanistan, Chile, Kampuchea (Cambodia), El Salvador and other countries have also been nagged to observe better standards.

Many of the principles of the Universal Declaration have been incorporated into the laws of individual countries through embodiment in constitutions, statutes and judicial decisions. But increasingly, from the mid-1950s onwards, it began to be felt that it was not sufficient simply to draft conventions and declarations without making any effective attempts to give them a more concrete legal base. Since then, the UN has drafted multilateral treaties on a variety of subjects as well as prepared two comprehensive covenants—on civil and political rights, and economic, social and cultural rights. Drafting these was a long and laborious process, which took well over ten years, being undertaken mainly in sessions of the Third Committee of the Assembly. Finally, texts were arrived at which were acceptable to the majority of the participating states. The two general covenants were not approved by the Assembly until December 1966, and both became operative only after ten years (1976) when the requisite 35 ratifications were finally obtained.

As far as the states were concerned, they could ratify either or both conventions, without assuming any more of an onerous obligation than the provision of a periodic report to the Secretary-General "on the measures they have adopted which give effect to the rights recognized therein and on the progress made in the enjoyment of those rights". Parties ratifying the Civil and Political Covenant have the option under Article 41 of recognizing the jurisdiction of the Covenant's Human Rights Committee to hear complaints from other states that have also accepted this procedure. The Committee may hold hearings and promote friendly settlements. What it apparently cannot do is form independent judgements about the merits of complaints. That power is reserved for cases, if any, arising under the so-called "Optional Protocol" to the Civil and Political Covenant. States adhering to it recognize the Committee's authority to hear petitions from individual citizens alleging violations of their rights under the covenant. After considering the petitions the Committee can forward its views to the parties concerned.

Core Human Rights Treaties

There are nine core human rights treaties. They contain implementation mechanisms and create treaty monitoring bodies within states besides being marked by a:

- Reporting Procedure
- Inter-state complaints procedure
- Individual complaint procedure

The nine treaties are as follows:

1. ICCPR, I 1966 adopted on 23 March 1976 & II Optional Protocol to ICCPR, 1989. The United Nations' International Covenant on Civil and Political Rights (ICCPR), requires the States that ratify it to renounce the use of the death penalty definitively.
2. International Covenant on Economic, Social & Cultural Rights (ICESCR), 1966.
3. International CERD (Convention on the Elimination of All Forms of Racial Discrimination, 1969.
4. Convention on the Elimination of All Forms of Discrimination against Women (CEDAW), 1979.
5. Convention Against Torture (CAT) and Other Cruel, Inhuman or Degrading Treatment or Punishment, 1984.
6. Convention on the Rights of the Child (CRC), 1989.
7. International Convention on the Rights of Migrant Workers and their Family Members, 1990.
8. Convention on the Rights of Persons, with Disabilities, 2006
9. International Convention for the Protection of All Persons from Enforced Disappearance (ICPPED), 2010.

International Covenants on Human Rights

Following the adoption of the Universal Declaration of Human Rights, work began on the drafting of two International Covenants on Human Rights – one on economic, social and cultural rights and the other on civil and political rights – to put into binding legal form the rights proclaimed in the Declaration.

The International Covenant on Economic, Social and Cultural Rights, the International Covenant on Civil and Political Rights and the Optional Protocol to the latter Covenant were adopted unanimously by the General Assembly on December 16, 1966.

Although the Covenants are based on the Universal Declaration of Human Rights, the rights covered by them are not identical. The most important right regulated in both covenants, but not contained in the Declaration is the right of peoples to self-determination, including the right of peoples to freely dispose of their natural wealth and resources.

The International Covenant on Economic, Social and Cultural Rights entered into force on January 3, 1976. By 30 June 1989, 92 states had acceded to or ratified it.

The Covenant deals with conditions of work, trade unions, social security, protection of the family, standards of living and health, education and cultural life. It provides for the progressive realization of these rights without discrimination. States-parties to the Covenant submit periodic reports to the Economic and Social Council. The Committee on Economic, Social and Cultural Rights, an 18-member body of independent experts set up by the Council to assist it in implementing the Covenant, studies the reports and discusses them with representatives of the governments concerned. The Committee makes recommendations to the Council on helping states-parties to put the rights incorporated in the Covenant into effect.

The International Covenant on Civil and Political Rights and the Optional Protocol entered into force on March 23, 1976. By June 30, 1989, 87 states had acceded to or ratified the International Covenant and 45 states had acceded or ratified the Optional Protocol.

The Covenant deals with such rights as freedom of movement, equality before the law, the presumption of innocence, freedom of conscience and religion, freedom of opinion and expression, peaceful assembly, freedom of association, participation in public affairs and elections, and minority rights. It prohibits arbitrary deprivation of life; torture, cruel or degrading treatment or punishment; slavery and forced labour; arbitrary arrest or detention and arbitrary interference with privacy; war propaganda, and advocacy of racial or religious hatred that constitutes incitement to discrimination or violence.

The Covenant established an 18-member Human Rights Committee, which considers reports submitted by states parties on measures taken to implement the Covenant's provisions, and also considers communications alleging violations under the Optional Protocol.

The Optional Protocol to the International Covenant on Civil and Political Rights provides for the consideration of communications from individuals who claim to be victims of violations of any rights outlined in the Covenant. Only claims against state parties to the Protocol can be considered.

Promotion of Human Rights through UN Bodies

The General Assembly reigns, of course, at the top of the UN pyramid. It has plenary authority to create subsidiary bodies for any purpose enumerated in the Charter—a power which was used, for example, to establish the office of the UNHCR in 1951 and the successive committees on apartheid since 1962. The General Assembly is free to act either through the bodies created by it or directly, on any human rights issue that engages the concern of its members. Within the institutional framework created by the Charter, the Economic and Social Council (ECOSOC) serves, subject to the ultimate authority of the Assembly, as the principal organ of the UN concerned with human rights.

Articles 62-63 of the UN Charter authorize ECOSOC to make recommendations to promote "respect for, and observance of, human rights and fundamental freedom for all", to prepare draft conventions for submission to the General Assembly to call international conferences, to coordinate the activities of the specialized agencies, and to obtain reports both from them and from member states. "On the steps taken to give effect to its recommendations". ECOSOC is essentially a political body, whose 54 members are elected by the General Assembly on the basis of adequate geographical distribution. Equally political in its form, as in its functions, is the Commission on Human Rights established by ECOSOC in 1946 to serve as the UN's principal focus for human rights activists, of whatever kind it might be. The Commission has since grown to 43 state representatives, elected on the basis of an "adequate geographical basis". In the performance of its several functions, the Human Rights Commission has frequently employed working groups and special rapporteurs. As of January 1987, eight of the former were conducting studies on topics as diverse as human rights in South Africa, enforced or involuntary disappearance of individuals, the right to development and rights of the child. An additional flock of working groups and rapporteurs indirectly service the Human Rights Commission through its principal subsidiary, the Sub-commission on the Prevention of Discrimination and the Protection of Minorities.

The Commission on the Status of Women set up by ECOSOC in 1946 has also been quietly and persuasively performing its tasks. Its mandate was

(a) to prepare recommendations and reports to ECOSOC on promoting women's rights in the political, economic, civil, social and educational fields, and

(b) to make recommendations to the Council on urgent problems requiring immediate attention in the field of women's rights with the object of implementing the principle that men and women shall have equal rights and to develop proposals to give effect to such recommendations. Among its achievements is the Declaration on the Elimination of Discrimination against Women, adopted by the General Assembly in 1967, and the Associated Convention approved by the Assembly in 1979. Other important conventions prepared by the Commission and adopted by the Assembly are one on the Political Rights of Women, and another on the Nationality of Married Women.

Article 28 of the Covenant on Civil and Political Rights provides for the establishment of an 18-member Human Rights Committee composed of nationals of states, which are parties to the Covenant and are elected by the parties from a list of nominees presented by them to the Secretary-General. The Committee's role is limited so far as most states are concerned. It is to consider the reports, that the parties are required to submit concerning the measures they have taken to give effect to the rights enumerated in the Covenant. The same committee has the power to hear complaints between states that have expressed acceptance of the committee on the jurisdiction, in such cases under Article 41 of the Covenant. The Committee also hears complaints by individuals against states which are parties to the Optional Protocol: well over 200 such complaints have come before it.

The Human Rights Committee has been functioning since 1977 under the Civil and Political Covenant. The Committee has a legal basis independent of the UN Charter. However, the Covenant makes the Secretary-General an integral part, both of its election and its reporting procedures. The Committee is dependent on the UN for logistical support, so it is regarded as a body functioning within the general framework of the UN system.

Humanitarian Assistance

This is the UN activity, which has had perhaps the most tangible and far-ranging impact on human rights; yet it is the least controversial. The two most indisputably effective and important instruments of direct assistance have been the United Nations International Children's Emergency Fund (UNICEF) and the United Nations High Commissioner for Refugees (UNHCR). Both these organizations have concentrated their resources, to begin with, on enabling the most desperate and vulnerable sectors of Third World populations to survive in times of severe crises and threats to their very existence. Although UNHCR's original mandate contemplated a short-term protective mission for rather limited numbers of people pending negotiation of conditions for their safe return to the countries of their origin, the vast numbers displaced by the Civil War and persecution, and the often indefinite prolongation of exile, have required the High Commissioner and his staff to marshal resources for maintaining, and in some cases, integrating, the displaced populations into new lands.

Observers of the operations of UNICEF and UNHCR are impressed by their efficiency, energy and commitment to work. It is their achievements alone, which would support the claim that, with all its institutional constraints, the United Nations has managed to play an important role in the defence of human rights.

Protection of Human Rights

Any discussion of the protection of human rights must take account of the limitations in the international power structure within which the United Nations operates. States, not international agencies, are the primary guarantors of individual rights. Unlike states, the United Nations has no courts to hear the complaints of individuals. Even the International Court of Justice permits only states to be parties to contentious cases brought before it. If a violation occurs, the UN can take recourse to negotiation, censure, or, in extreme cases the levying of sanctions (as it has done in the case of South Africa for practising apartheid). Though the Charter authorizes the use of force as a means of vindicating individual rights, this measure has never been used. What the UN does in a generally inoffensive way is to supply information and technical assistance. It has for years conducted a small programme of seminars, fellowships and advisory services for countries requesting special help. It also circulates information about human rights through UN conferences and studies, reports and other publications.

From the mid-1950s, attention began again to be focused on the subject of implementation. At first, this was not a very vigorous drive. In 1956, ECOSOC asked all delegations to submit every three years reports describing the developments and progress achieved in their own country in the field of human rights. Most member states submitted such reports, though only some were highly informative. The rest were deliberately evasive. No specific action was taken on any of them. A small breakthrough was made with the conclusion in 1966 of the International Convention on the Elimination of all Forms of Racial Discrimination. In this case, it was provided that when the Convention came into force a committee should be established to supervise the fulfilment of the obligations it contained by the various ratifying states. Each state had to submit a report on what it had done in this field, and it was subsequently subjected to cross-examination. For the first time, therefore (for many years only in ILO has this been done), a procedure was established for testing whether commitments were being fulfilled.

Even this, however, does not represent any machinery for examining complaints, even of the grossest violations by countries, which have not ratified the two Human Rights Covenants, nor of violations in fields not specified in them. For this reason, it has long been felt that there is a need for some procedure by which the complaints of individuals (or groups) can be looked at and seriously examined. Such complaints had been sent to the Human Rights Commission since the inception of the UN. For years, nothing much was done about them. From around 1970, there were demands that these communications should be considered in all seriousness.

Despite stiff resistance by many nations, it was eventually agreed that the complaints should be looked at by a special working group, which would consider how far they revealed evidence of "a systematic pattern of gross violations" of human rights. This so-called 1503 procedure (named after the resolution by which it was established) came into effect from 1973 onwards. However, the procedure was long and cumbersome. Even if the working group received many complaints that were particularly well documented, it could not itself take action. It could merely submit a report to the Sub-commission. The Sub-commission sometimes itself decided to take no action. Even if it did, it could only send the complaints on to the Commission of Human Rights itself. The Commission in turn passed them to yet another working group. And even then, after further sifting, when left with the very worst cases of all, it decided for the first two or three years to take no action. Thus, the main body entrusted with securing the protection of human rights was practically paralyzed with inaction. The only occasions when detailed investigations of situations within individual states were taken up were in such cases as those of Chile and South Africa.

Thus, the main weakness of the UN's work in the field of human rights is that it rarely looks into concrete cases. If the "protection" aspect of the UN's work is to be made more effective than it is now, there is a need for much greater resolution among the bodies responsible for such work within the system. If they continue to turn a blind eye to specific examples of gross violations, there will cease to be any respect for the work the UN does in this field. Either the organization will need to be more determined in applying the existing 1503 procedure when the circumstances justify it, or new measures, such as the UN High Commissioner for Human Rights which has been finally set up. Since some of the most effective bodies acting in the human rights, field have been regional ones, such as the European and Latin American Commissions on Human Rights the UN should consider taking steps to promote the establishment of similar bodies in other regions of the world. Many non-governmental organizations have also actively supplemented and supported UN efforts. These include the International Commission of Jurists, the International Federation for Human Rights and the Amnesty International, established in London in 1961, widely respected for its persistent efforts in mobilizing public opinion and encouraging government action to vindicate fundamental human rights.

These are some of how the UN could play a more effective role in the field of human rights.

High Commissioner for Human Rights

The United Nations High Commissioner for Human Rights is the United Nations official with principal responsibility for United Nations human rights activities. Appointed for a four-year term, the High Commissioner is in-charge of many tasks, including promoting and protecting the effective enjoyment by all of all human rights; promoting international cooperation for human rights; stimulating and coordinating action on human rights in the United Nations system; assisting in developing new human rights standards; and promoting ratification of human rights treaties. The High Commissioner is also promoted to respond to serious violations of human rights and to undertake action to prevent violations.

The Office of the High Commissioner for Human Rights (OHCHR) is the focal point for United Nations human rights activities and serves as the secretariat for the Commission on Human Rights, the treaty bodies (expert committees monitoring treaty compliance) and other United Nations human rights organs. It also undertakes human rights field activities and provides advisory services and technical assistance. In addition to the regular budget, some of its activities are financed through voluntary or trust funds.

The High Commissioner has taken concrete steps to institutionalize cooperation and coordination with other United Nations bodies involved in human rights, such as the United Nations Children's Fund (UNICEF), the United Nations Educational, Scientific and Cultural Organization (UNESCO), the United Nations Development Programme (UNDP), the Office of the United Nations High Commissioner for Refugees (UNHCR) and the United Nations Volunteers. Similarly, the office works in the area of peace and security in close cooperation with the departments of the United Nations Secretariat. The Office is part of the Inter-agency Standing Committee, which oversees the international response to humanitarian emergencies.

The Programme of Technical Cooperation for Human Rights, supervised by the Office of the High Commissioner, manages some 200 projects annually in some 50 countries. They are carried out mainly in developing countries and countries in transition towards democracy, which request the office's expertise to establish national human rights structures. The Programme, with an annual budget of some $1.7 million, is financed by the United Nations' regular budget as well as by voluntary contributions, which have totalled more than $20 million since 1987.

The office helps governments to identify the different aspects of their human rights problems, and to define policies especially by formulating and enacting broad national plans of action. Such plans define national priorities in human rights protection and promotion, set objectives and frames of reference, and involve human rights actors from both national institutions and NGOs.

The office provides advice for enacting legislative reforms that affect the enjoyment of human rights, such as penal codes, prison regulations, judicial and legal practices, and freedom of expression and association. Detailed technical assistance is provided in incorporating international human rights standards in national laws and policies, and in establishing national institutions promoting human rights, democracy and the rule of law. Among them are the Ombudsmen, who deal with complaints from individuals, and the National Commission for Human Rights, which monitors the actions of the government and can help it to observe the human rights obligations under national accords for human rights protection.

Human Rights Council

The UN General Assembly inaugurated the Human Rights Council (HRC) on 15 March 2006, as part of the reform programme then underway at the United Nations. It replaced the much-maligned Commission on Human Rights, which had been heavily criticized for a membership that included states with some of the worst human rights records and for being a highly politicized body that overlooked some of the worst human rights violations while condemning Israel and Western countries for their policies. Developing nations always had a working majority in the General Assembly. They also insisted on a broad, regionally balanced membership.

The council has forty-seven members-not much smaller than the fifty-three-member Commission on Human Rights that it replaced. Membership is regionally balanced, but each candidate is voted on separately in a secret ballot and must receive the affirmative votes of an absolute majority of the General Assembly. Each country serving on the Human Rights Council is required to undergo a review of its human rights record by the council during its term of membership. Member states are limited to two consecutive terms on the new council and are elected to staggered three-year terms. In addition, the General Assembly can suspend the council members of any state that "commits gross and systematic violations of human rights", though this requires a two-thirds vote.

It works closely with the Office of the High Commissioner for Human Rights. An important power of the Human Rights Council is the ability to appoint experts to investigate human rights abuses generally and in particular countries. In April 2015, fifty-five such individuals were reporting on broad themes, such as violence against women and human trafficking, and on specific countries' abuses, including states such as Myanmar, Iran, and Somalia.

Cited Works

Forsythe, David P., *Human Rights and World Politics*, Lincoln: University of Nebraska Press, 1983.

Meron, Theodore, (ed.) *Human Rights in International Law*, 2 vols, Oxford: Clarendon Press, 1984.

Moskowitz, Moses, *International Concern with Human Rights*, Dobbs Ferry, N.Y.: Oceana, 1974.

Moore, John Allphin, Jr., and Jerry, Pubantz, *The New United Nations, International Organization in the Twenty-First Century*, New York and London, Routledge, 2017.

Robertson, Arthur H., *Human Rights in the World: An Introduction to the International Protection of Human Rights*, New York: St. Martins' Press, 1982.

The United Nations and Human Rights, UN Publications.

United Nations, *United Nations Action in the Field of Human Rights*, New York: Uni pub, 1985.

Van Bover, Theo, *People Matter: Views on International Human Rights Policy*, Amsterdam, Menlenhoff, 1982.

Vijapur, Abdulrahim P. and Savitri, Kadloor, "The International Covenants on Human Rights: An Overview", *India Quarterly,* vol. 62, no. 2, 2006, pp. 1-37.

https://history.state.gov/historicaldocuments/frus1919Parisv13/ch10subch1

18

SUSTAINABLE DEVELOPMENT GOALS

Millennium Declaration and the Need for Action

The Millennium Summit Declaration was adopted by acclamation following three days of unprecedented meetings which brought together the largest gathering of world leaders in history. One hundred Heads of State, 47 Heads of Government, three crown princes, two highest-ranking officials, five vice-presidents and three deputy prime ministers took part in the event, which drew some 8,000 delegates and 5,500 journalists.

The Declaration spells out values and principles, as well as goals in the key priority areas of peace, development, the environment, human rights, protecting the vulnerable, the special needs of Africa, and strengthening the UN. In addition, leaders called for specific follow-up, requesting the General Assembly to regularly review progress in implementing the Declaration and asking the Secretary-General to issue periodic reports as a basis for further action.

"We believe that the central challenge we face today is to ensure that globalization becomes a positive force for the entire world's people," the Declaration states in its opening section. "For a while, globalization offers great opportunities, at present, its benefits are very unevenly shared, while its costs are unevenly distributed."

The opening section also identifies six core values as "essential" to international relations, namely freedom, equality, solidarity, tolerance, respect for nature and shared responsibility. In addition, the leaders reaffirmed their commitment to the UN and expressed their determination to establish a just and lasting peace all over the world under the UN Charter.

The Declaration sets out several measures in the area of peace and disarmament, including providing the UN with the necessary resources for conflict prevention, peacekeeping and related tasks.

"We will spare no effort to free our fellow men, women and children from the abject and dehumanizing conditions of extreme poverty," the Declaration states in its longest section, on development. Leaders set out a specific timetable for reducing poverty (halving the number of people in extreme poverty by the year 2015), ensuring universal primary education for boys and girls (by three quarters by 2015), halting the spread of HIV/AIDS (by 2015) and improving the lives of at least 100 million slum dwellers (by 2020).

Other measures to achieve poverty eradication concern promoting gender equality, working with the private sector, and providing access to information technology. In addition, the Declaration commits the Member States to "an open, equitable, rule-based, predictable and non-discriminatory multilateral trading and financial system."

On the environment, the Declaration calls for such measures as ensuring the entry into force of the Kyoto Protocol, which contains binding targets for the reduction of greenhouse gases and pressing for full implementation of treaties on biodiversity and desertification.

"We will spare no effort to promote democracy and strengthen the rule of law, as well as respect for all internationally recognized human rights and fundamental freedoms," the Declaration states. It calls for specific measures to secure the rights of all people, with particular mention of women, minorities and migrant workers, among others. Leaders undertake to eliminate acts of racism and xenophobia – on the rise in many societies – and to ensure media freedom as well as the public's right to information.

The Declaration also outlines a series of specific measures for meeting the special needs of Africa, including debt cancellation, improved market access, enhanced Official Development Assistance, and increased flows of Foreign Direct Investment as well as transfers of technology.

On strengthening the UN, the leaders reaffirmed the central position of the General Assembly as the chief deliberative, policy-making and representative UN organ. They also resolved "to intensify our efforts to achieve a comprehensive reform of the Security Council."

In addition, leaders resolved to ensure that the UN is provided with timely and predictable resources to do its job. The Declaration also calls for giving the private sector, non-governmental organizations and civil society more opportunities to realize the UN's goals. The leaders concluded their Declaration by pledging their "unstinting support for these common objectives," and "determination to achieve them."

In the report—"Road Map towards the Implementation of the United Nations Millennium Declaration" published in 2001, the Secretary-General examines in detail how member states, United Nations bodies, international organizations and civil society are putting into practice the goals set out in the Millennium Declaration.

The "Road Map" published in September 2001 reviews progress, suggests paths to follow and presents "strategies for moving forward" for each goal of the Declaration.

The road map makes clear the scale of the challenge that lies ahead and focuses on implementation. "What is needed", the Secretary-General says, "is not more technical or feasibility studies:" rather, "States need to demonstrate the political will to carry out commitments already given and to implement strategies already worked out". Its eight sections range from maintaining international peace and security, through development and poverty eradication, to strengthening the United Nations systems. The heading, "Peace, security and disarmament", outlines measures to help promote human security. These steps include strengthening the rule of law and taking action against transnational crime by helping States ratify treaties and harmonize their domestic laws with international obligations. Specifically, States must take concerted action against international terrorism, putting into practice their commitment to prevent and combat terrorist acts.

Other proactive measures include widening the jurisdiction of the International Court of Justice and promoting the rapid entry into force of the Rome Statute of the International Criminal Court. Addressing the need to take action when the rule of law fails – for example by deploying peacekeeping operations and peace-building missions – the Secretary-General stresses replacing the culture of reaction to conflict with one of prevention. This, the Road Map argues, will require to completion of ongoing United Nations peacekeeping reforms and support for peace-building efforts on the ground.

A further area for progress and reform is the "targeting" of sanctions to make them more effective and to reduce their impact on civilians. Of overriding importance is the need to pursue disarmament in all areas, from weapons of mass destruction to the illicit small-arms trade.

The second section of the Road Map is entitled "Development and Poverty Eradication: the Millennium Development Goals", while an annexed section pinpoints, in concrete and specific terms, the indicators that will measure the implementation of the eight Millennium Development Goals (MDGs). It is crucial, the report says, that the MDGs become national goals and serve to increase the coherence and consistency of national policies and programmes.

The major focus of this section is on eliminating poverty and meeting the Millennium Summit target of halving the proportion of people subsisting on one dollar a day or less by the year 2015. Any effort to achieve sustainable development, says the Secretary-General, must include the search for solutions to hunger, malnutrition and disease. Noting that the international community should "continue to cooperate on many fronts" to achieve these goals, the road map stresses the need to combat HIV/AIDS through such campaigns as the Global AIDS and Health Fund. It stresses the importance of education, and particularly of girls' empowerment through education, in poverty eradication. Ongoing programmes in support of education, such as "school meals" and "take-home rations", can have an impact on all the challenges we face: lack of access to education, health problems and poverty, the Secretary-General says. The section also emphasizes that people-centred initiatives must be supplemented with sound national policies. It reiterates the need for wealthier nations to fulfil their commitments on trade access and debt sustainability, as well as on official development assistance, currently in steady decline.

In addition, the road map also notes that the newly established United Nations Information and Communication Technologies Task Force will take steps to begin bridging the digital divide.

"Protecting our common environment" describes the devastating impact on the earth of climate change, and the consequent need for vigilant conservation and stewardship. Among essential actions in this area, the road map recommends completing ratification of the Kyoto Protocol on curbing greenhouse gas emissions. It recommends enhancing cooperation on forest-related issues, implementing the conventions on biodiversity and desertification, pursuing initiatives towards environmentally sound water management and reducing the impact of natural disasters. Further recommendation centres on respect for the principles of human dignity as research on the human genome proceeds: benefits from its advances should be made available to all.

"Human rights, democracy and good governance" reaffirms the need to work collectively for more inclusive political processes, with genuine political participation. Recommended strategies include fostering national human rights institutions and supporting a "rights-based" approach to economic and social development. They also include the continuation of electoral assistance to help consolidate new and restored democracies as well as further ratification and implementation of the Convention on Elimination of Discrimination Against Women and protection of the rights of migrants and their families. Another major target is helping ensure the independence of the media.

The sixth section, "Protecting the Vulnerable" focuses on groups, particularly women and children, forced into situations of abuse because of complex humanitarian emergencies. It identifies practical measures to protect civilians, including prosecuting violations of international humanitarian law, gaining access to vulnerable population and separating civilians and armed elements in situations of forced displacement. Among "essential next steps", includes fostering a culture of protection through the use of international humanitarian law, protecting refugees and internally displaced persons, and disseminating international standards such as the Guiding Principles on Internal Displacement. It advocates support for efforts to implement the Convention on the Rights of the Child and its Optional Protocols, with special stress on halting the use of children as soldiers.

"Meeting the special needs of Africa" addresses the challenges posed to the continent by extreme poverty, devastating debt burdens, disease, conflict and "wavering international interest". Noting that Africa's share in trade, investment and technological advances has diminished further over the past decade, the road map emphasizes that African leadership has galvanized local and international support for a range of forward-looking initiatives. These include the New African Initiatives adopted earlier this year by African Heads of State, a blueprint for radical new approaches to economic issues on the continent. Other initiatives include strengthening democratic governance and further developing peacekeeping capacity, in cooperation with regional organizations. Also recommended are continued efforts to promote sustainable development by increasing official development assistance, enhancing private capital flows and building capacities for trade. A final target is an enhanced response to the Abuja Summit Declaration to combat HIV/AIDS.

The final section of the road map, "Strengthening the United Nations", argues that 'renewing the capacity of the Organization to provide a space for genuine dialogue and a catalyst for effective action calls for improved coordination among its principal organs and enhanced partnerships with other multilateral organizations and civil society". Specifically, there is a need to reaffirm the central position of the General Assembly, achieve a comprehensive reform of the Security Council and strengthen the role of the Economic and Social Council.

Key reforms in this area, says the Secretary-General, will involve ensuring the safety of the United Nations and associated personnel. He also notes the importance of the Organization receiving needed financial resources on a timely and predictable basis. Among other recommendations for strengthening the Organization, the road map stresses continuing to adopt the best internal management practices. It recommends building a stronger relationship among the United Nations, the Bretton Woods institutions and the World Trade Organization through the United Nations body established for that purpose—the Administrative Committee on Coordination. Other strategies include deepening the relationship with the Inter-Parliamentary Union and engaging the private sector, Non-Governmental Organizations and the rest of civil society through the United Nations Foundation for International Partnerships and the Global Compact.

The Millennium Development Goals Report 2015

In 2015, the date targeted for the attainment of the Millennium Development Goals (MDGs), the United Nations issued a report on the goals' progress (from data compiled by over 28 UN and international agencies). The Millennium Development Goals Report 2015 acknowledged that shortfalls remained in realizing all of the 2000 goals' particulars. However, the MDGs had, according to the report, "produced the most successful anti-poverty movement in history", and served as a stimulus for a new sustainable development agenda that was adopted later in 2015. Secretary-General Ban Ki-moon, referring to the report, said that "Following profound and consistent gains, we now know that extreme poverty can be eradicated within one more generation governments, business and civil society can work together to achieve transformational breakthroughs.

Especially, as the report noted, extreme poverty had declined by more than half, falling from 1.9 billion in 1990 to 836 million in 2015. More girls were in school, and women had gained considerable ground in parliamentary representation in nearly 90 per cent of the 174 countries with data. The rate of child deaths before the fifth birthday had declined by more than half, and the maternity mortality ratio had gone down 45 per cent worldwide, with most of the progress recorded since 2000. At the same time, targeted investments in combating diseases such as HIV/AIDS and malaria and in improving sanitation-meeting MDG aspirations-had brought unprecedented positive results. Still, the report pointed out, progress had been uneven, inequalities persisted in parts of the world, and civil conflict remained the chief impediment to more substantial progress. Approaching the UN's seventy-fifth anniversary MDGs were at the forefront of global practice and strategy.

Sustainable Development Goals (SDGs)

The Sustainable Development Goals (SDGs) are found in a General Assembly Resolution (A/RES/70/1 of 25 September 2015). The resolution is an intergovernmental agreement considered a successor to the Millennium Development Goals. There are seventeen SDGs, with one hundred sixty-nine targets encompassing a wide range of issues. The final document followed several preliminary meetings and was adopted at the UN Sustainable Development Summit in September 2015 in New York-transpiring with the annual opening session of the United Nations. The title of the SDG programme is Transforming Our World: The 2030 Agenda for Sustainable Development. The full list of goals, with explication, is contained in paragraph 54 of Resolution A/RES/70/1.

The origin of the SDGs dates to many of the UN conferences and initiatives the 1972 UN Environment Conference, the 1983 World Commission on Environment and Development, and the Rio Earth Summit on Environment and Development in 1992. Two decades later, and over decades following the Millennium Summit, came the resolution known as "The Future We Want". Therein, member states agreed (in 2012) on certain key themes, including poverty eradication, upgrading energy, water and sanitation, and achieving progress in human settlement. Three years later, the world community was ready to commit to a broad set of goals, representing an extension beyond the Millennium Development Goals (2000-2015).

The Sustainable Development Goals are to be achieved by 2030

1. **Poverty:** end poverty in all its forms everywhere.
2. **Food:** end hunger, achieve food security, improve nutrition, and promote sustainable agriculture.

3. **Health:** cultivate healthy lives and nurture well-being for people of all ages.
4. **Education:** guarantee equitable, inclusive, and quality education, and advance lifelong learning.
5. **Women:** secure gender equality and empowerment for women and girls.
6. **Water:** safeguard sustainable and available water and sanitation, and appropriate management of water resources for all people.
7. **Energy:** Ensure access to affordable, reliable, sustainable, and modern energy for all people.
8. **Economy:** promote inclusive, sustainable and sustained economic growth, full employment, and decent and productive work for all people.
9. **Infrastructure:** construct sound and resilient infrastructure, certify inclusive and sustainable industrialization, and foster innovation.
10. **Inequality:** reduce inequality both within countries and among countries.
11. **Habitation:** render cities and human settlements inclusive, safe, and sustainable.
12. **Consumption:** ensure sustainable consumption and steady production patterns.
13. **Climate:** urgently combat climate change and its impacts.
14. **Marine ecosystems:** conserve the oceans, seas, and marine resources for sustainable development.
15. **Ecosystems:** restore, protect, and maintain terrestrial ecosystems, manage forests, combat desertification, stop land degradation, arrest biodiversity loss,
16. **Institutions:** promote peaceful and inclusive societies with access to justice for all, with accountable and inclusive institutions at every level.
17. **Sustainability:** the overarching theme; effectively implement sustainable development and strengthen the global partnership for forwarding sustainable development.

UN development policy has evolved and changed its focus in several ways during the last seventy-five years. UN efforts to meet the Charter's commitment to raising the standards of living and the socio-economic conditions of the world's poor have been played against the backdrop of both the East-West and the North-South struggles. These group struggles have shaped development policy, using diversity including that of the United Nations in the policy arena. However, the United Nations has also sought to make developmental policies by mobilizing the world on behalf of particular agendas and strategies. Through many types of multilateral forums—world conferences, panels of experts, media events, General Assembly special sessions, and public campaigns—the United Nations has blended environmental concerns with the search for economic development in the developing world, producing with time a new conception of economic progress known as "sustainable" development. Through its worldwide system of programs, funds, specialized agencies, and offices, the United Nations has also addressed policymaking in such personally human fields as health and individual rights and dignity, for sustainable development is possible only where sustainable human development is achieved. The United Nations has today completely transited towards a "people-centric" institution that sees its mission not only in terms of protecting the interests of the states but also that of its members. The entire UN System has moved to the centre of global developmental policy-making, on human security issues previously thought to lie on the periphery of international politics.

Cited Works

Moore, John Allphin, Jr., and Jerry, Pubantz, *The New United Nations, International Organization in the Twenty-First Century*, New York and London, Routledge, 2017.

Sachs, Jeffrey. *The Age of Sustainable Development*, New York: Columbia University Press, 2015.

UN General Assembly, *Implementation of the United Nations Millennium Declaration: Report of the Secretary-General*, UN document A/58/323 (New York: United Nations, September 2, 2003), para. 42.

Relevant Web Sites:

Millennium Development Goals *(www.un.org/millenniumgoals)*

Sustainable Development Goals *(www.undp.org/content/undp/en/home/sdgoverview/post-2015-development-agenda.html)*

PART V
ISSUES, REFORMS AND ROLE

19

ISSUES OF FINANCING

In every organization, some of the most difficult problems are with finances. This is no less true of international organizations. The basic questions that have arisen are how to raise and assess taxes, that is, contributions to international organizations (comparable to disputes within states over progressive or flat-rate taxation), how to ensure payment of the contributions after assessment (comparable to problems of tax collection and tax evasion within states) and how to supervise and control expenditure by the member states (similar to problems of effective parliamentary control of national expenditure).

About one-third of the expenditures of the entire UN system are funded through mandatory assessments from states which are members of the various organizations comprising the system. The other two-thirds come from voluntary contributions. Twenty states pay almost four-fifths of the total budget of the UN system. The US, China, Japan and Germany pay almost 49 per cent of the total UN budget.

In terms of order of the amounts contributed by the states to the United Nations, it is clear that a small proportion of the membership pays a large percentage of the expenses.

Budgetary Procedures

That part of the UN expenditure which is financed by mandatory assessments of member states is known as its "regular budget". All states which are members of the UN are obliged by the Charter to contribute to the regular budget. The rate of contribution to the regular budget of each member-state is fixed by the General Assembly on the advice of an 18-member committee on contributions. Normally, the scale is reviewed every third year on the basis of the latest available national income statistics. The total amount of the budget, the other factor determining the actual sum, each state must contribute, is decided by the Assembly, after considering a two-year budget proposed by the Secretary-General, together with the recommendations of a budgetary advisory committee and a programme and coordination committee.

The UN biennial budget and accompanying programmes are authorized by the General Assembly in resolutions, which set out estimates of income and fixed expenditure limits, including the number of appropriations for two years. The draft of the regular budget originates with proposals submitted by individual departments to the Budget Division and the Office for Programme Planning and Coordination of the Secretariat. These offices pass on their recommendations to the Programme Planning and Budgeting Board, a small body made up of senior secretariat officials and chaired by the Secretary-General. The budgetary board's recommendations determine the final contents of the Secretary-General's budget.

This budget is next rigorously scrutinized by two subsidiary bodies of the General Assembly. The first is the Advisory Committee on Administrative and Budgetary Questions (ACABQ)—a 16-member committee of experts in finance management and economics nominated by their Governments to serve in their capacity. The second is the Committee for Programme and Coordination (CPC)—a 34-member committee of experts who represent the views of their governments. These committees analyze the budget from the point of view of its conformity with inter-governmental legislative mandates.

The Secretary-General's proposed budget, plus the recommendations of the ACABQ and the CPC, go to the General Assembly's Fifth Administrative and Budgetary Committee, on which all the members of the UN are represented. Then over the three-month General Assembly session, the Committee scrutinizes the proposed budget, using the ACABQ's and CPC's recommendations as to the principal basis of its review, and incorporating into it any action taken by other committees of the Assembly which have financial implications. The Fifth Committee's recommendations on the budget are then forwarded to the General Assembly for final review and approval.

Economic, social and humanitarian activities account for nearly 90 per cent of the expenditure of the United Nations. UN budget operations are divided into four categories. The regular budget provides for the day-to-day costs of the organization, including buildings and equipment, conferences, travel, salaries and retirement salaries and other administrative costs of UN organs. Each specialized agency has its budget, which is presented independently to the General Assembly for formal approval. The budget for the voluntary programmes includes financial support for economic aid and technical assistance for programmes like the UN Development Programme (UNDP) and the UN Fund for Population Activities (UNFPA). In recent years the budget for peacekeeping operations has been the most controversial because of its political implications.

Problems of Financing

When the UN began its work in 1946, the need to find an equitable and satisfactory financing formula was accorded top priority. The task of preparing a scale of budgetary assessments was assigned to a special committee on contributions under guidelines laid down by the General Assembly. In performing this task, the committee was originally charged by the General Assembly to use the criterion of ability to pay as reflected by each state's total national income, per capita income, economic dislocation caused by the war after 1945, and foreign exchange earnings. These factors, except for dislocation caused by war, remain the main criteria for determining assessments today, although "floor" and "ceiling" limitations have been added. The United States is the largest contributor to the UN budget paying 22 per cent of the regular budget. At the other end of the scale, the Assembly has fixed a minimum rate of 0.001 per cent as the assessed contribution. More than 80 developing countries now pay this amount. A maximum assessment rate for the least developed countries is 0.01 per cent.

The poorer states of the world prefer that budget assessments be based strictly on each state's national income and ability to pay. The use of national per capita income as a factor in the assessment scale has met with objections from states with high national incomes and small populations. In deference to this objection, the Assembly set a rule that no state should be assessed more per capita than the largest contributor.

Since 1990, several of the major budget contributors have been criticizing the unfairness of the budgetary procedures of the UN. This is because the majority of nations of the developing world, which pay the least, have a decisive say about how much should be spent and for what. The seven richest countries pay 70 per cent of the total budget but can be outvoted by the majority who contribute only 30 per cent of it. Besides, the size of the UN budget has been increasing over the years, and no ceiling on expenditure has ever been laid down.

Ensuring Regular Payments by Contributors

Even if the problem of assessment could be tackled adequately, there would remain another problem, that of securing regular contributions. Till 1962, this had not been a major problem and most governments did not evade paying their dues. It arose for the first time in connection with the first United Nations Emergency Force (UNEF-I) established by the General Assembly as a buffer between Egyptian and Israeli lines from 1956 to 1967. The Soviet Union, along with 12 other countries, objected to the establishment of UNEF by the General Assembly on the ground that only the Security Council could legally raise such a force. When the UN operation in the Congo was sent to assist that country in its post-independence difficulties between 1960 and 1964, a group of nations led by the Soviet Union and France refused to pay their share of the peacekeeping expenses. They demanded in each case that the "aggressors" should pay the cost of the forces, that the operations had not been properly authorized and controlled, that the financing had not been satisfactorily agreed to in advance, and that the costs were unexpectedly high.

In 1961, the UN sold almost $170 million worth of bonds to 64 countries, using the proceeds to help finance deficits in the accounts of the Middle-East and the Congo forces. The same countries which had objected to the creation of the forces also objected to the repayment of the UN bond issue authorized by the Assembly. However, funds for repayment of principal and payment of interest on the bonds are included by the Assembly in each regular budget, with repayment scheduled to be completed in the next few years.

By December 1985, 15 countries were withholding $45.8 million from the regular budget because of the bonds. They included China, South Africa, the Soviet Union and some Eastern European countries. France, however, started to pay in 1971.

Some states have also withheld the assessed contributions for the most recent peacekeeping forces in the Middle-East. Arab states argued that the costs should be borne by Israel. China maintained that it had no obligation to pay for UN activities which were started before it got admitted to the UN in 1971.

Funds have also been withheld for reasons other than peacekeeping as well. Six countries – Bulgaria, the Byelorussian SSR, the German Democratic Republic, Hungary, the Ukrainian SSR and the erstwhile Soviet Union – have objected to the inclusion in the regular budget of appropriations for technical assistance activities, insisting that such work should be financed entirely voluntarily under the UN Development Programme. They have offered their assessed payments for these activities in their non-controvertible currencies rather than in dollars as stipulated in the UN Financial Regulations. The UN accepts these currencies only to the extent that these can be used for expenses such as purchases of equipment from the countries concerned. The unused portion is listed as a withholding. Israel has withheld funds concerned with the Palestine question and the Second Development Decade. South Africa is another major defaulter. It has said that it will start paying its dues when assured of its right to participate in the General Assembly which has been revoked since 1974.

Similarly, the United States has since 1982 refused to make payments for specialized agencies and general UN programmes in support of the Palestinians. In 1983 the US informed the Secretary-General that it would no longer pay its share of the regular budget costs associated with the UN treaty on the Law of the Sea, which it also refused to sign.

In the mid-1980s, a financial crisis of major proportions began to emerge. This most serious threat to UN solvency was caused by a substantial withholding of arrears by the US stemming from funding cuts mandated by Congress which desired a cut in US funding of the UN budget from 25 to 20 per cent, an action which involved withholding $42 million for 1987. Under the Kassebann Amendment adopted by Congress in 1985, this cut would be continued until the UN adopted a system of weighted voting on budgetary matters.

With the United States in default, many other countries rallied to support the United Nations. China gave the UN $435 million which it had owned for many years as part of its dues for peacekeeping expenses. The Soviets also made a special voluntary contribution to the regular budget, and some key developing countries, including India and Brazil, found the means to pay their long-overdue debts to the UN. This kept the UN functioning till the adoption by the General Assembly of some reforms in its budgetary procedures under the Report of the Group of 18 in 1986, an action which led the US to start paying back its dues as before.

Regular Budget and Working Capital Fund

By its resolution 73/271, the General Assembly decided that the scale of assessments for the period 2019-2021 shall be based on the following elements and criteria:

- Estimates of gross national income.
- Average statistical base periods of three and six years.
- Conversion rates based on market exchange rates, except where that would cause excessive fluctuations and distortions in the income of some Member States, when price-adjusted rates of exchange or other appropriate conversion rates should be employed, taking due account of its resolution 46/221 B.
- The debt-burden approach was employed in the scale of assessments for the period 2016-2018.
- A low per capita income adjustment of 80 per cent, with a threshold per capita income limit of the average per capita gross national income of all Member States for the statistical base periods.
- A minimum assessment rate of 0.001 per cent.
- A maximum assessment rate for the least developed countries of 0.01 per cent.

A maximum assessment rate of 22 per cent.

(a) The Working Capital Fund shall be established for the year 2022 for $150 million;

(b) The Member States shall make advances to the Working Capital Fund by the scale of assessments adopted by the Assembly for contributions of Member States to the budget for 2022;

(c) There shall be set off against this allocation of advances:

   (i) Credits to the Member States resulting from transfers made in 1959 and 1960 from the surplus account to the Working Capital Fund in an adjusted amount of $1,025,092;

   (ii) Cash advances paid by the Member States to the Working Capital Fund for the year 2021 by Assembly resolution 75/256 of 31 December 2020;

(d) Should the credits and advances paid by any Member State to the Working Capital Fund for the year 2021 exceed the amount of that Member State's advance under the provisions of paragraph 1 (b) above the excess would be set off against the amount of the contributions payable by the Member State in respect of the year 2022.

Control of Expenditure

Once funds are appropriated at the United Nations, internal controls come into play to ensure that money is spent only for authorized purposes and that it will be spent as economically as possible. The office of financial services of the secretariat is the main control mechanism for this. It designates the financial officers who authorize expenditure and keep records. Beyond this, the Assembly has created a Joint Inspection Unit (JIU), whose inspectors from 11 nations are appointed by the General Assembly to serve in their capacity. They are broadly empowered to investigate all matters bearing on the efficiency of services and proper use of funds. The recommendations of this unit are always discussed by the Fifth Committee or any other inter-governmental body directly concerned. Once approved by the Assembly the recommendations of the unit must be implemented by the officials concerned.

After any money is spent at the United Nations there is a complete audit of the accounts, first by the Secretariat's own internal auditors and then by a Board of External Auditors. The auditor's findings and recommendations are published, and their reports are submitted for approval and follow-up action by the Assembly.

Over the years, several attempts have been made by the United Nations, to solve the problem of withholding of funds by member states. In 1962, the General Assembly asked the International Court of Justice for an opinion on withholding assessments in the matter of the Congo and the Middle-East operations. The Court ruled that these two operations constituted "expenses of the organization" and that the problem, therefore, fell under paragraph 2 of Art. 17 of the Charter, which holds that the organization's expenses shall be borne by the members as apportioned by the General Assembly.

The same year, there was a move in the Assembly to invoke against withholding nations Article 19 of the Charter, which states that a Member which is in arrears in payment of its contribution by two full years is to be deprived of its vote in the General Assembly. The measure however was not adopted.

In 1965, a special committee on peacekeeping operations, examining the matter of delinquency, recommended that the question of Article 19 should not be raised in connection with the Middle-East and Congo operations and that the financial difficulties of the Organization should be solved through voluntary contributions by member states, with the highly developed countries making substantial contributions and later peacekeeping operations being assessed on a special scale (a method followed since then).

In response to repeated appeals by the General Assembly for assistance to meet the Organization's financial difficulties, 29 countries have made voluntary contributions. The amount received from them between 1965 and December 1985 was $42.6 million.

In a move to improve the efficiency of the Organization's administrative and financial functions, the General Assembly in 1985 agreed to a recommendation by Japan to set up an 18-member "Group of High-Level Intergovernmental Experts" to review UN administrative and financial matters and identify measures for further improving the efficiency of the administrative and financial functioning of the world body in dealing with political, economic and social issues. Its 40-page report (A/41/49), presented to the Secretary-General, Javier Perez de Cuellar, on 18 August 1986, formulated 71 recommendations which covered personnel measures, secretariat structure, monitoring budget and implementation procedures, and several economic measures to reduce expenditure.

The General Assembly members approved these recommendations in its 1986 session. As a result of the Assembly action on the Group Report, states have agreed to act by "consensus" on important budget issues which previously had proved divisive.

If the General Assembly Resolution (Resolution 41/213 of 19 December 1986) is followed strictly, the programme committee, CPC, will act by consensus and only proposals agreed to by the major donors will move further for final approval—thus limiting the capability of the majority of the small state to push through costly projects for the funding to which their contribution is minimal.

Under the terms of the General Assembly Resolution, the Secretary-General in off-budget years, is to submit an outline of the programme budget for the following biennium, indicating a preliminary estimate of resources needed to accommodate the proposed programme of activities for the biennium, priorities reflecting general sectoral trends; real growth, positive or negative, compared with the previous budget; and the size of a contingency fund, expressed as a percentage of the overall level of resources, to be set up to accommodate additional expenditures derived either from additional activities approved by the Assembly after the adoption of the budget or from the revision of original budget estimates.

The CPC is to consider the budget outline and make recommendations thereon to the Assembly. Based on the Assembly's decision, the Secretary-General will prepare his proposed programme budget for the following biennium. The resolution stresses that throughout this process, the mandate and functions of the Advisory Committee on Administrative and Budgetary Questions (ACABQ) would be respected.

During budget years, the resolution calls for the Secretary-General to submit his proposed programme budget to CPC and the administrative committee, it and CPC will examine it following their respective mandate and then submit their conclusions and recommendations to the Assembly.

If additional expenditures are proposed, which exceed the resources of the contingency fund, they are to be included in the budget only through redeployment of resources from low priority areas or modification of existing activities. Otherwise, they will have to be deferred until later.

The Secretary-General was asked to report later to the Assembly, the CPC and ACABQ on a comprehensive solution to the problem of additional expenditures, including those arising from factors such as inflation and currency fluctuations. Meanwhile, the Secretary-General is however instructed to absorb those expenditures through savings from the programme budget.

The position of UN finances will continue to be precarious since it is amply clear now that most members are not prepared to accept majority rule when it threatens their vital interests, and no decision can be forcibly imposed on its members. Financing of peacekeeping expenses continues to be disputed as the budget for peacekeeping continues to be an inflated one, sometimes exceeding the regular budget of the UN. By December 1985, the deficits in the regular budget and the peacekeeping accounts ran close to $391 million.

For those units of the United Nations system which are dependent on voluntary contributions from governments, organizations and even individuals – UNDP, UNFPA and UNHCR, for example – the situation is even more uncertain. UNICEF gets so large a portion of its budget (about 25 per cent) directly from individuals and non-governmental organizations that it is forced by the unpredictable nature of its funding to keep some money in the bank to meet its commitments in case the level of contributions drops.

Nearly all the nations that have lost their votes in the General Assembly at one time or another under Article 19 were among the poorest states with the lowest-percentage assessments. For example, in January 2015, thirteen nations, including Kyrgyzstan, the Former Yugoslav Republic of Macedonia, Vanuatu, Tonga, Rwanda, Grenada, Liberia, Marshall Islands, Comoros, Guinea-Bissau, Sao Tome and Principe, Somalia, and Yemen, fell far behind in their payments. Some of these states had been on the list for many years-Comoros, for example, since 2002. These nonpayments occurred even though in some cases the assessment was as little as $4,800. However, in the end, the General Assembly allowed all except Yemen to continue voting in the Chamber.

The growing unwillingness of the United States to pay its share of the budget as a result of consternation with UN policies or with specific UN agencies, coupled with the nonpayment of dues by other states, left the United Nations in a perennial funds shortfall. This deficit was particularly true in its peacekeeping budget, which along with the "regular" budget and the international criminal tribunal's budget, compose the organization's expenses for which members must pay. Even in the aftermath of the terrorist attacks of 11 September 2001, the United States moved slowly to make up its payments to those various budgets, owing in November of that year $265 million of the regular budget, $800 million to peacekeeping, and $14.6 million to the tribunals' account. The United States was not alone in its selective payments. Half the debt owed was held by members other than the United States. Between 1993 and 2011, the shortfall between actual payments and assessed contributions from all countries ranged between $200 million and $860 million annually for the regular budget, and up to $3.3 billion for peacekeeping.

The proposed UN budget for 2014-2015 was $5.34 billion, with approximately another $8 billion allocated for peacekeeping operations, the latter fund growing by 2.5 times since 2002. The General Assembly also established a Capital Master Plan fund approaching $2 billion for capital repairs to UN headquarters in New York. The minimum assessment was initially .04 per cent. It was lowered to .02 per cent in 1973, .01 per cent in 1978, and .001 per cent in 1997. This downward shift has resulted from recognition of the economic challenges confronting the least developed and low-income states. The consequence is that the major industrialized nations pay the preponderance of the UN budget, particularly its peacekeeping budget. In December 2000, the U.S. contribution was lowered from 25 per cent to 22 per cent of the regular budget and from 31 per cent to 27 per cent of the peacekeeping budget, which effectively set the ceiling for the largest contributor. As of 2014, after the United States (22 per cent of the UN budget), China (12.005 per cent) Japan paid 8.564 per cent of the UN budget, Germany, 7.1 per cent, France, 5.5 per cent and both Russia and Great Britain paid 5.5 per cent.

The financial crisis that set in during the 1960s lingered into the new millennium, which limited the UN's ability to fulfil its commitments. In 2004, for example, Secretary-General Kofi Annan worried about whether the UN's international tribunals would be able to even continue their work. They had to borrow money from the peacekeeping budget to stay afloat. The United Nations regularly had to shift funds from one account to another to pay operating expenses. It also had to turn to outside donor countries that were willing to make additional voluntary contributions, such as Canada, or private contributors, such as media mogul Ted Turner and Microsoft's Bill Gates-for funds to cover shortfalls or to pay for planned humanitarian programs.

The irony of the situation was that, given that in the 1960s the United States had led the effort to force the Soviet Union and others to pay their ascribed UN dues, the U.S. debt owed to the non-contributors was the factor that most severely weakened the United Nations. By the close of the millennium, the United States, always the UN's largest creditor had become its biggest debtor, owing to the organization over one billion dollars. The US's unwillingness to pay generated questions about the survival of the world organization.

- In "Renewing the United Nations", the Secretary-General has initiated a series of measures to reduce administrative costs to 25 per cent of the budget as compared to 38 per cent currently. Savings are anticipated to grow to at least $200 million for the biennium beginning in 2002.
- Savings derived from these administrative efficiencies will be utilized as a "development dividend" to fund the United Nations' highest priority—the alleviation of poverty and the generation of economic growth among developing countries.
- The Secretary-General proposed the creation of a revolving fund, to be capitalized up to $1 billion, as an interim solution to the United Nations' current fiscal crisis. This fund of voluntary contributions by governments would give the United Nations accessible operating capital at times when arrears in-country dues are causing significant cash-flow problems.
- Finally, the Secretary-General recommended the adoption of a results-based budgeting system. The United Nations currently operates under a system in which the General Assembly directs the Secretary-General not only about programme

objectives but also the specific means, including personnel, to be utilized. The Secretary-General seeks greater flexibility to determine the most effective and efficient means while being held accountable by the General Assembly for the results.

One answer to the financing problem is to find sources of income for the United Nations independent of its members. Although some of the sources suggested by UN scholars would require a Charter amendment, the need for the world body to have independent revenues has now been recognized as an absolute imperative. Some of the sources suggested are:

(i) Charges levied by UN agencies for services performed; for example, the World Meteorological Organization could charge a service fee for its weather data and the International Telecommunication Union could issue international radio licenses for fees.

(ii) Tolls charged for various transportation and communication facilities provided by UN programmes.

(iii) Profits earned through the implementation of the 1982 Law of the Sea Treaty by which a UN international investment corporation could exploit the mineral and other forms of wealth in international water and sea beds.

(iv) Charters sold to private companies or governmental agencies authorizing them to exploit the resources of sea beds, or giving them fishing, whaling and sealing rights in international waters, with royalty rights reserved by the UN.

(v) Rights to the use of outer space, or the operation of outer space programmes by the UN aimed at producing revenues through communication satellites, meteorological systems, etc.

(vi) Issuance of an international trading currency, backed by national reserves that could serve the dual function of financing UN programmes and providing a supplementary international monetary unit to encourage greater trade.

These are some of the proposals that have emanated from time to time to make the UN finances independent of the vagaries of its member states. It would be impossible to run an international organization effectively if members were free to pick and choose which of its programmes they were prepared to pay for. The readiness of nations to pay for international programmes, whether or not they supported them individually, is the only objective test of their commitment to the international system as a whole. Judged by this standard, UN members have shown a considerable, but not unlimited, commitment. Most members have paid most of the time despite rapidly rising budgets. The general commitment to voluntary programmes is also equally heartening. However, there will continue to be disputes about which programmes should be put on the regular budget and which outside it, and, above all, about the overall scale of expenditure. Such conflicts are inherent in any political organization which reflects opposing interests of members, especially those of the poor who want more expenditure, and the rich, who want less. These problems are likely to remain even in the future.

Cited Works

Annan, Kofi, *Renewing the United Nations: A Programme for Reform*, UN Document A/51/1950 (New York: United Nations, July 16, 1997).

Basic Facts about the United Nations, New York: UN Department of Public Information, published periodically.

Luard, Evan, *The United Nations: How it Works and What it Does*, London: Macmillan, 1979.

Riggs, Robert E. & Jack C. Plano., *The United Nations: International Organisation and World Politics* Chicago, Illinois: The Dorsey Press, 1988.

Stoessinger, John G., *Financing the United Nations System*, Washington D.C.: Brookings Institution, 1964.

United Nations, Image and Reality: Questions and Answers about Management, Finance and People, UN Publications, 1983.

20

REVISION OF THE UNITED NATIONS CHARTER

The UN Charter can be amended by a vote of two-thirds of the members of the General Assembly and ratification by two-thirds of the members of the United Nations, including the five permanent members of the Security Council. So far, four Charter Articles have been amended, one of them twice:

- In 1965, the membership of the Security Council was increased from 11 to 15 (Article 23) and the number of affirmative votes needed on procedural matters was increased from seven to nine: on all other matters, it was also increased to nine, including the concurring votes of the five permanent members (Article 27).
- In 1965, the membership of the Economic and Social Council was increased from 18 to 27 and, in 1973, was further increased to 54 (Article 61).
- In 1968, the number of votes required in the Security Council to convene a General Conference to review the Charter was increased from seven to nine (Article 109).

Four decades of the United Nations functioning have brought to light certain structural and functional defects in the organization which can be corrected through amendment and review of the Charter. A lot has changed in the world environment since the inception of the UN and some changes have become necessary in its system to make it more effective to bear increasing responsibilities in the future.

The United Nations Charter, which emerged from the deliberations of the San Francisco Conference of 1945, represented a series of compromises made by the various states having diverse interests, and varying political, economic and cultural backgrounds. Most of the functions of the United Nations were mentioned in general terms in the hope that these would be interpreted according to the exigencies of time. The framers of the Charter fully realized that the Charter was not a perfect instrument and should possess sufficient flexibility to grow and develop according to the changing conditions. Consequently, they made provisions for its amendment and review.

Though the Charter made provisions for its amendment and review, this could not be done because of political circumstances. However, this should not give the impression that no changes have been effected in the Charter. The Charter has been subjected to informal amendments in four ways.

1. Through the non-implementation or non-application of certain provisions of the Charter;
2. Through the interpretation of the Charter by various organs and members of the United Nations;
3. Through the conclusion of supplementary treaties or agreements; and
4. Through the creation of special organs and agencies.

Let us examine the changes that have been brought about in the UN Charter as a result of the experiences the world organization and its member states had to undergo since 1945.

1. Non-Implementation of Certain Provisions

Certain provisions of the Charter, which were considered very vital have not been implemented because the members either deliberately disregarded them or failed to implement them. Perhaps one of the best examples of this is Article 43, which forms the core of the collective security system. The members were expected to conclude agreements to make available to the Security Council the armed forces, assistance and facilities necessary for maintaining international peace and security. Yet due to East-West differences, the major powers were unable to agree on plans to make armed forces available at the call of the Council and the agreements referred to in Article 43 could never come into existence. Similarly, other provisions, like Articles 44, 45, 46, 48 and the major part of Article 47, which relate to the use of armed forces by the Security Council, have not been observed. The failure of these provisions meant that the Security Council could not discharge the policing function that the UN Charter had originally contemplated for it.

Article 106 lays down that till the Security Council can perform the peacekeeping functions assigned to it under Articles 42 and 43, the five permanent members will consult each other to take such joint action as may be necessary for maintaining international peace and security. In other words, Article 106 assigns the responsibility of maintaining peace, at least on a transitional basis, to the permanent members. But the East-West cleavage rendered this provision inoperative.

Let us consider the provisions of the UN Charter regarding the election of ten non-permanent members of the Security Council based on:

(i) the contributions of the members to the maintenance of peace and security and other purposes of the organization, and

(ii) equitable geographical distribution (Article 23). In practice, the General Assembly has ignored the first criterion and has mainly resorted to that of equitable geographical distribution. Usually, the five non-permanent members of the Security Council are taken from Africa and Asia, one from Eastern Europe, two from Latin America and two from Western Europe and other areas.

It may be noted that there is nothing in the Charter, which can prevent the General Assembly from disregarding the provisions of the Charter and there is no provision for an appeal against the action of the General Assembly. As a result, certain provisions of the Charter have become inoperative.

2. New Interpretations

The Charter has not vested the authority for interpretation of the Charter in any single agency. The only reference in this regard is found in Article 96 which lays down that the General Assembly or the Security Council may request the International Court of Justice to give an advisory opinion on any legal question. It may be noted that the opinion thus expressed by the International Court of Justice is not binding on the members. Otherwise, all the organs of the UN are left free to interpret the various articles of the Charter according to their discretion. Consequently, the various organs of the UN adopt the opinion which is acceptable to the majority of its members. This flexibility in the interpretation of the Charter has greatly extended the scope of the UN.

Let us examine certain instances to find out how far this new interpretation of the UN Charter has broadened the scope of the activities of the United Nations.

Voting in the Security Council

Article 27(3), which deals with the question of voting in the Security Council lays down that the decisions of the Security Council on all matters (other than procedural) shall be made by an affirmative vote of nine members, including the concurring votes of the permanent members. At a very early stage of its working, the Security Council was faced with the problem of whether it could make a decision when a permanent member abstained from voting. Any narrow interpretation of Article 27(3) would have meant that abstention does not constitute an affirmative vote and hence no decision could be taken. However, the Security Council took the position that an abstention or an absence of a permanent member did not constitute a negative vote. It was this liberal interpretation of the UN Charter, coupled with the absence of the Soviet Union from the Security Council, which made it possible for it to take action in Korea.

Similarly, the provisions of the Charter dealing with the definition of "procedural" and "substantive" questions are quite vague and have been interpreted with great elasticity by the General Assembly. The General Assembly has interpreted these provisions in a manner to restrict the area within which the veto can be applied. It may be noted that the "veto" can be applied only in matters which are substantive and not on procedural questions.

Secretary-General

The role of the Secretary-General has also been greatly modified by a liberal interpretation of the UN Charter. His role has been indicated in Articles 97-100. A quick reading of these articles will give the impression that the Secretary-General is merely the chief administrative officer of the United Nations possessing the authority to appoint his staff, and has not been vested with any important political functions. But in practice, the Secretary-General has come to exercise great influence in the United Nations. Both the

General Assembly and the Security Council have taken a broad view of the functions of the Secretary-General, and he has been permitted to play an important political role.

The General Assembly

Another important change in the United Nations has been the shifting of responsibility for peacekeeping from the Security Council to the Assembly. The Charter had laid much emphasis on the primary responsibility of the Council for the maintenance of world peace. The Council was deliberately made a small body so that it could act with speed in times of crisis. The Assembly, on the other hand, was designed to be merely a deliberative body authorized to make recommendations. But during all these years the General Assembly's prestige has been greatly increased and it has been playing a very important role. All this was made possible by the growing estrangement between the Soviet Union and the West. This Great Power rivalry led to the adoption of the Uniting for Peace Resolution in 1950 which provided that if the Security Council, because of lack of unanimity among its five permanent members fails to act on an apparent threat to peace, breach of peace or act of aggression, the Assembly itself may take up the matter within 24 hours and recommend collective measures including the use of armed forces. This amounted to a virtual amendment of the Charter, so extensive as to constitute a major shift of power between the organs of the UN.

The powers of the General Assembly continued to grow due to the East-West differences and the emergence of a large number of Afro-Asian countries who preferred to refer their political disputes to the General Assembly rather than to the Security Council, where the big powers had veto power.

However, in the past few years, the Security Council has once again assumed responsibilities that were imposed on it in the Charter. No veto has been used against the establishment of peacekeeping operations. The number of its meetings has tremendously increased. It played a decisive role in the Congo, Cyprus and recently in the Gulf War.

Non-Self-Governing Territories

The liberal interpretation of Article 73(e) dealing with the non-self-governing territories has led to the assumption of certain powers by the General Assembly which was not envisaged by the Charter. This Article makes it obligatory for the members of the United Nations who have assumed responsibilities for the administration of non-self-governing territories to transmit regularly to the Secretary-General, subject to such limitations as security and constitutional considerations may require, statistical and other information of a technical nature relating to the economic, social and educational conditions in the territories for which they are respectively responsible. Strictly interpreted, this provision does not accord authority to the United Nations to deal with the information furnished or to make recommendations in this regard. The General Assembly, however, despite opposition from the colonial powers, went considerably beyond this provision and created a special committee in 1949 to examine the information transmitted and to submit reports thereon to the Assembly. It has frequently debated the reports submitted for its information and has thus made the colonial powers fully accountable to the United Nations for the administration of their non-self-governing territories. The General Assembly played a positive role in securing independence for the non-self-governing territories by adopting a Declaration on the Granting of Independence to the Colonial Countries and Peoples in 1960. In this declaration, emphasis was laid not only on the right to self-determination but also on the need to grant independence in the larger interest of international peace and security. The General Assembly also set up a Committee of 24 which worked diligently for the independence of the non-self-governing territories.

Thus, the General Assembly has greatly extended its control over the non-self-governing territories by liberally interpreting the provisions of the Charter. It may be noted that the Charter never expected the General Assembly to play such a vital role in this regard. This change took place primarily because the General Assembly came to be dominated by the Afro-Asian countries which were keen to see that all people under colonial powers got independence. The work of the Trusteeship Council is over and it has suspended operations in 1994 upon the independence of the last Trust territory of Palau.

3. Conclusion of Supplementary Agreements

The Charter did not specify the privileges and immunities of the members of the international organization and laid down in Article 105(3) that the General Assembly may make recommendations to determine the details of the application of the privileges and immunities and may propose conventions to the members of the United Nations for this purpose. In pursuance of this Article 105, a convention on the "Privileges and Immunities" of the United Nations was concluded in February 1946, outlined in considerable detail the juridical personality of the United Nations, the immunity of UN property, funds, and assets, the right of the United Nations to use communication facilities, the privileges and immunities of the officials credited to the United Nations, etc. This Convention has been ratified by the majority of states.

Compulsory Jurisdiction of International Court of Justice

The Charter has also been greatly enlarged by the decision of several member states to voluntarily accept the compulsory jurisdiction of the International Court of Justice. The Charter had only emphasized that the member states must settle their disputes by peaceful means, without specifying the actual methods to be adopted. However, under Article 36 of the Statute, the states can declare that they recognize the compulsory jurisdiction of the Court in all legal disputes concerning:

(a) the interpretation of a treaty,
(b) any question of international law,
(c) the existence of any fact which if established would constitute a breach of an established obligation, and
(d) the nature or extent of the reparations to be made for the breach of an international obligation.

The decision of the member states to accept the so-called optional clause of the Statute has enlarged the competence of the United Nations.

Regional Pacts

The conclusion of regional pacts like the Brussels Pact, the Inter-American Treaty of Reciprocal Assistance, the North Atlantic Treaty, Warsaw Pact, Anzus Pact, Manila Pact, Balkan Pact, SEATO, etc. has also brought about changes in the UN. Originally, the responsibility for collective security was vested only in the United Nations (Security Council). But soon the cleavage between the Soviet Union and the Western powers rendered this provision unworkable. As a result, the member states were compelled to find out alternatives for security. This resulted in the conclusion of regional defence pacts. It may be noted that most of these regional pacts were concluded under Article 51 of the Charter, and the constitutions of some of these regional organizations make a specific reference to this Article.

Although it has been pointed out by certain critics that these regional arrangements violate the spirit of the Charter, it cannot be denied that the emergence of these pacts had led to the expansion of the scope of the United Nations Charter.

4. Creation of Subsidiary Organs

The creation of subsidiary and special organs within the United Nations system has also contributed to the development of the international organization. These organs have been created under Articles 22 to 29, which point out that the General Assembly and the Security Council may establish such subsidiary organs as are deemed necessary for the performance of their respective functions. In pursuance of the powers vested in them, the General Assembly and the Security Council set several committees which have greatly facilitated the proceedings of these two organs. In addition to these committees, a large number of other committees and commissions have been set up to perform certain specific functions. Some of these commissions, like the International Law Commission, the Disarmament Commission, etc. are permanent. In addition to these permanent commissions, several *ad hoc* organs like the Commission for India and Pakistan, the Special Committee on the Balkans, the Palestine Conciliation Commission, the Commission for Unification and Rehabilitation of Korea, the Committee on the Question of Defining Aggression, were also created. Some of the other important organs established since the inauguration of the UN Charter include the International Atomic Energy Agency (July 1957), World Meteorological Organization (1951), United Nations High Commissioner for Refugees, United Nations Relief and Work Agency, United Nations International Children's Emergency Fund, and a score of others. The chief benefit of having these organizations is that the UN has been able to use the services of experts in various fields.

The above discussion shows that the UN Charter, in theory, differs significantly from the UN Charter in practice. Numerous changes have been effected in it either by permitting certain provisions to lapse by non-implementation or through new interpretations of the Charter, the conclusion of supplementary agreements and the creation of special organs.

Proposals for Reform

Before we discuss proposals for reform of the UN, which have been advanced from time to time, a few words about the general direction in which the world organization should seek to move become relevant here. It is generally agreed that the UN should try to become far more effective than it is today by acting as what its Charter has described as "a centre for harmonizing the interests of nations". It should be better equipped to enable it to become such a centre. UN is not yet what was once hoped it would be—a world government, which can decide what nations should do and instruct them accordingly. What it can do, if properly used, is to modify interstate relations by maximizing the asset which it does possess: its influence. It can act as a guide, as an authority, and above all as a focus for discussion and contacts. If it uses the authority it already has in the most effective way it might be able to bring significant long-term changes in the attitudes and policies of governments. The general direction in which the UN should seek to move is towards anticipation of potential conflicts, promotion of negotiations and the formulation of general norms of international behaviour. What specific changes in structure and procedures would be required to bring about such a movement?

The first point to be borne in mind is that changes are unlikely to come through a revision of the UN Charter. Under Article 109, a conference to consider Charter amendments could be called at any time by a two-thirds vote of Assembly members, and a vote of nine members of the Security Council. Since amendments are subject to the veto, such an exercise is not likely to get very far. A special review conference could, however, provide the opportunity for a detailed debate on the reforms needed, and if sufficient impetus for change is generated, it could produce pressure for full-scale amendments. What are the changes needed? Let us discuss some of these.

To ensure that disputes are discussed before they have erupted into open war, it would be useful if the UN Secretariat were to institute a more systematic procedure for monitoring political situations all over the world. Better research and advisory staff within the Secretariat for this purpose might be needed to keep potential conflict situations under constant review.

Though under Chapter VI of the UN Charter a long series of procedures can be put into effect by the Security Council to examine situations, which have not yet reached the stage of open conflict they have seldom been used. The Security Council has chosen to ignore the full potentialities of Chapter VI most of the time in its long history. In most cases it does nothing at all until a conflict has reached the stage of open war; for example, the Security Council made no effort whatever to discuss the Iraq-Iran dispute during the summer of 1980, even though recurrent armed clashes were already taking place along their borders and there was every likelihood of an open armed conflict breaking shortly. In other words, the Council should activate the procedures incorporated in Chapter VI, whenever necessary, rather than try to intervene after the outbreak of actual war, when it is extremely difficult to stop the fighting. The Secretary-General should be accorded a stronger position and better means to exercise authority. He or she should have the constitutional power to act swiftly when an international crisis calls for it. He should be the first to know when a conflict is likely to develop and be able to take preventive action. To this end, permanent political offices in key regions, military observer teams, fact-finding missions and military collective security forces could constitute a global emergency system.

The UN should have a permanent fund to make its financial position secure. Whether the 1986 agreement – under which "consensus" will be required for all budgetary decisions – will permanently solve all financial problems of the UN is yet to be seen. "Consensus" in effect means that each state has a veto. Everything will depend on the way compromises are worked out. If the developed states choose to use their veto power unreasonably to prevent even moderate increases in the UN budget, or if developing countries continually try to push through proposals leading to unreasonable budgetary expansion, the problems will remain unsolved. This will continue as long as the UN does not have a system of raising revenues independently for its activities.

Another field in which the UN has not been particularly successful in achieving its objectives is that of human rights. Though it has a plethora of human rights bodies and a vast collection of conventions, covenants, and other formal instruments, its influence on the Governments that have ratified them has not always been very effective.

It is necessary to improve the capacity of the United Nations to coordinate a large number of social and economic activities, now being carried out by its organs and specialized agencies. The existing coordinating bodies (ACC and ECOSOC) have only marginal influence over the UN system. Ideally, any new high-powered committee or council responsible for budgetary control should be given an overall coordinating function within the UN system.

A global law enforcement role for the UN should be elaborated focusing on the role of sanctions and military enforcement measures. There must be a clear understanding of the enforcement measures, their sequencing and timing that can be implemented by the international community when international law has been violated. As military measures may sometimes become necessary, the potential of the Military Staff Committee of the Security Council should be reviewed. This committee, practically dormant during the years of the Cold War, could play a significantly more important role in the future. The role of UN peacekeeping forces should also be expanded. They should not only deal with monitoring ceasefires and other means of ending or containing conflicts but could also be used to ensure that countries are not destabilized across frontiers. There is a need for securing agreement in principle on the form these forces should take and how they should be controlled. There are certain points on which wider agreement can be reached. Future peacekeeping should normally be authorized and controlled by the

Security Council; they should play a neutral political role within the country where they are operating; financing should, where possible, be under the regular budget but on a special scale. The possibility of a permanent peacekeeping fund should be explored. Meanwhile, the voluntary earmarking of forces and greater cooperation and coordination in training such forces could continue. UN missions could be used to oversee elections as was the case in Namibia and Nicaragua recently. Military units in the armed forces of all nations could be earmarked for these peacekeeping tasks.

The decline in respect for General Assembly resolutions, where the majority consists largely of very small states, is a fact of life and the further influx of tiny states into the UN is posing a serious problem. The oft-proposed solution, the introduction of a system of weighted voting, is difficult to implement. The majority of over-represented small states are hardly likely to agree to give up their present privileged position. Nor would even the basic principles of any such scheme be easy to agree upon by all states. Would it be based on population, on the gross national product, on contributions to the UN or what? Yet the ultimate choice seems to be between a limited measure of weighted voting or a decline in the importance attached to UN resolutions. If no change is made, the effect will be to reduce the influence of the Assembly to enhance the role of the Security Council.

The frequent use of veto power in the Security Council has resulted in oft-repeated calls for the abolition of the veto. However, the veto problem cannot be solved by any revision of the Charter, because of the opposition of the Great Powers to such an amendment. Under the circumstances, the permanent members of the Security Council should accept certain voluntary restrictions on their right to veto decisions. Further, the veto should be used only on vital issues and procedural matters should be immune from it. It is also desirable that the veto could be concerning the admission of new members and the peaceful settlement of disputes. It is also desirable that the composition of the Security Council, concerning its permanent members, should be changed and should include other great and potentially Great Powers like Germany, Japan, India and Brazil in the immediate future. However, it would be more appropriate if the status of permanent membership is abolished to democratize the Council while making it more representative.

To make the International Court of Justice more effective the members should agree to submit their legal disputes to it. As the member states are reluctant to accept the optional clause, the United Nations should broaden the scope of the work of the Court on its initiative. For example, the Security Council and the General Assembly can refuse to consider legal disputes and recommend to the parties that such disputes be taken to the Court. Such an attitude on the part of the Council and the Assembly may not compel the states to take their disputes to the Courts, but it would certainly encourage them to reach some settlement. If UN bodies are to play a leading role in developmental work, efforts should be made to ensure that as large a share as possible of the national development programmes are channelled through the UN agencies. Multilateral programmes not only reduce the effect of political bias in determining aid distribution but also make possible more rational coordination of programmes. The cooperative world climate we enjoy at the moment offers political advantages as well as the opportunity to open up substantial resources, which had earlier been diverted for war purposes. Governments in industrialized countries should pledge to allocate a specific part of their defence budgets to international cooperation. One billion people – one in five living on this planet – exist in conditions of extreme poverty. The world community should set as its goal the eradication of such poverty within the next two decades. All industrialized nations should set timeframes for providing one per cent of their GNP towards cooperative international development and the UN must monitor such efforts.

The United Nations, to live up to the challenges of tomorrow, needs certain changes which must be achieved in some measure. This could only be possible with the adoption of certain structural changes in the UN system making it obligatory for states to agree to compulsory jurisdiction in the long run. If the UN is to become an effective body, the obligations which member states agreed upon when joining it must not be contravened. The UN also does not pay much attention to the growing need for regional cooperation. One of the major ways to achieve political security and economic advancement in most nations is through regional cooperation. Collective self-reliance on an international scale is possible only if it can be achieved on a limited scale on a regional basis. This is one of the neglected areas which require greater formal recognition in the UN Charter.

Like any other written foundational document, the UN Charter lays out an organizational and functional arrangement that required amendment and reinterpretation as times and conditions have changed. Although the Charter has been amended formally only five times in the UN's history, the majority of changes in the United Nations have resulted from informal revisions in UN practice. Most importantly, the growth in UN membership, Cold War pressures and its aftermath, financial woes, U.S. discontent with the United Nations and peacekeeping and new-era demands on the organization have forced concerted reform in the United Nation. The reform process has been closely associated with the secretary-generalship of Kofi Annan, who tried to refocus the organization on the challenges of human rights protection, development, democratization, and emerging international civil society.

Cited Works

Cohen, Benjamin V., *The United Nations: Constitutional Developments, Growth and Possibilities*, Cambridge, Mass: Harvard University Press, 1961.

Claude, Iris L., *Swords into Ploughshares*, New York: Random, 1971.

Goodrich, L.M., *UN in a Changing World*, New York: Columbia University Press, 1974.

Luard, Evan, *United Nations, How it Works and What it Does*, London: Macmillan, 1979.

Nicholas, H.G., *The United Nations as a Political Institution*, London: Oxford University Press, 1975.

Riggs, Robert E. & Jack C. Plano, *The United Nations: International Organization and World Politics*, Chicago, Illinois: Dorsey Press, 1988.

21

ACHIEVEMENTS AND LIMITATIONS

For over 75 years, the United Nations, despite all its alleged failures and shortcomings, has been a living institution, a "going concern," which has left a permanent imprint on nearly every major political, economic, social and humanitarian problem of our age in its efforts to find solutions to them. The post-1945 era in world politics has been one of the unprecedented changes in every part of the globe—an era of decolonization, the emergence of a host of newly independent nations on the world scene, the Cold War between the superpowers, and continuing nuclear arms race, struggle for modernization and development in the Third World, recurring regional conflicts and most importantly, several technological changes which have created closer and more extensive contacts among the peoples of the world than was ever possible in any previous period. The United Nations has played a role in each of these developments on the world scene, developments which have accelerated the need for cooperation among the peoples of the world. Let us now examine some of the major achievements of the UN before we turn to some of its major objectives which remain unfulfilled.

Indeed, the UN has not been able to prevent wars, which is evident from the fact that there have been more than five hundred regional conflicts since 1945, and the nation-states have not yet come to a stage of evolution where they can renounce war as an instrument of national policy. Though nuclear weapons have not been used since 1945, thus averting a major world catastrophe, conventional weapons have frequently been employed in regional conflicts and the race for conventional as well as nuclear arms is still on. However, despite all this, the United Nations as an organization has made some modest contributions to reduce or contain conflicts in various regions of the world. The outbreak of hostilities anywhere brings a UN response, generally as a moderator or pacifier. The use of the "Uniting for Peace Proposal" since the Suez Crisis has been one of the most important contributions of the organization, to the maintenance of international peace and security. Peacekeeping has been one of the most significant innovations under the UN Charter which had originally provided for the device of collective security (this has been used only twice, since the inception of the UN). Collective security however became unworkable and the UN resorted to "peacekeeping" to defuse tensions in various conflict regions of the world. It is this dynamism and innovative character of the UN which has helped it to survive in a world, and has changed so rapidly since 1945.

Besides peacekeeping, the UN has adopted other methods to maintain peace among its members. By becoming an important meeting and debating forum for nations, it has provided members with opportunities to air their views and understand the viewpoints of others. In this way, it has helped to promote a spirit of understanding and accommodation among nations. One of the major causes of war is misperceptions, the United Nations by providing a continuing forum for discussion, where every state can try to increase its understanding of a situation, has created an environment where there can be an open debate on every major world issue. The East-West *detente* has been possible because of the opportunities provided by the United Nations to settle differences through dialogue. The UN has also helped the colonial world to adjust itself to its earlier territories as equal members of the international system. The continuing North-South dialogue has been carried out mostly within the confines of the UN. The United Nations has also been frequently used as a forum for lobbying support for issues, both conservative and innovative, especially the latter. Propaganda against racism, colonialism and a new international economic order are some examples of *anti-status quo* issues (issues, which could change the current world political or economic structure), which have been voiced in UN bodies.

The United Nations has today become the most important forum for using the diplomacy of reconciliation between member states as well as for the use of preventive diplomacy. With regards to both, the UN has managed to bring about the minimum of peace and security required by the international system to survive.

Through its trusteeship and non-self-governing provisions, the United Nations has provided the basic machinery needed for the most important as well as the biggest revolutions of our time—decolonization. It is debatable whether this process could have taken place in a relatively peaceful manner had it not been for the efforts of the UN. Through its principle of trusteeship, it has been able to maintain the international accountability needed for the transformation of the colonial states into independent ones. In this regard, it has provided them with a forum where they can stand on an equal footing with their colonial masters, thus breaking down the barriers of the past centuries without recrimination.

It is however in the field of functional cooperation that the United Nations record has been most impressive. The work of UN agencies in such areas as health, transportation, communication, food, science and education has made the world body an indispensable organ of multinational cooperation. Its trade and monetary institutions have been somewhat more controversial in their operations, but they too have performed a major role in reducing trade barriers and facilitating international payments.

Through multilateral programmes in specific functional areas, the United Nations has given international protection and material assistance to millions of refugees and has aided children and other target groups to meet their special needs. The UN system has also helped in a substantial flow of technical assistance and development capital to needy countries. Although the wide gap between the rich and the poor has not been bridged, the UN has made a significant contribution to the growth of the idea that development is an international responsibility.

The UN's role in promoting human rights has been limited largely to rule-making. Violations of UN standards in this regard have been innumerable. Nevertheless, through discussions, declarations, reports and international covenants sponsored by the UN, the organization seems to have promoted the cause of human rights as never before.

The Limits of UN Action

Judged by its self-proclaimed aims and objectives, United Nations' achievements have been modest. Given the practical limits that exist on effective international action, this does not seem surprising. The divisive effects of differing ideologies, cultures, material interests and levels of development have very often hindered effective multilateral cooperation. In the more sensitive areas of peace and security, where national power, prestige, and resource allocation are at stake, the UN has since its very inception been hampered by serious and continuing divisions—East-West, North-South, colonial-anticolonial, regional and bilateral power rivalries, etc. This is not exactly a suitable setting for a speedy resolution of international conflicts by international organizations. Another serious limitation on UN performance in every field has been the inability of the United Nations to enforce its decisions on states reluctant to conform to them. This is true not only of the permanent members of the Security Council (armed with the veto, which can nullify any action against them) but also of, other recalcitrant states against whom it has not been possible to impose decisions. Any international organization, which has no binding force on its members, is entirely dependent on the goodwill of its members to support its decisions and encourage others to comply with them. The greatest limitation of the UN system was and will remain the sovereignty of states and until the force of "collective will" becomes strong enough to bear the weight of more authoritative decisions, the UN will continue to function pretty much as it does today.

Cited Works

Baehr, Peter R. and Leon Gordenker, *The United Nations*, New York: Praeger, 1984.

Bajpai, U. S., *Forty Years of the UN*, New Delhi: Lancer International, 1986.

Claude, Iris L., *Swords into Ploughshares*, New York: Random, 1971.

Goodrich, L. M., *UN in a Changing World*, New York: Columbia University Press, 1974.

Goodspeed, S. S., *The Nature and Functions of International Organization*, New York: OUP, 1967.

Hingst Karen A. & Margaret P. Karan, *The UN in Post-Cold War Years*, Colorado: West View Press, 1996.

Luard, Evan, *The United Nations: How it Works and What it Does*, London: Macmillan, 1979.

Nicholas H., *The United Nations as a Political Institution*, London: OUP, 1975.

Riggs, Robert E. & Jack C. Plano, *The United Nations: International Organisation and World Politics*, Chicago: The Dorsey Press, 1988.

Weiss, Thomas G., P. Forsythe, David, Coate, A. Roger, *The UN and Changing World Politics*, Colorado: Westview Press, 1996.

22

REFORMS, ROLE AND RELEVANCE

The United Nations is a multinational forum of institutional structures, specialized agencies, programmes, and funds dispersed around the world that have increasingly come to address the global (as per its charter mandate) and sometimes domestic issues, that were earlier not considered pivotal to its principal objective of maintaining international peace and security. Former Secretary-General Kofi Annan described a "new" United Nations in his Millennium Summit Report in September 2000, titled *We The People.* At this invited forum of world statesmen, Non-governmental organizations, and private citizens at UN headquarters, the Secretary-General noted that it is "thematic diplomacy" that made the United Nations a "forum for sharing information, conducting negotiations, elaborating norms and voicing expectations, coordinating the behaviour of states and other actors, and pursuing common plans of action". He envisioned the UN as a universal Intergovernmental Organization (IGO) committed to peace, human security, and economic development. The UN Charter, codified in the name of "We the People", advocated a new emphasis on the rights of "the person" in both domestic and international life. Annan called for a United Nations that acknowledged state sovereignty but would never let that principle stand in the way of defending individual rights or providing critical international humanitarian assistance in case of large-scale violation of those same rights within a state. This is what the current UN Secretary-General António Guterres has called for in the Ukraine crisis that started in February 2022: to aid the civilians in a war that has led to a large-scale violation of human rights.

The UN may be an institution in the throes of change in the 21st century. The UN agenda of the early 21st century includes a renewed interest in potential problems that confront states and their citizens on a global level and require multinational cooperation and the proactive involvement of international organizations for their solutions. e.g. Climate Change requires a heavy commitment to the global environment both by the developed and the developing countries. The argument that peace and human security may best be achieved by the "spill-over" effect of increasing cooperation among people in international organizations through the foundational cooperation on non-political issues, to begin with, has a rich 200-year history of theoretical debates followed by practices of international organizations. The United Nations is pursuing many areas of "thematic" diplomacy, but the following themes predominate—the environment, gender, the control of HIV/AIDS and other deadly diseases like Ebola or Covid-19, disarmament, sustainable development, globalization, human rights, nation-building, poverty eradication, population control, democratization, and international law.

Though the United Nations is a multinational organization, the non-state actors have gradually evolved a role in designing the UN policy and the success or failure of its programme implementation. The UN Charter had only given "consultative status" to the NGOs in the Economic and Social Council, but the NGO community now dominates the UN world conferences, formulates a global agenda that this organization gives ears to, and serves as the most sincere evaluator of the UN's socio-economic programmes. The second group of non-state actors includes the corporate sector or multinational companies working in different countries. Beginning with Secretary-General Annan's "Global Compact" initiative in 1999, thousands of private companies have voluntarily associated themselves with the work of the United Nations.

The United Nations' mandate has always been to impose the rule of law as much on citizens as it does amongst its member states. This is in contradistinction with the UN Charter's injunction in Article 2 (7) that "Nothing contained in the present Charter shall authorize the United Nations to intervene in matters which are essentially within the domestic jurisdiction of any state". International law permits voluntary adjudication of interstate conflicts, but it does not reach individuals within a state. Earlier, in rare cases only, like the Nuremberg tribunals, did the world community seek to apply legal penalties to individuals who violated standards of universal legal morality. Post-Covid interventions in the form of "state-building" which followed an earlier relatively neutral monitoring process of "peacekeeping" also reflect the new concern for individual citizen rights over state sovereignty. Evolved with varying degrees of effectiveness, this new kind of peacekeeping has faced many brickbats since it led to a reinvention of the charter mandate in the context of the twenty-first century. The United Nations appears to have transited from being essentially an IGO of sovereign states primarily concerned with keeping the immediate peace among its members; it has also become an agency to solve intrastate disputes.

The United Nations has chosen to make "democratization", the *leitmotif* of the 21st century. The United Nations was founded as an intergovernmental organization to maintain peace and security. However, other concerns reflected in the Charter provisions for a trusteeship system were decolonization, human rights, and the specialized agencies to address common economic and social problems shared by all human beings across the world. The United Nations has survived, so far, partly because of a timely effort to reinvent itself and partly because of democratization that reflects more efforts towards participation, accountability, and transparency. It has also changed its agenda, which implicitly recognizes that the maintenance of international peace and security in due course depends on fulfilling the needs of human security.

In this context, it would be interesting to enumerate the various roles the UN has played so far and examine their relevance for the future.

The United Nations as a Norm-Setter

The United Nations has always played a significant role in creating the atmosphere or climate in which adaptation of norms takes place in the international arena. This involves the process of progressive law creation in a global society with broad seminal consequences. It includes the development of both substantive norms of international politics and operative rules of the game for use in international relations. It often involves the formulation of specific procedures for the legitimation of the political activities of individual states in the global system. The position of the UN is of considerable importance for each of these functions. It offers a variety of opportunities for extensive multilateral contacts and even acts as a catalyst for change in the international system through its norm-setting activities.

Articulation and Aggregation of Interests

This is an important United Nations function. The UN is an instrument of conference diplomacy. Here states make their demands, express their fears, articulate their interests and through a process of aggregation or by universal consensus, thus seek to fulfil their demands. The UN provides an international forum for communication among states where all nations can meet and hold talks.

Though the climate of opinion prevailing in 1945 did not foster it, the possibility of using the United Nations as an instrument of partisan politics has always been a subject of interest to several states and groups of states. The fundamental point of interest arises from the potential of the UN as a legitimizer of intrinsically partisan interests and as a device for cumulating or focusing the influence of otherwise unstructured interest groups.

When the Cold War got underway in the late 1940s, the Western states discovered that they could effectively dominate the policy of the United Nations, and they had good reason to desire legitimation for many activities. There ensued, therefore, the Uniting for Peace Era, which lasted until the aftermath of the Korean episode. The changes, both in the composition of the organization and the international system itself, destroyed this relationship during the 1950s. But these very changes generated new efforts to use the UN for partisan purposes. The next period devoted much attention to the role the organization played as a guardian of the interests of weak states, especially those non-aligned or neutralists on East-West issues. This role, in turn, has proved to be divisive in recent years. African and Asian interests have become more and more divergent as the organization has become less willing to become involved in many Asian problems, and the Africans have increasingly asserted their growing numerical dominance. Consequently, the Africans alone are beginning to spearhead more significant efforts to use the UN as an ally in many of their political struggles. The re-emergence of Great

Powers' interest, while using the organization as a forum, at least for *de facto* political legitimization (as is happening currently in Ukraine in 2022), however, has now, simultaneously, restricted these efforts of the lesser powers—though they cannot produce a genuine reversion to the patterns of the early years. In short, therefore, there is currently a growing ambiguity surrounding the role of the UN for partisan purposes.

Conflict Management

This is probably the most obvious of United Nations functions. The UN, since its inception, has tried to eliminate conflicts or, if that is impossible, at least to control or keep them within tolerable limits.

Perhaps the greatest hope underlying the establishment of the United Nations was based on the idea that it would play a significant role in maintaining a minimum level of peace and stability in the international system. In this sense, the UN assumes the mantle of the League as a substitute for the more traditional practices of "power politics". The conception of the role of the UN, which has remained much of influence: in reality, has operated as a regulator: the organization should, as much as possible, refrain from influencing the outcomes of specific interactions in the international arena. Therefore, the role of the UN is that of a rules-keeper who imposes stringent regulations or restrictions on contestants by force if necessary or calls a halt to specific confrontations that may get out of hand.

Even though its relevance is strictly limited to some fundamental features of the global system, the regulator conception has remained unchanged over the years. Thus, it is impossible for an organization such as the United Nations, to effectively adopt a position above "power politics" in the contemporary world. Various forms of power politics are inevitable in a state system that invariably permeates the activities of international organizations concerned with highly politicized issues, such as those that fall under the heading of peace and security. And the growing importance of conflict patterns, stem from internal war situations in recent years, has only emphasized the difficulties of avoiding political interventions in conducting regulatory operations.

Consequently, the idea of the United Nations as a neutral regulator is increasingly coming into question. It is becoming quite hard in recent years to avoid the question of the feasibility of compartmentalizing activities: how can the UN continue to engage in essentially neutral regulatory operations while, at the same time, undertaking other actions which have a distinctly partisan flavour and are, therefore, incompatible with a regulatory conception?

UN Reform

Four factors which pushed the UN to a reformed mode towards the end of the 20th century:

- The US government demands for significant institutional changes since the developing countries majority in the UN system did not give any additional advantage in decision making to the US in any UN body despite its contribution of almost 25 per cent of the UN budget. Even the Security Council, shared the "veto" power with four other members.

- A long-term financial crisis was driven by many members' non-payment of their UN assessed dues, particularly the unwillingness of the United States to meet its financial obligations to UN Bodies.
- The expansion of UN budgetary obligations, particularly for peacekeeping, the UN Administrative and Budgetary Committee approved 8 billion dollars in 2014-2015, which included peacekeeping, engaging in nation-building, battling terrorism, and providing humanitarian assistance.

In 1996, Kofi Annan became the seventh Secretary-General of the United Nations and made a far-reaching reform programme. He delivered on his commitment, issuing *Renewing the United Nations*, the most radical set of administrative and financial reform proposals made in the institution's history. During the next six years and even later, reform would come in three broad areas: administrative, programmatic, and structural.

Most of the programmatic reforms came in the wake of the Millennium Summit of 2000. They maybe grouped into three categories viz., peacekeeping, development and democratization, and UN's relations with international civil society.

The United Nations, under Annan, gave special attention to peacekeeping and the Department of Peacekeeping Operations (DPKO), which he had headed from 1993 to 1995 when the United Nations experienced some of its worst failures in nation-building and peacemaking. After apparent peacekeeping successes in Angola (1988), Namibia (1989), and Cambodia (1992), confidence that the United Nations could intervene in disintegrating states and restore peace effectively to start the process of nation-building, gave a shot in the arm to UN activism in conflict zones.

By the end of the Millennium summit, Annan had convinced the assembled nations, often with divergent views about various issues like development and human rights, to approve a declaration of the world's aspirations for the twenty-first century. They agreed on six "fundamental values" essential to multistate relations, freedom, equality, solidarity, tolerance, respect for nature, and a sense of shared responsibility. These values, though inherent in the UN Charter, were never central to the day-to-day diplomacy within the international organization. The declaration set specific goals, including the following: to halve by 2015 the number of people living on less than one dollar a day, hunger, or have no access to clean water, ensure that all children complete primary school and that no gender inequality exists in education, to reduce maternal mortality by three-fourths and the deaths of children younger than five years old by two-thirds, to stop the spread of HIV/AIDS, malaria, and other infectious diseases, to achieve significant improvement in the lives of at least one hundred million slum dwellers, to promote gender equality and the empowerment of women, to encourage industry to provide the benefits of new technologies to all across the globe.

These goals were a combination of both development and democratization targets. As world conflicts shifted from interstate causes to intrastate ones to religious, ethnic, and economic origins in the developing world, Annan saw an opportunity for the UN to reinvent itself. Through a combination of peacekeeping and state-building, the United Nations could address the complex overwhelming internal problems of "fragile" states, could raise the standard of living for millions, and could promote international stability by ending human rights abuses within countries. Annan was instrumental in the advocacy of a new understanding of the concept of security. Once synonymous with the defence of territory from external attack, the requirements for security, he said, should come to include the protection of communities and individuals from internal violence. He argued for the United Nations to defend "personal sovereignty". Being determined to uphold the new era of peacekeeping, humanitarian intervention, and nation-building, he also made a case for not shielding crimes against humanity. He reiterated that the United Nations has a "moral duty" to intervene on behalf of the individual.

Later events have underscored the growing demand for international intervention in state matters. The violence of the civil wars in the Former Yugoslavia (the 1990s), genocide in Rwanda (1994), violence in Timor-Leste (1999), bloodbath in Darfur (2006-2007), anarchic civil strife in the Central African Republic (2014), and serious human rights violations in the Congo and currently in Ukraine (2022) in recent times have all contributed to the UN's growing willingness to intervene and attempt to create "sustainable" states.

The Responsibility to Protect, (R2P) is one of the most ambitious and interventionist conceptual doctrines, which emerged after the UN's World Summit (2005) advocated external actors (preferably with UN approval) to intervene in the internal affairs of a dysfunctional state that is unable or unwilling to protect its inhabitants from serious harm. R2P, a new and original notion in world politics and international law, heralds an extension of evolving moral sensibilities deriving from human rights traditions, wherein individual human rights have priority over other rights of a state.

Annan's successor, Ban Ki-moon, diversified on the programmatic reforms of advancing democracy and personal sovereignty through nation-building in post-conflict states. In 2009, he published a *Guidance Note on Democracy*, in which he advocated "holistic democracy". The document laid out a charter of the objectives, content, and procedures for the implementation of the democratization that failed in transitioning weak or non-democratic states. By 2009, democratic governance in all of its components had entered the largest zone of UNDP investment, accounting for 37 per cent of the agency's budget. In 2015, the UN Development Programme sanctioned $772 million for 723 "democratic governance" projects across the world.

In Annan's view, the United Nations could achieve its goals only through partnership with civil society on the international, national, and subnational levels. Early efforts of the Secretary-General to engage civil society included the creation of the Global Compact in 1999, which invited corporations to establish formal relationships with the United

Nations, the encouragement of NGO participation in world conferences and the work of UN agencies, and the cultivation of influential individuals in different countries with UN work.

In February 2003, Annan appointed a panel of eminent persons, headed by Fernando Henrique Cardoso, the former president of Brazil, to look at UN-Civil society relations and to make recommendations on how such relationships might improve. The panel issued the Cardoso Report in June 2004. The six Panel members called for a "paradigm shift" in the work of the United Nations, with reforms based on four principles:

- The United Nations should be the "convener" of multiple global issues, facilitating rather than "rowing".
- The United Nations should attempt to forge permanent "partnerships" whenever possible. The United Nations must recognize that global civil society now wields real power in the name of citizens.
- The United Nations must attempt to connect the global with the local, acting as the mediator between the citizen and the world. The United Nations will implement its programmes effectively only if it has a working relationship with the subnational actors present in a nation-state.
- The United Nations can strengthen global governance by becoming an "actor" itself in civil society.

Annan also advised the creation of two new bodies and a revitalization of the Secretariat, ECOSOC, and the General Assembly. To address the growing challenges of peacekeeping and nation-building, he urged the creation of a Peacebuilding Commission (PBC) which was to act as an agency to "help states with the transition from war to peace" a missing mechanism in the UN structure. This Commission would focus on creating new national institutions, ensuring necessary reconstruction financing, enhancing coordination among international agencies, and reviewing progress on post-conflict recovery. Annan also recommended a replacement of the existing Commission on Human Rights with a new, smaller Human Rights Council. He argued that the current body had lost legitimacy, given its rotating membership, which often included states accused of human rights abuses, which, therefore, needed to be replaced with a council having "a status, authority, and capability" commensurate with its importance. He urged that the new council at large be elected by a two-thirds vote in the General Assembly.

Post Covid-19 Emerging New World Order: Issues

The Covid-19 pandemic has been the most consequential global event of 2020, whose impact will cascade over at least the next decade. The pandemic brought home the costs of historical failures, such as the neglect of public health systems in most countries worldwide.

The human cost has been huge. Around 1.76 million people have lost their lives, in addition to almost 80 million cases that were confirmed to have protracted it. The virus was a social leveller, neither wealth nor power offered protection. Lockdowns and physical distancing crippled the global economy. The cumulative damage could be up to $28 trillion over five years (2020-2025) to the pre-pandemic trend. Globally, millions have slipped back into poverty.

The geopolitical rivalry between the US and China sharpened with the pandemic. China's gaming of the global system had already started impacting Western democracies. But with the onset of the pandemic, China, where the virus had originated, took a decisive turn to be a benign hegemon. President Donald Trump was a political victim of the virus, however, his defeat paved the way for the US to regain its global leadership role, ending the disarray among Western democracies.

The pandemic marks the end of the post-Cold War phase of globalization, we are heading towards more focused groupings of the like-minded, rather than one where everyone was welcome in a loose group with a vague hope of eventual convergence. The unprecedented medical response through international vaccine development showed the importance of collaboration. But that still leaves the world with an unanswered question. If in 2020, our choices had unleashed a zoonotic disaster, there is still a big challenge ahead. Climate change needs global collaboration and compromise in a big way. Will the geopolitical rivalry still provide space to combat shared threats?

The US in the New Era

So much has been written on Afghanistan, marking the end of the US Empire in 2021. The US reluctance to act like an empire, often as an afterthought exhibits the strong isolationist streak that has always been a powerful force in US thinking. The US has long been a unique mix of imperial and anti-imperial tendencies that defy easy categorization.

During the Cold War, the US was a quite powerful military machine, yet it lacked the imperial thirst for the territory that not just requires the willingness but the determination to fight long wars. While the US was strong enough to force regime changes in many countries, it was stalled or beaten repeatedly by much smaller powers in long-drawn-out regional conflicts.

However, attacking the US territory, crossed a line that could not be ignored. The US struck back in Afghanistan. Its quick success in ousting the Taliban in 2001 led an over-confident Bush to invade Iraq, supposedly to capture weapons of mass destruction (these did not exist) and create a modern democracy (which proved almost impossible). The conflicts in Afghanistan and Iraq did not end quickly, and the US public lost interest in both. US President Obama pledged to build up troops and then exit Afghanistan. Thus, the US withdrawal was foretold. The Afghan government's abrupt fall and the Taliban takeover of Afghanistan in 2021 took the world by surprise.

The UN states that Afghanistan is mired in a humanitarian crisis affecting 18 million people, or half its population. UN aid efforts can finance help for only 38 per cent of the country's population, so the world body urgently needs nearly $800 million, according to the UN Reports to perform its task of humanitarian assistance.

Recent developments in Afghanistan have brought back the attention to long-standing conflicts and the impact of such prolonged problems on nations. Globally, many countries are still affected by terrorism, which has disturbed peace and economies, and Afghanistan has been among the worst-affected countries for many years now. She has also incurred heavy economic losses from terrorism. As a result, the number of terror incidents saw a massive increase over the past decade resulting in more deaths.

The global economic impact of terrorism was estimated to be $26.4 billion in 2019–25 per cent less than in 2018. This is the fifth consecutive year it has declined. The declining trend of terrorism in Iran, Nigeria, Pakistan and Syria was largely due to the improvement over the last four years.

The worst 5 countries on the Global Terrorism Index – 2020

- Afghanistan
- Iraq
- Nigeria
- Syria
- Somalia

Following World War II, the United States provided the vision and the resources to create the postwar liberal order based on the UN system, the Bretton Woods institutions, and the rule of law. Can the United States, as a superpower in relative decline today, provide the necessary leadership when it has so often thwarted international law over the years, failed to ratify key human rights treaties, and reinterpreted other conventions in its national interest? The United States itself is now so significantly hampered by domestic political divisions and government paralysis that it is hard to imagine it providing much leadership for elements of global governance.

Russia and the New World Order

In a historic resolution, backed by 141 of its 193 members, the United Nations General Assembly (UNGA) on 2nd March 2022 "deplored in the strongest terms" Russia's aggression in Ukraine, reaffirmed its commitment to the sovereignty and territorial integrity of Ukraine and demanded Russia "immediate cease of use of force" and completely and unconditionally" withdraw all its troops from Ukraine's internationally recognised borders. Only five countries – Russia, Belarus, Eritrea, North Korea, and Syria – voted against the resolution, and 34 abstained.

The UNGA resolution "condemned" Russia's decision of 24 February 2022, to launch a "special military operation" in Ukraine, saying that `no territorial acquisition from the threat or use of force would be recognised as "legal". Calling for an "immediate peaceful resolution" of the conflict through "political dialogue, negotiations, mediation and other peaceful means", the UNGA resolution called upon Russia to abide by principles of the UN Charter and also called upon all parties to abide by the Minsk Agreement (the peace framework to resolve the conflict in eastern Ukraine signed in 2014 and 2015) and supported attempts at de-escalation of the current situation.

Ukraine's President, Volodymyr Zelensky, spoke at the United Nations Security Council (UNSC) soon after in the backdrop of the discovery of mass graves and summary civilian executions in Bucha in Kyiv's suburbs – with evidence suggesting that Russian troops were responsible for the atrocities. Mr Zelensky called for drastic reforms of the UN system, where the UNSC remains a reflection of the realities of the post-World War II moment rather than the 21st century, having failed to discharge its responsibility of maintaining international peace and security.

Most international groups and western countries are united in proclaiming that war crimes were committed in Bucha and that Russian soldiers left behind evidence of violations of international laws and the Geneva Conventions. In most of these cases, where armies targeted civilians, the UN had either chosen to ignore or merely issued repeated appeals for peace. The world community and the UN, in particular, must ensure that this apathy does not get repeated in Ukraine. The international community must assist investigators in collecting evidence of alleged war crimes and build a case against the perpetrators of the atrocities in forums such as the International Court of Justice and the International Criminal Court (ICC). To be sure, such mechanisms can still be ineffective - Russia has long rejected the authority of the ICC and Moscow's veto as a permanent member of the UN Security Council adds further complications. Several deadlocked votes in the UN, over the past months, have shown just how international law enforcement is held hostage to strategic national interest.

Despite the US invasion and occupation of Iraq (2003-2011) and Russia's annexation of Crimea in 2014 one had hoped that interstate wars, involving great powers were not expected to recur in the 21st century. The tactical movers of contemporary world politics were supposed to emerge from global financial networks, religious revivalism, enduring inequality, terrorism, lethal technologies, and/or the anthropogenic climate crisis in the vulnerable planetary ecosystem. A global pandemic was the last to join this daunting list of public policy challenges for the 21st century.

However Russia's full-scale invasion of Ukraine revives the great power war debates. What do Russia's invasion and Ukraine's resistance convey to the rest of us and the remainder of the 21st century? War, reflecting the relations, patterns, and balances of military power between States, is understandably dominated by great powers, i.e., States with system-shaping capabilities and intentions. Nuclear deterrence has reduced the incidence of war between great powers in the last half-century but not their proclivities for war-making and lack of hesitation to use force to secure their vital national interests.

The Russia-Ukraine war continues unabated. The largest ground war in Europe since World War II has forced nearly five million people to flee Ukraine, with another seven million simmering as internal refugees. Despite the Russian withdrawal from the northern areas of Ukraine, cities in the eastern and southern regions remain under siege.

There are several speculations about the causes of the war. The eastward expansion of the North Atlantic Treaty Organization (NATO) and Ukraine's NATO ambitions were viewed as a serious existential threat by Russian President Vladimir Putin. For several years and several times before the war, Putin had stated that Ukraine never had "real statehood" and that the country was an integral part of Russia's "own history, culture, and spiritual space". Any western encroachment into this space would, therefore, not be tolerated. The ease with which Russia annexed Crimea from Ukraine in 2014 could have influenced Putin to believe that a quick victory was possible through military force and that the western response to such a transgression would be near absent.

All these reasons stand true to some extent, but one underlying cause of this war is the behaviour of great powers in the international system. The realist school of thought believes that the international system is anarchic due to the absence of any legitimate authority to regulate disputes between sovereign States. This induces nation-States to compete for more and more power.

American political scientist John J Mearsheimer put forth the theory of "Offensive Realism", in which he argues that the international system creates powerful incentives for states to look for opportunities to gain power at the expense of others. Every state's secret dream is to be the hegemon in the world system. Great powers do everything to weaken other rising powers. This dynamic has been playing out between the United States (US) and Russia in Europe since the end of The Cold War.

Following the breakup of the erstwhile Soviet Union, the US emerged as the unchallenged superpower. With a weakened Russia, between 1999 and 2009, 12 Eastern Europe and Baltic countries joined NATO, moving towards the Russian border. When the first decade of the 21st century was coming to a close, Russia was pushing back to reassert authority over its sphere of influence with military interventions in Georgia and Ukraine and cyber-attacks in Estonia and Ukraine.

The US's focus has also shifted from the global war on terrorism to great power competition. President Joe Biden's 2021 Interim National Security Strategy has talked about the changing "distribution of power across the world" and "growing rivalry with China, Russia, and other authoritarian states". Russia invaded Ukraine to display its authority over its traditional sphere of influence. The lack of major military victories in the first two months of conflict has provided an opportunity to use the US to weaken Russia by getting it embroiled in a long and bloody war. Apart from crippling economic sanctions against Russia, the US and NATO have provided more than $3 billion in military aid to Ukraine. Whichever way the war unfolds, it is clear that Russia will emerge as a much feebler power in the future. Ukraine is putting up a heroic resistance but may suffer devastating destruction. United Nations Secretary-General Antonio Guterres has warned that rising food and oil prices caused by the Ukraine conflict could throw up to 1.7 billion people – over one-fifth of humanity – into poverty, destitution, and hunger on a scale not seen in decades.

The new power balance, likely to emerge after the Ukraine war, will undoubtedly influence the ongoing great power rivalry between the US and China. It is premature to assess how this could play out the broad aims of the two sides will remain unchanged. China will continue to strive for regional hegemony while the US will attempt to prevent China from becoming a peer competitor. Europe is facing its most dangerous crisis in decades by way of the Russian aggression on Ukraine. Putin has moved to establish a Russian power role in Eurasia. The United States President Joe Biden's position followed by NATO is drastically different. They believe that Russia was and will always be a potential threat to the West. Firstly, the US and Europeans will continue to weaponize their allies in Europe and elsewhere for the containment and isolation of Russia and China. Secondly, the US will set the agenda and lead security in Europe.

The US will not send its forces into Ukraine, but fortify NATO forces or bases on its flanks. The US prefers regional wars in Europe, such as Serbia and Bosnia, or interventionist wars in Iraq, Libya, Syria, and Afghanistan. The Centre for Economic Policy Research (India) estimates that it will cost between $220 billion and $540 billion to rebuild Ukraine after the war. Accurate figures for military losses are never easy to collate, but it is evident that the Russian armed forces have also suffered severe damage. In addition, World Bank projections display that Russia's economy has plunged into recession, with output projected to contract by 11.2 per cent in 2022.

Mostly the Global South is weary of the great powers and their muscle-flexing. They are arguing for a return to diplomacy and are in favour of mechanisms that will ensure security and an honourable exit from conflict by both warring parties.

As the wars go on, the innocent civilians will suffer due to inequalities, economic deprivations and lack of guaranteed civil order or civil rights, as it happens in regions embroiled in interstate or intrastate conflicts.

China in the New Order

China will play an increasingly dominant role in the UN in the coming years. Very little thought has been given by countries to the consequences of a China-dominated international order. All permanent members have misused the veto to escape censure in the Security Council and control other organs of the UN. But China displays utter contempt for the most basic obligation under the Charter "to refrain in their international relations from the threat or use of force". Its sabre-rattling against Taiwan is against the letter and spirit of the UN Charter, even if it considers it to be a Chinese province. China demonstrates no commitment to other values of the UN like democracy, human rights and the peaceful settlement of disputes. It is the only major country which is not a party to the Convention on Civil and Political Rights. It has also refused to honour the ruling of international arbitration in the dispute in the South China Sea. China seeks to dominate the UN system as no other country has done. Four of the 15 specialized agencies of the UN are now headed by Chinese nationals. China emulates Western countries in making voluntary donations and placing its nationals in the secretariats of international organizations.

Can China play a leadership role? There could be a change from its record in the 1980s and 1990s of playing a low-key role, showing little interest in or respect for the norms, principles, and even rules of the international organizations it joined. There is increasing evidence of China's "selective multilateralism", in its relationship to ASEAN and its initiatives in the SCO and with the BRICS. There is also clear evidence since 2013 of China's assertiveness as a rising power, it is flouting the law of the sea, and thwarting efforts to impose standards of good governance and sustainability in development aid and investment. Its leadership role in the creation of new international economic and financial institutions such as the Asian Infrastructure Bank and the New Development Bank challenges the dominance of the Bretton Woods institutions and the United States.

The reality is that, in today's world, no single state or another actor will dominate or provide leadership in the manner the United States did after World War II. Leadership will come from many quarters-from individual states (large and small or middle-sized) transnational advocacy groups, public-private partnerships, corporations and perhaps even prominent individuals. There are multiple authorities in global politics that "draw their authority from expertise, morality, competence, and other sources that are independent of the state". It may be that a more robust, universal-membership body will replace the UN, should a global crisis of sufficient magnitude provide the impetus. In short, there is no assurance that any particular form of global governance is or will be inherently "good", and any assessment surely depends on the purposes it serves, its effectiveness in making a real difference, and see who benefits.

Concluding Observations: UN as a Catalyst for Change

There are other ideas concerning possible roles for the United Nations in achieving authoritative adjustments in the effective distribution of world values. One of the fundamental problems in a decentralized state system is the achievement of political change without radically disrupting the system itself. This problem has become increasingly complex in the contemporary world with the large-scale use of violence as a means of achieving political change. Nevertheless, it remains extremely difficult for the UN to play an effective role in this area because political change frequently involves the redistribution of values, for at least some of the actors in the international system. And it is hardly expected that influential actors will find it easy to preside over their decline even if the process is facilitated by the neutral position of the UN.

Throughout its history, therefore, the United Nations has been hesitant in assuming active roles relating explicitly to the achievement of political change even though activities of this kind constitute, in a real sense, a logical corollary to the passive role of the regulator. This has been especially evident in cases where a military force would be necessary to achieve political change. Consequently, the UN has sometimes displayed a tendency to freeze dangerous conflicts in the interests of regulation without doing much to resolve the underlying issues.

Despite this fundamental limitation, however, the United Nations has affected processes of political change in some areas over the years. It has played a significant role in liquidating colonial relationships. Besides, on some occasions, it has played several key disguised roles in bringing about political change, for example, in popularizing the ideas of "human security" and "personal sovereignty" over the old cardinal principles used in International Relations: ideas of state-centric security and state sovereignty. But these activities are often delicate and their significance seems to lie more in *ad hoc* considerations associated with specific cases than in their impact on the long-term evolution of the UN role itself. In recent years, on the other hand, the developing countries (and especially the Africans) have launched, perhaps for the first time in UN history, a concerted drive to utilize the organization as a genuine legislative force in international politics—not only on specific problems such as democratization in Africa but also on more general issues arising from the unequal distribution of economic resources between the developed North and the developing South. It seems likely that the activities of the UN in the area of political change will be a focus of contention concerning appropriate roles for the organization in the foreseeable future.

Since the end of the 20th century and the beginning of the 21st, there has been a strong emphasis in many circles on the need to supplement international regulatory procedures with longer-term efforts aimed at fulfilling the underlying requirements of sustainability in a state's system. The Charter of the United Nations places considerable emphasis on these longer-term activities, especially in such areas, as economic development and human rights.

The United Nations has, on the whole, played a role of considerable significance in long-term activities. It is, of course, true that it has not yet been able to stimulate a massive increase in aid programmes for the underdeveloped world or presided over a wholesale transfer of existing programmes from bilateral to multilateral bases. Moreover, these longer-term UN activities are certainly more impressive than past multilateral efforts. It is now increasingly accepted that the totality of UN programmes directed towards promoting national development efforts thus generate effects more far-reaching than their financial dimensions would suggest. Several new programmes (for example, UNDP) indicate the strength of this link between changes in the overall international system and the evolving pattern in the distribution of UN resources.

There are virtually no general conclusions to draw from this discussion of the current flux both in \the international system and the United Nations except to stress the absence of clarity. The current confusion surrounding the UN indeed stems from the rapidly changing quality of the international system. The indeterminate nature of current trends in world politics makes it extraordinarily difficult to project a probable evolutionary course for the future.

The clearly defined contours of the bipolar international system under which the UN Charter system worked for the most of the 20th century, most ineffectively, due to the irreconcilable ideological antagonism and superpower rivalry, which have virtually disappeared today. One of the superpowers, the Soviet Union, disintegrated, and the emergence of the United States as the only superpower gave rise to speculation about the possible emergence of a unipolar world. However, a widely shared view today is that the emerging world order is multipolar. Many scholars believe that the United States is a declining economic power. New power centres like China, Germany and India are emerging and all of them are economic titans. The shift in international politics is from military power rivalry to economic power confrontation.

We are already at the threshold of a new balance of power system. The United States, Russia, China and some members of the developing world would constitute this new power configuration. Apart from the declining military rivalry and ascending economic competition, the new world order is also witnessing a rise in ethnic violence and the resurgence of war as a serious tool of national interest after the Russian invasion of Ukraine in 2022.

So, the new world order is, in any case, not going to be a millennium of peace and order. If we also take into account, terrorism – global and local – the new world order is going to see a lot of violence, both structural and institutional, which will have a tremendous dehumanizing effect. It is going to be an unequal world order coexisting with a lot of nuclear and conventional weapons despite the progress made in the direction of democracy, human rights and institution-building. The burning issues which transcend democracy and human rights stem from economic disparity dividing the rich and poor nations—the squalor and degradation in the quality of life prevailing in parts of the developing world.

The rapidly shifting nature of the underlying context of world politics and the consequent emergence of a variety of qualitatively new concerns in international politics also contribute to the prevailing sense of fluidity in both the overall global system and the politics of the United Nations. There are fundamentally new concerns arising from rapid developments in many areas, such as exploring possible uses of the oceans, population growth, an urban agglomeration, climate change, and so forth. At the same time, virtually all relationships in world politics are sharply affected by the phenomenon of continuous innovation associated with constant, rapid, and accelerating developments in a wide range, of both military and non-military technologies. In other words, the emerging political flux discussed in the preceding paragraphs is playing itself out in an international system whose fundamental contextual conditions are also changing at an unprecedented rate.

This fluidity in the international system creates both—opportunities and pitfalls for the United Nations. By its very nature, the situation emphasizes the norm creation and the role of collective legitimization of the organization. The fact that many of the emerging problems are relatively new ones, but makes them seem more promising areas for UN activity than many of the long-standing and intractable political difficulties confronting the organization. The UN may well be able to play a role in creating regulatory arrangements for new human endeavours.

As to the pitfalls, the temptation to move into each new area as a major participant, despite the clear-cut political limitations on the capacities of the organization in the present international system, raises serious dangers of over-commitment. Though the source of this problem is understandable in terms of the Universalist thrust of the UN, its potential consequences are sufficiently important in terms of realistic political calculations to warrant self-limitation of its role in many cases.

Lastly, by far the most important prerequisite for making the United Nations a more effective institution is the willingness of its members to let it work. This requires a sufficient commitment on the part of all members to allow collective decision-making to succeed, i.e., a readiness to accept decisions that are often contrary to their immediate desires and interests. An argument often repeated is that if the more powerful states are to cooperate with the organization, their voice will have to be given weightage commensurate with their power. But these states should also not take this as a license to abuse their power in such a way as to alienate themselves from the weak. The interests of the rich, as well as the poor, can and should be reconciled if both are willing to compromise in the name of peace. The UN was built on the bedrock of Great Power consensus. However, as events have shown (the most recent being the Russian invasion of Ukraine) there will be no easily mobilized five-power consensus. If it is to occur at all, it will normally have to be produced. Each power will have its views, its interests and its client governments to defend. What this means is that agreed solutions will only come about by careful and patient negotiations to secure a balance of interest. The UN's role will be in promoting and guiding such negotiations. The belief that the UN aims to produce resolutions or to win votes needs to be replaced by a recognition that it aims to produce accommodations through encouraging patient negotiations and diplomacy.

What this means is that the United Nations should seek to become far more effective than it is today, in the words of its Charter: a "centre for harmonizing the interests of nations". It should be better equipped to grow into precisely such a centre. For the UN is not, whatever was once hoped, a world government which can take authoritative decisions binding on its members. It has not yet been able to transform fundamentally the nature of inter-state relations and the bases on which they exist. What it can do, if its activities are properly channelized, is to modify those relations by the power of influence it alone can still command. The period we have entered is Janus-faced. It wears both the aspect of hope and the countenance of dangerous unrestraint. In one major segment of world affairs, we have witnessed a political change of a phenomenal character e.g. the entire process of transition from decolonization to today's globalization. In large parts of the globe, however, the scene continues to be one of simmering resentments, violent collisions and, at best, a precarious peace. The question of whether the more beneficial recent developments like the withering of East-West tensions will have a healthy impact on the totality of the world situation remains to be watched.

The ending of the Cold War has meant the abandonment of the many assumptions that had blocked progress in international affairs, bred chronic suspicion and fear and polarized the world. The lessons it conveys for both social thought and purposes of practical policy are manifold. From the viewpoint of the UN, however, three of its characteristics have a global significance.

First, the revolutionary developments in Eastern and Central Europe have given powerful expression to two of the cardinal principles of the Charter of the United Nations: self-determination of peoples and respect for human rights. Second, it has been strikingly demonstrated that a *status quo* based primarily on the military factor is bound to prove unstable.

Third, the wider and saner concept of security, encompassing all its dimensions, which has begun to emerge, is precisely the one the United Nations has been expounding all these years. It has been the constant theme at the UN that an obsessive arms race distorts priorities, hampers social and economic progress, constrains political dialogue, affects the institutions of the state to their long-term detriment, and aggravates the sense of insecurity among all nations. What often appeared to be a voice in the wilderness has now gained the seriousness it has long deserved.

Thus, the very change that has rendered obsolete the whole infrastructure of the Cold War serves to reveal afresh the design for peace which the United Nations is meant to execute. Nothing in the constructive refashioning that has taken place in Europe after the disintegration of the Soviet Union nor in the destructive trends that have now emerged after the Ukrainian crisis, requires a modification of the purposes and principles of the organization as laid down in its Charter. In fact, in this respect, the Charter gains a richer meaning as political evolution progressively enlarges and clarifies the scope of its principles.

The United Nations, therefore, enters the post globalized era in the 21st century as a central point of constancy in flux. Through years of patient effort, it has achieved a complementarity in the working of its different organs which makes it far better suited to fulfil its arduous tasks. The exercise of the authority of the Security Council in the manner envisaged in the Charter, the many instances of the General Assembly and the Council reinforcing each other's efforts, the close cooperation between the Council as a whole and the Secretary-General, the growing role of the Secretariat as represented by the Secretary-General in undertaking increasingly diversified missions of peace and the revitalized role that is being contemplated for the Economic and Social Council—all these testify to a strengthening of the institutions embodied in the organization.

With its ability thus enhanced and its relevance emphasized by the process of change, three broad objectives define the mandate of the UN today. It has to try to eliminate the seeds of war in all areas of the globe, and, in so doing, squarely face the fact that new sources of conflict are emerging in our age. It has to serve as the prime instrument for extending the spirit of cooperation to those spheres – economic relations between nations and humanity's social problems – which are seemingly non-political but have profound political implications. It has to strive continuously to ensure that international relations are governed by the rule of law and universal respect for human rights. This is a tall agenda but in today's rapidly changing world, there can be no shorter mandate for the United Nations.

We are now entering a world of greater plurilateralism, one that recognizes the shortcomings of multilateralism, the limits of bilateralism and the untenability of unilateralism. The current global situation has opened up spaces for more decentralized globalization offering more opportunities to many more middle powers to participate actively in the international arena. These would be accentuated by a stronger desire to foster localization and promote regionalism.

On the other hand, China's extraordinary growth (10 per cent for 3 decades is a world record) has given the world a superpower challenger in more ways than one - a country that is deeply embedded in the global economy but showcasing an authoritarian political system internally that is different from democracies. Moreover, the retreat of globalization, the rise of right-wing populism, the failure of institutions of global governance to come up with an overwhelming response to the Covid-19 pandemic, the continuing onslaught of the climate crisis, and the rapidly changing demographics of the old-world system may trigger off the inadvertent emergence of a new order among the global comity of nations. The Ukrainian crisis has led to a clamour for a rule-based multinational system and a revulsion against the use of force and Super Power empire-building in global politics.

What will that new order look like? It will be multipolar with issue-based groupings rather than permanent alliance systems. Chinese power games and the Russian invasion of Ukraine should not take the global system away from what is touted as a rules-based international system, at one time believed to be working to the advantage of those in the old order who anchor it. On the other hand, Chinese belligerence is also unjust and is imposing costs on countries that work with China. Similarly, on reforming or fixing the United Nations system, pacts would have to be solidified among those nations which seek to give stronger contemporary flavour to UN institutions than before, for instance, the World Health Organization (WHO), that have come up short during the pandemic. Similarly, on the climate question, net-zero will require finance to flow from the global North to the South. It will not happen till there is enough unity of purpose among nations that have been compelled to adjust their positions from the original paradigm of separate but differentiated responsibilities.

In short, by the force of circumstances, the blueprint of the new world order is likely to be a loose shifting amalgam of issue-based coalitions and alliances, woven together by the commonality of interests rather than the inflexibility of ideology. Over the decades, multilateralism has evolved into a web of specialized institutions, in almost every area of global common concern (collective good). Each of these areas has spawned a web of global norms and standard-setting, ranging from a comprehensive body of human rights covenants and treaties, Sustainable Development Goals, the Paris climate agreement, and the World Summit on the Information Society to soft laws on every subject of global concern.

It has inspired advocacy and social movements, building around each cause and global best practices including peacekeeping: 72 operations since 1948 and 13 active missions in three continents, relief for 60 million refugees, reducing maternal mortality, ending polio, promoting gender equality, supporting developing countries and using its moral power for the governance of new and evolving areas such as Tech 4.0 and cyber security.

However, the UN system has been undermined by its institutional capture by major powers and the unrepresentative nature of key decision-making bodies. The UN Security Council (UNSC) permanent members especially China, show no inclination to expand permanent membership or bring in substantive reforms in the Security Council despite major changes in global power groupings demanding representation. The International Monetary Fund/World Bank's quota of reforms has also been largely static. The shaping and running of the world's monetary, financial and trading systems remain dominated as before by a few. Sovereignty is invoked by the powerful, while the weak are often denied the protection of a rule-based, equitable multilateral order as promised by the UN bodies.

The UN Security Council's conflict prevention, peace-making and building role in regional conflicts, interstate and intrastate wars, and terrorism are serious developments coexisting with elitism, cross-veto, and implementation gaps. Universal membership of 193 countries makes consensus-building elusive. Big powers resort to unilateralism, regionalism, plurilateral, and issue-based strategic groupings (G7, G20, BRICS) acting on their perceived national interests. The UN lacks teeth today, as always due to conflicting member interests, evident in its operational procedures over the last 75 years.

Cited Works

Beres, Louis R., *People, States and World Order,* Ithaca: Peacock Publishers, 1981.

Epps, Valerie, Graham, Lorie, *Examples & Explanations for International Law, Examples &* Explanations *Series*, 2nd edn., Wolters Kluwer, 2014.

Falk, Richard A., *A Study of Future Worlds*, New York: Free Press, 1975.

Gordenker, Leon (ed.), *The United Nations in International Politics,* Princeton University Press, New Jersey, 1971& 2017.

Kan, Harman & J. Weiner, et. al., *The Year 2000: A Framework for Speculation on the Next Thirty-three Years,* New York: Macmillan, 1967.

Moore, John Allphin, Jr., and Jerry, Pubantz, *The New United Nations, International Organization in the Twenty-First Century*, New York and London, Routledge, 2017.

Roberts Adam & Benedict Kingsbury, *UN, Divided World—the UN's Rules in International Relations*, Oxford: Clarendon, 1988.

Basic facts about the UN: 42nd Edition, New York: UN, DPI, 2017.

Appendix

THE CHARTER OF THE UNITED NATIONS

We the peoples of the United Nations determined

to save succeeding generations from the scourge of war, which twice in our lifetime has brought untold sorrow to mankind, and

to reaffirm faith in fundamental human rights, in the dignity and worth of the human person, in the equal rights of men and women and

of nations large and small, and to establish conditions under which justice and respect for the obligations arising from treaties and

other sources of international law can be maintained, and to promote social progress and better standards of life in larger freedom,

And for these ends

to practise tolerance and live together in peace with one another as good neighbours, and

to unite our strength to maintain international peace and security, and

to ensure, by the acceptance of principles and the institution of methods, that armed force shall not be used, save in the common interest, and

to employ international machinery for the promotion of the economic and social advancement of all peoples,

Have resolved to combine our efforts to accomplish these aims

accordingly, our respective Governments, through representatives assembled in the city of San Francisco, who have exhibited their full powers found to be in good and due form, have agreed to the present Charter of the United Nations and do hereby establish an international organisation to be known as the United Nations.

Chapter–I
Purposes and Principles

Article 1

The Purposes of the United Nations are:

1. To maintain international peace and security, and to that end: to take effective collective measures for the prevention and removal of threats to the peace, and for the suppression of acts of aggression or other breaches of the peace, and to bring about by peaceful means, and in conformity with the principles of justice and international law, adjustment or settlement of international disputes or situations which might lead to a breach of the peace;
2. To develop friendly relations among nations based on respect for the principle of equal rights and self-determination of peoples, and to take other appropriate measures to strengthen universal peace;
3. To achieve international cooperation in solving international problems of an economic, social, cultural, or humanitarian character, and in promoting and encouraging respect for human rights and for fundamental freedoms for all without distinction as to race, sex, language, or religion; and
4. To be a centre for harmonising the actions of nations in the attainment of these common ends.

Article 2

The Organisation and its Members, in pursuit of the Purposes stated in Article 1, shall act in accordance with the following Principles:

1. The Organisation is based on the principle of the sovereign equality of all its Members.
2. All Members, in order to ensure to all of them the rights and benefits resulting from membership, shall fulfil in good faith the obligations assumed by them in accordance with the present Charter.
3. All Members shall settle their international disputes by peaceful means in such a manner that international peace and security, and justice, are not endangered.
4. All Members shall refrain in their international relations from the threat or use of force against the territorial integrity or consistent with the Purposes of the United Nations.
5. All Members shall give the United Nations every assistance in any action it takes in accordance with the present Charter, and shall refrain from giving assistance to any state against which the United Nations is taking preventive or enforcement action.
6. The Organisation shall ensure that states which are not Members of the United Nations act in accordance with these Principles so far as may be necessary for the maintenance of international peace and security.
7. Nothing contained in the present Charter shall authorise the United Nations to intervene in matters which are essentially within the domestic jurisdiction of any state or shall require the Members to submit such matters to settlement

under the present Charter; but this principle shall not prejudice the application of enforcement measures under Chapter VII.

Chapter–II
Membership

Article 3

The original members of the United Nations shall be the states which, having participated in the United Nations Conference of International Organisation at San Francisco, or having previously signed the Declaration by United Nations of 1 January, 1942, sign the present Charter and ratify it in accordance with Article 110.

Article 4

1. Membership in the United Nations is open to all other peace-loving states which accept the obligations contained in the present Charter and, in the judgement of the Organisation, are able and willing to carry out these obligations.
2. The admission of any such state to membership in the United Nations will be effected by a decision of the General Assembly upon the recommendation of the Security Council.

Article 5

A Member of the United Nations against which preventive or enforcement action has been taken by the Security Council may be suspended from the exercise of the rights and privileges of membership by the General Assembly upon the recommendation of the Security Council. The exercise of these rights and privileges may be restored by the Security Council.

Article 6

A Member of the United Nations which has persistently violated the Principles contained in the present Charter may be expelled from the Organisation by the General Assembly upon the recommendation of the Security Council.

Chapter–III
Organs

Article 7

1. There are established as the principal organs of the United Nations: a General Assembly, a Security Council, an Economic and Social Council, a Trusteeship Council, an International Court of Justice, and a Secretariat.
2. Such subsidiary organs as may be found necessary may be established in accordance with the present Charter.

Article 8

The United Nations shall place no restrictions on the eligibility of men and women to participate in any capacity and under conditions of equality in its principal and subsidiary organs.

Chapter–IV
The General Assembly

Composition

Article 9

1. The General Assembly shall consist of all the Members of the United Nations.
2. Each Member shall have not more than five representatives in the General Assembly.

Functions and Powers

Article 10

The General Assembly may discuss any questions or any matters within the scope of the present Charter or relating to the powers and functions of any organs provided for in the present Charter, and, except as provided in Article 12, may make recommendations to the Members of the United Nations or to the Security Council or to both on any such questions or matters.

Article 11

1. The General Assembly may consider the general principles of cooperation in the maintenance of international peace and security, including the principles governing disarmament and the regulation of armaments, and may make recommendations with regard to such principles to the Members or to the Security Council or to both.
2. The General Assembly may discuss any questions relating to the maintenance of international peace and security brought before it by any Member of the United Nations, or by the Security Council, or by a state which is not a Member of the United Nations in accordance with Article 35, paragraph 2, and, except as provided in Article 12, may make recommendations with regard to any such questions to the state or states concerned or to the Security Council or to both. Any such question on which action is necessary shall be referred to the Security Council by the General Assembly either or after discussion.
3. The General Assembly may call the attention of the Security Council to situations which are likely to endanger international peace and security.
4. The powers of the General Assembly set forth in its Article shall not limit the general scope of Article 10.

Article 12

1. While the Security Council is exercising in respect of any dispute or situation the functions assigned to it in the present Charter, the General Assembly shall not make any recommendation with regard to that dispute or situation unless the Security Council so requests.
2. The Secretary-General, with the consent of the Security Council, shall notify the General Assembly at each session of any matters relative to the maintenance of international peace and security which are being dealt with by the Security Council and shall similarly notify the General Assembly, or the members of the United Nations if the General Assembly is not in session, immediately the Security Council ceases to deal with such matters.

Article 13

1. The General Assembly shall initiate studies and make recommendations for purpose of:
   (a) promoting international cooperation in the political field and encouraging the progressive development of international law and its codification;
   (b) promoting international cooperation in the economic, social, cultural, educational and health fields, and assisting in the realisation of human rights and fundamental freedoms for all without distinction as to race, sex, language, or religion.
2. The further responsibilities, functions and powers of the General Assembly with respect to matters mentioned in paragraph 1(b) above are set forth in Chapters IX and X.

Article 14

Subject to the provisions of Article 12, the General Assembly may recommend measures for the peaceful adjustment of any situation, regardless of origin, which it deems likely to impair the general welfare or friendly relations among nations, including situations resulting from a violation of the provisions of the present Charter setting forth the Purposes and Principles of the United Nations.

Article 15

1. The General Assembly shall receive and consider annual and special reports from the Security Council; these reports shall include an account of the measures that the Security Council has decided upon or taken to maintain international peace and security.
2. The General Assembly shall receive and consider reports from the other organs of the United Nations.

Article 16

The General Assembly shall perform such functions with respect to the international Trusteeship system as are assigned to it under Chapters XII and XIII, including the approval of the trusteeship agreements for areas not designated as strategic.

Article 17

1. The General Assembly shall consider and approve the budget of the Organisation.
2. The expenses of the Organisation shall be borne by the Members as apportioned by the General Assembly.
3. The General Assembly shall consider and approve any financial and budgetary arrangements with specialised agencies referred to in Article 57 and shall examine the administrative budgets of such specialised agencies with a view to making recommendations to the agencies concerned.

Voting

Article 18

1. Each member of the General Assembly shall have one vote.
2. Decisions of the General Assembly on important questions shall be made by

a two-thirds majority of the members present and voting. These questions hall include: recommendations with respect to the maintenance of international peace and security, the election of the non-permanent members of the Security Council, the election of the members of the Economic and Social Council, the election of members of the Trusteeship Council in accordance with paragraph 1(c) of Article 86, the admission of new Members to the United Nations, the suspension of the rights and privileges of membership, the expulsion of Members, questions relating to the operation of the Trusteeship system, and budgetary questions.

3. Decisions on other questions, including the determination of additional categories of questions to be decided by a two-thirds majority, shall be made by a majority of the members present and voting.

Article 19

A Member of the United Nations which is in arrears in the payment of its financial contributions to the Organisation shall have no vote in the General Assembly if the amount of its arrears equals or exceeds the amount of the contributions due from it for the preceding two full years. The General Assembly may, nevertheless, permit such a Member to vote if it is satisfied that the failure to pay is due to conditions beyond the control of the Member.

Procedure

Article 20

The General Assembly shall meet in regular annual sessions and in such special sessions as the occasion may require. Special sessions shall be invoked by the Secretary-General at the request of the Security Council or of a majority of the Members of the United Nations.

Article 21

The General Assembly shall adopt its own rules of procedure. It shall elect its President for each session.

Article 22

The General Assembly may establish such subsidiary organs as it deems necessary for the performance of its functions.

Chapter–V
The Security Council

Composition

Article 23

1. The Security Council shall consist of fifteen Members of the United Nations. The Republic of China, France, the Union of Soviet Socialist Republics, the United Kingdom of Great Britain and Northern Ireland, and the United States of America

shall be permanent members of the Security Council. They shall elect ten other Members of the United Nations to be non-permanent members of the Security Council, due regard being specially paid, in the first instance, to the contribution of members of the United Nations to the maintenance of international peace and security and to the other purposes of the Organisation, and also to equitable geographical distribution.

2. The non-permanent members of the Security Council shall be elected for a term of two years. In the first election of the non-permanent members after the increase of the membership of the Security Council from eleven to fifteen, two of the four additional members shall be chosen for a term of one year. A retiring member shall not be eligible for immediate re-election.
3. Each member of the Security Council shall have one representative.

Functions and Powers

Article 24

1. In order to ensure prompt and effective action by the United Nations, its Members confer on the Security Council primary responsibility for the maintenance of international peace and security, and agree that in carrying out its duties under this responsibility the Security Council acts on their behalf.
2. In discharging these duties the Security Council shall act in accordance with the Purposes and Principles of the United Nations. The specific powers granted to the Security Council for the discharge of these duties are laid down in Chapters VI, VII, VIII and XII.
3. The Security Council shall submit annual and when necessary, special reports to the General Assembly for its consideration.

Article 25

The Members of the United Nations agree to accept and carry out the decisions of the Security Council in accordance with the present Charter.

Article 26

In order to promote the establishment and maintenance of international peace and security with the least diversion for armaments of the world's human and economic resources, the Security Council shall be responsible for formulating, with the assistance of the Military Staff Committee referred to in Article 47, plans to be submitted to the Members of the United Nations for the establishment of a system for the regulation of armaments.

Voting

Article 27

1. Each member of the Security Council shall have one vote.
2. Decisions of the Security Council on procedural matters shall be made by an affirmative vote of nine members.
3. Decisions of the Security Council on all other matters shall be made by an affirmative vote of nine members including the concurring votes of the permanent

members; provided that, in decisions under Chapter VI, and under paragraph 3 of Article 52, a party to a dispute shall abstain from voting.

Procedure

Article 28

1. The Security Council shall be so organised as to be able to function continuously. Each member of the Security Council shall for this purpose be represented at all times at the seat of the Organisation.
2. The Security Council shall hold periodic meetings at which each of its members may, if it so desires, be represented by a member of the government or by some other specially designated representative.
3. The Security Council may hold meetings at such places other than the seat of the Organisation as in its judgement will best facilitate its work.

Article 29

The Security Council may establish such subsidiary organs as it deems necessary for the performance of its functions.

Article 30

The Security Council shall adopt its own rules of procedure, including the method of selecting its President.

Article 31

Any Member of the United Nations which is not a member of the Security Council may participate, without vote, in the discussion of any question brought before the Security Council whenever the latter considers that the interests of that Member are specially affected.

Article 32

Any Member of the United Nations which is not a member of the Security Council or any state which is not a Member of the United Nations, if it is a party to a dispute under consideration by the Security Council, shall be invited to participate, without vote, in the discussion relating to the dispute. The Security Council shall lay down such conditions as it deems just for the participation of a state which is not a member of the United Nations.

Chapter–VI
Pacific Settlement of Disputes

Article 33

1. The parties to any dispute, the continuance of which is likely to endanger the maintenance of international peace and security shall, first of all, seek a solution by negotiation, enquiry, mediation, conciliation, arbitration, judicial settlement,

resort to regional agencies or arrangements, or other peaceful means of their own choice.

2. The Security Council shall, when it deems necessary, call upon the parties to settle their dispute by such means.

Article 34

The Security Council may investigate any dispute, or any situation which might lead to international friction or give rise to a dispute, in order to determine whether the continuance of the dispute or situation is likely to endanger the maintenance of international peace and security.

Article 35

1. Any Member of the United Nations may bring any dispute, or any situation of the nature referred to in Article 34, to the attention of the Security Council or of the General Assembly.
2. A state which is not a member of the United Nations may bring to the attention of the Security Council or the General Assembly any dispute to which it is a party if it accepts in advance, for the purposes of the dispute, the obligations of pacific settlement provided in the present Charter.
3. The proceedings of the General Assembly in respect of matters brought to its attention under this Article will be subject to the provisions of Articles 11 and 12.

Article 36

1. The Security Council may, at any stage of a dispute of the nature referred to in Article 33 or of a situation of like nature, recommend appropriate procedures or methods of adjustment.
2. The Security Council should take into consideration any procedures for the settlement of the dispute which have already been adopted by the parties.
3. In making recommendations under this Article the Security Council should also take into consideration that legal disputes should as a general rule be referred by the parties to the International Court of Justice in accordance with the provisions of the Statute of the Court.

Article 37

1. Should the parties to a dispute of the nature referred in Article 33 fail to settle it by the means indicated in that Article, they shall refer it to the Security Council.
2. If the Security Council deems that the continuance of the dispute is in fact likely to endanger the maintenance of international peace and security, it shall decide whether to take action under Article 36 or to recommend such terms of settlement as it may consider appropriate.

Article 38

Without prejudice to the provisions of the Articles 33 to 37 the Security Council may, if all the parties to any dispute so request, make recommendations to the parties with a view to a pacific settlement of the dispute.

Chapter–VII
Action with Respect to Threats to the Peace, Breaches of the Peace, and Acts of Aggression

Article 39

The Security Council shall determine the existence of any threat to the peace, breach of the peace, or act of aggression and shall make recommendations, or decide what measures shall be taken in accordance with Articles 41 and 42, to maintain or restore international peace and security.

Article 40

In order to prevent an aggravation of the situation, the Security Council may, before making the recommendations or deciding upon the measures provided for in Article 39, call upon the parties concerned to comply with such provisional measures as it deems necessary or desirable. Such provisional measures shall be without prejudice to the rights, claims, or position of the parties concerned. The Security Council shall duly take account of failure to comply with such provisional measures.

Article 41

The Security Council may decide what measures not involving the use of armed force are to be employed to give effect to its decisions, and it may call upon the Members of the United Nations to apply such measures. These may include complete or partial interruption of economic relations and of rail, sea, air, postal, telegraphic, radio, and other means of communication and the severance of diplomatic relations.

Article 42

Should the Security Council consider that measures provided for in Article 41 would be inadequate or have proved to be inadequate, it may take such action by air, sea, or land forces as may be necessary to maintain or restore international peace and security. Such action may include demonstrations, blockade, and other operations by air, sea, or land forces of Members of the United Nations.

Article 43

1. All Members of the United Nations, in order to contribute to the maintenance of international peace and security, undertake to make available to the Security Council, on its call and in accordance with a special agreement or agreements, armed forces, assistance and facilities, including rights of passage, necessary for the purpose of maintaining international peace and security.
2. Such agreement or agreements shall govern the numbers and types of force, their degree of readiness and general location, and the nature of the facilities and assistance to be provided.
3. The agreement or agreements shall be negotiated as soon as possible on the initiative of the Security Council. They shall be concluded between the Security Council and Members or between the Security Council and groups of Members

and shall be subject to ratification by the signatory states in accordance with their respective constitutional processes.

Article 44

When the Security Council has decided to use force it shall, before calling upon a Member not represented on it to provide armed forces in fulfilment of the obligations assumed under Article 43, invite that Member, if the Member so desires, to participate in the decisions of the Security Council concerning the employment of contingents of that Member's armed forces.

Article 45

In order to enable the United Nations to take urgent military measures, Members shall hold immediate available national air-force contingents for combined international enforcement action. The strength and degree of readiness of these contingents and plans for their combined action shall be determined, within the limits laid down in the special agreement or agreements referred to in Article 43, by the Security Council with the assistance of the Military Staff Committee.

Article 46

Plans for the application of armed force shall be made by the Security Council with the assistance of the Military Staff Committee.

Article 47

1. There shall be established a Military Staff Committee to advise and assist the Security Council on all questions relating to the Security Council's military requirements for the maintenance of international peace and security, the employment and command of forces placed at its disposal the regulation of armaments, and possible disarmament.
2. The Military Staff Committee shall consist of the Chiefs of Staff of the permanent members of the Security Council or their representatives. Any Member of the United Nations not permanently represented on the Committee shall be invited by the Committee to be associated with it when the efficient discharge of the Committee's responsibilities requires the participation of that Member in its work.
3. The Military Staff Committee shall be responsible under the Security Council for the strategic direction of any armed forces placed at the disposal of the Security Council. Questions relating to the command of such forces shall be worked out subsequently.
4. The Military Staff Committee, with the authorisation of the Security Council, and after consultation with appropriate regional agencies, may establish regional sub-committees.

Article 48

1. The action required to carry out the decisions of the Security Council for the maintenance of international peace and security shall be taken by all the Members of the United Nations or by some of them, as the Security Council may determine.

2. Such decisions shall be carried out by the Members of the United Nations directly and through their action in the appropriate international agencies of which they are members.

Article 49

The Members of the United Nations shall join in affording mutual assistance in carrying out the measures decided upon by the Security Council.

Article 50

If preventive or enforcement measures against any state are taken by the Security Council, any other state, whether a Member of the United Nations or not, which finds itself confronted with special economic problems arising from the carrying out of those measures shall have the right to consult the Security Council with regard to a solution of those problems.

Article 51

Nothing in the present Charter shall impair the inherent right of individual or collective self-defence if an armed attack occurs against a Member of the United Nations, until the Security Council has taken measures necessary to maintain international peace and security. Measures taken by Members in the exercise of this right of self-defence shall be immediately reported to the Security Council and shall not in any way affect the authority and responsibility of the Security Council under the present Charter to take at any time such action as it deems necessary in order to maintain or restore international peace and security.

Chapter–VIII
Regional Arrangements

Article 52

1. Nothing in the present Charter precludes the existence of regional arrangements or agencies for dealing with such matters relating to the maintenance of international peace and security as are appropriate for regional action, provided that such arrangements or agencies and their activities are consistent with the Purposes and Principles of the United Nations.
2. The Members of the United Nations entering into such arrangements or constituting such agencies shall make every effort to achieve pacific settlement of local disputes through such regional arrangements or by such regional agencies before referring them to the Security Council.
3. The Security Council shall encourage the development of pacific settlement of local disputes through such regional arrangements or by such regional agencies either on the initiative of the states concerned or by reference from the Security Council.
4. This Article in no way impairs the application of Articles 34 and 35.

Article 53

1. The Security Council shall, where appropriate, utilise such regional arrangements or agencies for enforcement action under its authority. But no enforcement action shall be taken under regional arrangements or by regional agencies without the authorisation of the Security Council, with the exception of measures against any enemy state, as defined in paragraph 2 of this Article, provided for pursuant to Article 107 or in regional arrangements directed against renewal of aggressive policy on the part of any such state, until such time as the Organisation may, on request of the Governments concerned, be charged with the responsibility for preventing further aggression by such a state.
2. The term enemy state as used in paragraph 1 of this Article applies to any state which during the Second World War has been an enemy of any signatory of the present Charter.

Article 54

The Security Council shall at all times be kept fully informed of activities undertaken or in contemplation under regional arrangements or by regional agencies for the maintenance of international peace and security.

Chapter–IX
International Economic and Social Cooperation

Article 55

With a view to the creation of conditions of stability and well-being which are necessary for peaceful and friendly relations among nations based on respect for the principle of equal rights and self-determination of peoples, the United Nations shall promote:

1. Higher standards of living, full employment and conditions of economic and social progress and development;
2. Solutions of international economic, social, health, and related problems; and international cultural and educational cooperation; and
3. Universal respect for, and observance of, human rights and fundamental freedoms for all without distinction as to race, sex, language or religion.

Article 56

All Members pledge themselves to take joint and separate action in cooperation with the Organisation for the achievement of the purposes set forth in Article 55.

Article 57

1. The various specialised agencies, established by inter-governmental agreement and having wide international responsibilities, as defined in their basic instruments, in economic, social, cultural, educational, health, and related fields, shall be brought into relationship with the United Nations in accordance with the provisions of Article 63.
2. Such agencies thus brought into relationship with the United Nations are hereinafter referred to as specialised agencies.

Article 58

The Organisation shall make recommendations for the coordination of the policies and activities of the specialised agencies.

Article 59

The Organisation shall, where appropriate, initiate negotiations among the states concerned for the creation of any new specialised agencies required for the accomplishment of the purposes set forth in Article 55.

Article 60

Responsibility for the discharge of the functions of the Organisation set forth in this Chapter shall be vested in the General Assembly and under the authority of the General Assembly, in the Economic and Social Council, which shall have for this purpose the power set forth in Chapter X.

Chapter–X
The Economic and Social Council

Composition

Article 61

1. The Economic and Social Council shall consist of fifty-four Members of the United Nations elected by the General Assembly.
2. Subject to the provisions of paragraph 3, eighteen members of the Economic and Social Council shall be elected each year for a term of three years. A retiring member shall be eligible for immediate re-election.
3. At the first election after the increase in the membership of the Economic and Social Council from twenty-seven to fifty-four members, in term of office, expires at the end of that year, twenty-seven additional members shall be elected. Of these twenty-seven additional members, the term of nine members so elected shall expire at the end of one year, and of nine other members at the end of two years, in accordance with arrangements made by the General Assembly.
4. Each member of the Economic and Social Council shall have one representative.

Functions and Powers

Article 62

1. The Economic and Social Council may make or initiate studies and reports with respect to international economic, social, cultural, education, health, and related matters and may make recommendations with respect to any such matters to the General Assembly, to the Member of the United Nations, and to the specialised agencies concerned.
2. It may make recommendations for the purpose of promoting respect for, and observance of, human rights and fundamental freedoms for all.

3. It may prepare draft conventions for submission to the General Assembly, with respect to matters falling within its competence.
4. It may call, in accordance with the rules prescribed by the United Nations, international conference on matters falling within its competence.

Article 63

1. The Economic and Social Council may enter into agreements with any of the agencies referred to in Article 57, defining the terms on which the agency concerned shall be brought into relationship with the United Nations. Such agreements shall be subject to approval by the General Assembly.
2. It may coordinate the activities of the specialised agencies through consultation with and recommendations to such agencies and through recommendations to the General Assembly and to the Members of the United Nations.

Article 64

1. The Economic and Social Council may take appropriate steps to obtain regular reports from the specialised agencies. It may make arrangements with the Members of the United Nations and with the specialised agencies to obtain reports on the steps taken to give effect to its own recommendations and to make recommendations on matters falling within its competence made by the General Assembly.
2. It may communicate its observation on these reports to the General Assembly.

Article 65

The Economic and Social Council may furnish information to the Security Council and shall assist the Security Council upon its request.

Article 66

1. The Economic and Social Council shall perform such functions as fall within its competence in connection with the carrying out of the recommendations of the General Assembly.
2. It may, with the approval of the General Assembly, perform services at the request of members of the United Nations and at the request of specialised agencies.
3. It shall perform such other functions as are specified elsewhere in the present Charter or as may be assigned to it by the General Assembly.

Voting

Article 67

1. Each member of the Economic and Social Council shall have one vote.
2. Decisions of the Economic and Social Council shall be made by a majority of the members present and voting.

Procedure

Article 68

The Economic and Social Council shall set up commissions in economic and social fields and for the promotion of human rights, and such other commissions as may be required for the performance of its functions.

Article 69

The Economic and Social Council shall invite the member of the United Nations to participate, without vote, in its deliberations on any matter of particular concern to that Member.

Article 70

The Economic and Social Council may make arrangements for representatives of the specialised agencies to participate, without vote, in its deliberations and in those of the commissions established by it, and for its representatives to participate in the deliberations of the specialised agencies.

Article 71

The Economic and Social Council may make suitable arrangements for consultation with non-governmental organisations which are concerned with matters within its competence. Such arrangements may be made with international organisations and, where appropriate, with national organisations after consultation with the Member of the United Nations concerned.

Article 72

1. The Economic and Social Council shall adopt its own rules of procedure, including the method of selecting its President.
2. The Economic and Social Council shall meet as required in accordance with its rules, which shall include provision for the convening of meetings on the request of a majority of its members.

Chapter–XI
Declaration Regarding Non-Self-Governing

Territories

Article 73

Members of the United Nations which have or assume responsibilities for the administration of territories whose peoples have not yet attained a full measure of self-government recognise the principle that the interests of the inhabitants of these territories are paramount, and accept as a sacred trust the obligation to promote to the utmost, within the system of international peace and security established by the present Charter, the well-being of the inhabitants of these territories, and, to this end:

(a) to ensure, with due respect for the culture of the peoples concerned, their political, economic, social and educational advancement, their just treatment, and their protection against abuses;

(b) to develop self-government, to take due account of the political aspirations of the peoples, and to assist them in a progressive development of their free political institutions, according to the particular circumstances of each territory and its peoples and their varying stages of advancement;

(c) to further international peace and security;
(d) to promote constructive measures of development, to encourage research, and to cooperate with one another and, when and where appropriate, with specialised international bodies with a view to the practical achievement of the social, economic, and scientific purposes set forth in this Article; and
(e) to transmit regularly to the Secretary-General for information purposes, subject to such limitation as security and constitutional considerations may require, statistical and other information of a technical nature relating to economic, social, and educational conditions in the territories for which they are respectively responsible other than those territories to which Chapters XII and XIII apply.

Article 74

Members of the United Nations also agree that their policy in respect of the territories to which this Chapter applies, or less than in respect of their metropolitan areas, must be based on the general principle of good-neighbourliness, due account being taken of the interests and well-being of the rest of the world, in social, economic, and commercial matters.

Chapter–XII
International Trusteeship System

Article 75

The United Nations shall establish under its authority an international Trusteeship system for the administration and supervision of such territories as may be placed thereunder by subsequent individual agreements. These territories are hereinafter referred to as trust territories.

Article 761

The basic objectives of the Trusteeship system, in accordance with the purposes of the United Nations laid down in Article 1 of the present Charter, shall be:

(a) to further international peace and security;
(b) to promote the political, economic, social and educational advancement of the inhabitants of the trust territories, and their progressive development towards self-government or independence as may be appropriate to the particular circumstances of each territory and its peoples and the freely expressed wishes of the peoples concerned, and as may be provided by the terms of each trusteeship agreement;
(c) to encourage respect for human rights and for fundamental freedoms for all without distinction as to race, sex, language or religion, and to encourage recognition of the interdependence of the peoples of the world; and
(d) to ensure equal treatment in social, economic, and commercial matters for all Members of the United Nations and their nationals, and also equal treatment for the latter in the administration of justice, without prejudice to the attainment of the foregoing objectives and subject to the provisions of Article 80.

Article 77

1. The Trusteeship system shall apply to such territories in the following categories as may be placed thereunder by means of trusteeship agreements:
   (a) territories now held under mandate;
   (b) territories which may be detached from enemy states as a result of the Second World War; and
   (c) territories voluntarily placed under the system by states responsible for their administration.
2. It will be a matter for subsequent agreement as to which territories in the foregoing categories will be brought under the Trusteeship system and upon what terms.

Article 78

The terms of the trusteeship for each territory to be placed under the Trusteeship system, including any alteration or amendment, shall be agreed upon by the states directly concerned, including the mandatory power in the case of territories held under mandate by the Member of the United Nations, and shall be approved as provided for in Articles 83 and 85.

Article 79

The terms of trusteeship for each territory to be placed under the Trusteeship system, including any alteration on amendment, shall be agreed upon by the states directly concerned, including the mandatory power in the case of territories held under mandate by a member of the United Nations, and shall be approved as provided for in Acts 83 and 85.

Article 80

1. Except as may be agreed upon in individual trusteeship agreements, made under Articles 77, 79, and 81, placing each territory under the Trusteeship system, and until such agreements have been concluded, nothing in this Chapter shall be construed in or of itself to alter in any manner the rights whatsoever of any states or any peoples or the terms of existing international instruments to which Members of the United Nations may respectively be parties.

Article 81

The trusteeship agreement shall in each case include the terms under which the trust territory will be administered and designate the authority which will exercise the administration of the trust territory. Such authority, hereinafter called the administering authority, may be one or more states or the Organisation itself.

Article 82

There may be designated, in any trusteeship agreement, a strategic area or areas which may include part or all of the trust territory to which the agreement applies, without prejudice to any special agreement or agreements made under Article 43.

Article 83

1. All functions of the United Nations relating to strategic areas, including the approval of the terms of the trusteeship agreements and of their alteration or amendment, shall be exercised by the Security Council.

2. The basic objectives set forth in Article 76 shall be applicable to the people of each strategic area.
3. The Security Council shall, subject to the provisions of the trusteeship agreements and without prejudice to security considerations, avail itself of the assistance of the Trusteeship Council to perform those functions of the United Nations under the Trusteeship system relating to political, economic, social, and educational matters in the strategic areas.

Article 84

It shall be the duty of the administering authority to ensure that the trust territory shall play its part in the maintenance of international peace and security. To this end the administering authority may make use of volunteer forces, facilities, and assistance from the trust territory in carrying out the obligations towards the Security Council undertaken in this regard by the administering authority, as well as for local defence and the maintenance of law and order within the trust territory.

Article 85

1. The functions of the United Nations with regards to trusteeship agreements for all areas not designated as strategic, including the approval of the terms of the trusteeship agreements and of their alteration or amendment shall be exercised by the General Assembly.
2. The Trusteeship Council, operating under the authority of the General Assembly, shall assist the General Assembly in carrying out these functions.

Chapter–XIII
The Trusteeship Council

Composition

Article 86

1. The Trusteeship Council shall consist of the following Members of the United Nations:
   (a) those Members administering trust territories;
   (b) such of those Members mentioned by name in Article 23 as are not administering trust territories; and
   (c) as many other Members elected for three-year terms by the General Assembly as may be necessary to ensure that the total number of members of the Trusteeship Council is equally divided between those Members of the United Nations which administer trust territories and those which do not.
2. Each member of the Trusteeship Council shall designate one specially qualified person to represent therein.

Functions and Powers

Article 87

The General Assembly and, under its authority, the Trusteeship Council, in carrying out their functions, may:

(a) consider reports submitted by the administering authority;
(b) accept petitions and examine them in consultation with the administering authority;
(c) provide for periodic visits to the respective trust territories at times agreed upon with the administering authority; and
(d) take these and other actions in conformity with the terms of the trusteeship agreements.

Article 88

The Trusteeship Council shall formulate a questionnaire on the political, economic, social, and educational advancement of the inhabitants of each trust territory, and the administering authority for each trust territory within the competence of the General Assembly shall make an annual report to the General Assembly upon the basis of such questionnaire.

Voting

Article 89

1. Each member of the Trusteeship Council shall have one vote.
2. Decisions of the Trusteeship Council shall be made by a majority of the members present and voting.

Procedure

Article 90

1. The Trusteeship Council shall adopt its own rules of procedure, including the method of selecting its President.
2. The Trusteeship Council shall meet as required in accordance with its rules, which shall include provision for the convening of meetings on the request of a majority of its members.

Article 91

The Trusteeship Council shall, when appropriate, avail itself of the assistance of the Economic and Social Council and of the specialised agencies in regard to matters with which they are respectively concerned.

Chapter–XIV
The International Court of Justice

Article 92

The International Court of Justice shall be the principal judicial organ of the United Nations. It shall function in accordance with the annexed Statute, which is based upon the Statute of the Permanent Court of International Justice and forms an integral part of the present Charter.

Article 93

1. All Members of the United Nations are *ipso facto* parties to the Statute of the International Court of Justice.
2. A state which is not a Member of the United Nations may become a party to the Statute of the International Court of Justice on conditions to be determined in each case by the General Assembly upon the recommendation of the Security Council.

Article 94

1. Each Member of the United Nations undertakes to comply with the decision of the International Court of Justice in any case to which it is a party.
2. If any party to a case fails to perform the obligations incumbent upon it under a judgement rendered by the Court, the other party may have recourse to the Security Council, which may, if it deems necessary, make recommendations or decide upon measures to be taken to give effect to the judgement.

Article 95

Nothing in the present Charter shall prevent Members of the United Nations from entrusting the solution of their differences to other tribunals by virtue of agreements already in existence or which may be concluded in the future.

Article 96

1. The General Assembly or the Security Council may request the International Court of Justice to give an advisory opinion on any legal question.
2. Other organs of the United Nations and specialised agencies, which may at any time be so authorised by the General Assembly, may also request advisory opinions of the Court on legal questions arising within the scope of their activities.

Chapter–XV
The Secretariat

Article 97

The Secretariat shall comprise a Secretary-General and such staff as the Organisation may require. The Secretary-General shall be appointed by the General Assembly upon the recommendation of the Security Council. He shall be the chief administrative officer of the Organisation.

Article 98

The Secretary-General shall act in that capacity in all meetings of the General Assembly of the Security Council, of the Economic and Social Council, and of the Trusteeship Council, and shall perform such other functions as are entrusted to him by these organs. The Secretary-General shall make an annual report to the General Assembly on the work of the Organisation.

Article 99

The Secretary-General may bring to the attention of the Security Council any matter which in his opinion may threaten the maintenance of international peace and security.

Article 100

1. In the performance of their duties the Secretary-General and staff shall not seek or receive instructions from any government or from any other authority external to the Organisation. They shall refrain from any action which might reflect on their position as international officials responsible only to the Organisation.
2. Each Member of the United Nations undertakes to respect the exclusively international character of the responsibilities of the Secretary-General and the staff and not to seek to influence them in the discharge of their responsibilities.

Article 101

1. The staff shall be appointed by the Secretary-General under regulations established by the General Assembly.
2. Appropriate staffs shall be permanently assigned to the Economic and Social Council, the Trusteeship Council, and, as required, to other organs of the United Nations. These staffs shall form a part of the Secretariat.
3. The paramount consideration in the employment of the staff and in the determination of the conditions of service shall be the necessity of securing the highest standards of efficiency, competence, and integrity. Due regard shall be paid to the importance of recruiting the staff on as wide a geographical basis as possible.

Chapter–XVI
Miscellaneous Provisions

Article 102

1. Every treaty and every international agreement entered into by any Member of the United Nations after the present Charter comes into force shall as soon as possible be registered with the Secretariat and published by it.
2. No party to any such treaty or international agreement which has not been registered in accordance with the provisions of paragraph 1 of this Article may invoke that treaty or agreement before any organ of the United Nations.

Article 103

In the event of a conflict between the obligations of the Members of the United Nations under the present Charter and their obligations under any other international agreement, their obligations under the present Charter shall prevail.

Article 104

The Organisation shall enjoy in the territory of each of its Members such legal capacity as may be necessary for the exercise of its functions and the fulfilment of its purposes.

Article 105

1. The Organisation shall enjoy in the territory of each of its Members such privileges and immunities as are necessary for the fulfilment of its purposes.
2. Representatives of the Members of the United Nations and officials of the Organisation shall similarly enjoy such privileges and immunities as are necessary for the independent exercise of their functions in connection with the Organisation.
3. The General Assembly may make recommendations with a view to determining the details of the application of paragraphs 1 and 2 of this Article or may propose conventions to the Members of the United Nations for this purpose.

Chapter–XVII
Transitional Security Arrangements

Article 106

Pending the coming into force of such special agreements referred to in Article 43 as in the opinion of the Security Council enable it to begin the exercise of its responsibilities under Article 42, the parties to the Four-Nation Declaration, signed at Moscow, 30 October 1943, and France, shall, in accordance with the provisions of paragraph 5 of the Declaration, consult with one another and as occasion requires with other Members of the United Nations with a view to such joint action on behalf of the Organisation as may be necessary for the purpose of maintaining international peace and security.

Article 107

Nothing in the present Charter shall invalidate or preclude action, in relation to any state which during the Second World War has been an enemy of any signatory to the present Charter, taken or authorised as a result of that war by the Governments having responsibility for such action.

Chapter–XVIII
Amendments

Article 108

Amendments to the present Charter shall come into force for all Members of the United Nations when they have been adopted by a vote of two thirds of the members of the General Assembly and ratified in accordance with their respective constitutional processes by two-thirds of the Members of the United Nations, including all the permanent members of the Security Council.

Article 109

1. A General Conference of the Members of the United Nations for the purpose of reviewing the present Charter may be held at a date and place to be fixed by a two-thirds vote of the members of the General Assembly and by a vote of any nine

members of the Security Council. Each Member of the United Nations shall have no vote in the conference.

2. Any alteration of the present Charter recommended by a two-thirds vote of the conference shall take effect when ratified in accordance with their respective constitutional processes by two-thirds of the Members of the United Nations including all the permanent members of the Security Council.
3. If such a conference has not been held before the tenth annual session of the General Assembly following the coming into force of the present Charter, the proposal to call such a conference shall be placed on the agenda of that session of the General Assembly, and the conference shall be held if so decided by a majority vote of the members of the General Assembly and by a vote of any seven members of the Security Council.

Chapter–XIX
Ratification and Signature

Article 110

1. The present Charter shall be ratified by the signatory states in accordance with their respective constitutional processes.
2. The ratifications shall be deposited with the Government of the United States of America, which shall notify all the signatory states of each deposit as well as the Secretary-General of the Organisation when he has been appointed.
3. The present Charter shall come into force upon the deposit of ratifications by the Republic of China, France, the Union of Soviet Socialist Republics, the United Kingdom of Great Britain and Northern Ireland, and the United States of America, and by a majority of the other signatory states. A protocol of the ratifications deposited shall thereupon be drawn up by the Government of the United States of America which all communicate copies thereof to all the signatory states.
4. The states signatory to the present Charter which ratify it after it has come into force will become original Members of the United Nations on the date of the deposit of their respective ratifications.

Article 111

The present Charter, of which the Chinese, French, Russian, English, and Spanish texts are equally authentic, shall remain deposited in the archives of the Government of the United States of America. Duly certified copies thereof shall be transmitted by that Government to the Governments of the other signatory states.

In faith whereof the representatives of the Governments of the United Nations have signed the present Charter.

Done at the city of San Francisco the twenty-sixth day of June, one thousand nine hundred and forty-five.

Our Other Books on Political Science

978 81 207 5758 5
₹ 450

978 81 207 4378 6
₹ 450

978 93 86245 14 4
₹ 450

978 81 207 6992 2
₹ 475

978 81 207 8078 1
₹ 475

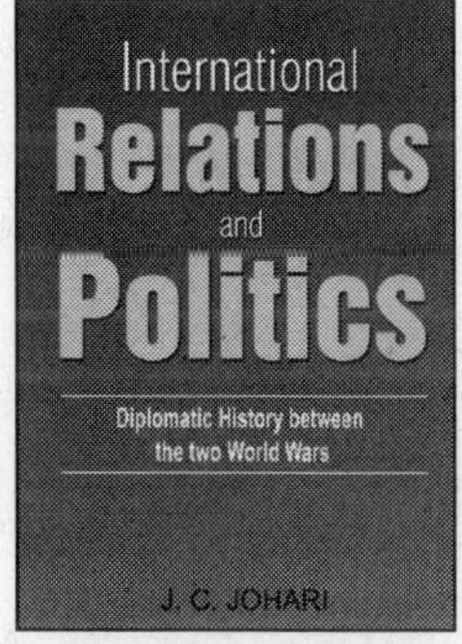

978 81 207 1560 8
₹ 250

Our Other Books on Public Administration

978 93 86245 11 3
₹ 350

978 93 86245 41 0
₹ 300

978 81 954046 5 0
₹ 325

978 81 207 2763 2
₹ 350

978 81 207 7752 1
₹ 300

978 81 207 9513 6
₹ 350

STERLING

mail@sterlingpublishers.in

www.sterlingpublishers.in